THE EPISTLES OF ST. PAUL

TO THE

THESSALONIANS, GALATIANS
ROMANS

TRANSLATIONS AND COMMENTARY

THE
EPISTLES OF ST. PAUL
TO THE
THESSALONIANS, GALATIANS AND ROMANS

TRANSLATION AND COMMENTARY

BY THE LATE

BENJAMIN JOWETT, M.A.
MASTER OF BALLIOL COLLEGE
REGIUS PROFESSOR OF GREEK IN THE UNIVERSITY OF OXFORD
DOCTOR IN THEOLOGY OF THE UNIVERSITY OF LEYDEN

THIRD EDITION, EDITED AND CONDENSED BY

LEWIS CAMPBELL, M.A., LL.D.
EMERITUS PROFESSOR OF GREEK IN THE UNIVERSITY OF ST. ANDREWS

Wipf and Stock Publishers
EUGENE, OREGON

Wipf and Stock Publishers
199 West 8th Avenue, Suite 3
Eugene, Oregon 97401

The Epistles of St. Paul to the Thessalonians, Galatians, and Romans
Translation and Commentary
By Jowett, Benjamin
ISBN: 1-59244-262-5
Publication date: June, 2003
Previously published by John Murray, January, 1894 .

PREFACE

The book which is now presented to the reader in an abridged form, was first published in June 1855; and the second Edition from which this reprint is taken appeared in 1859. Both editions were dedicated to Dr. Temple, the present Bishop of London.

The writer was one on whom the responsibilities of authorship pressed with unusual weight. He had reached the age of thirty-seven before the publication of this his first book; and when to his surprise his work gave grave offence to some classes of his countrymen, he sought earnestly to bring it nearer to perfection. The second Edition gave proof of much assiduous toil in the revision. Many parts of it, particularly the Essay on the *Atonement*, were entirely re-written, with the view rather of elucidating what had been misunderstood, than of merely conciliating opposition. Years passed, the book was out of print, a secondhand copy fetched more than the original price, and by-and-by became wholly unprocurable. Yet no hint was given of renewed publication. The author would not reprint without revising, and a multitude of occupations made revision, as he understood revision, impossible. Not that his mind was ever wholly absorbed in other work, or that his interest in theology was at all abated. But a position, of which he saw the vast possibilities, had at last opened to him, and engaged his active powers.

Great tasks connected with his Professorship of Greek had been undertaken, and were pursued with characteristic tenacity. The resumption of yet deeper studies was reserved for a time of leisure which never came to him—*Senectuti seposuit*. But when 'the days closed around him, and the years,' he more than once expressed a wish that his theological writings might again be given to the world, and this re-publication of them has been undertaken in obedience to his last commands.

In projecting the Edition of St. Paul's Epistles, which Arthur Penrhyn Stanley and Benjamin Jowett undertook conjointly, there is little doubt that they were originally inspired by the example of Dr. Arnold [1].

The two friends had worked on a concerted plan, and the amount of general agreement and difference between their methods has been well stated by Dean Stanley's biographer (vol. i. p. 473). Jowett's work had characteristics of a deeper and more far-reaching kind than that of the graphic delineator of the Apostolical age and of so much besides. He had chosen for his province what may be called the pivot-documents of Augustinian, of Lutheran and of Calvinistic theology; and his endeavour had been nothing less than to penetrate the clouds of tradition, and

[1] That this is more than a surmise, appears from the following passage in the *Life of Arnold* (6th Edition, 1846, p. 163). 'Strong as was his natural taste for history, it was to Theology that he looked as the highest sphere of his exertions, and as the province which most needed them. The chief object which he here proposed to himself—in fact, the object which he conceived as the proper end of Theology itself—was the interpretation and application of the Scriptures. From the time of his early studies at Oxford, when he analysed and commented on the Epistles of St. Paul, with Chrysostom's Homilies, down to the last year of his life, when he was endeavouring to set on foot a Rugby edition of them, under his own superintendence, he never lost sight of this design.'

apprehend the original meaning of the Apostle. He found every chapter, every word, enveloped with many layers of uncritical commentary, and even of passionate controversy; coloured over with the reflected lights of many ages. The duty of the interpreter, which he was one of the first to realize, was to get away from Paulinism, and to find St. Paul — just as afterwards he got away from Platonism and found Plato :—

> 'As when a painter, poring on a face,
> Divinely thro' all hindrance finds the man
> Behind it.'

How much of imaginative sympathy, of independent judgement, of varied learning and calm critical insight, the Oxford tutor brought to such an arduous task, will be partly felt by those who read now for the first time the notes which are here selected, or the Essay on the *Character of St. Paul*. His method as an interpreter is one which had never before been applied so strenuously, and to this day has hardly been again employed with the same simple boldness. He steeped himself in his author, and while laying hold of every aid that was available, still sought to interpret him mainly from himself—working from within outwards, not building up, however closely, round.

But he was not content with mere interpretation. As the thoughts which burned in the Apostle of the Gentiles were of universal import, they could not be without their application to the present age ; and when seen once more in themselves, apart from the accumulations of tradition, they could not fail to be suggestive of fruitful thoughts, arising out of the contemplation of eternal themes. The note on the words 'It is one God' ($\epsilon\hat{\iota}s$ δ $\theta\epsilon\delta s$) in Rom. iii. 30, may serve to illustrate this germinal consideration, which lies at the root also of such extended speculations as those on *Natural Religion*, on *Casuistry* and on *Predestination and Free-will*.

In the Essay on *Philo* he endeavoured to bring out the incidental light which Alexandrine Judaism casts on the interpretation of St. Paul—the similarities of language—even of forms of thought—and the deep-lying spiritual difference.

The reception of the book showed plainly that it was before its time. Evangelical and Tractarian authorities alike anathematized it. Even Frederick Maurice, who himself had suffered for independence of theological speculation, could not bear to have it said, that an Apostle in his lifetime had been mistaken—for example, in looking for the immediate advent of his Lord. Professor Jowett met all attacks with silence, and simply laboured in re-writing his book, to make his meaning clearer. Echoes of the intervening controversy are heard only in undertones, as in the concluding passage of the revised Essay on the *Atonement*, and in various parts of the Essay on the *Interpretation of Scripture*. That Essay had been originally designed to form part of the edition of 1859, but the pertinacity of his opponents, while somewhat hindering his labours, so stimulated public interest, that the second edition was called for before the new Essay could be completed. And when the Rev. H. B. Wilson, whose Bampton Lectures had met with similar obloquy, sought contributions for a volume, which should vindicate the 'free handling in a becoming spirit' of theological subjects, Mr. Jowett sent in this dissertation after re-writing and enlarging it.

The storm which broke out in 1860 over *Essays and Reviews* is hardly yet forgotten, and has to some extent effaced the impression of Professor Jowett's earlier work. But it is long since over, and has cleared the air: and it is hoped that these writings may now obtain a hearing on their merits, with 'better quiet

Better opinion, better confirmation,'

than was possible during the heat of the struggle. Had their author lived, and found the necessary leisure, he would have brought his work again into the front line of critical and historical inquiry. He would have again re-written much in his later style of admirably lucid prose. He might have illuminated his subject by the comparison not only of Alexandrianism, but of other great religions, such as Buddhism or Zoroastrianism. He might have expressed his thoughts on 'the religion of all good men; that which all know, but none will tell.'—He gave authority for the re-publication of his work 'altered or unaltered.' I have not ventured to change a single line. But (1) Lachmann's Greek text on which the work was based has not been reprinted in full. It was immensely in advance of what preceded it, but the investigations of Tischendorf, Tregelles and others, the discovery of the Codex Sinaiticus, and the elaborate discussion of the documents by Westcott and Hort, have again superseded Lachmann. The differences, however, between Lachmann's and the Cambridge text are only in a few places really significant, and it has been thought sufficient, in reprinting Jowett's revised version, to add in a footnote to such places the special reading of Lachmann.

(2) In attempting to bring the volumes within convenient compass, it was necessary to make further omissions, and to rearrange the contents. The choice of passages for omission has been determined in some instances by Professor Jowett's expressed wish; for the rest, those parts have been left

out which could most easily be dispensed with, either as assuming facts which subsequent inquiries have rendered doubtful, or as involving repetition, or as explaining what the translation now makes sufficiently obvious to a well-informed student. Old lovers of the book may regret the absence of many things: but this was true of the author's own second edition: some would like to have renewed acquaintance with the impassioned outburst against a crude phase of contemporary theology, which drew down such anathemas on the work when it first appeared. Others would recapture, if they could, the brief excursus on the *Conversion of St. Paul*. But Professor Jowett himself decided all this otherwise.

(3) The examination of Paley's *Horae Paulinae* has not been reprinted, although it is full of sound and subtle reasoning. Paley is but little studied in the present day; and these chapters could only interest those who have studied Paley[1].

(4) The contents have been slightly rearranged. The Epistles themselves with Introductions, notes and shorter Essays now fill volume one; and volume two consists of the more general Dissertations. The connexion of these with the subjects of the Epistles is indicated where this appeared to be required. The readings of the Authorized Version are subjoined to the English text as before, and are printed in italics, where they represent a different Greek reading.

The work is once more commended to all students of early Christianity, to all who desire that religion should be real and permanent, and to all those who care to contemplate under enlightened guidance 'what is highest in man.'

A fear is sometimes expressed lest sixty years of theo-

---

[1] See *The Times* for Oct. 15, 1859.

logical controversy, while hardening superstitious prejudices, may have left the reading public cold—lest the 'visible Church' should be growing narrower, and the world more and more indifferent to Christianity. But there are not wanting signs of very different augury — symptoms of widening thought within the Christian Churches, of a re-awakening of religious aspiration amongst mankind at large. And it is with the hope which such indications have suggested, that these volumes are now sent forth.

A review of the First Edition by Dr. James Martineau, which has been since reprinted amongst his *Studies of Christianity* (Longmans & Co.), caught with rare insight the characteristic excellence of the book. The following sentences especially deserve quotation here:—

'The text being chosen on grounds purely critical, the notes are written in a spirit purely exegetical; they aim, simply and with rare self-abnegation, to bring out, by every happy change of light and turn of reflective sympathy, the great Apostle's real thought and feeling. How very far this faithful historic purpose in itself raises the interpreter above the crowd of erudite and commenting divines, can scarcely be understood till it has formed a new generation, and fixed itself as a distinct intellectual type.'

But again

'it is not in the notes—which are wholly occupied in recovering St. Paul's own thought — but in the interposed disquisitions, which avowedly deal with the theology of to-day, that a certain breadth and balance of statement, and delicate ease in manœuvring the forms and antitheses of abstract thought, and fine appreciation of human experience, make us feel the double presence of metaphysical power and historical tact. The author, accordingly, appears to us, not only to have seized the great Apostle's attitude of mind more happily than any preceding English critic, but also to have separated the essence from the accidents of the Pauline Christianity, and disengaged its divine elements for transfusion into the organism of our immediate life.'

Thanks are due to several friends for encouragement in the preparation of this edition, and particularly to Mr. Claud G. Montefiore, for help in verifying some allusions to Hebrew custom and tradition.

LEWIS CAMPBELL.

35 KENSINGTON COURT MANSIONS, W.
Dec. 28, 1893.

CONTENTS

	PAGE
FIRST EPISTLE TO THE THESSALONIANS	1–66
Introduction	1–3
Genuineness	4–17
Thessalonica	17–20
Subject of the Epistle	20–22
Evils in the Church of the Apostolical age	22–32
TRANSLATION AND NOTES	33–52
Belief in the coming of Christ	53–66
SECOND EPISTLE TO THE THESSALONIANS	67–111
Introduction	67–70
Genuineness	70–76
TRANSLATION AND NOTES	77–85
Essay on the Man of Sin	86–103
Questions set aside as irrelevant	86
Connexion with other prophecies	89
Has St. Paul in view a real person?	90
Apocalyptic tendencies	91
Distinctive features of New Testament prophecy	96
Relation to actual events	98
'He that letteth'	99
General remarks	101
The lost Epistles	104–111
THE EPISTLE TO THE GALATIANS	112–202
Introduction	112–117
Were the Galatians Gentiles or Jews originally?	113–115
Probably Gentiles who had been Jewish proselytes	115–117
Galatia	118, 119
Subject of the Epistle	120
Genuineness	120, 121
Analysis	122–127

CONTENTS

	PAGE
TRANSLATION AND NOTES	128–164
Essay on the Character of St. Paul	165–184
Prevailing conceptions illusory	166, 167
The great fact of his conversion	167
Contrast to his former self	168
General reflections	169–171
The temperament of religious reformers	171, 172
The Hero, the Prophet, the Apostle	172, 173
Contrasted elements in St. Paul	174–176
St. Paul and Luther	176
The thorn in the flesh	177
His noble forms of courtesy	178
Enthusiasm, prudence, moderation	178–180
His relation to the churches	181, 182
Strength out of weakness	182–184
Essay on the Quotations from the Old Testament in the Writings of St. Paul	185–202
Habit of reference to ancient writings	185–187
Gnostic and Alexandrian tendencies	187
Deeper connexion of Old and New Testament	188, 189
Use of earlier books by Psalmist and Prophet	189, 190
Classification of quotations	191–199
General results	199–202
THE EPISTLE TO THE ROMANS	203–351
Introduction	203–213
What was the Roman church?	204
Transition from Judaism	205
In what sense Gentile?	207
Authorities	208
Jewish proselytism	209
Alexandrianism	211
Jewish in feeling, Gentile in origin	212
Re-action from Jewish narrowness	213
Subject of the Epistle	214–220
Righteousness by faith and admission of Gentiles	215
Universal, individual, national	217–219
Conclusion	220
Time and Place	220–224
Analysis	
Chapters II–VI	224–235
VII, VIII	236–240
IX–XI	240–246
XII–XVI	246–257
TRANSLATION AND NOTES	258–351

CONTENTS

	PAGE
ESSAY ON THE ABSTRACT IDEAS OF THE NEW TESTAMENT	352–366
Theology and Philosophy	352–354
The growth of abstract ideas	354–356
Degrees of abstraction	356
The language of the Fathers	357
Illustration from the Epistles	357–359
Different modes of thought	359, 360
Personifying tendency	360, 361
Deeper significance	361–364
Definition through use	364, 365
An objection answered	365, 366
ESSAY ON St. PAUL AND THE TWELVE	367–381
The origin of every society obscure	367, 368
Prepossessions of Eusebius	368, 369
No record of the earliest heretics, nor of the earliest church	369–371
Speculative reconstructions	371, 372
Nature of apostolical authority	372–374
The attitude of the Apostles and of their followers	375
Irenaeus, Justin, Tertullian	376
Concealment of differences in third century	377
Statements to be considered	378
'Simon Magus'	379
Disappearance of St. Paul from history	379, 380
Yet his principle triumphed	380
The dawn of Ecclesiastical History	380, 381
ESSAY ON St. PAUL AND PHILO	382–434
External view of Christianity	382–384
The Jewish and the Alexandrian Philosophy	384, 385
Philo on the edge of Christianity in point of time	385, 386
Character of the Alexandrian school	386, 387
Allegorical interpretation	387, 388
Mysticism the end, logic the means	388, 389
Yet Philo was a great and good man	389, 390
Concentration on the Pentateuch	390, 391
Comparison of the early Fathers	391, 392
The allegorical method not yet extinct	392, 393
The nature and being of God	393–399
The Logos	399–410
Few traces of Messianic hopes	410–412
Conception of the Creation	412–414
Virtue, how attainable?	414–416
Faith, Hope, and Love	416–419

CONTENTS

	PAGE
The Law idealized	419
Yet belief in sacrifice	419, 420
Not a system, but a method	420, 421
The method existed before and after Philo	421, 422
Wide diffusion of Alexandrian modes of thought	422, 423
Anticipations in the Old Testament	423, 424
Clement and Origen	424
Philo claimed by the Fathers as a Christian	424–426
Differences between Philo and St. Paul	426–430
The Word and the Spirit	430, 431
His doctrine more theoretical than practical	431, 432
Faith, in Philo and St. Paul	432
Difference of result	432, 433
Relation to Fourth Gospel and Epistle to the Hebrews	433, 434
Conclusion	434

THE FIRST EPISTLE

TO THE

THESSALONIANS

INTRODUCTION.

THE greater number of the Epistles of St. Paul may be arranged conveniently in two groups: the first comprehending the Galatians, Corinthians, Romans; the second, the Epistles of the Imprisonment, including under this term the Ephesians, Colossians, Philippians, and Philemon.

Reading the Epistles in chronological order, many will be tempted to trace in them a gradual development of idea and doctrine. Others, again, will seek to impress upon them the same fixed type of truth held from the beginning, 'the faith once delivered to the saints.' Could a person lay aside previous conceptions, and resign himself to the letter of the text, he would not find either of these views supported by an examination of the Epistles themselves. There is no system which is presupposed in them; nor can any be constructed out of them without marring their simplicity. They have almost wholly a practical aim, and are fragmentary and occasional. Ordinary letters arise out of the incidents of the day; so these have to do with real events and feelings passing between the Apostle and the churches. There is a growth in the Epistles of St. Paul, it is true; but it is the growth of Christian life, not of intellectual progress,—not of reflection, but of spiritual experience, enlarging as the world widens before the Apostle's eyes, passing from life to death, or from strife to peace, with the changes in the Apostle's own life, or the circumstances of his converts. There is a rest also in the Epistles of St. Paul, discernible not in forms of thought or types of doctrine, but in the person of Christ Himself, who is his centre in every Epistle, however various may be his modes of expression, or his treatment of controversial questions.

There is one mode of expression we naturally adopt when near, another at a distance—one in the fullness and vigour of life, another in the near approach of death—one in joy, another in sorrow—one in sympathy with others, another when at variance with them. Change of sphere will often produce a corresponding change in the style and cast of our thoughts. What we have long or often meditated upon, we express differently from what flashes upon us for the first time; what comes to us sealed by the experience of many years, assumes a different character in our minds from what with equal confidence we believed and acted upon in the fervour of first conviction.

These are the kind of differences which separate the first from the second of the two main divisions of the writings of St. Paul.

And before this there is a prior stage, in which he is on the threshold of the conflict, and not wholly (shall we say?) aware of the great thoughts which were hereafter, by the will of God, to spring up within him. Such is the inference which we are led to draw when, from the perusal of the later Epistles, we turn to those which are universally agreed to be first in date,—the Epistles to the Thessalonians,— and read them not as 'dead words,' but as witnesses of the Apostle's mind and life.

It is a comparatively short period of time which can be allowed—not more than four or five years at the utmost—

between the date of the First Epistle to the Thessalonians, written from Athens or Corinth, and the Epistle to the Galatians, written probably during the Apostle's stay at Ephesus or in its neighbourhood. More than half the Apostle's ministry had already elapsed ere he set his hand to this the first of his extant writings,—one among many, as he implies in a passage in the Second Epistle, iii. 17, and therefore not to be looked upon too curiously, as part of a scheme which was to be completed in the series of Epistles. It is a fragment, the earliest we possess, of the Apostle's life and the History of the Church. Nothing is gained for the interpretation of the Epistle, by attempting to combine it artificially with his later writings. No such connexion could have been present to the mind of the Apostle. The real light which they receive from one another is that of contrast. Two writings of the same author could not be more different than the Epistles to the Thessalonians and that which follows next in order, the Epistle to the Galatians. The latter is fervid and abrupt, full of interrogation and argument, and abounding in allusions to the Old Testament; it has the tone of one speaking with authority; parts of it are written under what may be termed the feeling of persecution (vi. 14–18), the subdued, painful sense that 'he bore in his body the marks of the Lord Jesus.' The Epistles to the Thessalonians are perhaps the least impassioned, and most regular in style, of any of St. Paul's Epistles: they contain no single quotation from the Old Testament, and very few questions; they are not argumentative at all; they advise rather than command; nor are they marked by any of the Apostle's deepest and most inward feelings.

GENUINENESS OF THE FIRST EPISTLE.

THE First Epistle to the Thessalonians is not deficient in external evidence for its genuineness. It is quoted by Irenaeus, Clement, and Tertullian; is named in the Muratori fragment; and had a place among the ten Pauline Epistles, which were admitted into the Canon of Marcion, by whom it was ranked fifth in the list of St. Paul's writings. Like all the other books of the New Testament, it is said to have been corrupted by him, or rather, if Epiphanius may be trusted (*Haereses*, p. 371), he left nothing of the original. The question of the relation of Marcion to the canon of Scripture is obscure, and one which, as we have no means of determining it from the Epistle to the Thessalonians, it would be out of place to discuss here. The fact, however, that he inserted the Epistle in his canon, is a proof that a writing under this name, identified by quotations of Irenaeus, Clement, and Tertullian, as the one which we possess, must have been received as a genuine work of St. Paul, at least as early as the middle of the second century.

It is not in consequence of any deficiency of external, but, as is supposed, of internal evidence, that doubts have been raised of late years respecting the genuineness of the Epistle. In some respects it has been thought too like, in others too unlike, undoubted writings of the Apostle, for us to maintain that it is from his hand. The critic by whom these difficulties have been chiefly urged, is Dr. Baur, of Tübingen, whose objections may be regarded as a summary of all that can be said on that side of the argument[1]. They may be conveniently arranged under the following heads:—

i. Absence of individuality, and of doctrinal statements.

ii. The tone of a later age discernible in ii. 14–16.

[1] Baur, *Paulus*, pp. 480-492.

iii. Inconsistency with the Acts of the Apostles, in relation to some points of fact.

iv. Perpetual reference to the events recorded in the Acts of the Apostles, indicative of the sources whence the Epistle was compiled.

v. Verbal similarities to passages in the other Epistles of St. Paul, leading to a suspicion of designed imitation.

vi. Discrepancies from the other Epistles in modes of thought, especially traceable in iv. 13–18.

i. Absence of individuality (eigenthümlichkeit) and of doctrinal statements. 'It is made up of nothing but wishes, instructions, admonitions—contains no doctrinal subject-matter at all, with the single exception of the mention of the coming of Christ, iv. 13–18.'

There is a difficulty in meeting such objections as these, because, whatever real weight they may have, they ultimately resolve themselves into the impression of an individual critic, who, if he be gifted with the faculty of writing clearly, easily masters the judgement of his reader. Sometimes they come to us with overwhelming force; at other times we wonder that we can have been influenced by them at all. How an author *ought* to have written, is a question in which imagination has a wide range; a meagre induction, gathered from a few short works, is not a sufficient criterion of how he must have written everywhere and at all times. Baur's objections labour under the fallacy of presenting one side of the question only. Grounds of suspicion are endless; and in answer we can only accumulate the probabilities opposed to them. On the same ground with Baur, it may be argued with great truth, that the very absence of individuality agrees with the incidental character of the Epistles. Why should we expect them all to bear marks of 'originality?' Might not the Apostle write as a man writes to his friends, without seeking to impart any new truth? Does not the First Epistle to the Thessalonians arise naturally from a real occasion—the return of Timothy with news respecting the converts—an occasion just similar to that of the Second Epistle to the Corinthians? Is not one doctrine enough in the space of five short chapters? And is the disproportion between the doctrinal and practical sections any greater than in the case of some of the other Epistles?

Slight as these presumptions are, they may be fairly placed in the scale against an argument such as Baur's. If it were admitted that the absence of doctrinal ideas makes the Epistle unworthy of St. Paul, it makes it also a forgery without an object.

ii. The tone of a later age discernible in chap. ii. 16: 'For the wrath is come upon them to the uttermost;' which is supposed to be an after-reflection on the destruction of Jerusalem.

To the Apostle, reading the future in the present, the state of Judea at any time during the last thirty years before the destruction of the city, would have been sufficient to justify the expression, 'wrath is come upon them to the uttermost.' The fearful looking for of judgement was natural, not only to Christians, but to Jews themselves, to Josephus as well as to St. Paul. The passage must not, however, be strained beyond its natural meaning. The word $\dot{o}\rho\gamma\acute{\eta}$, wrath, in other places (Rom. i. 18; ii. 8) refers at least as much to final impenitence and hardness of heart, 'the spiritual wrath of God,' as to temporal judgements. And the connexion in which it occurs here, 'forbidding us to speak to the Gentiles, that they might be saved, to fill up their sins alway,' shows the Apostle to be speaking, not of punishment, but of reprobation[1].

iii. Inconsistencies with the Acts of the Apostles in some points of fact. These are: (1) The statement of the Acts that Silas and Timotheus, being left behind at Berea, came

---

[1] [Recent critics suspect interpolation here.—ED.]

up with the Apostle at Corinth, after he had left them (Acts xviii. 5), compared with the fact recorded in the Epistle that Timothy was sent back from Athens to Thessalonica, 1 Thess. iii. 1; (2) the impression conveyed by the Acts xvii. 1–5, that the Thessalonian Church was of Jewish origin, compared with the impression conveyed by 1 Thess. ii. 14 that it was Gentile; and (3) the statement that the persecution which the Thessalonians endured was of their own countrymen, which is nevertheless recorded in the Acts to have been stirred up by Jews.

What reconciliation of these opposite views is possible need not be considered [in the present connexion]. It is sufficient here to observe, that the discrepancies alluded to are not greater than those between the Acts of the Apostles and the Epistle to the Galatians, in the account of the council. If these latter discrepancies have never led any critic to doubt the Epistle to the Galatians, neither is there any reason why similar discrepancies should be assumed as fatal to the Epistle to the Thessalonians.

Another objection is based on the indications afforded by the Epistle, that the Church to which it is addressed had been already long established. Their faith is known in every place, i. 9; they had a regular Church government, v. 12; and some of their members had died since the Apostle's visit to them, iv. 13, although, according to the narrative of the Acts, but a few weeks, or at the most a few months, could have elapsed. Compare Acts xvii. 1–8, xviii. 1–5.

The answer to this objection is to be sought in the peculiar circumstances of the early Church, in which a year might be said to be like a day, and a whole life to be crowded into the moment of conversion. Men living in expectation of the coming of the Lord lost their measure of time; every hour was fraught to them with feelings and events. Nor must the language of the Apostle himself be too strictly interpreted when speaking of the Church, as seen by the eye of faith and love idealised before him. Compare 1 Cor. i. 9, especially as contrasted with the after tone of the Epistle; Rom. i. 8. Further it may be observed, that some kind of organization was established by St. Paul, immediately on his first declaration of the Gospel everywhere among the new converts, Acts xiv. 23; and that nothing is implied in the word προιστάμενοι but what must have existed in the Jewish Synagogue, and would naturally spring up in the Christian Church. The death of even one or two members of the Church might be sufficient to suggest the inquiry what became of the departed.

iv. Reference to the events recorded in the Acts of the Apostles, indicative of the sources whence the Epistle was compiled.

Baur supposes the forger of the Epistle to have had before him, either the Acts of the Apostles themselves, or earlier documents from which the Acts of the Apostles were compiled. The Epistle appears to him to add nothing to the events narrated there.

Opposite probabilities are: (1) The natural manner in which the events referred to are introduced. To go back to what happened while he was yet with them, is quite in character with the writings of the Apostle. In 1 Thessalonians, as in the Epistle to the Galatians, he recalls his converts to the moment of their first conversion; as in the Corinthians he appeals to the witness of his own life, and awakens their sympathies by the mention of persecutions which he suffered for their sakes. There is scarcely one of his Epistles which has not several allusions of this kind. Hence there is no sort of improbability that many such might occur in the Thessalonians. But, on the other hand, it must be observed, (2) that these resemblances to the Acts relate only to the persecution which the Apostle had endured at Philippi (ii. 2), to the persecution of the Thessalonian Church (ii. 14), and to his own stay at Athens;

and (3) that the discrepancies just noticed are of themselves opposite probabilities. For is it likely that a forger, carefully reading the Acts of the Apostles when compiling his Epistle, could have committed so clumsy an error as to send back Timothy and Silas, not from Corinth, but from Athens? or would he have lighted upon so crude an invention as to send back Timothy at all, to satisfy the longing desire of the Apostle about his converts, when Timothy had just come from the place to which he was sent? Or again, is it probable that he would have fallen into the inconsistency of representing that [as] a Gentile which the Acts rather intimates to have been a Jewish Church? Or that persecution as raised by Gentiles, which the Acts informs us originated with Jews? The greatest carelessness must be attributed to him, to account for such oversights. But the greatest ingenuity would have been required to imitate the style and topics of St. Paul, as he must be supposed to have done. It is a refinement not to be thought of, that he purposely differed from the Acts of the Apostles, with the view of concealing the sources from which his information was derived.

v. The next argument of Baur is of a more subtle kind, and can only be justly appreciated by a careful comparison of the passages on which it is based. He thinks that in 1 Thessalonians he can trace a repetition of the same thoughts that occur elsewhere in the writings of St. Paul; or, in other words, he supposes the Epistle to be a sort of *cento* ingeniously made up from other places.

The instances given by him are as follows:—

1 Thess. i. 5.

τὸ εὐαγγέλιον ἡμῶν οὐκ ἐγενήθη πρὸς ὑμᾶς ἐν λόγῳ μόνον, ἀλλὰ καὶ ἐν δυνάμει, καὶ ἐν πνεύματι ἁγίῳ καὶ ἐν πληροφορίᾳ πολλῇ.

1 Cor. ii. 4.

καὶ ὁ λόγος μου καὶ τὸ κήρυγμά μου οὐκ ἐν πειθοῖς σοφίας λόγοις, ἀλλὰ ἐν ἀποδείξει πνεύματος καὶ δυνάμεως.

1 Thess. i. 6.

καὶ ὑμεῖς μιμηταὶ ἡμῶν ἐγενήθητε καὶ τοῦ κυρίου, δεξάμενοι τὸν λόγον ἐν θλίψει πολλῇ.

i. 8.

ἀφ' ὑμῶν γὰρ ἐξήχηται ὁ λόγος τοῦ κυρίου οὐ μόνον ἐν τῇ Μακεδονίᾳ καὶ ἐν τῇ Ἀχαΐᾳ, ἀλλὰ καὶ ἐν παντὶ τόπῳ ἡ πίστις ὑμῶν ἡ πρὸς τὸν θεὸν ἐξελήλυθεν, ὥστε μὴ χρείαν ἔχειν ἡμᾶς λαλεῖν τι.

ii. 4–10.

⁴ ἀλλὰ καθὼς δεδοκιμάσμεθα ὑπὸ τοῦ θεοῦ πιστευθῆναι τὸ εὐαγγέλιον, οὕτως λαλοῦμεν, οὐχ ὡς ἀνθρώποις ἀρέσκοντες, ἀλλὰ [τῷ] θεῷ τῷ δοκιμάζοντι τὰς καρδίας ἡμῶν. ⁵οὔτε γάρ ποτε ἐν λόγῳ κολακείας ἐγενήθημεν, καθὼς οἴδατε, οὔτε ἐν προφάσει πλεονεξίας (θεὸς μάρτυς), ⁶οὔτε ζητοῦντες ἐξ ἀνθρώπων δόξαν, οὔτε ἀφ' ὑμῶν οὔτε ἀπ' ἄλλων, δυνάμενοι ἐν βάρει εἶναι ὡς χριστοῦ ἀπόστολοι, ⁷ἀλλ' ἐγενήθημεν νήπιοι ἐν μέσῳ ὑμῶν, ὡς ἐὰν τροφὸς θάλπῃ τὰ ἑαυτῆς τέκνα, ⁸οὕτως ὁμειρόμενοι ὑμῶν, εὐδοκοῦμεν μεταδοῦναι ὑμῖν οὐ μόνον τὸ εὐαγγέλιον τοῦ θεοῦ, ἀλλὰ καὶ τὰς ἑαυτῶν ψυχάς, διότι ἀγαπητοὶ ἡμῖν ἐγενήθητε. ⁹μνημονεύετε γάρ, ἀδελφοί, τὸν κόπον ἡμῶν καὶ τὸν μόχθον· νυκτὸς καὶ ἡμέρας ἐργαζόμενοι πρὸς τὸ μὴ ἐπιβαρῆσαί

1 Cor. xi. 1.

μιμηταί μου γίνεσθε, καθὼς κἀγὼ χριστοῦ.

Rom. i. 8.

ἡ πίστις ὑμῶν καταγγέλλεται ἐν ὅλῳ τῷ κόσμῳ.

1 Cor. ii. 4. See above.

1 Cor. iv. 3–4.

ἐμοὶ δὲ εἰς ἐλάχιστόν ἐστιν ἵνα ὑφ' ὑμῶν ἀνακριθῶ ἢ ὑπὸ ἀνθρωπίνης ἡμέρας· ἀλλ' οὐδὲ ἐμαυτὸν ἀνακρίνω (οὐδὲν γὰρ ἐμαυτῷ σύνοιδα, ἀλλ' οὐκ ἐν τούτῳ δεδικαίωμαι), ὁ δὲ ἀνακρίνων με κύριός ἐστιν.

ix. 15.

ἐγὼ δὲ οὐ κέχρημαι οὐδενὶ τούτων· οὐκ ἔγραψα δὲ ταῦτα, ἵνα οὕτως γένηται ἐν ἐμοί· καλὸν γάρ μοι μᾶλλον ἀποθανεῖν, ἢ τὸ καύχημά μου· οὐδεὶς κενώσει.

2 Cor. ii. 17.

οὐ γάρ ἐσμεν ὡς οἱ πολλοὶ καπηλεύοντες τὸν λόγον τοῦ θεοῦ, ἀλλ' ὡς ἐξ εἰλικρινείας, ἀλλ' ὡς ἐκ θεοῦ κατέναντι θεοῦ ἐν χριστῷ λαλοῦμεν.

1 Thess. ii. 4–10.

τινα ὑμῶν ἐκηρύξαμεν εἰς ὑμᾶς τὸ εὐαγγέλιον τοῦ θεοῦ. ¹⁰ ὑμεῖς μάρτυρες καὶ ὁ θεός, ὡς ὁσίως καὶ δικαίως καὶ ἀμέμπτως ὑμῖν τοῖς πιστεύουσιν ἐγενήθημεν.

2 Cor. v. 11.

Εἰδότες οὖν τὸν ον φόβτοῦ κυρίου, ἀνθρώπους πείθομεν, θεῷ δὲ πεφανερώμεθα· ἐλπίζω δὲ καὶ ἐν ταῖς συνειδήσεσιν ὑμῶν πεφανερῶσθαι.

xi. 9.

καὶ ἐν παντὶ ἀβαρῆ ἐμαυτὸν ὑμῖν ἐτήρησα καὶ τηρήσω.

That these are striking similarities is not to be doubted. The whole question turns upon the point, Of what nature is the similarity?

There is one kind of resemblance between two passages which indicates that one of them is an imitation or transcript of the other, while another kind proves them only to have been the production of the same mind. Even exact verbal agreements do not necessarily show more than that the same words have been used twice over by the same person. St. Paul, when writing nearly at the same time to the Ephesians and Colossians, might to both Churches repeat the same topics expressed in the same words, without this repetition necessarily shaking the genuineness of either Epistle. On the other hand, the portion of the Second Epistle of St. Peter and of the Epistle of St. Jude which is common to both is such as to demand a different explanation.

Which of these two alternatives we adopt, will depend chiefly on what we know of the author. The recurrence of the same thoughts or topics in two different works, may or may not be a presumption against the genuineness of both or either of them.

(1) Is it the way of an author to repeat himself? If we were able to say no, a strong presumption would be raised against the genuineness of a work which seemed to be but a repetition of his other writings. But if he were in the

habit of repeating himself, the repetitions would be no disproof of the genuineness of the work in which they occurred.

They would be a slight presumption in its favour, or even a considerable one if made in a manner which was characteristic of the writer.

(2) The argument from similarity against the genuineness of one of two writings has a very different force when applied to a classical author or to the fluent rhetorician of a later age, and to a writer like St. Paul, whose style is constrained and vocabulary limited. Great masters of language are never at a loss for words; it is otherwise with those who are stammering in a foreign tongue.

(3) Similarities in words and terms only are not a presumption in favour of forgery, but rather the reverse, in the case of two works bearing the name of the same person. The forged book in ancient times was not a tessellated work of phrases and expressions derived from other writings of the supposed author. Whole passages were interpolated with an object, or perhaps without one, as they chanced to be remembered. But nothing would have been gained by stealing words.

Now, it must be observed: (a) That the parallels which we have quoted in no instance extend to whole verses, like that of St. Jude and St. Peter; (b) that they occur in a writer who, in his undoubtedly genuine Epistles, is remarkable for such repetitions. Not to mention the parallelism of the Ephesians and the Colossians, the very passages, which we have already quoted from the two Epistles to the Corinthians, closely resemble similar expressions in the Epistles to the Galatians and Romans. Compare 1 Cor. ii. 4, iv. 3, 4 with Gal. i. 10; or 2 Cor. xii. 7 with Gal. iv. 14; or Rom. xiv with 1 Cor. viii; or the deferred intention in 2 Cor. xiii. 1 with Rom. i. 13; or the unwillingness to enter on another man's labours in Rom. xv. 18–24 with 2 Cor. x. 14–16 ; or Gal. iii. 6–12 with Rom. iv. 3–11. Almost every Epistle of St. Paul has a network of thoughts and expressions derived from the rest. And hence we infer that the passages in the Thessalonians quoted by Baur are rather to be regarded as an indication of the genuineness than of the spuriousness of the Epistle ; because they are quoted in the manner in which St. Paul repeats himself; and (c) they are not of a kind which a forger could easily have invented.

It might be truly said of the early Ecclesiastical forgeries that nothing could exceed the readiness with which they were received ; but, on the other hand, nothing could exceed the clumsiness of their falsification. They made no attempt to imitate the style of the author whose name they bore ; they commonly carried on their face the object with which they were written. A forgery so ingenious as the First Epistle to the Thessalonians, containing so many latent resemblances to the genuine writings of the Apostle, would be unique in Ecclesiastical literature.

Paley remarks, that a writer of the second century would never have thought of attributing to St. Paul the expectation of the immediate end of the world, which had already been refuted by the course of events. Put in a slightly different point of view, the argument is perfectly just. He who may be supposed to have written the First Epistle to the Thessalonians in the second century, was probably a believer in the immediate advent of Christ. But whatever may have been his own belief, he would have felt the anachronism of putting into the mouth of one long since dead, words that implied that he would be alive when it took place. And the whole spirit of such a belief would have led him to have supported it by present immediate inspiration rather than by the testimony of an Apostle who had himself fallen asleep.

(4) Lastly : Many positive evidences may be urged in favour of the genuineness of the First Epistle to the

Thessalonians. Among these we reckon the last of Baur's objections (above, p. 5).

vi. Without laying greater stress on this argument than it deserves, we pass on to enumerate other internal evidences that the Epistle is St. Paul's. Such are:—

(1) The desire to see the face of his converts, iii. 6, 10, and delayed intention to come to them, ii. 18. Compare Rom. i. 13, xv. 22; 1 Cor. xvi. 1; 2 Cor. i. 16, xiii. 1; Phil. i. 8; Philem. 22.

(2) The lively sympathy with them throughout the Epistle. Such passages as ii. 17, iii. 5, 10, are good instances of this. He is taken from them in presence, not in heart; he lives if they stand fast in the Lord; they desire to see him, even as he them. These expressions show the same sort of reciprocity between the Apostle and his converts as is traceable in the Second Epistle to the Corinthians. In both there is the same sensitiveness to every human as well as spiritual consolation, the same loneliness when separated from them, and the same joy at the good news of Titus and Timothy. Compare 1 Thess. ii. 17, iii. 6, with 2 Cor. vii. 5, 7, ii. 12, 13; also Phil. iii. 25, 29; Col. i. 7, 8. Yet great as is the similarity of thought, there is no similarity of language, such as that into which an imitator would naturally have fallen.

(3) The frequent and characteristic mention of himself. As in the Galatians, he perpetually recurs to the time when he was yet with them. It is through himself, in the remembrance of himself, that he would implant in them the image of Christ. And yet that which he especially seeks to recall, is the very absence of any claim or pretension on his part. He did not seek praise when he might have done so; he did not receive the maintenance to which, as an Apostle, he had a right, 2 Cor. xi. 9, xiii. 13, 14. Does not this remind us of him who did glory and did not glory, seeming, as it were, to assert and deny himself at once? And yet the favourite word καυχᾶσθαι nowhere occurs in the First Epistle to the Thessalonians.

GENUINENESS OF THE FIRST EPISTLE

(4) The delicate manner in which reproof and admonition are conveyed, as what they already knew and practised, and had no need that the Apostle should teach them, iv. 9, v. 2.

(5) The germs of thoughts and of precepts which may be traced in a more developed form in later Epistles. Thus the practical exhortations at the end of the Epistle, are more fully worked out in the twelfth chapter of the Romans; the figure in v. 8 is expanded in Eph. vi. 13-17. A slighter example of the same growth is traceable in the expression, 'Whether we wake or sleep we may live together with him,' in v. 10, compared with the common phraseology of the Romans, Galatians, and the later Epistles. Another is the reference to the heathen origin of the Thessalonians, in i. 9; compare 1 Cor. xii. 2; Eph. ii. 11; Gal. iv. 8; also the mention made of the relation of the Church to those that are without, iv. 12 (compare Col. iv. 5; Cor. vi. 1), as well as of unity within, v. 13. A similar growth is observable in the allusion to the duty of the Church to support the teachers of the Gospel, when placed side by side with the larger manner in which the same subject is treated in 1 Cor. ix; 2 Cor. xi. 8, 9; xii. 13. In all these instances there is the kind of difference that we should expect to find between a thought or precept often dwelt upon and frequently repeated, and the same thought expressed for the first time in few words by a comparatively unpractised writer.

It has been objected against the genuineness of this Epistle, that it contains only a single statement of doctrine. But liveliness, personality, similar traits of disposition, are far more difficult to invent than statements of doctrine. A later age might have supplied these, but it could hardly have caught the very likeness and portrait of the Apostle. The strength of this argument is considerably increased when it is placed side by side with another of a wholly different kind, derived from mannerisms of style and language. Such are :—

(1) The expansion and association of words traceable in

passages, such as i. 2-6, 7, 8; 'Going off upon a word' or thought, ii. 18, v. 4; 'harping back upon one,' ii. 1; cf. i. 9, iii. 5; cf. 1; elucidation of one expression or one verse by another in apposition with it, as in i. 9, iv. 3, 6; the aggravation and accumulation of language in such passages as i. 2, 3, 5, 8; the apparent unmeaningness of some emphatic expressions, ii. 5, iii. 11, v. 27; the recurrence of the same forms of speech and thought at the commencement of successive verses and paragraphs, i. 9, ii. 1, ii. 3, 5, ii. 7, 11, iii. 1, 5, often traceable at a great distance, as in i. 6, ii. 14; play of words, iv. 9; exaggeration, iv. 10; climax, ii. 8, i. 5, in the latter passage with the favourite οὐ μόνον ἀλλὰ καί; negative and positive statements of the same thought, ii. 1, 2, 3, 4, 5, 6, 7; interrogative and positive statements, ii. 19, 20.

(2) Peculiarities of another class, found in the Epistles to the Thessalonians as well as in other writings of St. Paul, are the following:—

The play of words δεδοκιμάσμεθα, δοκιμάζοντι, in ii. 4; the paradox in i. 6 ἐν θλίψει πολλῇ μετὰ χαρᾶς πνεύματος ἁγίου (compare Col. i. 24; 2 Cor. vii. 10, viii. 1); the mixed metaphor respecting the day of the Lord in v. 5, also in the same passage the double use of κλέπτης, κλέπτας (compare Rom. xiii. 12; 1 Cor. iii. 15; and the inversion of thought in Rom. vii. 1-7); the substitution of the present for the future, in iii. 19 (compare Rom. ii. 16); verbal antithesis of prepositions, i. 5 ἐν ὑμῖν δι' ὑμᾶς, iv. 7 ἐπὶ ἀκαθαρσίᾳ, ἀλλ' ἐν ἁγιασμῷ, ii. 3 οὐκ ἐκ πλάνης οὐδὲ ἐν δόλῳ; pleonasms as in i. 3, ii. 9, v. 23; repetition of γάρ in several successive verses, i. 8—ii. 1; use of γάρ in question, ii. 19, iii. 9; resumption of sentence after a digression with διὰ τοῦτο, iii. 5, iii. 7; the use of the double ἵνα, iv. 1; peculiar uses of words and expressions such as εὐαγγέλιον for the preaching of the Gospel, 1 Thess. i. 5; ἀγών Col. iii. 1; 1 Thess. ii. 2, to express the passionate earnestness of his feelings towards his converts; χαρὰ ἢ στέφανος 1 Thess. ii. 19; Phil. iv. 1, said also of his converts; ἵνα μὴ ἐπιβαρῶ 2 Cor. ii. 5; δυνάμενοι ἐν βάρει εἶναι 1 Thess. ii. 6, of his burdening the Church with his maintenance. Compare also the following:—

ἀπὼν τῷ σώματι, παρὼν δὲ τῷ πνεύματι 1 Cor. v. 3; ἐν προσώπῳ καὶ μὴ ἐν καρδίᾳ 2 Cor. v. 12; προσώπῳ οὐ καρδίᾳ 1 Thess. ii. 17.

Such intricate similarities of language, such lively traits of character, it is not within the power of any forger to invent, and, least of all, of a forger of the second century.

THESSALONICA.

THESSALONICA, called in more ancient times Halia, Emathia, and Therma, now Salonichi, was a populous city, the capital of one of the Roman divisions of Macedonia, situated at the north-east corner of the Thermaic Gulf.

It is not one of the objects of the present work to enter minutely either into the history of the cities to which the Epistles were addressed, or into the local features of the country in which they were situated. To fill the mind with historical pictures or descriptions of scenery, will not in any degree help us to feel as the Apostles felt, or think as they thought, any more than the history of the reign of George the Third, or a description of the scenery of Somersetshire or Cornwall, would enable us to understand the life and character of Wesley or Whitfield. Interesting as such pictures may be, they tend to withdraw us from a higher interest, which is to be found only in the private character of the Gospel narrative itself.

It is not in the first, but in the second century, that the Church comes into contact with the world. The life of Christ and His Apostles stands in no relation to the public history of their time. None of the great events of the world appears to touch them; no edict of the Roman emperors, with the single exception of the command of Claudius that the Jews should depart from Rome, has the least effect on the fortunes of the infant communion. Even in this case, we arrive at no other result than that Aquila and Priscilla met with St. Paul at Corinth, and may conjecture of the possible influence of the dispersion of so many Jews throughout the empire. No name of any Christian convert in the New Testament can be certainly identified with the name of any one known to us from profane history.

Neither are the descriptions of particular cities or countries at all more instructive. The fact, that at Thessalonica there were many thousand Jews, is of very slight importance in connexion with an Epistle addressed to Gentiles; it is not more than a probability, that we can trace in the erring Galatians the spirit of the worshippers of Cybele or of the followers of Montanus. No amount of research into the history of the time, would inform us of the first question respecting all the Epistles, whether they were addressed to Jews or Gentiles.

Such historical or topographical inquiries are of interest to the antiquarian; they are like the relaxation of foreign travel after severe study: but they have no real connexion with the interpretation of Scripture; and they tend to withdraw the mind from the true sources of illustration of the Epistles, and the true nature of the earliest Christianity. They lead us away from the internal relation of all Jewish and heathen thought to the truths of the Gospel, to a relation between the Church and the world which is purely accidental and external. They tend to give a national and historical character to Christianity, ere yet it appeared to the eye of man as a phenomenon of history. It is not the least danger of such inquiries that they fill up the void of materials by innumerable conjectures.

The traveller in Greece or in Asia who has followed in the footsteps of the Apostles, who has beheld with his own eyes the same scenes that were looked upon by St. Paul and St. John, is loth to believe that he can add nothing to our knowledge of the Seven Churches, or of the labours of the Apostle of the Gentiles. Those scenes have a never-dying interest; but it is for themselves alone. Fain would we imagine the sight upon which St. Paul looked, when standing on Mars' Hill, he beheld 'the city wholly given to idolatry;' fain would we see in fancy the desert rocks of the sea-girt isle, on which St. John gazed when he wrote the Apocalypse. But we must not transfer to the ancient world our own impressions of nature or of art. Of that sensibility to the beauties of scenery, or of that romantic recollection of the past, which are such remarkable characteristics of our own day, there is no trace in the writings of the New Testament, nor any reason to suppose that they had a place in the minds of its authors.

Taking the other aspect of the subject, we are far from denying that the birth of Christianity is the most interesting of historical facts; but its interest is also for itself alone: it is not derived from any political influence which the Gospel at first exercised, or from any political causes which may have favoured or given rise to it. In the vastness of the Roman world, it is as a small isolated spot, the light, as it were, of a candle, which must be sought for, not in the court of Caesar, nor amid the factions of Jerusalem, but in the upper chamber in which the disciples met when 'the number of the names together was about an hundred and twenty, and the doors were shut for fear of the Jews.' It is one of those minute facts which escape the eye of the contemporary historian, and must not be drawn before its time into the circle of political events. Its first greatness is the very contrast which it presents with the greatness of history. Strange it is to think of the contemporary heathen world, of Tiberius at Capreae, of the Roman senate, of the solid framework of the Roman empire itself. But when this first feeling of surprise has passed away, we become aware that the page of Tacitus, or even of Josephus, adds nothing worth speaking of to our knowledge of the earliest Christianity. The most remarkable fact supplied by them is their unconsciousness of its importance.

SUBJECT OF THE EPISTLE.

It does not detract from the value of the First Epistle to the Thessalonians to say that it is without an object. That is, it has no other object but to confirm their faith and remind them of what they owed to the Apostle, as a motive for their continuance in the lesson which he had taught them. The greater part of it is a simple narrative of 'his manner of entering into them' and its results. As though he had said, 'Remember who it was who showed you these things; who spoke to you disinterested words; who drew you towards him with cords of love, as a nurse among her children, as a father with his sons.' The burden of the first three chapters is his love to them and theirs to him; his anxiety to hear of them and to see them. But love cannot abstain from exhortation; not that it has new commands to give, or fresh lessons to impart, but the very excess of love pours itself forth in thrice-told admonitions and consolations. Trite precepts are repeated by the Apostle as by a parent, not because his children know them not, but in the hope that this time they may strike home upon them with some peculiar force or influence.

From the personal narrative which, in the first half of the Epistle, he has made the vehicle of his instruction, he passes on to a more general lesson. There is no peculiar appropriateness in the manner in which the topics of the fourth

SUBJECT OF THE EPISTLE

and fifth chapters follow one another. They are, first, purity; secondly, love of the brethren; thirdly, the state of the departed, and the coming of Christ; fourthly, peace and order; these are followed by particular and apparently disjointed precepts. It is not impossible to trace a connexion of the second and fourth with the third in the series; for affection for one another may have led to an inquiry 'concerning them which are asleep,' and the belief in the approaching Advent, with which the anxiety about the dead was connected, was probably the source of disorder in the Church. Compare 2 Thess. ii. 2. But however interesting such an association may be, we cannot feel certain that it had any real existence in the Apostle's mind. More naturally we may suppose that, as in the First Epistle to the Corinthians, he writes without connexion, as the several subjects occur to him, or may have been suggested by the news of Timothy, as in the former case by certain of the household of Chloe.

The subject which stands out most prominently in this latter portion of the Epistle, is the state of the departed. The formula with which it is introduced reminds us of the similar formula at the commencement of the tenth chapter of the First of Corinthians, 'Moreover, brethren, I would not have you ignorant;' which, in the same way, forms a transition to a fresh topic. It is closely connected with that which is the undercurrent of the whole Epistle, the near approach of the coming of Christ; and probably arises out of some inquiry made of the Apostle by those who were sorrowing for lost friends or kinsmen, who seemed to them not only to have passed, like the Israelites of old, from the presence of God, but from the hope of Messiah's kingdom.

The ground of consolation (1 Thess. iv. 14, 'If we believe that Jesus died and rose again, even so them also which sleep in Jesus will Christ bring with him') is the same as that of 1 Cor. xv. 21, 'Since by man came death, by man came also the resurrection of the dead;' though the form is different. It is the object of the Apostle to do away with the dreary thought which we infer the Thessalonians to have entertained, that they were for ever separated from the dead. Their heaven was on earth, where they were expecting the reign of the Lord Jesus Christ. The Apostle comforts them with the assurance that, even if they should not go to the dead, the dead should return to them; that in that kingdom they were not to be parted, but together, the living with the dead and both with Christ.

EVILS IN THE CHURCH OF THE APOSTOLICAL AGE.

WERE we, with the view of forming a judgement of the moral state of the early Church, to examine the subjects of rebuke most frequently referred to by the Apostle, these would be found to range themselves under four heads:— first, licentiousness; secondly, disorder; thirdly, scruples of conscience; fourthly, strifes about doctrine and teachers. The consideration of these four subjects, the two former falling in with the argument of the Epistle to the Thessalonians, the two latter more closely connected with the Romans and the Galatians, will give what may be termed the darker side of the primitive Church.

1. Licentiousness was the besetting sin of the Roman world. Except by a miracle, it was impossible that the new converts could be at once and wholly freed from it. It lingered in the flesh when the spirit had cast it off. It had interwoven itself in the pagan religions; and, if we may believe the writings of adversaries, was ever reappearing on the confines of the Church in the earliest heresies. It was possible for men 'to resist unto death, striving against sin,' yet to fall beneath its power. Even within the pale of the

Church, it might assume the form of a mystic Christianity. The very ecstasy of conversion would often lead to a reaction. Nothing is more natural than that in a licentious city, like Corinth or Ephesus, those who were impressed by St. Paul's teaching should have gone their way, and returned to their former life. In this case it would seldom happen that they apostatized into the ranks of the heathen: the same impulse which led them to the Gospel, would lead them also to bridge the gulf which separated them from its purer morality. Many may have sinned and repented again and again, unable to stand themselves in the general corruption, yet unable to cast aside utterly the image of innocence and goodness which the Apostle had set before them. There were those, again, who consciously sought to lead the double life, and imagined themselves to have found in licentiousness the true freedom of the Gospel.

How the consciences of men were aroused to the sense that sins of the flesh were really sins, may be seen by the manner in which the Apostle speaks of them. His tone respecting them is very different from that of moralists, or of common conversation even among serious men in modern times. He says nothing of the distrust which they infuse into society, or the consequences to the individual himself.

It is a new and hitherto unheard of language in which the Apostle denounces sins of impurity. They are not moral evils, but spiritual. They corrupt the soul; they defile the temple of the Holy Ghost; they cut men off from the body of Christ. Of morality, as distinct from religion, there is hardly a trace in the Epistles of St. Paul. He cannot appeal to public opinion, for public opinion does not exist; the Gospel itself has to make the standard to the level of which it will raise the world. Fornication and uncleanness were mildly, when at all, censured by heathen philosophy. From within, not from without, the nature of sin has to be explained; as it appears in the depths of the human soul, in the awakening conscience of mankind. Even its consequences in another state of being are but slightly touched upon, in comparison with that living death which [sin] itself is. It is not merely a vice or crime, or even an offence against the law of God, to be punished here or hereafter. It is more than this. It is what men feel in themselves, not what they observe in those around them ; not what shall be, but what is ; a terrible consciousness, a mystery of iniquity, a communion with unseen powers of evil.

But although such is the tone of the Apostle, there is no violence to human nature in his commands respecting it. He knew how easily extremes meet, how hard it is for asceticism to make clean that which is within, how quickly it might itself pass into its opposite. Nothing can be more different from the spirit of early ecclesiastical history on this subject, than the moderation of St. Paul. The remedy for sin is not celibacy, but marriage. Even second marriages are, for the prevention of sin, to be encouraged. In the same spirit is his treatment of the incestuous person. He had committed a sin not even named among the Gentiles, for which he was to be delivered unto Satan, for which all the Church should humble themselves ; yet upon his true repentance, no ban is to separate him from the rest of the brethren, no doom of endless penance is recorded against him. Whatever might have been the enormity of his offence, he was to be forgiven, as in heaven, so on earth.

The manner in which the Corinthian Church are described as regarding this offence before the Apostle's rebuke to them, no less than the lenient sentence of the Apostle himself afterwards, as well as his constant admonitions on the same subject in all his Epistles, must be regarded as indications of the state of morality among the first converts. Above all other things, the Apostle insisted on purity as the first note of the Christian character ; and yet the very earnestness and frequency of his warnings show that he is speaking, not of a sin hardly named among saints, but of one the victory over which was the greatest and most difficult triumph of the cross of Christ.

2. It is hard to resist the impression which naturally arises in our minds, that the early Church was without spot, or wrinkle, or any such thing; as it were, a bride adorned for her husband, the type of Christian purity, the model of Apostolical order. The real image is marred with human frailty; its evils, perhaps, arising more from this cause than any other, that in its commencement it was a kingdom not of this world; in other words, it had no political existence or legal support; hence there is no evil more frequently referred to in the Epistles than disorder.

This spirit of disorder was manifested in various ways. In the Church of Corinth, the communion of the Lord's Supper was administered so as to be a scandal; 'one was hungry, and another was drunken.' There was as yet no rite or custom to which all conformed. In the same Church, the spiritual gifts were manifested without rule or order. It seemed as if God was not the author of peace, but of confusion. All spoke together, men and women, apparently without distinction, singing, praying, teaching, uttering words unintelligible to the rest, with no regular succession or subordination (1 Cor. xiv). The scene in their assemblies was such, that if an unbeliever had come in, he would have said they were mad. There is no other Church into which we have the same particular insight; but it is not likely that more regularity was observed in the Galatian Church, which was distracted between St. Paul and the false teachers, than in the Corinthian, which still, though in disorder, acknowledged his authority. In the Church to which the Epistle of Jude is addressed, the worst heretics are described as joining in the love feasts of its members, 'feeding without fear.' The Second Epistle of Peter uses nearly the same words to the Jews of the dispersion. (Jude 12; 2 Pet. ii. 13.)

Evils of this kind in a great measure arose from the

absence of Church authority. Even the Apostle himself persuades more often than commands, and often uses language which implies a sort of hesitation whether his rule would be acknowledged or not. The freedom with which the Church of Corinth challenges particulars in his life and conduct (1 Cor. ix) reminds us rather of the license of a modern congregation in censuring a minister of the Gospel, who was under its control, than of the position which we should expect an Apostle to have held in the minds of the first converts. The diverse offices, the figure of the members and the body, do not refer to what was, but to what ought to have been; to an ideal of harmonious life and action, which the Apostle holds up before them, which in practice was far from being realized. The Church was not organized, but was in process of organization. Its only punishment was excommunication, which, as in modern so in primitive times, could not be enforced against the wishes of the majority. In two cases only are members of the Church 'delivered unto Satan' (1 Cor. v. 5; 1 Tim. i. 20). It was a moral and spiritual, not a legal control that was exercised. Hence the frequent admonitions given, doubtless, because they were needed: 'Obey them that have the rule over you.'

A second kind of disorder arose from unsettlement of mind. Of such unsettlement we find traces in the levity and vanity of the Corinthians; in the fickleness with which the Galatians left St. Paul for the false teachers; almost (may we not say?) in the very passion with which the Apostle addresses them; above all, in the case of the Thessalonians. How few, among all the converts, were there capable of truly discerning their relation to the world around! or of supporting themselves alone when the fervour of conversion had passed away and the Apostle was no longer present with them! They had entered into a state so different from that of their fellow-men, that it might well be termed supernatural. The ordinary experience of men was no longer their guide. They left their daily employments. The great change which they felt within, seemed to extend itself without and involve the world in its shadow. So 'palpable to sense' was the vision of Christ's coming again, that their only fear or doubt was how the departed would have a share in it. No religious belief could be more unsettling than this: that to-day, or to-morrow, or the third day, before the sun set or the dawn arose, the sign of the Son of man might appear in the clouds of heaven. It was not possible to take thought for the morrow, to study to be quiet and get their own living, when men hardly expected the morrow. Death comes to individuals now, as nature prepares them for it; but the immediate expectation of Christ's coming is out of the course of nature. Young and old alike look for it. It is a resurrection of the world itself, and implies a corresponding revolution in the thoughts, feelings, and purposes of men.

A third kind of disorder may have arisen from the same causes, but seems to have assumed another character. As among the Jews, so among the first Christians, there were those who needed to be perpetually reminded, that the powers that be were ordained of God. The heathen converts could not at once lay aside the licentiousness of manners amid which they had been brought up; no more could the Jewish converts give up their aspirations, that at this time 'the kingdom was to be restored to Israel,' which had perhaps been in some cases their first attraction to the Gospel. A community springing up in Palestine under the dominion of the Romans, could not be expected exactly to draw the line between the things that were Caesar's and the things that were God's, or to understand in what sense 'the children were free,' in what sense it was nevertheless their duty to pay tribute. The spirit of those Galileans, 'who called no man Lord,' must have sometimes found its way into the early Christian Church. When men are 'wrestling against principalities and powers, and spiritual wickedness in heavenly places,' they do not find it easy to reconcile their course of action with the bidding of those 'who sit in Moses's seat.' That one of the chief apprehensions of the Apostle was this tendency to rebellion, is proved by the frequency of the exhortations to obey magistrates, and the energy with which he sets himself against it.

3. The third head of our inquiry related to scruples of conscience, which were chiefly of two kinds ; regarding either the observance of days, or the eating with the unclean or unbelievers. Were they, or were they not, to observe the Jewish Sabbath, or new moon, or passover ? Such questions as these are not to be considered the fancies or opinions of individuals ; but, as mankind are quick enough to discover, involve general principles, and are but the outward signs of some deep and radical difference. In the question of the observance of Jewish feasts, and still more in the question of going in unto men uncircumcised and eating with them, was implied the whole question of the relation of the disciple of Christ to the Jew, just as the question of sitting at meat in the idol's temple was the question of the relation of the disciple of Christ to the Gentile. Was the Christian to preserve his caste, and remain within the pale of Judaism ? Was he in his daily life to carry his religious scruples so far as to exclude himself from the social life of the heathen world ? How much prudence and liberty and charity was necessary for the solution of such difficulties!

Freedom is the key-note of the Gospel, as preached by St. Paul. 'All things are lawful.' 'There is no distinction of Jew or Greek, barbarian or Scythian, bond or free.' 'Let no man judge you of a new moon or a Sabbath.' 'Where the spirit of the Lord is, there is liberty.' And yet, if we go back to its origin, the Christian Church was born into the world marked and diversified with the features of the religions that had preceded it, bound within the curtains of the tabernacle, coloured with Oriental opinions

EVILS IN THE CHURCH OF THE APOSTOLICAL AGE 29

that refused to be washed out of the minds of men. The scruples of individuals are but indications of the elements out of which the Church was composed. There were narrow paths in which men walked, customs which clung to them long after the reason of them had ceased, observances which they were unable to give up, though conscience and reason alike disowned them, which were based on the traditions of half the world, and could not be relinquished, however alien to the spirit of the Gospel. Slowly and gradually, as Christianity itself became more spread, these remnants of Judaism or Orientalism disappeared, and the spirit which had been taught from the beginning made itself felt in the hearts of men and in the institutions of the Church.

4. The heresies of the Apostolical age are a subject too wide for illustration in a note. We shall attempt no more than to bring together the names and heads of opinion which occur in Scripture, with the view of completing the preceding sketch.

There was the party of Peter and of Paul, of the circumcision and of the uncircumcision. There were those who knew 'Christ according to the flesh;' those who, like St. Paul, knew Him only as revealed within. There were others who, after casting aside circumcision, were still struggling between the old dispensation and the new. There were those who never went beyond the baptism of John; others, again, to whom the Gospel of Christ clothed itself in Alexandrian language. There were prophets, speakers with tongues, discerners of spirits, interpreters of tongues. There were seekers after 'knowledge, falsely so called;' 'spoilers of others with philosophy and vain deceit,' 'worshippers of angels, intruders into things they had not seen.' There were those who looked daily for the coming of Christ; others who 'said that the Resurrection was passed already.' There were some who maintained an Oriental asceticism in their lives, 'forbidding to marry, commanding to abstain from meats.' There were individuals, like Hymenaeus and Alexander, who had 'made shipwreck of their faith;' like Phygellus and Hermogenes, who had 'turned away' from St. Paul; like Diotrephes, the leader in the Church of Ephesus, who refused to 'receive' St. John. There were national differences, Jewish Sectarian tendencies, heathen systems of philosophy; stones of another workmanship built into the fabric of the Christian Church. There was the doctrine of the Nicolaitans, the synagogue of Satan, who 'said that they were Jews, and are not,' 'the woman Jezebel, which calleth herself a prophetess.' There were wild heretics, 'many Antichrists,' 'grievous wolves, entering into the fold,' apostasy of whole churches at once. There were mingled anarchy and licentiousness, 'filthy dreamers, despising dominion, speaking evil of dignities,' of whom no language is too strong for St. Paul or St. John to use, though they seem to have been separated by no definite line from the Church itself. There were fainter contrasts, too, of those who agreed in the unity of the same spirit, aspects, and points of view, as we term them, of faith and works, of the Epistle to the Romans and the Epistle to the Hebrews.

How this outline is to be filled up must for ever remain, in a great degree, matter of speculation. Yet there is not a single trait here mentioned which does not reappear in the second century, either within the Church or without it, more or less prominent as favoured by circumstances or the reverse. The beginning of Ebionitism, Sabaism, Gnosticism, Montanism, Alexandrianism, Orientalism, and of the licentiousness which marked the track of some of them, are all discernible in the Apostolical age. They would be more correctly regarded, not as offshoots of Christianity, but as the soil in which it grew up. We are surrounded by them, in the Epistles of St. Paul, as truly as the Israelites were surrounded by their enemies when they first took possession of the Promised Land. They are not errors which arose when men began to speculate on the truths of the Gospel: Gnosticism, in particular, would be more nearly described as the mental atmosphere of the Greek cities of Asia, a conducting medium between heathenism and Christianity, in the magic light of which all religions faded and reappeared. None of them pass away at once; some even acquire a temporary principle of life, and grow up parallel with the Church itself. As opinions and tendencies of the human mind, many linger among us to the present day. Only after the destruction of Jerusalem, with the spread of the Gospel over the world, as the spirit of the East moves towards the West, Judaism dies away, to rise again, as some hold, in the glorified form of a mediaeval Church.

Such is the reverse side of the picture of the Apostolical age; what proportions we should give to each feature it is impossible to determine. We need not infer that all Churches were in the same disorder as Corinth and Galatia; or like Sardis, in which only 'a few names had not defiled their garments;' nor can we say how far the more flagrant evils were tamely submitted to by the Church itself. There was much of good that we can never know; much also of evil. The first Christians stood alone in the world: many of them were ready to venture their lives for the faith; most of them had probably suffered persecution—a difference between ourselves and them than which none can be greater. And perhaps the general lesson which we gather from the preceding considerations is, not that the state of the primitive Church was better or worse than our first thoughts would have suggested, but that its state was one in which good and evil exercised a more vital power, were more subtly intermingled with, and more easily passed into, each other. All things were coming to the birth, some in one way, some in another. The supports of custom, of opinion, of tradition, had given way; human nature was thrown upon itself and the guidance of the Spirit of God. There were as many diversities of human character in the world then as now;

more strange influences of religion and race than have ever since met in one ; a far greater yearning of the human intellect to solve the problems of existence. There was no settled principle of morality independent of and above religious convictions. All these causes are sufficient to account for the diversities of opinion or practice, as well as for the extremes which met in the bosom of the primitive Church.

THE FIRST EPISTLE

TO THE

THESSALONIANS

1 PAUL, and Silvanus, and Timotheus, unto the Church of the Thessalonians in God the Father and the Lord Jesus Christ; Grace unto you, and peace [from God our Father, and the Lord Jesus Christ].

2 We give thanks to God always for you all, making

1. ἐν θεῷ πατρί, *in God the Father*] is closely connected with the preceding words. All things in their highest aspect, churches, individuals, the actions, feelings, and words of men, are in God and Christ; they pass out of themselves into union with the Divine nature; they rest in God, have their place in Him, 'take up their abode' in Him (compare John xiv. 10, 20; Phil. iv. 2; Eph. vi. 1). The nearest approach in classical Greek to this 'Christian' signification of the preposition ἐν is its use with the person (ἐν σοί, ἐμοί, ἑαυτῷ) in the sense of 'in the power of.' Language of this sort can hardly be said to exist among ourselves; it is only repeated from the New Testament. Yet so it was the early Church thought and felt.

2-10. Few passages are more characteristic of the style of St. Paul than that on which we are entering. First, as it is the overflowing of his soul in thankfulness for his converts, about whom he can never say too much. Secondly, in the very form and structure of the sentences, which seem to grow under his hand, gaining force in each successive clause by the repetition and expansion of the preceding. A classical or modern writer distinguishes his several propositions, assigning to each its exact relation to what goes before and follows, that he may give meaning and articulation to the whole. The manner of St. Paul is the reverse of this. He overlays one proposition with another, the second just emerging beyond the first, and arising out of association with it, but not always standing in a clear relation to it. Thus in the passage which we are considering, ἀδιαλείπτως μνημονεύοντες, in ver. 3, is a repetition of εὐχαριστοῦμεν πάντοτε and μνείαν ποιούμενοι, in ver. 2. Again, with

VOL. I. D

3 mention of you ^aat^{*g*} our prayers; remembering without ceasing your work of faith, and labour of love, and patience of hope ^bof^{*g*} our Lord Jesus Christ, in the
4 sight of ^c our God and^{*g*} Father; knowing, brethren
5 beloved ^d of God, your election, that^{*g*} our gospel came not unto you in word only, but also in power, and in the Holy Ghost, and in much assurance; as ye know

^a in   ^b in   ^c God and our   ^d your election of God. For

reference to the latter words themselves, it is not clear whether μνείαν ποιούμενοι is an addition to, or a limitation on, εὐχαριστοῦμεν. A little lower down, ver. 5, the clause ὅτι τὸ εὐαγγέλιον, κ.τ.λ., is a sort of after-thought on τὴν ἐκλογήν. In like manner, whether in the words καὶ ὑμεῖς μιμηταί, in the 6th verse, the Apostle carries in his thoughts the preceding οἴδατε, or not, is uncertain. Ver. 8 is an amplification of ver. 7, and in ver. 8 itself the language of the second clause is varied from that of the first, without any variation of meaning; in ver. 9 the words δουλεύειν θεῷ ζῶντι καὶ ἀληθινῷ, are an extension of the preceding ἐπεστρέψατε πρὸς τὸν θεὸν ἀπὸ τῶν εἰδώλων. At the commencement of chap. ii we appear to break off and pass on to a new subject, and yet are but resuming the thread of ver. 5 and 6 in the preceding.

Leaving the form, let us go on to the substance. The Apostle is full of thankfulness to God for the conversion of the Thessalonians, which has brought forth such unmistakable fruits of righteousness. These are just in accordance with the manner of their reception of the Gospel, the manner in which he preached and they believed. It seemed to have a peculiar power over them, received with joy amid persecutions; they were as burning and shining lights in all that land. Their conversion was in all men's mouths, who could not help, of their own accord, telling even the Apostle himself how these idolaters had come to the knowledge of the true God; and how they, like the other disciples, had learned to sit waiting for the day of the Lord. In such manner does the Apostle, in the excess of his affection for them, not without knowledge of the way in which to approach human nature, transform the language of compliment into a spiritual lesson.

3. τοῦ ἔργου τῆς πίστεως, *work of faith*,] has been variously explained as meaning the reality of your faith, or the fact of your receiving the Gospel, or the working of your faith. Better your work of faith, that is, the Christian life which springs from faith. (Comp. 2 Thess. i. 11.)

6. The suffering that comes from without, cannot depress the spirit of a man who is faithful in a good cause. It is only when 'from within are fears' that the mind is enslaved. For in the spiritual world joy and

what manner of men we were among you for your
sake; and ye became followers of us, and of the Lord,
having received the word in much affliction, with joy
of the Holy Ghost: so that ye were ᵉan ensample ⁽⁾ to
all that believe in Macedonia and ᶠin ⁽⁾ Achaia. For
from you ᵍhas been ⁽⁾ sounded out the word of the
Lord not only in Macedonia and ᶠin ⁽⁾ Achaia, but ʰ⁻⁽⁾ in
every place your faith to God-ward is spread abroad;
so that we need not to speak any thing. For they
themselves shew of us what manner of entering in we
had unto you, and how ye turned to God from idols to
serve the living and true God, and to wait for his Son

ᵉ *ensamples*   ᶠ omit *in*   ᵍ *omit* has been   ʰ add *also*

sorrow are not two, but one. The servant of Christ feels a sort of exhilaration at the contrast between himself and the world, similar to that of the soldier on the battle-field, in the presence of danger and death. He is not like another man, but at once above and below others; he has the sentence of death in himself, and is yet more than a conqueror. It is this peculiarity of the Christian character that the Apostle expresses by 'joy of the Holy Ghost,' 'glorying in the Lord,' 'fulness of consolation:' 'rejoicing in his sufferings, and filling up what was wanting of the afflictions of Christ in his flesh.' See also the alternations of feeling in 2 Cor. vi. 10: 'As sorrowful, yet alway rejoicing.' Herein too the Thessalonians were 'followers of St. Paul as he was of Christ.' Compare John xii. 23, 'The hour is come, that the Son of man should be glorified;' and the double character of the discourse in the following chapters which precedes our Lord's passion.

8. ἐν παντὶ τόπῳ, *in every place.*] How could it be said, that the faith of the Thessalonians was known everywhere? It has been sometimes attempted to remove this difficulty by taking οὐ μόνον (not only) with ἐξήχηται (for from you has not only been sounded out), which is objectionable, however, both upon the ground of the order of the words and the poorness of the sense. It is better to admit that the language of St. Paul, uttered in the fullness of his heart, is not to be construed strictly, any more than where he says, in like manner, that the faith of the Romans was known over the whole world (Rom. i. 8), or that the Gospel of which he was a minister was preached to every creature under heaven. He means, in other words, that not only in Greece, but in Asia, wherever there were believers, the news of the Thessalonian

from heaven, whom he raised from the dead, Jesus, which ⁱ delivereth ⁰ us from the wrath to come.

2 For yourselves, brethren, know our entrance in ² unto you, that it was not in vain: but ᵏ⁻⁰ after that we had suffered before, and were shamefully entreated, as ye know, at Philippi, we were bold in our God to

ⁱ delivered   ᵏ add *even*

conversion had spread, or rather must have spread; he had no need to speak of them, for the report of them had preceded him on his way.

It is not necessary that these latter words should be connected with ἐν παντὶ τόπῳ; the meaning would be assisted if, instead of adopting Lachmann's punctuation, the clause, ὥστε μὴ χρείαν ἔχειν ἡμᾶς λαλεῖν τι, were separated by a colon from ἐξελήλυθεν, and closely joined with the following verse.

2. The personal narrative which follows, may be compared with that in the Galatians i. 11 to ii. 14. Alluding to the spirit in which he preached to them, he glances, for an instant, at the persecution which he had just before endured at Philippi, and which had not deterred him from speaking the truth boldly, though at Thessalonica too the conflict was hot. He had spoken as to God and not to men, without covetousness, or guile, or flattery, or vain glory, or any such thing. He had given up his right to support as an Apostle from the excess of his love to them; a love, which would fain have made him lay down his life for their sake. They must surely remember how they had seen him toiling day and night to get his own livelihood; they were the witnesses (and there was a higher witness) of the innocence of his life, and of his gentle and fatherly admonitions to them.

Then changing the person, he gives thanks to God as at first, for their reception of the Word of God; they had become followers of the Churches in Judea, and stood in the same relation to their own countrymen, as these did to the Jews. The persecutions that they suffered, did but recall the thought of what these latter had done to the Lord Jesus, and to their own prophets; enemies, as they were, of God and man, forbidding to preach to the Gentiles that they might be saved. Their evil was tending to a consummation, and the wrath of God was fulfilled upon them.

In the verses which follow, there appears to be an abrupt transition to the longing desire that the Apostle had to see them, and the efforts that he had made to accomplish this purpose. The 15th and 16th verses are a digression which may be regarded as an outburst of indignation at the Jews. As in conversation we sometimes ask, 'What leads another to say that?' so here we can but guess the secret thread of

speak unto you the gospel of God with much con-
3 tention. For our exhortation was not of deceit, nor
4 of uncleanness, nor in guile; but as we were ¹ approved⁗
of God to be put in trust with the gospel, even so we
speak; not as pleasing men, but God which ᵐ proveth⁗
5 our hearts. For neither at any time used we flattering
words, as ye know, nor a cloke of covetousness; God
6 is witness: nor of men sought we glory, neither of
you, nor of others, when we might have been burden-
7 some, as the apostles of Christ. But we were ⁿ babes⁗
among you, even as a nurse cherisheth her ᵒ own⁗
8 children: so being affectionately desirous of you, we
were willing to have imparted unto you, not the gospel
of God only, but also our own souls, because ye were

¹ alowed   ᵐ trieth   ⁿ *gentle*   ᵒ *omit* own

association which carries on the mind of the Apostle from one topic to another. The real connexion in what follows may probably be the persecutions of the Thessalonian Church, just slightly touched upon in ver. 14, which quickened the Apostle's desire to see them, and increased his sense of loneliness in being parted from them. This thread reappears again in the following chapter, iii. 2–9.

3. The two senses of παράκλησις, exhortation and consolation, so easily passing into one another (compare ver. 11), are suggestive of the external state of the early Church, sorrowing amid the evils of the world, and needing as its first lesson to be comforted, and not less suggestive of the first lesson of the Gospel to the individual soul of peace in believing.

Many passages in the New Testament lead us to infer, that there existed, in the age of the Apostles, a connexion between the form of spirituality and licentiousness. It is this of which the Apostle declares his innocence, and with which elsewhere he upbraids the false teachers. Compare iv. 7; Tit. iii. 8; James iii. 13; 1 Tim. vi. 3; Jude 4–18.

6. Why should the Apostle so repeatedly repudiate the imputation that he sought glory of men? He was one of those who instinctively know the impression produced by his character and conduct on the hearts of others. What was the motive of this 'vain babbler' would be a common topic of conversation in the cities at which he preached. 'To get money, to make himself somebody,' would be the ordinary solution. Against this the Apostle protests. His whole life and conversation were a disproof of it. It may have been that he

9 dear unto us. For ye remember, brethren, our labour and travail: ᵖ⁻⁾ labouring night and day, because we would not be ᑫ burdensome ᶠ unto any of you, we 10 preached unto you the gospel of God. Ye are witnesses, and God also, how holily and ʳ righteously ᵍ and unblameably we behaved ˢ⁻⁾ among you that

ᵖ add *for*   ᑫ chargeable   ʳ justly   ˢ *add* ourselves

was aware also of something in his manner which might have suggested such a thought. It was not good for him to glory, and yet he sometimes 'spake as a fool.' Rightly understood this glorying was but an elevation of the soul to God and Christ, or at worst the assertion of himself, in moments of depression or ill-treatment, but to others he might have been conscious that it must have seemed a weakness, and may have been made a ground of imputations from his adversaries.

9. It throws a singular light on the life of St. Paul, which reflects itself in some degree on the early Church, to observe that his labours as a preacher of the Gospel were not the sole business which engaged him, but were added to his daily occupation. Such, at least, we know to have been his custom at Corinth, at Thessalonica, at Ephesus, and probably elsewhere. Of the twelve hours of the day, perhaps not more than one, of the seven days of the week, perhaps only the Sabbath, was devoted to the exercise of his spiritual calling. It is natural to ask, what motive could have led him, a man of station and education, unused to toil, brought up in the school of a Rabbi, at an age when the bodily frame refuses to perform any new office, to submit himself to manual labour? Was it that he desired to set the example of Christian life, as well as to teach Christian doctrine, to show that there was no opposition between the Gospel and the daily course of the world? Or may it have been to identify himself with the poorer members of his flock? or to provide for their necessities? or as a religious exercise to keep under his body, and bring it into subjection? or to distinguish himself from the strolling soothsayers who wandered over Greece and Asia, 'telling some new thing'? or to draw a line between himself and the Judaizing teachers? or from necessity, or, as we should say, to preserve his independence? Whatever higher motives led the Apostle to toil for his bread, the last-mentioned one falls in with that peculiar sensitiveness respecting the charge of receiving money, which is traceable in the Second Epistle to the Corinthians, both in reference to himself and Titus receiving support from the Church, as in reference to the collections for the saints. In the Second Epistle to the Thessalonians, iii. 4, another motive is also indicated, the desire to set an example to his

11 believe: as ye know how we exhorted and comforted and charged every one of you, as a father doth his
12 children, that ye would walk worthy of God, who ᵗ calleth ⁰ you unto his kingdom and glory.
13 And for this cause ᵘ we also thank ⁰ God without ceasing, because, when ye received the word of God which ye heard of us, ye received it not as the word of men, but as it is in truth, the word of God, which
14 effectually worketh also in you that believe. For ye, brethren, became followers of the churches of God which in Judæa are in Christ Jesus: for ye also have suffered like things of your own countrymen, even as
15 they have of the Jews: who both killed the Lord Jesus, and ˣ the ⁰ prophets, have persecuted us; and they please not God, and are contrary to all men:

ᵗ hath called ᵘ also thank we ˣ *their own*

converts. A third motive, that of charity, is mentioned in the discourse to the elders of the Church of Ephesus. (Acts xx. 34.)

14. Wherever the Apostle had gone on his second journey, he had been persecuted by the Jews; and the longer he travelled about among Gentile cities, the more he must have been sensible of the feeling with which his countrymen were regarded. Isolated as they were from the rest of the world in every city, a people within a people, it was impossible that they should not be united for their own self-defence, and regarded with suspicion by the rest of mankind. But their inner nature was not less repugnant to the nobler, as well as the baser feelings of Greece and Rome. Their fierce nationality had outlived itself; though worshippers of the true God, they knew Him not to be the God of all nations of the earth; hated and despised by others, they could but cherish in return an impotent contempt and hatred of other men. What wonder that, for an instant, the Apostle should have felt that this Gentile feeling was not wholly groundless? or that he should use words which recall the expression of Tacitus: 'Adversus omnes alios hostile odium?'—Hist. v. 5.

For the feelings which the Apostle entertained towards his countrymen at a later period, compare Rom. x. 1:—'Brethren, my heart's desire and prayer to God for Israel is, that they may be saved.' Yet, both states of mind may have existed together; the one on the surface, called forth by passing events; the other in his 'heart of hearts,' deep and silent.

16 forbidding us to speak to the Gentiles that they might be saved, to fill up their sins alway. ʸ But ⁿ the wrath ᶻ has ⁿ come upon them to the uttermost.

17 BUT we, brethren, being ᵃ bereaved in being ⁿ taken from you for a short time in presence, not in heart, ᵇ were the more abundantly earnest ⁿ to see your face 18 with great desire. Wherefore we would have come unto you, even I Paul, once and again; but Satan 19 hindered us. For what is our hope, or joy, or crown of rejoicing? Are not even ye in the presence of our 20 Lord Jesus Christ at his coming? For ye are our

ʸ For   ᶻ *is*   ᵃ *omit* bereaved in being   ᵇ endeavoured the more abundantly

16. It has been maintained that this verse must have been written after the destruction of Jerusalem. (See Introductory Essay, on the Genuineness of the Epistle.) Had it been so, it is probable that allusions to the destruction of Jerusalem would have appeared elsewhere in the Epistle, and that this very passage would have spoken more plainly. In all ages, without the gift of prophecy, men have been prone to read the signs of evil in the world. There was enough in the outward state of the Jewish people, as we read the narrative of it in Josephus, or in the impenitency and obstinacy of the Jewish nature, as it revealed itself to the Apostle from within, to be the shadow of events to come. Yet the language of the Apostle seems to indicate, not that they were actually suffering or to suffer punishment, but only that they had reached their final point of reprobation from whence there is no more a way back.

19. For you are our hope and joy and crown of glory in the day of judgment. As he says elsewhere:—'Who is weak, and I am not weak?' or, in other words, who feels, and I do not feel with him?—so in this passage, their hope is his hope, their joy is his joy; they are his crown of glory at the last day. He does not mean that he is to be rewarded for converting them; it is a higher thought than this which fills the Apostle's soul. Remembering that hour on which his mind is dwelling, he transfers them to it, and is rapt in his love of them. Compare, for the time, note on Rom. ii. 16; for a similar use of a figure, 2 Cor. iii. 2, 'Ye are our Epistle;' and for the general meaning, 2 Tim. iv. 8. 'Henceforth there is laid up for me a crown of righteousness, which the Lord, the righteous judge, shall give me at that day;' and, as the Apostle characteristically adds, 'not to me only, but to all that love his appearing.'

3 glory and joy. Wherefore when we could no longer
   ᶜcontain,ǁ we thought it good to be left at Athens
2 alone; and sent Timotheus, ¹our brother, and fellow-
   worker with God, in the gospel of Christ, to establish
3 you, and to comfort you concerning your faith, that
   no man should be moved by these ᵈtribulations ǁ; for
4 yourselves know that we are appointed thereunto, for
   verily, when we were with you, we told you before
   that we should suffer tribulation; even as it came to
5 pass, and ye know. For this cause, when I could no
   longer forbear, I also sent to know your faith, lest by
   some means the tempter have tempted you, and our
6 labour been in vain. But now when Timotheus came
   from you unto us, and brought us good tidings of your
   faith and ᵉlove,ǁ and that ye have good remembrance
   of us always, desiring greatly to see us, as we also to
7 see you: therefore, brethren, we were comforted ᶠin ǁ

| ᶜ forbear | ᵈ afflictions | ᵉ charity | ᶠ over |

3. καταλειφθῆναι, κ.τ.λ., *to be left*, &c.] It may be remarked, that these words half agree with the Acts, and half with the Epistle. For they imply that the Apostle was left without companions, and yet there is no mention of his sending away Silas, who was with him at the time of his writing the Epistle, but only Timothy.

Admitting the genuineness of the Epistle, and the confirmation afforded by it to many of the statements of the Acts, we are naturally led to speculate by what arrangement of events the error may be made smallest.

Suppose Silas only to have been left in Macedonia, with a charge to join Paul shortly; Paul, impatient to hear of his new converts, sends Timothy from Athens, who returns with Silas. The only incorrectness then in the narrative of the Acts arises from the ignorance of the writer, that Timothy was not left behind. The account of the Epistle, that Paul *was* left alone at Athens, although he only sent away Timothy and although Silas and Timothy were with him shortly afterwards, as well as the tone of the Acts, respecting Paul's eagerness that Silas and Timothy should follow him, agrees with this hypothesis.

7. διὰ τοῦτο] takes up the sentence after the long participial clauses. *For this good news.*

ἄρτι παρεκλήθημεν, now we are comforted. Implying that the

¹ Reading τὸν ἀδελφὸν ἡμῶν καὶ συνεργὸν τοῦ θεοῦ

you, in all our affliction and distress by your faith:
8 for now we live, if ye stand fast in the Lord. For
9 what thanks can we render to God again for you, for
all the joy wherewith we joy for your sakes before
10 our God; night and day praying exceedingly that we
might see your face, and might perfect that which is
11 lacking in your faith? Now our God and Father
himself, and our Lord Jesus Christ direct our way
12 unto you. And the Lord make you to increase and
abound in love one toward another, and toward all
13 men, even as we do toward you: to the end he may

Epistle was written immediately after the return of Timothy. The Apostle, though speaking now of what was almost present to himself, still uses the historical tense; possibly, like ἔγραψα in 1 Cor. v. 9, and elsewhere, in reference to the time at which the Thessalonians would receive his letter—as in Latin.

8. ὅτι νῦν ζῶμεν, *for now we live.*] The Apostle regards his affliction as a sort of death, from which he is roused to life by the news of his converts. Compare 2 Cor. i. 8-10, and Gal. ii. 20, for a similar figure.

νῦν refers to the change of feeling occasioned by the arrival of Timothy. When he thought of the persecutions that surrounded him, and the possibility of their falling off from the faith, he was as one 'having the sentence of death in himself:' but now in their life he lives.

13. All ages which have witnessed a revival of religious feeling, have witnessed also the outbreak of religious passions; the pure light of the one becomes the spark by which the other is kindled. Reasons of state sometimes create a faint and distant suspicion of a new faith; the feelings of the mass rise to overwhelm it.

Allowing for the difference of times and seasons, the feelings of the Roman governors were not altogether unlike those with which the followers of John Wesley, in the last century, might have been regarded by the magistrates of an English town. And making still greater allowance for the malignity and depth of the passions by which men were agitated as the old religions were breaking up, a parallel not less just might be drawn also between the feelings of the multitude. There was in both cases a kind of sympathy by which the lower class were attracted towards the new teachers. Natural feeling suggested that these men had come for their good; they were grateful for the love shown of them, and for the ministration to their temporal wants. There was a time when it was said of the first believers, that they were in favour with all the people (Acts ii. 47), and that 'all men glorified God for that which was done' stablish your hearts unblameable in holiness before ᵍ our God and Father, ⁰ at the coming of our Lord Jesus Christ with all his saints.

ᵍ *God, our Father*

(iv. 21). But at the preaching of Stephen the scene changes; the deep irreconcilable hostility of the two principles is beginning to be felt; 'it is not peace, but a sword;' not 'I am come to fulfil the law,' but 'not one stone shall be left upon another.'

The moment this was clearly perceived, not only would the far-sighted jealousy of chief priests and rulers be alarmed at the preaching of the Apostles; but the very instincts of the multitude itself would rise at them. More than anything that we have witnessed in modern times of religious intolerance, would be the feeling against those who sought to relax the bond of circumcision as enemies to their country, their religion, and their God. But there was another aspect of the new religion, which served to bring home these feelings even yet more nearly. It was the disruption of the family. As our Lord foretold, the father was against the son, the son against the father, the mother-in-law against the daughter-in-law, the daughter-in-law against her mother-in-law. A new power had arisen in the world, which seemed to cut across and dissever natural affections (Matt. x. 34). Consider what is implied in the words 'of believing women not a few;' what animosities of parents, and brethren, and husbands! what hatreds, and fears, and jealousies! An unknown tie, closer than that of kindred, drew away the individuals of a family, and joined them to an external society. It was not only that they were members of another Church, or attendants on a separate worship. The difference went beyond this. In the daily intercourse of life, at every meal, the unbelieving brother or sister was conscious of the presence of the unclean. It was an injury not readily to be forgotten, or forgiven its authors, the greatest, perhaps, which could be offered in this world. The fanatic priest, led on by every personal and religious motive— the man of the world, caring for none of those things, but not the less resenting the intrusion on the peace of his home—the craftsman, fearing for his gains—the accursed multitude, knowing not the law, but irritated at the very notion of this mysterious society of such real though hidden strength—would all work together towards the overthrow of those who seemed to them to be turning upside down the political, religious, and social order of the world. The utterance of this instinct of dislike, is heard in the words, 'These men being Jews, do exceedingly trouble our city, and teach customs which are not lawful for us to receive, neither to observe, being Romans.' Acts xvi. 20, 21. (Compare, to complete the picture, the description in the previous verses of the damsel possessed with a spirit of

4 ¹FURTHERMORE then we beseech you, brethren, and exhort you by the Lord Jesus, that as ye received of us how ye ought to walk and to please God, even as ye do walk, that ye would abound more and more. 2 For ye know what commandments we gave you by 3 the Lord Jesus. For this is the will of God, your sanctification, that ye should abstain from fornication: 4 that every one of you should know how to ᵇ get himself

ᵇ possess his

divination, who cried after Paul many days, 'These men are the servants of the most High God.')

These considerations, though based only on general principles of human nature, are necessary to make us understand the undercurrent of the Apostolical history, as well as to form a just estimate of the question which we are considering. The actual persecution of the Roman government was slight, but what may be termed the social persecution and the illegal violence employed towards the first disciples unceasing. 'Of the Jews five times received I forty stripes save one;' who would know or care what went on in the Jewish quarter of a great city? How precarious must have been their fate who, with the passions of men arrayed against them, had no protection from the law! They were liable to be persecuted by the Jews, to suffer persecution as Jews, to arm the feelings of all nations against themselves as the professors of an unnatural religion. Little reflection is necessary to fill up the details of that image of peril, which the Apostle presents to us in all his Epistles. It is the same vision which is again held up to us in the Book of the Revelation, of the common tribulation of St. John and the Churches, of the sufferings that were to come upon the Church of Smyrna, of the faithfulness of Pergamos in the days when the martyr Antipas was slain, of the two witnesses, and of the souls beneath the altar, saying 'How long?' It is the same which reappears in the earliest ecclesiastical history, in the narrative of Hegesippus respecting James the Just. It is the state of life described in the Epistle to the Hebrews of those who 'had not yet resisted unto blood, striving against sin' (xii. 4), whose leaders seem to have already suffered (xiii. 7, 23). Except on some accidental occasion, such as the Neronian persecution, there is no reason to suppose that the power of Rome was systematically employed against the first disciples of the Apostles. But it does not diminish their sufferings, that they were the result of illegal violence, such as the tumults at Thessalonica, at Ephesus, or at Jerusalem.

4. 4. τὸ ἑαυτοῦ σκεῦος κτᾶσθαι, *to get his own vessel.*] It is doubted

¹ Reading λοιπὸν οὖν

4. 8] FIRST EPISTLE TO THE THESSALONIANS 45

5 his own " vessel in sanctification and honour: not in
the lust of concupiscence, even as the Gentiles which
6 know not God: that no man go beyond and defraud
his brother in the matter: because that the Lord is
the avenger of all these things, as we also forewarned
7 you and testified. For God called us not unto un-
8 cleanness, but in sanctification. He therefore that
despiseth, despiseth not man, but God, who giveth
unto you his holy Spirit.

whether under the image of a vessel is meant 'the body' or 'a wife.' The meaning of the word κτᾶσθαι, and the opposition of ἑαυτοῦ to πορνείας, and also to πλεονεκτεῖν τὸν ἀδελφόν, in ver. 6, is decidedly in favour of the latter interpretation. Compare 1 Cor. vii. 2, for a similar opposition, διὰ δὲ τὰς πορνείας ἕκαστος τὴν ἑαυτοῦ γυναῖκα ἐχέτω. For the figure, compare 1 Peter iii. 7. See also parallels in Schöttgen, which prove the common Jewish use of σκεῦος for a wife. On the other hand, it may be urged that there would be no propriety here, as there is elsewhere, in the description of the 'body' under the metaphor of a vessel; when in Rom. ix. 21, the term σκεῦος ὀργῆς occurs, this is a continuation of the figure of the potter; when in 2 Cor. iv. 7, the body is called ὀστράκινον σκεῦος, this is to denote its frailty; so in 2 Tim. ii. 20, 21 the metaphor is helped by the surrounding words. But none of these uses shows that σκεῦος in this place could simply mean body.

The exact force of the whole passage may be expressed as follows:—'This is the will of God—your sanctification:' by this is meant, 'your abstaining from fornication, your knowing how to live chastely in a married state.' This is opposed to ver. 6, the general sense of which is 'not to covet another man's wife.' Two difficulties occur, however, in the attempt to disentangle the connexion. First, it might seem as if St. Paul was enjoining all men to marry. This, however, is modified by ver. 6. Every man is to have his own wife, rather than to defraud his neighbour. In other words, the precept is not absolute; but relative to the sin of adultery and fornication. The second difficulty is the insertion of μὴ ἐν πάθει ἐπιθυμίας, in ver. 5, because it might be said, that though the heathen were distinguished from Christians by immorality, they were not so by an abuse of the marriage-bed in particular. But the words, ἐν πάθει ἐπιθυμίας, though forming an antithesis to ἐν ἁγιασμῷ καὶ τιμῇ, need not necessarily, when applied to the heathen, carry us back to κτᾶσθαι τὸ σκεῦος. In ver. 5 these latter words are lost sight of and some general idea gathered from them, such as 'living' ἐν πάθει ἐπιθυμίας.

9 But as touching brotherly love [1] we need not to write unto you: for ye yourselves are taught of God 10 to love one another. And indeed ye do it toward all the brethren which are in all Macedonia: but we beseech you, brethren, to increase more and more; 11 and to study to be quiet, and do your own business, and work with your hands, as we commanded you; 12 that ye may walk honestly towards them that are without, and may have lack of nothing.

13 But we would not have you to be ignorant, brethren,

13. The Apostle passes on, with a formula that he employs elsewhere (οὐ θέλομεν δὲ ὑμᾶς ἀγνοεῖν, ἀδελφοί), to a new subject, the state of the departed. The train of thought may possibly have been suggested by the previous exhortation to be diligent in their daily occupations, the missing link being that their occupations had been interrupted by the expectation of the coming of Christ. Compare chap. v. 11, 12. It may also have been a reply to an inquiry, or may have originated in the Apostle hearing of the anxiety of the converts, who found that a gloom was cast upon their faith in Christ, by the death of some one of their number. Their sadness was not as to whether or not there was a future state, but whether those who were already dead should participate in the coming reign of Christ. To the Jew of old, death seemed sad, because it took men away from the presence of God. Yet more sad must it have appeared to the uninstructed mind of the first converts, because it took them away in the very hour when it seemed good to live, 'waiting for the Son from heaven.'

καθὼς καὶ οἱ λοιποί, *as the others.*] The heathen, as in Ephesians ii. 3, who sorrow as the Apostle, regarding them partly from his own point of view, says of them, or have reason to sorrow for their ignorance of the future.

It would be easy to multiply quotations from classical writers in illustration of this expression, like the words of Theocritus, Idyll. iv. 42 ἐλπίδες ἐν ζωοῖσιν, ἀνέλπιστοι δὲ θανόντες: or the mournful strain of Catullus, v. 4 'Soles occidere et redire possent. Nobis quum semel occidit brevis lux nox est perpetua una dormienda;' or the life-like touch of Lucretius, iii. 942 'Nec quisquam expergitus exstat, frigida quem semel est vitai pausa secuta;' or the sad complaints of Cicero and Quintilian over the loss of their children; or the dreary hope of an immortality of fame in Tacitus or Thucydides, or the still more dreary acquiescence

[1] Reading ἔχομεν

concerning them which are asleep, that ye sorrow not, 14 even as the others which have no hope. For if we believe that Jesus died and rose again, even so them also which sleep in Jesus will God bring with him. 15 For this we say unto you by the word of the Lord, that

in the belief of a future state as a useful terror to man in general, by Chrysippus and others; or the trifling dispute in the Ethics of Aristotle affecting not the fact but a question of words. The silence of the earlier books of the Old Testament is not less awful; and its language where it speaks, though more religious, is in many passages hardly more cheering: 'The living, the living, he shall praise thee. What profit is there in the grave? Shall they that go down into the pit, declare thy truth?'

15. τοῦτο γὰρ ὑμῖν] The Apostle adds emphatically:—'*And this I say to you not of myself, but by the word of Christ.*' It has been asked respecting this passage, as well as in reference to 1 Cor. vii. 10, whether St. Paul is referring to some special saying of our Lord on these subjects, i.e. resurrection and divorce, or to a revelation which he had received from Him. Neither of the passages supposed to be alluded to (Matt. xxiv. 31, or John v. 25) is sufficiently near in sense to make it safe for us to identify them; while a strong negative argument may be urged on the other side, from the fact of no other quotations in St. Paul's writings being apparently derived from our canonical Gospels. It may be further adduced as an argument in favour of the supposition that St. Paul is referring to actual words of Christ, that he nowhere speaks of any special truths or doctrines as imparted to himself. When he uses the expression, 'not I, but the Lord,' 1 Cor. vii. 12, he is speaking of matters of discipline, not of doctrine.

The question suggests a wider one, which is equally incapable of receiving a precise answer:— 'What did St. Paul know of the life of Christ?' Two passages only throw any considerable light on this subject. First, 1 Cor. xv. 3-10, in which the Apostle describes himself, not only as preaching to the Corinthians the doctrine of the resurrection of Christ, but as dwelling on the minute circumstances which attested it. Had he told them in like manner of other events in the life of Christ? Had the parables and discourses of Christ interwoven themselves in his teaching? Were the miracles of Christ a witness to which he appealed?

It is instructive to put these questions, even though they remain without an answer. St. Paul must have known numberless persons who had followed the footsteps of the Lord on earth; and yet the only memorial which he has preserved is the short fragment, 'It is more blessed to give than to receive,' which forms the second of the two quo-

we which are alive and remain unto the coming of the
16 Lord shall not prevent them which sleep ; because the
Lord himself shall descend from heaven with a shout,
with the voice of the archangel, and with the trump of
17 God: and the dead in Christ shall rise first: then we
which are alive and remain shall be caught up together
with them in the clouds, to meet the Lord in the air :

tations alluded to above (Acts xx. 35. Compare 1 Tim. vi. 13 ; the mention of the institution of the Lord's Supper, in 1 Cor. xi. 24 ; also Phil. ii. 7, 2 Cor. viii. 9). Had all the things that were known of Christ in the days of the Apostle been written down, 'the world itself,' it might be said, would hardly have contained 'the books that should be written;' and yet, as far as we can trace, it was not the sayings or events of the life of Christ, but the witness of the Old Testament prophets, that formed the larger part of St. Paul's teaching, the 'external' evidence by which he supported, in himself and others, the inward and living sense of union with Christ, the medium through which he preached 'Christ crucified.'

ὅτι ἡμεῖς οἱ ζῶντες, *that we which are alive.*] Is St. Paul speaking here of his own generation only ? or are the living at a particular time put for the living in general, these being spoken of in the first person by way of contrast with the dead from whom they are parted ? In 1 Cor. xv. 51, according to one reading, the Apostle seems to number himself, not among the living, but among the dead, at the coming of Christ. The mode of thought in the present passage is not precisely similar, but yet not entirely different. We may consider ἡμεῖς οἱ ζῶντες as a figure of the living in general, just as οἱ κοιμώμενοι, though primarily referring to the dead in the Thessalonian Church, is also put for the dead in general. It is nevertheless true, that the words imply the immediate expectation of Christ's coming. The Apostle could not have said 'we,' if he had had a distinct perception that the coming of Christ was still far distant.

The Apostle had been speaking of the coming of Christ in the clouds of heaven. The question would naturally arise in the minds of the Thessalonians,'When shall these things be?' But this they already know as far as it can be known. (Compare the turn of iv. 9.) And all that can be known is that 'The day of the Lord cometh as a thief in the night.' The world is lying in darkness, asleep, ready to be surprised. But they are the children of the day, having a light within anticipating the dawn ; they may not be asleep, they cannot be surprised ; they are to arm themselves as soldiers of Christ, taking the breastplate of faith and the helmet of salvation ; for to salvation they are appointed through Christ Jesus, with whom they are one in life and death.

18 and so shall we ever be with the Lord. Wherefore comfort one another with these words.

5 But of the times and the seasons, brethren, ye have 2 no need that I write unto you. For yourselves know perfectly that the day of the Lord so cometh as a thief 3 in the night. ¹But when they shall say, Peace and safety; then sudden destruction cometh upon them, as travail upon a woman with child; and they shall not 4 escape. But ye, brethren, are not in darkness, that 5 that day should overtake you as ⁱthieves⁰ : ᵏfor⁰ ye are all the children of light, and the children of the day. 6 We are not of the night, nor of darkness. Therefore let us not sleep, as do others; but let us watch and 7 be sober. For they that sleep sleep in the night; and 8 they that be drunken are drunken in the night. But let us who are of the day, be sober, putting on the breastplate of faith and love; and for an helmet, the 9 hope of salvation. For God hath not appointed us to wrath, but to ¹obtaining of⁰ salvation by our Lord 10 Jesus Christ, who died for us, that, whether we wake

ⁱ *a thief*   ᵏ omit *for*   ˡ *obtain*

5. 1. Many characteristics of St. Paul are crowded in this passage. First, the rhetorical turn, οὐ χρείαν ἔχετε. Secondly, the subtle transition in the use of the metaphor of the day of the Lord to the moral lesson that they are to walk as children of the day. (Compare Rom. xiii. 1-14.) Thirdly, the imagery of v. 8 (compare Ephes. vi); also the going off upon the word σωτηρία, which is made the link of the following verse. Fourthly, the thought of our identity with Christ, in which is still retained the allusion to sleeping and waking. And lastly, in the 11th verse, the resumption of the precept which closes the preceding chapter.

4. κλέπτας.] The reading of Lachmann [and the Cambridge Text] has equal or rather greater MS. authority than κλέπτης, which is the reading of the 'Textus Receptus.' The question remains somewhat uncertain when argued further on grounds of internal evidence.

On behalf of Lachmann may be urged the old canon of the more difficult reading; the copyist was

¹ Reading ὅταν δέ

11 or sleep, we may live together with him. Wherefore comfort yourselves together, and edify one another, even as also ye do.

12 And we beseech you, brethren, to know them which labour among you, and are over you in the Lord, and
13 admonish you; and to esteem them very highly in love for their work's sake. ᵐ⁻ᵈ Be at peace among yourselves.
14 Now we exhort you, brethren, warn them that are unruly, comfort the feeble-minded, support the weak,
15 be patient toward all men. See that none render evil for evil unto any man; but ever follow that which is
16 good, both among yourselves, and to all men. Rejoice
17,18 evermore; pray without ceasing: in every thing give thanks: for this is the will of God in Jesus Christ
19,20 concerning you. Quench not the Spirit; despise not

ᵐ add *And*

far more likely to repeat the same case which had occurred in a proverbial expression just quoted than to alter it. The change in the figure itself is also rather in favour of the accusative κλέπτας. For St. Paul transposes figures of speech in other places, as, for example, Rom. vii. 1-6, where the image begins with the law dying, and ends with men dying to the law; or 1 Thess. ii. 7 and 17; or 2 Cor. iii. 16-18. The echo of the word is still in his ears; to avoid repetition, he changes its use. Lastly, the reading κλέπτας gives a point to υἱοὶ φωτός. Also the appropriateness of the figure itself, daylight breaking on the thief. Cf. Hom. Il. iii. 11 κλέπτῃ δέ τε νυκτὸς ἀμείνω.

15. ὁρᾶτε μή τις.] These words do not mean, 'Take heed of some one else;' but 'Let each one take heed not to return evil for evil, but everywhere pursue after goodness, both in relation to the brethren and to those without the Church.'

It is not strictly true to say that Christianity alone or first forbade to return evil for evil. Plato knew that it was not the true definition of justice to do harm to one's enemies. The Stoics, who taught the extirpation of the passions, were far enough from admitting of revenge to be the only one which should be allowed to remain. It is a higher as well as a truer claim to make for the Gospel, that it kindled that spirit of kindness and goodwill in the breast of man (which could not be wholly extinguished even towards an enemy), until it became a practical principle; and that it preached as a rule of life for all, what had previously been the

21 prophesyings. ⁿ But⁗ prove all things; hold fast that
22 which is good; abstain from ᵒ every kind⁗ of evil.
23 And the very God of peace sanctify you wholly, and may your whole spirit and soul and body be preserved blameless in the coming of our Lord
24 Jesus Christ. Faithful is he that calleth you, who also will do it.

ⁿ omit *But*   ᵒ all appearance

supreme virtue, or the mere theory of philosophers.

21, 22. The general meaning of these two verses may be paraphrased thus :—' Discern between good and evil; choose the good, avoid the evil.' Yet the English translation, 'try all things,' naturally suggests thoughts very unlike those of the first century. However apt their application may sound, the true meaning is not 'make a rational inquiry into all things.' The organ of discernment was of another and a spiritual kind. In 1 Cor. xii. 10, St. Paul speaks of a gift of the discernment of spirits, and it is in a similar connexion the precept occurs hereafter; the Apostle has been speaking of prophecy and of the spirit, as in the Corinthians the discerning of spirits is spoken of with immediate reference to the spiritual gifts. Bearing in mind, that the whole state of the first believers was extraordinary and spiritual, we shall find the meaning in both passages much the same. The distinction of right and wrong, no less than of matters of faith was to them a discerning of spirits. Let us imagine a community of prophets, agitated by every various spiritual impulse, yet remaining men of a common nature with ourselves, and liable to mistake merely physical effects for spiritual power; what extravagances must have been the result, what mixed good and evil must have blended together under the name of the spirit ! To separate and distinguish this among those who held the name of Christ, and yet may have sometimes mingled with it 'the doctrines of devils,' must have been the chief office of a discerner of spirits in the first century. It is this discernment of spirits that is partly spoken of in the words πάντα δοκιμάζετε.

23. Still the Apostle is thinking of the coming of Christ, against which he prays that they may be preserved, not only in soul and spirit, but in body. Had he a distinct thought attached to each of these words? Probably not. He is not writing a treatise on the soul, but pouring forth, from the fullness of his heart, a prayer for his converts. Language thus used should not be too closely analysed. His words may be compared to similar expressions among ourselves : e.g. 'with my heart and soul.' Who would distinguish between the two? Neither did the age in which St. Paul lived admit of

25 Brethren, pray for us [p] too.‖ Greet all the brethren
26 with an holy kiss. I charge you by the Lord that
27 this epistle be read unto all the [q]–‖ brethren.
28 The grace of our Lord Jesus Christ be with you.
Amen.[r]–‖

[p] omit *too* [q] add *holy*
[r] add *the first Epistle unto the Thessalonians was written from Athens.*

any great accuracy in speaking of the human soul; nor does the fluctuating use of such terms in other parts of Scripture imply any precise or exact distinction. Who could define the difference between soul and spirit in the Alexandrian, scholastic, or any other philosophy? least of all should we attempt to do so in Scripture, which no more anticipates the metaphysical distinctions of later ages than their discoveries in astronomy or geology.

ON THE BELIEF

IN THE

COMING OF CHRIST IN THE APOSTOLICAL AGE

1 THESS. III, IV.

'Neither shall they say, Lo here! or, lo there! for, behold, the kingdom of God is within you.' (Luke xvii. 21.)

THE belief in the near approach of the coming of Christ is spoken of or implied in almost every book of the New Testament; in the discourses of our Lord himself, as well as in the Acts of the Apostles; in the Epistles of St. Paul no less than in the Book of the Revelation. The remains of such a belief are discernible in the Montanism of the second century, which is separated by a scarcely definable line from the Church itself. Nor is there wanting in our own day a dim and meagre shadow of the same primitive faith, moving around, and sometimes within, the pale of our own communion. There are still those who argue, from the very lapse of time, that 'now is their salvation nearer than when they believed.' All religious men have at times blended in their thoughts earth and heaven; while there are some who have raised their passing feelings into a system of doctrinal truth, and have seemed to see in the temporary state of the first converts the type of Christian life in all ages.

The influence which this belief exercised on the beginnings of the Church, and the manner in which it is interwoven in the writings of the New Testament, render the consideration of it necessary for the right understanding of St. Paul's Epistles. Yet it is a subject from which the interpreter of Scripture would gladly turn aside. For it seems as if he were compelled to allow 'that St. Paul was mistaken, and that in support of his mistake he could appeal to the words of Christ Himself.' Nothing can be plainer than the Apostle's meaning; he says, that men living in his own day will be 'caught up to meet the Lord in the air;' and yet, after eighteen centuries, the world is as it was. The language which is attributed in the Epistle of St. Peter to unbelievers of that age has become the language of believers in our own:—'Since the fathers have fallen asleep, all things remain the same from the beginning.' No one can now be looking daily for the visible coming of Christ any more than, in a land where nature is at rest, he would live in expectation of an earthquake. Not 'the hardness of men's hearts,' but the experience of eighteen hundred years has made it impossible, consistently with the laws of the human mind, that the belief of the first Christians should continue among ourselves.

Why, then, were the traces of such a belief permitted to appear in the New Testament? That is a question which we debate with ourselves the moment the difficulty is perceived, which receives various answers. There are some who say, 'as a trial of our faith;' while others have recourse to the double senses of prophecy, to divide the past from the future, the day of judgement from the destruction of Jerusalem. Others cite its existence as a proof that the books of Scripture were compiled at a time when such a belief was still living, and this not without, but within the circle of the Church itself. It may be also regarded as an indication that we were not intended to interpret Scripture apart from the light of experience, or violently to bend life and truth into agreement with isolated texts. Lastly, so far as we can venture to move such a question of our Lord himself, we may observe that his teaching here, as in other places, is on a level with the modes of thought of his age, clothed in figures, as it must necessarily be, to express 'the things that eye hath not seen;' limited by time, as if to give the sense of reality to what otherwise would be vague and infinite, yet mysterious in this respect too, for of 'that hour knoweth no man;' and that, however these figures of speech are explained, or these opposite aspects reconciled, their meaning, breaking through the horizon of earth, has been the stay and hope of the believer in all ages, who knows, nevertheless, that the Apostles have passed away, and no 'sign has yet appeared in the clouds,' and that 'the round world is set so fast that it cannot be moved.'

But instead of regarding this or any other fact of Scripture as a difficulty to be explained away, it will be more instructive for us to consider the nature of the belief and its probable effect on the infant communion. In its origin it was simple and childlike, the belief of men who saw but a little way into the purposes of Providence, who never dreamed of a vista of futurity. It was not what we should term an article of faith, but natural and necessary, flowing immediately out of the life and state of the earliest believers. It was the feeling of men who looked for the coming of Christ as we might look for the return of a lost friend, many of whom had seen Him on earth, and could not believe that He was taken from them for ever. Those who remembered the Lord would often say one to another, 'Yet a little while, and we do not see Him; and again a little while, and we shall see Him.' And sometimes, as years rolled on, they would ask the question which they had once asked in His lifetime, 'What was this that He said? we cannot tell what this was which He said.' Let us imagine them, 'with their lamps lighted and their loins girded,' in the spirit of our Lord's discourses, waiting for His appearing. The night is far spent, the day is at hand; already they see the streaks of the morning light. And then again the light fails and fades; it was the light as of a distant city: the hour is not yet come; their own wishes had made them fancy it nearer than it was. Time passes; one by one the fathers fall asleep; at last, 'a lingering star with lessening ray, the beloved Apostle alone remains;—the saying goes forth 'that that disciple should not die;' and the daylight indeed appears, but it is the light not of another world but of this.

So we may trace in a figure the thoughts of the first disciples respecting the coming of the Lord, towards whom they yearned, and the end of the world; the course of events silently rebuking them and saying, 'It is not for you to know the times and the seasons which the Father hath put in His own power.' But the belief in the expectation of the coming of Christ has other aspects also which are equally interesting and important. It was the beginning of the Church. It was the feeling of men who, in the language of St. Paul, were 'baptized into one body and drunk of one spirit;' the kingdom of God creating itself in the heart of man, when, in modern language, it was still an idea and not an outward institution,— the liquid ore, as it were, melted by the heavenly flame, but not cast in the mould. It was the feeling of men who had an intense sense of the change that had been wrought in themselves, and to whom this change seemed like the beginning of a greater change that was overflowing on the world around them. It was the feeling of men who looked back upon the past, of which they knew so little, and discerned in it the workings of the same spirit, one and continuous, which they felt in their own souls; to whom the world within and the world without were reflected upon one another, and the history of the Jewish race was a parable, an 'open secret,' of the things to come. It was the feeling of men who were living not amid the aspirations of prophecy, but in the hour of its fulfilment; who clothed their own times in its glorious

BELIEF IN THE COMING OF CHRIST

imagery; to whom the veil that was on the face of Moses was done away in Christ. It was the putting of the garment of the old dispensation upon the new. It was the feeling of men who were saying, Lord, how long? whom their own sufferings assured that there was a righteous judge who would not always delay. It was the feeling of men who were living far above and away from earth, in a spiritual kingdom, who scarcely thought either of the past or the future in the eternity of the present.

Let those who think this is an imaginary picture recall to mind and compare with Scripture, either what they may have read in books or experienced in themselves as the workings of a mind suddenly converted to the Gospel. Such an one seems to lose his measure of events and his true relation to the world. While other men are going on with their daily occupations, he only is out of sympathy with nature, and has fears and joys in himself, which he can neither communicate nor explain to his fellows. It is not that he is thinking of the endless ages in which he will partake of heavenly bliss; rather the present consciousness of sin, or the present sense of forgiveness and of peace in Christ, is already a sort of hell or heaven within him, which excludes the future. It is not that he has an increased insight into the original meaning of Scripture; rather he seems to absorb Scripture into himself. Least of all have persons in such a state of mind distinct or accurate conceptions of the world to come. The images in which they express themselves are carnal and visible, often inconsistent with each other, scarcely intelligible to minds which are not in sympathy with them, yet not the less the realization to them of a true and lively faith. The last thing that they desire, or could comprehend, is an intellectual theory of another life. They seem hardly to need either statements of doctrine or the religious ministrations of others; their concern is with God only.

Substitute now for a single individual, the three thousand

who were converted on the day of Pentecost, the 'multitude of Jews that believed, zealous for the law;' conceive them changed at the same instant by one spirit, and we seem to see on a larger scale the same effects following. Their conversion is an exception to the course of nature; itself a revelation and inspiration, a wonder of which they can give no account to themselves or others, not the least wonderful part of which is their communion with one another. The same Divine power, which originally formed men into nations, forms them into a church now, and almost literally gives them a new language and a new speech. They come into being with common hopes and fears, at one with each other, separated from mankind at large, in new relations to their own country and kindred. They see God looking upon themselves and other men, not, as heretofore, 'winking at the times of that ignorance,' but distinctly conscious of all their acts. What they feel within themselves spreads itself over the world. All men are in the presence of God: good and evil quicken into life beneath His searching eye; there is a fellowship of the saints on one side, and a mystery of iniquity on the other. They do not read history, or comprehend the sort of imperfect necessity under which men act as creatures of their age. The same guilt which they acknowledge in themselves, they attach to other men; the same judgement which would await them, is awaiting the world everywhere. In the events around them, in their own sufferings, in their daily life, they see the preparations for the great conflict between good and evil, between Christ and Belial, if, indeed, it be not already begun. The circle of their own life includes in it the destinies of the human race itself, of which it is, as it were, the microcosm, seen by the eye of faith and the light of inward experience. This is what the law and the prophets seem to them to have meant when they spoke of God's judgements on His enemies, of the Lord coming with ten thousand of His saints. And the signs which were to accompany these things are already seen among them, 'not in word only, but in power, and in the Holy Spirit, and in much assurance.'

To us the preaching of the Gospel is a new beginning, from which we date all things, beyond which we neither desire nor are able to inquire. To the first believers it was otherwise; not the beginning of a new world, but the end of a former one. They looked back to the past, because the veil of the future was not yet lifted up. They were living in 'the latter days,' the confluence of all times, the meeting-point of the purposes of God. They read all things in the light of the approaching end of the world. They were not taught, and could not have imagined, that for eighteen centuries servants of God should continue on the earth, waiting, like themselves, for the promise of His coming. They were not taught, and could not have imagined, that after three centuries the Church, which they saw poverty-stricken and persecuted, should be the mistress of the earth, and that, in another sense than they had hoped, the kingdoms of this world should become the kingdoms of the Lord and of His Christ. Instead of it they beheld in a figure the heavens opening, and the angels of God ascending and descending; the present outpouring of the Spirit, and the evil and perplexity of the world itself, being the earnest of the things which were shortly to come to pass.

It has been often remarked, that the belief in the coming of Christ stood in the same relation to the Apostolic Church that the expectation of death does to ourselves. Certainly the absence of exhortations based upon the shortness of life, which are not unfrequent in the Old Testament, and are so familiar to our own day, forms a remarkable feature in the writings of the New Testament, and in a measure seems to confirm such an opinion. And yet the similarity is rather apparent than real; or, at any rate, the difference between the two is not less remarkable. For the feeble apprehension which each man entertains of his own mortality, can bear no comparison with that living sense of the day of the Lord which was the habitual thought of the first Christians, which was not so much a 'coming' as a 'presence' to them, as its very name implied (παρουσία). How different also was the event looked for, no less than the anticipation of it! There is nothing terrible in death; it is the repose of wearied nature; it steals men away one by one, while the world goes still on its way. We fear it at a distance, but not near. Only in youth sometimes it seems hard to die; the language of old men is, 'I have lived long enough.' But the day of the Lord was an inversion of the course of nature; it was a change, not to the individual only, but to the world; a scene of great fear and great joy at once to the whole Church and to all mankind, which was in its very nature sudden, unexpected, coming 'as a thief in the night, and as travail upon a woman with child.' Yet it might be said to be expected too, for the first disciples were sitting waiting for it 'with their lamps lighted and their loins girded.' It was not darkness, nor sleep, nor death, but a day of light and life, in the expectation of which men were to walk as children of the light, yet fearful by its very suddenness and the vengeance to be poured on the wicked.

Such a belief could not be without its effect on the lives of the first converts and on the state of the Church. While it increased the awfulness of life, it almost unavoidably withdrew men's thoughts from its ordinary duties. It naturally led to the state described in the Corinthian Church, in which spiritual gifts had taken the place of moral duties, and of those very gifts, the less spiritual were preferred to the more spiritual. It took the mind away from the kingdom of God within, to fix it on signs and wonders, 'the things spoken of by the prophet Joel,' when the sun should be turned into darkness, and the moon into blood. It made men almost ready to act contrary to the decrees of Caesar, from the sense of what they saw, or seemed to see, in the world around them. The intensity of the spiritual state in which they lived, so far beyond that of our daily life, is itself the explanation of the spiritual disorder which seems so strange to us in men who were ready to hazard their lives for the truth, and which was but the natural reaction against their former state.

It is obvious that such a belief was inconsistent with an established Ecclesiastical order. A succession of bishops could have had no meaning in a world that was to vanish away. Episcopacy, it has been truly remarked, was in natural antagonism to Montanism; and in the age of the Apostles as well, there is an opposition, traceable in the Epistles themselves, between the supernatural gifts and the order and discipline of the Church. Ecclesiastical as well as political institutions are not made, but grow. What we are apt to regard as their first idea and design, is in reality their after-development, what in the fullness of time they become, not what they originally were, the former being faintly, if at all, discernible in the new birth of the Church and of the world.

Nor is it unreasonable to suppose that the meagreness of those historical memorials of the first age which survived it, has been the result of such a belief. What interest would be attached to the events of this world, if they were so soon to be lost in another? or to the lessons of history, when the nations of the earth were in a few years to appear before the judgement-seat of Christ? Even the narrative of the acts and sayings of the Saviour of mankind must have had a different degree of importance to those who expected to see with their eyes the Word of life, and to us, to whom they are the great example, for after-ages, of faith and practice. Among many causes which may be assigned for the great historical chasm which separates the life of Christ and His Apostles from after-ages, this is not the least probable. The age of the Apostles was an age, not of history, but of prophecy.

And now 'the fathers have fallen asleep, all things

remain the same as at the beginning.' More clearly than in former times, we see the discrepancy between the meaning of Scripture and the order of events which history discloses to us. The fact stares us in the face. We feel no satisfaction or security in attempting to conceal it; we cannot do so if we would. It is right, therefore, that we should be assured, that even if the Apostles were mistaken, 'our faith' is not 'vain.' Our hope of life and immortality is not taken away, because the language of St. Paul in some passages seem to fix the times and the seasons which our Saviour, in His last words on earth, tells His Apostles, 'it is not for you to know.'

The subject of the preceding essay may be considered apologetically; that is, with a view to meet objections in two ways—either as affecting theology, or belief and practice.

I. Most of the difficulties of theology are self-made, and ready to vanish away when we consider them naturally. They generally arise out of certain hypotheses which we vainly try to reconcile with obvious facts; often they are the opinions of a past day lingering on into the present. The belief of St. Paul in the immediate coming of Christ is not at all different from what we should have expected, or in any degree inconsistent with the laws of the human mind, or, again, unlike the analogy of prophecy and of religion generally. It was a natural interpretation of the old prophetic writings. Our difficulty is really of a different kind—how to reconcile such a belief with the infallibility of the Apostle. He never claims this infallibility; it is we ourselves who love to ascribe it to him. It is true that the Apostle, if infallible, could not have erred respecting the end of the world; and if we could prove that he was infallible, we might deny that he was in error. But the ascription of infallibility to him involves further and almost endless difficulties. For it seems, to use an expression of Bishop Butler's, as if 'there would be no stopping,' until revelation was wholly different from what it is. Its truths should no longer be expressed in human language, or under the limitation of human faculties; they must have dropped from heaven; that is, have found their way into the world out of the course of nature, unconnected with history, in no relation to the thoughts of men, and therefore powerless to assimilate the human heart to themselves.

Not in this way has it 'pleased God to reveal his Son in us.' The New Testament came through the Old; it did not rudely break with the former Dispensation. It appropriated the figures of the law, it clothed itself in the imagery of the prophets. It was preached to the poor, and therefore it was on a level with the modes of thought which prevailed in the age in which it was given. It is foolish to admit this in words, and to deny the inferences which unavoidably flow from it. The lesson which it taught was pure and divine, and so far as it was connected at all with facts of history, historically true: but it was not supernaturally guarded against error. It left the Jewish belief in Messiah's kingdom as it had been before; only it purified, sanctified, spiritualized it. Herein is the great difference between what, without detracting from the divine character of Christianity, we may be permitted to call the error of the Apostles and erroneous assumptions of modern interpreters of prophecy respecting the end of the world. The first was natural, arising out of the circumstances and modes of thought of the first Christians; the other is an intrusion into the unseen future, which experience has shown to be irreverent and unmeaning. The difference is of the same kind as between voluntary error and the unavoidable imperfection of human knowledge in a particular age or country.

But neither is the New Testament to be interpreted apart from the course of events. The world is left to itself to clear up as it goes on; many lessons even in divinity are only learnt by experience. Time may often enlarge faith;

it may also correct it. The belief and practice of the early Church, respecting the admission of the Gentiles, were greatly altered by the fact that the Gentiles themselves flocked in : 'the kingdom of heaven suffered violence, and the violent took it by force.' In like manner, the faith respecting the coming of Christ was modified by the continuance of the world itself. Common sense suggests that those who were in the first ecstasy of conversion, and those who after the lapse of years saw the world unchanged and the fabric of the Church on earth rising around them, could not regard the day of the Lord with the same feelings. While to the one it seemed near and present, at any moment ready to burst forth; to the other it was a long way off, separated by time and, as it were by place : a world beyond the stars, yet also having its dwelling in the heart of man ; as to ourselves it is a world inseparably bound up with our consciousness of a Divine Being. Not at once, but gradually did the cloud clear up, and the one mode of faith take the place of the other. Apart from the prophets, through them, beyond them, springing up in a new and living way in the soul of man, corrected by long experience, as 'the fathers' one by one 'fell asleep,' as the hope of the Jewish race declined, as ecstatic gifts ceased, as a regular hierarchy was established in the Church, the belief in the coming of Christ was transformed from being outward to becoming inward, from being national to becoming individual and universal, from being Jewish to becoming Christian.

The belief in a future life is not derived from revelation, though greatly strengthened by it. It is the growing sense of human nature respecting itself. Scarcely any one passes out of existence fearing that he will cease to be ; perhaps no one whose mind may be regarded as in a natural state. Absurd superstitions, even the painful efforts to get rid of self, in some of the Eastern religions, indirectly bear witness to the same truth. They seem to say, 'Stamp upon the Soul, crush it as you will, the poor worm will still creep out into the sunshine of the Almighty.' Nor is the consciousness of another life a mere instinct which, however distorted, still remains : to those who reason it is inseparably connected with our highest, that is, with our moral notions. We feel that God cannot have given us capacities and affections, that they should find no other fulfilment than they attain here; that He cannot intend the unequal measure of good and evil which He has assigned to men on earth to be the end of all : nor can we believe that the crimes or sins which go unpunished in this world, are to pass away as though they had never been ; that the cries of saints and heroes, and the work of the Saviour Himself, have gone up unheard before His throne. That can never be. Equally impossible is it to suppose that creatures whom He has endowed with reason are, like the great multitude of the human race, to be sunk for ever in hopeless ignorance and unconsciousness. It is true that the nature of the change which is to come over them and us is not disclosed : 'The times and the seasons the Father has put in his own power.' Had it been otherwise, immortality must have overpowered us ; the thought of another state would have swallowed up this.

And this sense of a future life and judgement to come has been so quickened in us by Christianity, that it may be said almost to have been created by it. It is the witness of Christ Himself, than which to the Christian no assurance can be greater. He who meditates on this divine life in the brief narrative which has been preserved of it, will find the belief in another world come again to him when many physical and metaphysical proofs are beginning to be as broken reeds. He will find more than enough to balance the difficulties of the manner 'how' or the time 'when ;' he will find, as he draws nearer to Christ, a sort of impossibility of believing otherwise. When we ask, 'How are the dead raised up, and with what body do they come?' St. Paul answers, 'Thou fool, that which thou sowest is not quickened except it die;' when we raise objections to the narrative which has been preserved of our Saviour's discourse respecting the last things and the end of the world, may not the answer to this as well as to many other difficulties be gathered from His own words—'It is the Spirit that quickeneth, the flesh profiteth nothing; the words that I speak unto you they are Spirit, and they are truth?'

There was a sense in which our Saviour said that it was better for His disciples that He should be taken from them, that the Comforter should come unto them. There is also a blessing recorded in the Gospels on those who had not seen and yet had believed. Is there not a sense in which it is more blessed to live at a distance from those events which are the beginning of Christianity, than under their immediate influence, to see them as they truly are in the light of this world as well as of another? If it was an illusion in the first Christians to believe in the immediate coming of Christ, is it not a cause of thankfulness that now we see clearly? Of truth, as well as of love, it may be said there is no fear in truth, but perfect truth casteth out fear. The eye which is strong enough to pierce through the shadow of death, is not troubled because the golden mist is dispelled and it looks on the open heaven.

And though prophecy may fail and tongues cease, though to those who look back upon them when they are with the past, they are different from what they were to those who melted under their influence, the pure moral and spiritual nature of Christianity, the 'kingdom of God within,' remains as at the first, the law of Christian love becoming more and more, and all in all.

THE SECOND EPISTLE

TO THE

THESSALONIANS

INTRODUCTION.

It was thought by Grotius, and it is also the opinion of Ewald, that what is termed the Second Epistle must have preceded the First. The best arguments by which this opinion can be defended, are the references in the Second Epistle to the teaching of the Apostle while 'he was yet with them,' and the absence of any allusions to the First Epistle. (See ch. ii. ver. 2.) These grounds are far from being conclusive. It is improbable (observe, however, 2 Thess. ii. 15) that a previous Epistle could have interposed itself between the visit of the Apostle and chapters two and three of the First Epistle. (Compare Acts xvii, xviii.) The allusions to the conversion of the Thessalonians also mark the First Epistle as commonly received to be the earlier of the two. But the opinion, though probably an error, may serve to remind us that, in one sense the Second Epistle anticipates the first ; that is to say, it is based on the lesson which the Apostle had taught the Thessalonians, while he was yet with them, ii. 5. The subject of Antichrist was not new to them; they had been told who was meant, and what withheld him now, that he should be revealed in his own time. Whereas, in the former Epistle, he had led their minds exclusively to the heavenly vision, 'the saints meeting in the air with Christ, and the dead whom he would bring with him.'

Something like a definite object is indicated in the second chapter of the Epistle. That object seems to have been to inform the converts, or rather to remind them of what they already knew, respecting the coming of Christ and the previous revelation of Antichrist, and 'that which let.' It might, indeed, be questioned here, as in Rom. ix—xi, compared with i—viii, whether the first chapter is introductory to the second, or the second supplementary to the first. But the particularity of the second chapter, and the nearness of that 'which already worketh,' as well as the earnestness of the Apostle's language, tend to show that what is in form subordinate, is really the centre of the Epistle. As in 1 Cor. x, the thought which is nearest the Apostle's heart is overlaid with what is merely introductory to it.

But whether there is or is not any doubt about the primary object of the Epistle, the mind and feelings with which the Apostle wrote are plainly impressed upon it, and hardly less so the state of the Church to which it was addressed. The aspect in which the Gospel presented itself to the Apostle, was not unlike that in which it was described by John the Baptist: 'He shall burn up the chaff with fire unquenchable.' Within the Church it might be possible to think only of the elect, whose prayers and hopes seemed to bring the day of the Lord nearer and nearer, until the horizon of earth melted away in the clouds of heaven. But it was impossible to turn away the sight from the aspect of the world itself, especially that portion of it which was on the confines of the Church, whether the Jewish persecutors, who harassed the Apostle in every city, 'who pleased not God, and were contrary to man,' or the wild forms of heresy or licentiousness which at one moment seemed to set themselves with giant force to arrest his course; at another time, by seductive influences to steal away the hearts of his converts. In the distance, too, were the heathen world mingling in the vision of sin; ripe for the revelation of wrath, no less than for the revelation of mercy. (Compare Rom. i. 8.)

The whole of the Epistle, like the Epistles of the imprisonment, is written under what may be termed 'the feeling of persecution;' that is to say, the sense of resignation, on the one hand, to the present will of God; on the other hand, a sure and certain hope that 'times of refreshment' were at hand. Such was the feeling of the Apostle himself, and he implies the existence of a similar feeling in the Church to which he was writing. Sadness and consolation, hope and fear, the array of glory and of terror, were present with them or passing before them. They were not living the common life of other men; they did not see with the eyes of other men.

A life thus divided between this world and another was naturally liable to become a life of excitement and disorder. Times of persecution needed extraordinary religious supports; the withdrawal of those supports, the momentary clouding of the heaven above, would from time to time lead to reaction. Those who sat 'waiting for the day of the Lord,' and in this very expectation perhaps neglecting their employments, had lost that quietness of mind which is given by daily occupation. The perils of such a state were not unknown to the Apostle. It might at any time pass into its opposite, the very good that was in it becoming only material for evil. Half organized as the Church was then, the only means of avoiding such dangers was to withdraw from the disorderly, in the hope that the shunning of their society might have a moral influence on them. And yet even this gentle discipline must be exercised with moderation, in the remembrance that a brother was a brother still. More urgently, and as a lesson more congenial to himself, does the Apostle seek to impress upon them his own spirit, the spirit of honest industry, the spirit of peace and order, which is at once his benediction and admonition to them.

GENUINENESS OF THE SECOND EPISTLE.

The second Epistle to the Thessalonians is not deficient in external evidence of its genuineness. As in the case of the former Epistle, the doubts that have been raised respecting it are based solely on an examination of its language and contents. They may be summed up under the following heads, the consideration of which will tend to establish the genuineness of the Epistle, as well as to throw light on its character and object :—

i. Inconsistency with the First Epistle, in deferring the coming of Christ.

ii. Doctrine of Antichrist, which is said to be an anachronism, either as indicating a later Montanist origin, or as betraying an allusion to later historical events.

iii. The absence of situation and circumstance, as well as of traits of individual character.

iv. The token at the end of the Epistle, which is the sign in all the Epistles.

v. Likeness to, and difference from, the style of St. Paul.

i. Inconsistency with the First Epistle in deferring the coming of Christ, 1 Thess. v. 2, 'Yourselves know perfectly that the day of the Lord cometh as a thief in the night;' 2 Thess. ii. 3, 'That day shall not come, except there come a falling away first.' It may be replied, that no argument against the genuineness of writings of St. Paul is more unsafe than that from supposed inconsistency. No writer is more apt to present us with opposite views of the same subject, even in the same Epistle, or to modify one side of a precept or of an argument by the other. (Compare the treatment of the question of meats offered to idols in 1 Cor. viii; or of the Rejection of the Jews in the Epistle to the Romans.) The coming of Christ is a subject in which such a difference is most likely to appear, because it is future, and therefore necessarily indistinct. And the difference between the two passages is just similar to that which occurs elsewhere, even in successive verses of the same chapter and in the discourses of our Lord Himself.

ii. Doctrine of Antichrist: Supposed to indicate a later Montanist origin. To this it may be answered that the doctrine of Antichrist is not Montanist, but Jewish, and in its general outline is found in the writings of Philo and the Rabbis, no less than in those of Paul and John. (Compare, though later, 2 Esdras.) Even were there no express proof of its existence, it might have been safely conjectured, from the analogy of prophecy, to have followed the belief in Messiah's kingdom.

iii. The absence of situation and circumstance, and of traits of individual character.

One Epistle has not as many historical allusions as another, or there is a difference of length in different Epistles. But the shortness of an Epistle, or the absence of historical allusions, does not prove it to be spurious; it only lessens or does away with a single proof of genuineness. In this case it may be argued further, that the tone of the Epistle agrees with what we gather from the Acts respecting the Spirit and feelings of the earliest believers, living 'amid the things spoken of by the prophet Joel'; and that the early date of the Epistle offers a general coincidence with its Old Testament and prophetic character. Some value may be also attributed to the connexion of the First and Second Epistles. Arguments which are comparatively slight may be fairly set against slight objections. Lastly, considering the deep feeling which throughout marks the Epistle, it cannot be said to be devoid of character.

It is the opinion of Ewald (*Die Sendschreiben des Apostels Paulus*), 'that none of the writings of the New Testament have so much of the living freshness of the first age of the Gospel, or present so vivid a picture of the hopes of the first believers, as the Epistles to the Thessalonians. Their chief subject is the Apocalyptic vision in its first native power working on the minds of men, not yet formed into an artistic whole, as in the Book of Revelation. In other respects also a coincidence may be observed between the contents of the Epistle and the earlier stages of the Apostle's life. Circumstances have not yet drawn out the sense of the opposition between Judaism and the Gospel. He preaches love and not faith ; the words "righteousness" and "justification" never occur. He is contending with Jews or heathens (1 Thess. ii. 14–16); Jewish Christians (2 Thess. iii. 2 ?) have not yet appeared on the scene' (pp. 13–18).

iv. The token at the end of the Epistle, which is the sign in all the Epistles.

It is argued that at this date there were no forgeries, and therefore no reason for guarding against forgery, and that the Apostle had as yet written but one Epistle.

This is the strongest objection urged by Baur against the genuineness of the Epistle. In answer it may be remarked : (1) that the autograph salutation occurs in 1 Cor. xvi. 21 and Col. iv. 18 ; that it would require minute observation to have remarked this, and yet the Epistle to which it is supposed to be transferred, exhibits no imitation either in words or train of thought of those Epistles. (2) That it is most probable that the words of Gal. vi. 11, 'Ye see in how large letters I have written to you with my own hand,' are similarly a sign of the genuineness of that Epistle. It is true that to appeal to the allusion in 2 Thess. ii. 2 itself, as

GENUINENESS OF THE SECOND EPISTLE 73

a proof of the existence of forged epistles in St. Paul's time, would be [to reason in] a circle. (3) But the consistency of that allusion with the token of salutation, and the slightness of it, are presumptions of the Epistle having arisen from a real occasion. (4) The readiness to practise forgery and pious fraud in an age when such forgeries were apt to be thought innocent and laudable, can hardly be estimated. Compare Rev. xxii. 18-19. Lastly, the incidental character of the Epistles we have, leads us naturally to suppose that there were others also, which have not come down to us, and gives a rational meaning to the words 'in every Epistle,' even though occurring in one of the first of those extant.

v. Likeness to, and difference from, the style and writings of St. Paul.

The likeness is supposed to be such as betrays an imitator; the difference, such as renders it impossible that the epistle could have been written by St. Paul. But, on the other hand, it may be retorted that the difference is no greater than might naturally be expected in the same author writing at different times; and the likeness of a kind such as indicates the hand, not of an imitator, but of St. Paul himself.

(a) The examples of difference of style and language are very uncertain. The following expressions are quoted in confirmation of the objection [1]:—

1. εὐχαριστεῖν ὀφείλομεν i. 3, ii. 13, especially in the first passage, where it is weakened by καθὼς ἄξιόν ἐστιν.

2. ὑπεραυξάνει ἡ πίστις ὑμῶν i. 3 is said to be inconsistent with καταρτίσαι τὰ ὑστερήματα τῆς πίστεως ὑμῶν in 1 Thess. iii. 10.

3. αἱρεῖσθαι, used of election in ii. 13.

4. καὶ διὰ τοῦτο, for διὰ τοῦτο, ii. 11.

5. Forced construction of ἐπιστεύθη τὸ μαρτύριον ἡμῶν ἐφ' ὑμᾶς i. 10.

[1] Baur, *Paulus*, pp. 489, 490.

6. πᾶσα εὐδοκία ἀγαθωσύνης, ἔργον πίστεως i. 11 ; ἐπιφάνεια τῆς παρουσίας ii. 8 ; δέχεσθαι τὴν ἀγάπην τῆς ἀληθείας ii. 10; ἀξιώσῃ τῆς κλήσεως i. 11 ; καλοποιεῖν iii. 13.

Objections of this kind are, for the most part, matters of taste or feeling, about which it is useless to dispute. It may be observed on No. 1, that although εὐχαριστεῖν ὀφείλομεν, i. 3, ii. 13, does not occur elsewhere in the writings of St. Paul, it cannot be regarded as unlike his style. The form of duty is one which all thoughts naturally take in his mind. He is under obligation, compulsion, &c., to do many things. Nor can any pleonasm or dilution of language be regarded as an evidence of the spuriousness of a writing of St. Paul's age if it be not rather, as far as it goes, a proof of its genuineness. This latter remark strictly applies to No. 2, which reminds us of the amplification of language which occurs at the commencement of his other Epistles. Neither is the supposed inconsistency in this last-mentioned passage with 1 Thess. iii. 10 so great as the difference in tone of 1 Cor. i. 5-9 and the rest of the Epistle, the wavering and variation of which are themselves characteristic of the Apostle.

On No. 3 it may be observed, that although the word αἱρεῖσθαι nowhere occurs in the New Testament in the sense of election, it has this sense in Deut. xxvi. 18, whence it is not unreasonable to suppose that St. Paul, or any other writer of the New Testament, may have transferred it to his own use. No. 4. There is no more objection to καί before διὰ τοῦτο than to any other pleonastic use of καί, such, for example, as that in Col. iii. 13. No. 5. Compare Rom. iv. 9 for a similar use of ἐπί. No. 6. Compare Eph. i. 5 for a pleonastic use of εὐδοκία : Eph. i. 3, 8 for a similar use of πᾶς. Instances do not occur precisely parallel with the remaining examples ; still, neither the want of clearness of expression in some of these, nor the pleonastic character

GENUINENESS OF THE SECOND EPISTLE 75

of others, are at all inconsistent with the style of the Apostle.

(b) Against such supposed dissimilarities, it is fair to set also the resemblances in manner and phraseology to the Apostle's writings. The following are characteristically, if not exclusively, St. Paul's:—

The pleonastic and vehement mode of speaking of the faith and love of his converts, in i. 3, as elsewhere, at the commencement of his Epistles, yet, as in the Corinthians, passing into reproof of some at the close of the Epistle.

The antithetical turn of thought in ver. 6, 7, and real, though latent, parallelism with Phil. i. 28, 29.

The mode of connecting ἐνδοξασθῆναι with the word ἐν δόξῃ in i. 10; the echo of ἐνδοξασθῆναι in ἐνδοξασθῇ, ver. 12; the verbal connexion of ἐπιστεύθη with πιστεύσασιν in ver. 10; the reciprocal expression ἐν ὑμῖν καὶ ὑμεῖς ἐν αὐτῷ in ver. 12.

The ἵνα in i. 11, and the more remote ὅπως in ver. 12, like Rom. vii. 13.

The anacoluthon in ii. 3.

The expression in ii. 3 μή τις ὑμᾶς ἐξαπατήσῃ, like the warning in Eph. v. 6 μηδεὶς ὑμᾶς ἀπατάτω κενοῖς λόγοις.

The recurrence to his visit to them, as in Cor., Gal., Phil., 1 Thess.

The following parallelisms: 2 Thess. ii. 7 μόνον ὁ κατέχων, participle without a verb; so Rom. xii. 16, 17, 19. 2 Thess. ii. 10 τοῖς ἀπολλυμένοις; so 1 Cor. i. 18; 2 Cor. ii. 15. 2 Thess. ii. 12 εὐδοκήσαντες [ἐν] τῇ ἀδικίᾳ; Rom. i. 32 συνευδοκοῦσι τοῖς πράσσουσι.

The defective antithesis in ii. 12.

The expressions 2 Thess. ii. 13 εὐχαριστεῖν πάντοτε; compare 1 Cor. i. 4 εὐχαριστῶ τῷ θεῷ μου πάντοτε. 2 Thess. ii. 15 ἄρα οὖν, ἀδελφοί; so Rom. viii. 12 ἄρα οὖν, ἀδελφοί; Gal. iv. 31 ἄρα, ἀδελφοί. 2 Thess. ii. 16

παράκλησιν ... καὶ ἐλπίδα; Rom. xv. 4 τῆς παρακλήσεως τῶν γραφῶν τὴν ἐλπίδα ἔχωμεν. 2 Thess. iii. 2 ἵνα ῥυσθῶμεν; Rom. xv. 31 ἵνα ῥυσθῶ.

The juxtaposition of παρακαλεῖν and στηρίζειν in ii. 17 as in Rom. i. 11, 12.

The echo of sound, rather than of sense, in πίστις and πιστός, in iii. 3, and of πιστός in πεποίθαμεν in ver. 3, 4 ; compare Rom. xii. 13, 14.

The expression in 2 Thess. iii. 6 παραγγέλλομεν ... ἐν ὀνόματι τοῦ κυρίου; so 1 Cor. vii. 10 παραγγέλλω οὐκ ἐγὼ ἀλλ' ὁ κύριος.

The words οὐχ ὅτι οὐκ ἔχομεν ἐξουσίαν iii. 9, which occur also in 1 Cor. ix. 4, there as a part of the main argument, but here incidentally; also the passage which follows, and the use of the word ἐπιβαρῆσαι just before, in the same sense as ἀβαρής 2 Cor. xi. 9.

The sudden alternation from the language of severity to that of love, in iii. 14, 15; compare 1 Cor. v. and 2 Cor. ii. 6. 2 Thess. iii. 13 μὴ ἐκκακήσητε καλοποιοῦντες. So Gal. vi. 9 τὸ δὲ καλὸν ποιοῦντες μὴ ἐκκακῶμεν. 2 Thess. iii. 16 ὁ κύριος εἰρήνης, towards the end of the Epistle. So Rom. xvi. 20; 2 Cor. xiii. 11; Gal. vi. 16.

The play of words (iii. 11), μηδὲν ἐργαζομένους, ἀλλὰ περιεργαζομένους. Compare Rom. i. 20, 28, ii. 1, &c.

THE SECOND EPISTLE

TO THE

THESSALONIANS

1 PAUL, and Silvanus, and Timotheus, unto the Church of the Thessalonians in God our Father and the
2 Lord Jesus Christ: Grace unto you, and peace, from God our Father and the Lord Jesus Christ.
3 WE are bound to thank God always for you, brethren, as it is meet, because that your faith groweth exceedingly, and the ᵃ love ᵃ of every one of
4 you all toward each other aboundeth; so that we ourselves glory in you in the churches of God for your patience and faith in all your persecutions and

ᵃ charity

1. The substance of the first chapter may be summed up as follows:—The Apostle commends the Thessalonian converts, for their increasing faith and the love which draws them closer to one another amid persecutions. This commendation he utters in the form of a thanksgiving on their behalf, in which, as elsewhere, the power of expression falls short of the fullness of his heart. The patience with which the Thessalonians endured their sufferings is a source of pride to him in the churches of God. Those very sufferings of theirs are a manifestation of the righteousness of God; their object being to make them worthy of the kingdom of God. For they must be considered as part of a whole, the present balancing with the future; the state of believers here alternating with that of their enemies in the world to come. 'Son, thou in thy life hadst thy good things and likewise Lazarus evil things, but now he is comforted, and thou

₅ tribulations that ye endure: which is a manifest
token of the righteous judgment of God, that ye may
be counted worthy of the kingdom of God, for which
₆ ye also suffer: seeing it is a righteous thing with
God to recompense tribulation to them that trouble
₇ you; and to you who are troubled rest with us, when
the Lord Jesus shall be revealed from heaven with
₈ his mighty angels, in ᵇ flame of ᵈ fire taking vengeance
on them that know not God, and that obey not
₉ the gospel of our Lord Jesus Christ: who shall be
punished with everlasting destruction from the
presence of the Lord, and from the glory of his
₁₀ power; when he shall come to be glorified in his
saints, and to be admired in all them that believe
because our testimony ᶜ to ᵈ you was believed in that
₁₁ day. Wherefore also we pray always for you, that
our God would count you worthy of this calling, and
fulfil all the good pleasure of his goodness, and the

ᵇ *flaming*   ᶜ among

art tormented.' This is the law of compensation, in God's dealings with the heathen and the despisers of the Gospel, in the day when they shall pass away for ever from His presence, and His saints who have believed the word of the Apostle, shall magnify Him. For which end the Apostle prays without ceasing, that God may make them worthy of their calling and the name of Christ be glorified in them.

8. ἐν φλογὶ πυρός, *in flaming fire.*] Compare Exod. iii. 2: Dan. vii. 9, 10: Is. xxix. 6.

The Gospel 'of the coming of Christ' is clothed in language taken from the Old Testament. 'The flame of fire' and the punishment of the wicked, 'from the presence of God and from the glory of his might,' are literally expressions of Isaiah (ii. 10, 19, 21, and xxix. 6; xxx. 27), as the description of the man of sin in the next chapter is in part also borrowed from Ezekiel and Daniel. The array of His saints is also an image familiar to the prophets. (Comp. Jude, ver. 14.) Almost we may fancy we hear Elias saying by the mouth of John the Baptist, 'He shall thoroughly purge his floor and burn up the chaff with unquenchable fire.' And yet that which most distinguishes the truth of Christ even from Evangelical prophecy is not wanting.

12 work of faith with power: that the name of our Lord
Jesus Christ may be glorified in you, and ye in him,
according to the grace of our God and the Lord Jesus
Christ.

2 NOW we beseech you, brethren, ᵈ concerning ᶠ the
coming of our Lord Jesus Christ, and our gathering
2 together unto him, that ye be not soon shaken ᵉ from
your ᶠ mind, or be troubled, neither by spirit, nor by
word, nor by letter as from us, as that the day of the
3 Lord is at hand. Let no man deceive you by any
means: for except there come ᶠ the ᶠ falling away first,

ᵈ by   ᵉ in   ᶠ a

They who are to be 'glorified in Christ' in company ($\mu\epsilon\theta'$ $\dot{\eta}\mu\hat{\omega}\nu$) with the Apostles and prophets, are not the chosen people, but a heathen community. That earlier Gospel of St. Paul 'which was not another,' had a kind of Old Testament force and simplicity. Its phraseology was yet unformed; it embodied in vision of sense the 'things that eye hath not seen;' the Apostle when he preached it was 'drunk into the Spirit' of the old prophets of Israel. But it was a Gospel for the Gentile as well as the Jew; it spoke of faith in Christ and salvation through His name; it witnessed to the Apostle's own call and that of his converts; it was 'very near,' though it seemed also 'to bring down Christ from above.'

2. 1-10 is suggested by the mention of the judgement in the previous chapter, and has reference to opinions existing in the Thessalonian Church. They had suffered persecution, and this led the Apostle to the thought, that the judgement of God would be upon their enemies, in the day of the Lord. But a sort of counter-thought arises in his mind, that this coming of the day of the Lord was the very subject upon which he had to warn them to be calm, and not think, day after day, that the course of the world was to be interrupted. 'God is about to take vengeance on your enemies and that speedily' would be the natural sequence. But the Apostle goes on to teach them, that in fact 'it would not be speedily,' for an increase of evil must come first. And he proceeds to recall to their minds the lesson which he had taught while yet with them, respecting the man of sin and 'that which let.'

3. $\dot{\eta}$ $\dot{\alpha}\pi o\sigma\tau\alpha\sigma\acute{\iota}\alpha$, *the falling away,*] either that of which he had spoken to them while he was yet with them, or the falling away which was the common belief of Christians or which in his own mind was inseparable from the coming of Christ, which was to follow. For the use of the

and [g]the[⁷] man of sin be revealed, the son of perdition; who opposeth and exalteth himself [h]over[ʲ] all that is called God, or that is worshipped; so that he [i–ʲ] sitteth in the temple of God, shewing himself that he is God,—Remember ye not, that, when I was yet with you, I told you these things? And now ye know what withholdeth, that he [k]may[ʲ] be revealed

[g] that   [h] above   [ⁱ] add *as God*   [k] might

article, compare Apoc. xx. 3 ἄχρι τελεσθῇ τὰ χίλια ἔτη. Of what nature was this falling away? What vision of apostasy rose before him as he wrote this? Was it within or without? permanent or passing? persecution by the heathen, or the disorganization of the body of Christ itself? Was it the transition of the Church from its first love to a more secular and earthly state, or the letting loose of a spiritual world of evil, such as the Apostle describes in Eph. vi. 12? So ideal a picture cannot properly be limited to any person or institution. That it is an inward, not an outward evil that is depicted, is implied in the name apostasy. It is not the evil of the heathen world, sunk in grossness and unconsciousness, but evil rebelling against good, conflicting with good in the spiritual world itself. And the conflict is of the same nature, though in a wider sphere, as the strife of good and evil in the heart of the individual. It is that same strife, not as represented in the seventh of Romans, but at a later stage, when evil is fast becoming good, and the remembrance of the past itself is carrying men away from the truth.

4. εἰς τὸν ναὸν τοῦ θεοῦ, *in the temple of God.*] Either: (1) the temple at Jerusalem; or (2) the Christian Church; or (3) more truly both, the one being the image of the other, as in our Lord's words—'Destroy this temple.' The use of the image may have been suggested by the recent attempt of Caligula to place his statue in the Temple, as well as by the common practice of deifying the Roman emperors. 'In medio mihi Caesar erit, templumque tenebit.' Compare Dan. ix. 27 ἐπὶ τὸ ἱερὸν τὸ βδέλυγμα τῆς ἐρημώσεως, quoted by our Lord in Matt. xxiv. 15. Antichrist, ὁ ἀντικείμενος, is not without, but within the Church, usurping the place of God. The Jewish Temple being regarded as the symbol of the Christian Church, or of the world itself, that other temple of God, the man of sin is the personified and concentrated might of evil possessing it by force.

6. That τὸ κατέχον refers to the hindrance of Antichrist is plain from ὁ κατέχων in the succeeding verse. As in the case of Anti-

---

[1] Reading ὁ ἄνθρωπος τῆς ἁμαρτίας.

7 in his ¹proper" time. For the mystery of iniquity doth already work: only ᵐ there is he who letteth
8 now," until he be taken out of the way. And then shall that Wicked be revealed, whom the Lord shall ⁿ slay" with the spirit of his mouth, and shall destroy
9 with the brightness of his coming: whose coming is after the working of Satan with all power and ᵒ lying
10 signs and wonders," and with all deceivableness of unrighteousness ᵖ for" them that perish; because they received not the love of the truth, that they
11 might be saved. And for this cause God doth send them strong delusion, that they should believe a lie:
12 that they all might be damned who believed not the truth, but had pleasure in unrighteousness.
13 BUT we are bound to give thanks always to God for you, brethren beloved of the Lord, because God chose

¹ *omit* proper   ᵐ he who now letteth will let
ⁿ *consume*   ᵒ signs and lying wonders   ᵖ in

christ itself, the change of gender indicates that the hindrance spoken of may be regarded indifferently as a thing or as a person.

'That which letteth' has been variously explained to mean the prayers of Christians, or the ministry of the Apostle himself, or the Roman empire, about the destruction of which the Apostle expresses himself in dark and enigmatic terms; or, more generally, the purpose of God to delay its appearance. That the Roman empire was a limit to the anarchy and licentiousness of the world is a natural view to us. But we do not find anywhere else in the writings of St. Paul any similar view, nor is it easy to see how the Roman empire could be said to curb or restrain forms of spiritual evil, although it might seem to stand between the world and the papacy, or between the world and the irruption of the barbarians. Compare Essay on the Man of Sin.

The subject admits also of being regarded in a more general way. Again and again, in Scripture occurs the idea of an order and series of events, not to be anticipated in the providence of God. Thus our Saviour says—'It is not for you to know the times and the seasons which the Father hath put in his own power.' The Gospel itself comes 'in the fulness of time.' There is a fitness of times and seasons, preparations and tendencies going before, and the final event follow-you ¹a firstfruits to salvation through sanctification of the Spirit and belief of the truth: whereunto he called you by our gospel, to the obtaining of the glory of our Lord Jesus Christ. Therefore, brethren, stand fast, and hold the lessons which ye have been taught, whether by word, or our epistle. Now our Lord Jesus Christ himself, and God ^{q-}" our Father, which hath loved us, and hath given us everlasting consolation and good hope through grace, ^r comfort and stablish your hearts " in every good ^s work and word."

3 Finally, brethren, pray for us, that the word of the Lord may have free course, and be glorified, even as it is with you: and that we may be delivered from ^t the strange and wicked ones:" for all men have not faith.

^q add *even*   ^r *comfort your hearts, and stablish you*
^s *word and work*   ^t unreasonable and wicked men

ing them. As in the Old Testament, 'the iniquity of the Amorites is not yet full,' so in the New, God is described as waiting and interposing hindrances that the order of Providence may not be inverted.

15. It might seem as if, when election is spoken of, God had already done all, and nothing was left for man to do. The opposite inference is that of the Apostle. Unconscious of what we should term the logical inconsistency, he immediately adds—'Stand fast therefore;' be not shaken in mind or troubled, and hold fast what I taught you, either by word, or by Epistle. You might be shaken if you did not know the purpose of God towards you; but knowing it, be therefore at rest.

16-17. The Greek philosopher spoke of wisdom as an ἰατρεία

ψυχῆς, as we speak of the Gospel as remedial to the ills of human nature. St. Paul uses stronger language; with him the Gospel is a consolation. Within and without, the Christian is suffering in this evil world (ἐν τῷ παρεστῶτι αἰῶνι πονηρῷ). The Gospel makes him sensible of this state, and at the same time turns his sorrow into joy. If his suffering abounds, his consolation much more abounds; and God, who is spoken of under many titles as the Author of the Gospel, has this one especially in the writings of St. Paul—that He is the God of all consolation. (Rom. xv. 5 : 2 Cor. i. 3.)

3, 2. καὶ ἵνα ῥυσθῶμεν, *and that we may be delivered.*] The first thought of the Apostle was for the success of the Gospel; then followed the shrinking of the

¹ Reading ἀπαρχήν

3. 5] SECOND EPISTLE TO THE THESSALONIANS 83

3 But [1] u God " is faithful, who shall stablish you, and keep
4 you from evil. And we have confidence in the Lord
touching you, that ye both do and will do the things
5 which we command you [2] x and ye have done." And
the Lord direct your hearts into the love of God, and
into the patient waiting for Christ.

u *the Lord*   x omit *and ye have done*

flesh from the dangers which awaited him.

The same shrinking of the flesh is traceable elsewhere, in Rom. xv. 31 : 2 Cor. i. 8, 9. It was not a fear of death, nor was it merely the wish to be preserved for his master's service ; but a natural human feeling, which, in later life, had passed away. (Phil. ii. 17: 2 Tim. iv. 7.) It may be not unreasonably connected with his bodily presence, which his adversaries said was weak and his speech contemptible. (2 Cor. x. 10.) In this passage the adversaries to whom he refers are not his opponents at Thessalonica, which he had left, but at Corinth, where he probably was at this time, the false brethren of the Second Epistle to the Corinthians. The words themselves indicate that he is speaking of those who are in a certain sense Christians. For why should he say οὐ γὰρ πάντων ἡ πίστις, of mere heathens or mere Jews ? It would be like saying, 'Pray God to deliver me from my enemies, for all men are not Christians ;' or, 'Pray God to deliver me from Jews or heathens, for they are unconverted ;'—a self-evident remark, which it would be unmeaning to attribute to him. We are, therefore, led to infer that the words relate to the false brethren, the apparent friends, but secret enemies, such as those who came, in Gal. ii, to spy out the liberty of the Gospel, and were not separated by any marked line from the disciples. Supposing this view to be the true one, we may paraphrase as follows :—'Pray God that we may be delivered from evil men ; for not all professors are true Christians.' Comp. Rom. xv. 31.

3. Though men are unfaithful, yet God is faithful. Compare Rom. iii. 4. Though there are false brethren who have not the faith, yet God is faithful, and will deliver you from the evil. The connecting-link between this verse and the preceding is formed by the two words πίστις and πονηρός. The Apostle, more anxious for others than for himself, changes the person, and passes suddenly from the thought of his own danger to that of the Thessalonians.

Commentators are not agreed whether τοῦ πονηροῦ is to be taken as neuter or masculine ; and whether, in the latter case, it refers to Satan or the man of sin, or is a collective name for bad

[1] Reading ὁ θεός   [2] Reading καὶ ἐποιήσατε καί

G 2

6 Now we command you, brethren, in the name of our Lord Jesus Christ, that ye withdraw yourselves from every brother that walketh disorderly, and not after 7 the ʸlesson ‖ which ᶻye ‖ received of us. For yourselves know how ye ought to follow us: for we behaved not 8 ourselves disorderly among you; neither did we eat any man's bread for nought; but wrought with labour and travail night and day, that we might not be 9 chargeable to any of you: not because we have not power, but to make ourselves an ensample unto you 10 to follow us. For ᵃ⁻ᵈ when we were with you, this we commanded you, that if any would not work, neither 11 ᵇlet him ʲ eat. For we hear that there are some which walk among you disorderly, ᶜbusy only with what is

ʸ tradition   ᶻ *he*   ᵃ add *even*   ᵇ should he
ᶜ working not at all, but are busybodies

men in general. The transition from the plural in the preceding verse to the singular is certainly possible: the form of Antichrist may be again for a moment rising before the Apostle's eyes. But it is simpler to take the words as a neuter, 'from evil.' (Compare Matt. v. 39; vi. 13.) It is an evil common to himself and them, the evil of persecution, and from which, feeling for them rather than for himself, he prays that they may be delivered.

6. From the ἃ παραγγέλλομεν of the fourth verse, the Apostle passes on to particular instructions; ἐν ὀνόματι τοῦ κυρίου ἡμῶν, 'I solemnly enjoin you.'

The remaining paragraph of this Epistle is important, as bearing on the degree and manner of authority which the Apostle exercised over the Churches. It seems to have been of a mixed kind, partly official and partly moral, springing from the sense of what the Apostle had done for the Church, in bringing them to the knowledge of the Lord Jesus, yet also claimed by him as a right. In any voluntary society like the early Christian Church, the enforcement of such an authority must have depended on feeling and opinion. There was no other way of enforcement in the last resort but the separation of the individual offending, or, rather, the separation of the society itself from the individual. Of this we find several traces, not in the set form of excommunication or exclusion from the Lord's supper (although such exclusion was doubtless implied in it); rather it is a counsel or sentence of the Apostle, more or less formal in different cases, intended to exert a moral, and apparently

3. 18]   SECOND EPISTLE TO THE THESSALONIANS   85

12 not their own business.^|| Now them that are such we command and exhort ^d in the ^|| Lord Jesus Christ, that with quietness they work, and eat their own bread.
13 But ye, brethren, be not weary in well doing. And
14 if any man obey not our word by this epistle, note that man, and have no company with him, that he may
15 be ashamed. Yet count him not as an enemy, but
16 admonish him as a brother. ^eAnd may ^|| the Lord of peace himself give you peace always ^1 ^f everywhere.^|| The Lord be with you all.
17 The salutation of Paul with mine own hand, which
18 is the token in every epistle: so I write. The grace of our Lord Jesus Christ be with you all. ^2 Amen.^b—^||

    ^d *by our*   ^e now   ^f *by all means*
^g add *The second epistle to the Thessalonians was written from Athens*

even a physical effect, and not always given where it appears to have been deserved. The incestuous person is to be delivered to Satan, not that he may perish everlastingly, but for 'the destruction of the flesh, that the spirit may be saved in the day of the Lord.' So Hymenaeus and Philetus, 'that they may learn not to blaspheme.' In the Galatian Church, on the other hand, notwithstanding the rebellion against the Apostle's authority, nothing is said of his opponents ceasing to be the Church. In the Philippians, he tolerates those who preach 'Christ of contention.' To the Thessalonian Church he says, that if there are any wild enthusiasts neglecting their daily occupation, they are to hold no communication with them, as he wrote to the Corinthians, 'not to keep company with fornicators.' But it is remarkable that, in the Epistle in which this very precept occurs, he says nothing of the expulsion of those who maintained that the Resurrection was passed already. 1 Cor. xv. 12.

    ^1 Reading ἐν παντὶ τόπῳ   ^2 Reading ἀμήν

ESSAY

ON

THE MAN OF SIN

2 THESS. II.

WHETHER the prophecy of the man of sin is fulfilled or unfulfilled—whether it is to be explained from the immediate circle of the Apostle's life, or from the distant future—whether it relates to an individual or to an idea, to the Pharisees or to the Gnostics—whether 'the man of sin' himself be Nero as Chrysostom imagined, or the impersonation of heresy as Theodoret and others, or the pope as the reformers, or the reformers as the pope, or Mahomet as the Greek Church, or the Emperor Caligula as Grotius, or Titus as Wetstein, or Simon Magus as Hammond, or Simon the son of Gioras as Usteri and Le Clerc, or Cromwell as Englishmen who were his subjects sometimes said, or the French revolution, or Napoleon, as the last generation, or some embodiment or power of evil which is yet to come, as was the opinion of several of the Fathers, and is also that of some modern writers;—whether 'that which letteth, and he which letteth, and will let until he be taken out of the way,' is the Roman Empire, which was likewise a common opinion of the Fathers, or the German Empire, as was maintained by the early opponents of the papacy, or the purpose of God that the Gospel should be first preached, as was held by Theodore of Mopsuestia and Theodoret, or the outpouring of spiritual gifts as Chrysostom inclined to think, or Nero as Wetstein, or Vitellius, who was proconsul of Judea in Caligula's time, as Grotius, or Elijah the prophet, who 'must first come' according to the Jewish belief, or St. Paul himself as a recent interpreter ;—whether the temple of God is the Christian Church or the temple at Jerusalem, or both, or neither, that is to say some temple hereafter to be built, or the temple of the human soul, a figure which the Apostle elsewhere employs ;—whether the coming of Christ be His coming to judge the world at the last day, or the anticipation of that judgement on the Jews in the destruction of Jerusalem, or the one the lesser, the other the greater fulfilment of the same prediction ;— are some of the principal questions which in ancient or modern times have been raised by interpreters respecting the second chapter of the Second Epistle to the Thessalonians.

Most of these questions may be set aside, as having no real bearing upon the interpretation of the Epistle. They are not found but brought there. When it is remembered that at this period of his life, as the words of the Epistle imply, St. Paul himself expected 'to remain and be alive' (1 Thess. iv. 17) in the day of the Lord, and that he expressly states that the coming of Christ was to be preceded by Antichrist, and that the coming of Antichrist was again restrained by that which let, it is clear that the vision of the future must be confined within narrow bounds, that is, within ten, twenty, or thirty years at the utmost, if it be not that the acts of the drama are contemporary, or certainly very near, 'for the mystery of iniquity already worketh.' It is not, therefore, in the wider sphere of the history of the world, but in the life of the Apostle, in the cities of Asia or Judea, perhaps at Rome in the days of Caligula or Nero, that we must look for the events, or shadow of events, which form the basis of the prophecy.

It is necessary to warn the reader, that we are not about to add another to the multitude of guesses which exist already. Our inquiry will relate rather to the style and structure of the prophecy, than to the opinions of interpreters respecting the facts which may be regarded as its fulfilment. The real facts may not have been recorded; they may have been too minute to be observed by us; they may also have been transfigured before the spiritual eye, until they are no longer recognizable as historical events. What we are attempting is not the solution of a riddle, or the reading of a hieroglyphic, but the comparison of one part of Scripture with another; and the comprehension of it, if possible, not in the letter but in the spirit.

And although it is true that there may be a disadvantage in excluding from our consideration all those topics from which the study of this remarkable passage has hitherto derived its interest and zest, let us pause to remember also how many dangers are avoided. We shall run no risk of attributing an exaggerated importance to the history of our own time. We shall be under no temptation to point the words of St. Paul against an ancient enemy. We shall have no inclination to adapt the proportions of lesser events to the main event or figure which we make the centre of our system. We may hope to escape the charge which has been brought against writers on these subjects, that they explain 'history by prophecy.' There will be no fear of our forging weapons of persecution for one body or party of Christians to use against another. We shall be in no danger of losing the simplicity of the Gospel in Apocalyptic fancies. Our own opinions, perhaps even changes of opinion, will not be imposed on others as an interpretation of Scripture, with a degree of authority which is only the veil of their extreme uncertainty. All these reproaches, however unconsciously and innocently they may be incurred by good and learned men, are injuries to the truth and dishonours to the word of God.

'The man of sin' is not a mere detached prophecy. It formed a leading subject of the Apostle's teaching. He introduces it with express reference to the fact, that on his visit to the Thessalonians he had warned them of it; and this not only in general terms, but with special mention of the times of his appearing, and the influences by which his revelation was withheld. 'Remember ye not, that when I was yet with you I told you these things?' What he had told them is contained in the description which precedes, and which is definite and precise; that man of sin, 'the son of perdition; who opposeth and exalteth himself above all that is called God, or that is worshipped; so that he as God sitteth in the temple of God, shewing himself that he is God.' All this was not new to the Thessalonian converts; they even knew of that which withheld, that he might be revealed in his own time. The Apostle adds a few other traits in the verses which follow; 'whose coming is after the working of Satan, with all power and lying signs and wonders, and with all deceivableness of unrighteousness in them that perish.'

The sources of our information are so limited, that we are able to pronounce at once that we know of no person or power existing in the lifetime of the Apostle, to which most of the above features will apply. We cannot say that 'the man of sin' was Caligula, whose reign had terminated about twelve years before this; or Nero, who had just mounted the imperial throne, or Simon the son of Gioras, the leader of the fanatics at Jerusalem, who had hardly come forth into public view; still less Vitellius, Vespasian, or Titus. Such guesses are only more probable than the wider ones, because they relate to persons who were actually or almost within the horizon of the Apostle's eye; but they are inconsistent with the general character of the prophecy, and offer no remarkable coincidences with its details. In any succession of historical events, it is possible to find war and peace, order and anarchy, a king and an usurper, a lawless force and a restraining power. General resemblances of this kind prove nothing; the good and evil of every age find an expression in the language of prophecy. In times of crisis or revolution men naturally apply the words of the Apostle to themselves. Even the quiet tenor of ordinary life has been 'set on fire' by the torch of enthusiasm. But we must not confuse the original meaning of the prophecy with the application of it which is on the lips of the preacher after 1800 years. The vision of evil which the Apostle saw was around and very near him; it hung like a cloud over the first age of the Church; it cannot be dispersed in generalities; we look in vain for it in the distant future.

If, confessing that no known person or event agrees with the description of the prophecy, we try another method, and interpret the second chapter of the Second Epistle to the Thessalonians entirely from itself, we shall probably infer that by the terms 'man of sin,' 'son of perdition,' St. Paul has in view a real person, and that by his 'sitting in the temple of God' is meant literally his enthronement in the temple at Jerusalem. The grossness of the delusion which is attributed to his followers falls in with such an interpretation. The word 'apostasy' is a further indication that the new God or teacher stands in some relation either to Judaism or Christianity. He is not a mere ordinary individual coming forth from the crowd and practising an imposture, any more than he is a statue of wood or stone, but the author or symbol of some new form of spiritual evil;— a false Christ or false prophet, a Simon Magus, an Elcasai, or a Barcochab. The way has been preparing for him, underground in the hearts of men; he is waiting for his appointed hour. The founder of a false religion, claiming divine honours, announcing himself as the new God of the Jewish Temple, influencing the minds of men by every sort of magic art and spiritual deception, would most adequately correspond to the description of the Apostle. Such a one, he would seem to say, was to exist for a short time, and then vanish away, not before the superior power of truth, but before the actual force of Christ and His angels, in flaming fire taking vengeance.

Natural as such an interpretation may appear, it would probably be erroneous, and for this reason, that, like many other interpretations of prophecy, it would rest too much on the words themselves, without considering the style of the language or the parallelisms in St. Paul's own writings. The first question respecting all prophecies is, whether the language of them is figurative or literal, or how far figurative and how far literal. Figurative language will commonly detect itself, as in the trumpets, vials, numbers, of the Book of Revelation. The very symmetry of it will indicate its true nature. Events in history are not carried on by sevens, or by twelves; nor are they exactly limited by periods of time. Nor are the powers of nature or the kingdoms of this world divisible into four or ten. Accordingly, in such instances, we readily separate the framework and compartments of the picture from the life and motion of the figures. But there are other passages in which the form and the thought are more closely united, in which the garment clings to the person, and cannot be put off without destroying the life of the prophecy. Interpretation of prophecy will, in these cases, be an imperfect analysis of what it is really impossible to analyse. Especially will this be so where the figures are traditional, and have acquired from use and familiarity a sort of permanent and apparently historical character. The vision of events themselves is then circumscribed by the circle of prophetic symbols.

Taking in this important element, we find in Ezekiel and Daniel, in the discourses of our Lord respecting the end of the world, in the Epistles to the Thessalonians and to Timothy, as well as in the Epistles of St. Peter and St. Jude and in the Book of Revelation, a series of images of the evil which was to come upon the world in the latter days, all together furnishing a sort of chain of prophecy between the Old Testament and the New, which gradually extends and seems to pass from the realms of history into the spiritual and unseen world. One of the first links in this chain is Ezekiel's description of Gog and Magog, the symbol of the tribes of the North, whom God will bring against the land of Israel, that He may be glorified in their destruction (xxxviii. 16, 17). This prophecy, which is the beginning of many others, itself implies that it was not uttered by Ezekiel for the first time: 'Art thou he of whom I have spoken in old time by my servants the prophets of Israel, which prophesied in those days many years that I would bring thee against them?' (Compare Jer. ii—iv.) The minds of the Jewish prophets in Babylon had been led to dwell on the powers of the North, since the Scythian tribes had spread themselves over Asia. Where could they find a more striking image of the power of God than in this mighty people, 'covering' the world 'like a cloud,' and suddenly, like a cloud, passing away— which had probably in Josiah's reign overspread Palestine itself? They had almost been seen by Ezekiel in the days of his youth, and the remembrance of them had stamped themselves for ages on the Eastern world. His prophecy of them is little more than history, inspired only by the consciousness that there is One that ruleth among the children of men. There is no indication that Gog is other than a person, the chief prince of Meshech and Tubal. Nor is there apparently any form of spiritual evil that is symbolized in him; he is but the great enemy of Israel, who comes up with all his hosts against the people of God.

Later in the series are the prophecies of Daniel, respecting the little horn and the kings of the North and South (vii and xi), which, though retaining a certain degree of resemblance to the prophecy of Ezekiel, present also a striking difference. It is a difference in spirit as well as in style and subject. We seem to have advanced another step in the revelation of God to man; with the vision of the kingdoms of this world mingles also the vision of the final judgement. Every one admits and loves to trace the connexion between the evangelical prophecies, as they are often termed, and the Gospel itself. But perhaps it has not been equally observed that the Apocalyptic prophecies are also a link of connexion between the Old Testament and the New. As the former anticipate the moral and spiritual nature of the kingdom of Christ, so do the latter anticipate the universality of the Gospel. No two books of the Old Testament itself bear a closer resemblance to each other, than the book of Daniel, the Apocalypse of the Old Testament, and the book of Revelation, which may be termed by its Greek name the Apocalypse of the New. Were the one placed at the end of the Old Testament, and the other at the beginning of the New, they would seem, more than any of the canonical writings, to bridge the chasm which separates, or appears to separate, the two parts of the Sacred Volume. Both alike differ from the older prophecies, in extending the purposes of God to all time and to all mankind. The earlier history of the Jews was itself a kind of prophecy, the earlier prophecies were a kind of history of the Jews and their neighbours. There was a time when other nations seemed to be out of the way, and only occasionally to share in the mercies and judgements of God. But now the prophet lifted up his eyes east and west, north and south, to all countries of the earth, and saw in the history of the world the prelude to the final judgement.

This is the kind of difference which separates the two prophecies of Daniel from that of Ezekiel respecting Gog and Magog. The one is a part of the history of the Jews; the other is a prophecy of the latter days, an anticipation of the judgement to come. That of Ezekiel is the germ of the other, and stands in the same relation to it, as the vision of the dry bones, in the same prophet, to the description of the general resurrection in the seventh and twelfth chapters of Daniel, or the vision of the Temple and the portions of the tribes, to the new Jerusalem and the 144,000, in the Book of Revelation. In Ezekiel we have not yet burst the bonds of the temporal dispensation; in Daniel we already pass within the veil into another world. They occupy different places in Jewish history, the very dispersion of the Jews in Asia and Egypt tending to break down the force of local feelings, and leading them to include all nations within the circle of God's providence.

Parallel with this enlargement of the symbols of prophecy is the new and nobler meaning which is given to the worship of the tabernacle and to the Jewish history, in the Epistle to the Hebrews. A light is shed on both, derived, perhaps, from a wider experience of mankind, yet not the less coming down 'from the author and father of lights.' First the prophets, then the law, become instinct with the life of the Gospel. The only difference is that in prophecy the new takes the place of the old, in a more gradual and less perceptible manner. The law is done away in Christ; the temple made with hands is destroyed, that another temple, not made with hands, may be raised up; and the discourses of Christ respecting the end of the world, gather together in one all the threads of Old Testament prophecy.

Thus, through the whole of the books of Scripture, from the earliest to the latest, the spirit of prophecy might be said to be changing with the increasing purpose of God to man. But though the spirit changed, the imagery remained the same. The two prophecies which have been referred to, present more than one minute similarity with the second chapter of the Second Epistle to the Thessalonians; as, for example, the insolence and impiety of the king 'who shall exalt and magnify himself above every god,' xi. 36, which may be compared with 2 Thess. ii. 4, 'Who opposeth and exalteth himself above all that is called God or worshipped,' and 'the pollution of the sanctuary of strength, and the abomination of desolation standing in the holy place,' xi. 31, quoted by our Lord, which recalls 'the man of sin sitting in the temple of God ;' also the words 'have intelligence with them which forsake the holy covenant,' which are a periphrasis for 'the apostasy.' It is not quite certain, nor is it important for our object to know, what was the original meaning of the passages of Daniel; but whether they allude to the kings of Syria and Egypt, or in part also to the Romans, to relate to some unknown course of events, their original meaning in the Book of Daniel has no necessary connexion with their use and application by the Apostle. We might say, in the language of Bossuet, that St. Paul spoke by the spirit of Daniel, as St. Peter spoke by the mouth of Joel on the day of Pentecost, or as St. John himself spoke by the spirit of Ezekiel in Rev. xx. 8, where the names Gog and Magog are retained, though the meaning is generalized. Many other instances may be found in which the general subject is changed, though the ornaments remain. The same symbols which once referred to the Temple or to the tribes of Israel, are again employed, without any precise meaning, of the Church and the world at large.

It does not, therefore, follow, because the words of the prophecy of Daniel, or of our Lord, refer to the Romans, that they necessarily received this explanation from St. Paul, any more than in the Book of Revelation, because mention is made of the hundred and forty and four thousand of the tribes of Israel, it follows that salvation was first to be given to the house of Israel. The forms of good and evil are idealized in the language of prophecy. The same images are handed down from one generation of prophets to another; but the state of the world, which is symbolized by them, may change and become different. As in the interpretation of prophecy, many successions of events have, in different ages of the world, been thought to correspond with the words of Daniel, or of the Apocalypse; so with the prophets themselves, there is a growth and adaptation of the same prophecy to various stages of human history. Not only are there many mirrors of the meaning of prophecy in the history of the world, but more than this—the last prophecy is itself, as it were, the glass through which the prophet looks forward into the future.

Hence the imagery of a prophecy in the New Testament will not be the clue to its true nature. Nay, it may be very far removed from it, sometimes even absolutely opposed to it. For it may refer to what is literal and historical, but the thing signified in the New Testament may be spiritual and ideal. Ordinary quotations from the Old Testament are to be explained by their context in the New Testament, not by their place in the Old. The same rule is applicable to the prophecies of the Old Testament when transferred to the New. In both, the spirit has commonly taken the place of the letter, the evangelical truth has lighted up the prophetic symbol. So that the true key to the interpretation of a prophecy of St. Paul, is not the meaning of the same imagery in the Old Testament, but the character of his own writings, 'Non, nisi ex ipso Paulo, Paulum potes interpretari.' The special sense is to be gathered from those points which he has distinct from the Old Testament, rather than those which he has in common with it. We do not feel certain that the man of sin, sitting in the temple of God, is more than a personification of the abomination of desolation spoken of by Daniel the prophet; suggested, perhaps, by the worship of the Emperor which St. Paul had seen in the cities to which he had travelled, or by the attempt of Caligula, a few years previously, to place his statue in the temple at Jerusalem. But he that 'letteth, and will let, until he be taken out of the way,' and the lying signs and wonders, with which the man of sin was to be accompanied, are traits which are peculiar to the Apostle, some of which are found elsewhere in his Epistles. Here, then, whether we are able to discern it or not, is something which we may naturally look for, not in the clouds of heaven, but in the history of the Apostolic age.

In many other places of the New Testament, and even of the writings of St. Paul himself, mention occurs of strange forms of evil. It is observable that all of them are spiritual. There are differences in the description of them, not unlike the difference which we may suppose to have existed between the author of the Epistles in which they are spoken of, St. Paul, and St. John ; but they nowhere convey the impression that they represent political changes or revolutions in the kingdoms of men. The one Apostle is, as it were, hastening, amid many impediments, to the coming of the day of the Lord ; the other is calmly waiting for the events that must shortly come to pass. Both seem to feel the evil of the world as a sign of 'the last time ;' the one, near and present, as if involved in the conflict ; the other, far off, separated from it rather than warring with it. Already there are many Antichrists, says St. John, and 'Antichrist is he that denieth the Father and the Son.' So in the first Epistle to Timothy, iv. 1–3, it is said, 'that in the latter times some shall depart from the faith, giving heed to seducing spirits, and doctrines of devils speaking lies in hypocrisy, having their conscience seared with a hot iron, forbidding to marry, and commanding to abstain from meats, which God hath created to be received with thanksgiving of them which believe and know the truth.' Compare 2 Tim. iii. 1. The Apostle appears to apprehend the same danger in Col. ii. 8, 16. And in the Second Epistle of Peter, ii. 1 ; iii. 3, there is the same pervading idea of the latter days, in which 'false prophets shall rise up, who privily shall bring in damnable heresies, denying the Lord that bought them.' The evil of which the New Testament prophecies speak, is not the idolatry of the heathen, nor the conquests of great empires, but the apostasy of sometime believers, or the fanaticism of the Jews. Of something of this kind, not of Roman governors, or Jewish high priests, the Apostle is speaking when he says: 'We wrestle not against flesh and blood, but against principalities, against powers, against the rulers of the darkness of this world, against spiritual wickedness in heavenly places.' The temporal Antichrist, like the temporal Israel, has passed into a spiritual one.

Such passages are a much safer guide to the interpretation of the one we are considering, than the meaning of similar passages in the Old Testament. For they indicate to us the habitual thought of the Apostle's mind; 'a falling away first,' suggested, probably, by the wavering which he saw around him among his own converts, the grievous wolves that were entering into the Church of Ephesus, Acts xx. 29; the turning away of all them of Asia, in 2 Tim. i. 15. When we consider that his own converts, and his Jewish opponents, or half converts, were all the world to him, that through them, as it were in a glass, he appeared to himself to see the workings of human nature generally, we understand how this double image of good and evil should have presented itself to him, and the kind of necessity which he felt that Christ and Antichrist should alternate with each other. It was not that he foresaw some great conflict, decisive of the destinies of mankind. What he anticipated far more nearly resembled the spiritual combat in the seventh chapter of the Romans. It was the same struggle, written in large letters, as Plato might have said, not on the tables of the heart, but on the scene around; the world turned inside out, as it might be described; evil as it is in the sight of God, and as it realizes itself to the conscience, putting on an external shape, transforming itself into a person.

Separating the prophecy, then, into two parts, its external form and internal meaning, the one part is to be explained from the Old Testament; that is to say, it is the repetition of the images of Ezekiel and Daniel, which naturally receive a more precise character from the associations of the time in which St. Paul lived; while the other part, or inward meaning, is to be illustrated by other passages in St. Paul's own writings, in which he speaks of the perilous times of the latter days; of false prophets transforming themselves into Apostles of Christ; of Satan transfigured into an angel of light; of religious licentiousness; of all them of Asia falling away from him. Of all these opponents of the Gospel the man of sin is the concentrated image; they are already working, but are at present underground, not yet bursting forth to envelop mankind. Gnosticism, or Orientalism, or Judaism, the evil of the world as it awoke to the consciousness of higher truths, the swarming heresy of an age of religious excitement, and the persecution of the followers of Christ and His Apostles, all probably, as in the Book of Revelation, mingled in the vision 'of the things that should shortly come to pass.'

Thus there are altogether four elements which enter into the conception of the man of sin:—(1) the traditional imagery of the elder prophets; (2) the style of the Apostle and his age; (3) the impression of recent historical events— which supply the form; (4) the state of the world and the Church, and the consciousness that, where good is, evil must ever be in aggravated proportions, which supply the matter of the prophecy.

Still we have not made a nearer approach to the true interpretation of 'him that letteth,' an expression on which no light is thrown, either by the writings of St. Paul, or by the symbolical language of the Old Testament. We cannot err in supposing that it intimates St. Paul's belief that the coming of Antichrist was not yet. Though already working, it was restrained by a superior power. The Thessalonians were exhorted not to be troubled in mind, as though the day of the Lord was at hand, for it was to be preceded by the manifestation of the man of sin. But it was still further delayed by the interposition of 'him that letteth.' So far all is consistent. Christ, Antichrist, the restrainer of Antichrist, are the triple links of the chain by which the world is held together. In what person or thing to find the last of the three is the point of difficulty.

No stress can be laid on the use of the masculine, 'him that letteth,' because it is immediately followed by that of the neuter, 'that which letteth,' and may be accounted for by parallelism with the man of sin in a preceding verse. More truly might it be argued that the use of the neuter excludes the idea of a person. Nero might have been ὁ κατέχων, but could not have been τὸ κατέχον. The double use of the masculine and the neuter in some degree favours the interpretation of the prophecy which identifies the Roman empire with the restraining power. For some interpretation seems to be required which is applicable to a thing as well as to a person, as, for example, in the case of the Roman empire, τὸ κατέχον and ὁ κατέχων may contain an allusion to the empire and to the emperor. A more important circumstance than this strikes us in the examination of the passage: it is the apparent secrecy which the Apostle observes in speaking of the restraining power. It is an enigma which he will not reveal, which he had explained while he was yet with them, and dare not now write 'with pen and ink.' It reminds us of the number of the beast in the Book of Revelation. It recalls the words of Daniel, xii. 10: 'None of the wicked shall understand, but the wise shall understand.' It quickens our curiosity to know what that power could have been, which was contemporary with the Apostle, and which he would not openly mention to his converts.

Two answers suggest themselves; conjectures, it is true, because it is impossible to do more than form conjectures which may be consistent or not inconsistent with the spirit of the prophecy; but they are not, however, to be rejected on that ground, if nothing better can be offered. The first is the Roman empire; the second, the Jewish law. According to the view which separates the traditional form from the substance of the prophecy, it would be no fatal objection to the first of these two interpretations, that the figure of Antichrist himself is taken from the image of the Roman emperors sitting in the temples as gods, while he that letteth is again the Roman emperor regarded from a new point of view. More real is the difficulty of supposing that St. Paul could have expected that, within a few years, the solid frame of the Roman empire was to break up and pass away. It is unlikely that he should have even taken the kingdoms of this world into the horizon of his spiritual vision. To say that the heresies of the Ebionites or Nicolaitanes were restrained by the continuance of the Roman government, would be farfetched : the two are not '*in pari materiâ.*' It might remove this difficulty if we could suppose the revelation of the man of sin to represent the rebellion of the Jews, but would leave the original one, how to account for the mystery which the Apostle observes about him which letteth. More natural is it to explain 'that which letteth' as the Jewish law, the check on spiritual licentiousness which for a little while was holding in its chains the swarms of Jewish heretics, who were soon to be let loose and sweep over the earth. Whatever other objections may be entertained to the last of the two interpretations, it has, at any rate, the advantage of consistency. It does not confuse the spiritual and historical, or take us away from the world of the human heart of which the Scripture speaks, to the world of objects and events.

Good and evil seem often to lie together flat upon the world's surface. At other times they start up, like armed men, and prepare for the last struggle. There is a state in the individual soul, in which it has entered into rest, and has its conversation in heaven, and is a partaker of the kingdom of God. There is a state also in which it is divided between two, not unconscious of good, but overpowered by evil, living in what St. Paul terms the body of death. There is a third state in which it is neither conscious of good nor overpowered by evil, but in which it 'leads the life of all men' acting under the influence of habit, law, opinion. All these three states have their parallels in the history of the world. In all of them, whether in the individual or in the world, whether arising out of the purpose of God or the nature of man, there sometimes seems to be a kind of necessity which will not suffer them to be other than they are. The first is that state for which the believer looks when the kingdoms of this world shall become the kingdoms of God and Christ. The second is that state of the world, seen also to him, but unseen to men in general, in which, in the language of prophecy, 'the wicked is revealed,' in which the elements of good and evil separate and decompose themselves, in anticipation of the final judgement. The third is that fixed order of the world in which we live, which surrounds us on every side with its restraints, social, legal, moral, which, if it be not very good, is not very evil; which 'letteth and will let' as long as human nature lasts. Such 'a let' to the evil of men was the Roman empire; such 'a let,' even when it had lost its inspired character, was the law of the Jews. Whether either of these, or both of them combined in the same way that in the Book of Revelation Rome and Jerusalem combine to form the image of the last enemy, suggested to the Apostle the thought of 'that which let;' whether the political order of the world, which was typified by them, seemed to him for a time to interpose itself against the manifestation of the man of sin, is uncertain. Such is a natural adaptation for us to make of the words of the prophecy; it is also a consistent interpretation of them when translated out of the symbolism of Ezekiel and Daniel into more general language. To suppose that there is to be some greater deluge of evil than any that has already poured over the world, at the fall of the Roman Empire, or in the tenth century, some louder shriek of the human race in its agony than at the destruction of Jerusalem, to be heard again at the expiration of two thousand years, adds nothing to the credibility of the Apostle. Least of all can we imagine him to refer to a 'gigantic' development of the human intellect, which is at present believed to be held with a chain by the governments of mankind. Such opinions draw us away from the healthy atmosphere of history and experience into the unseen future; they project to an unimaginable distance, what to the Apostle was near and present. No test can be applied to them; their truth or falsehood, when we are in our graves, we shall never know. They gain no additional witness from the willingness of their authors to stake the inspiration of Scripture on the historic certainty of the event. So long as we delight to trace coincidences, or to make pictures in religion; so long as the human mind continues to prefer the extraordinary to the common, such interpretations of prophecy, in forms more or less idealized or refined, adapted to different age or capacities, will never fail. But the Spirit of prophecy in every age lives not in signs and wonders, but in the divine sense of good and evil in our own hearts, and in the world around us.

ON THE PROBABILITY

THAT

MANY OF ST. PAUL'S EPISTLES HAVE BEEN LOST

'Ἐν πάσῃ ἐπιστολῇ—'In every Epistle.'—2 Thess. iii. 17.

THESE three words, dropping out by the way, open a field for reflection to those who maintain the genuineness of the Epistle in which they occur, because they imply, or at least make it probable, that St. Paul wrote other Epistles, which were never reckoned among the Canonical books, and of which all trace must therefore have disappeared in ecclesiastical history, even in that early age in which the Canon was beginning to be fixed.

Other expressions in the writings of the Apostle lead to the same inference. In the second chapter of the Epistle from which they are taken, which it is important to observe is almost the earliest of those extant, and the words of which cannot therefore refer to the Epistles which are familiar to us, he twice speaks of 'a letter as from us,' as a common and possible occurrence (ver. 2, 15). In the Second Epistle to the Corinthians, x. 10, the Apostle supposes his adversaries to say 'that his letters are weighty and powerful;' to which he replies in the next verse, 'Such as we are in word by letters when absent, such will we also be in deed when we are present.' Is it likely that the Apostle is here referring to the First Epistle only? The words of 1 Cor. v. 9, 'I wrote unto you in the epistle,' probably allude, notwithstanding the tense, to the letter which he was writing at the time, and have, therefore, nothing to do with our present inquiry. But the general character of both Epistles to the Corinthians leads to the conviction that he was in habits of correspondence with the teachers of the Church of Corinth. It appears also from 1 Cor. xvi. 3 that he was intending (although the intention in this instance was not fulfilled) to send messengers with letters of introduction, as we term them, to the Church at Jerusalem;—letters of Christian courtesy, of which one only—the short Epistle to Philemon—has been preserved to after-ages. Similar occasions must often have occurred in the course of a long life and ministry; St. Paul did not cease to be St. Paul in his feelings towards others, because what he wrote in the privacy of the closet was not destined to be read afterwards by the whole Christian world. Once more, in the Epistle to the Colossians, iv. 16, the Apostle enjoins the Churches of Colossae and Laodicea to interchange the letters which they had received from him. It is only a conjecture, and one which is not favoured by the similarity of the Epistles to the Colossians and Ephesians, that the Epistle here referred to as the Epistle to the Laodiceans is the extant Epistle to the Ephesians. Here then are signs of another lost Epistle. The allusion in the Second Epistle of St. Peter, iii. 15, 16, 'Even as our beloved brother Paul also, according unto the wisdom given unto him, hath written unto you; as also in all his epistles, speaking in them of these things; in which are some things hard to be understood, which they that are unlearned and unstable wrest, as they do also the other scriptures, unto their own destruction,' may be mentioned also, though it has only a general bearing on our present subject.

(ii) The character of the Apostle is a further presumption

on the same side of the question. He who lives in himself the life of all the Churches, who is praying for his converts night and day, and who allows no other concerns to occupy his mind—of such an one is it reasonable to suppose that, during his whole ministry, to all his followers in many lands, he would write no other Epistles but those which have come down to us? One might have thought that every year, almost every month, he would have found some exhortation to give to them; that he would have received news of them from some quarter or other touching divisions which required healing, or persecution under which his children needed comfort, or advances of the truth which called for his counsel and sympathy. One might have thought that his affection for them, and his extreme (may we call it?) sensitiveness to their feelings towards himself, would have led him to make use of every opportunity for writing to them or hearing from them. He who had no rest in his soul until he had sent Timothy to know their state, could not have borne to have passed a great portion of his life without knowledge of them or intercourse with them. But if so, the Canonical Epistles or Letters cannot be the only ones of which the Apostle was the author. For, including the Pastoral Epistles, their number is but thirteen, not one in two years for the entire active portion of the Apostle's life, and these very unequally spread over different periods. Of the first ten or fifteen years no Epistle is extant; then two short ones begin the series; after an interval of some years succeeded by another short one: then in a single year follow the three larger Epistles together, more than half the whole: lastly, in the years of his imprisonment, we have not much more than a short Epistle for every year. Is it likely that there were no others?—or are we suffering ourselves to be imposed upon by the fear of disturbing a natural but superficial impression?

(iii) The Epistles which are extant, with the exception of the Epistle to the Romans, are unlike the compositions of

ST. PAUL'S EPISTLES HAVE BEEN LOST 107

one who in his whole life wrote only ten letters. They are too lively and draw too near to the hearts of men. Those especially to the Thessalonians, Corinthians, Galatians, and Colossians (compare Philemon) imply habits of familiar intercourse between the Apostle and the distant Churches. Messengers are passing from him to them, and he is minutely informed of their circumstances. There is no trace of ignorance on the Apostle's part of what is going on among them. There is none of that natural formality which grows up in letters between unknown persons. Would the Apostle have written to a Church which he only addressed once in his life in a style which is more like talking than writing?—and without the least allusion anywhere to the singularity of the circumstance of his writing to them?

But if, as the allusions which have been mentioned and the reason of the thing, and the style of the extant Epistles themselves, lead us to suppose, St. Paul wrote other Epistles, which have not been handed down to us, then many reflections arise in our minds, some of which have an important bearing on the interpretation of Scripture.

1. It has been observed that within a single year of his life the Apostle wrote the Epistle to the Romans and the two Epistles to the Corinthians, which are in quantity equal to more than half the whole of his Epistles, and not much short of a seventh portion of the entire New Testament. Nor is it certain that these were the only Epistles written by him in the same year: the reverse is more likely. Now suppose we take this as the criterion of the probable amount of his lost writings, and that during each year of his ministry, which extended over a period of at least twenty-five years, he wrote an equal quantity—though it would not be true to say that 'the world itself would not contain the books that would have been written,' yet the result would have been a volume three times the size of the New Testament. There is nothing extravagant in this speculation, although

there is no proof of it; the allusions to lost Epistles make the idea extremely probable. Nor would any one think it extravagant if the Apostle had not been one of the Canonical writers, whose writings we are accustomed to regard as supernaturally preserved to us.

2. Suppose, further, that in a distant part of the world, in some Syriac, or Armenian, or Aethiopic transcript, or even in its original language, buried in the unexcavated portions of Herculaneum or Pompeii, one of these lost Epistles were suddenly brought to light: with what feelings would it be received by the astonished world! The return of the Apostle himself to earth would hardly be a more surprising event. There are minds to whom such a discovery would seem to involve more danger than the loss of an Epistle which we already have. It is not impossible that it might be suppressed or ever it found its way to the Christian public. Suppose it to escape this fate; it is printed and translated: with what anxiety do men turn over its pages, to find in them something which has a bearing on this or that controverted point! If touching upon disputed matters, is it too much to conceive that it would not find equal acceptance with disputants on both sides—supposing that it favoured one of them rather than the other? Time would elapse before the new Epistle would find its way into the language of theology. There would be no Fathers or Commentators to overlay it with traditional interpretations. It is strange but also true that it could never receive the deference and respect which has attached to those more legitimate Epistles in the possession of which the Christian Church has gloried for above eighteen centuries. And some one standing aloof might ask whether any article of faith which such an accident might disturb could be necessary to salvation.

3. Another supposition may be raised of the discovery not of one but of many lost Epistles of St. Paul, which suggests a new question. Would the balance of Christian

truth be thereby altered? Not so. A moment's reflection will remind us that the servant is not above his Lord, nor the disciple above his Master. If we have failed to gather from the words of Christ the spirit of the Gospel, a new Epistle of St. Paul would hardly enlighten us; if we are partakers of that spirit we have more religious knowledge than it is possible to exhaust on earth. The alarm is no sooner raised than dispelled. The chief use of bringing the supposition before our minds is to remind us of the simplicity of the faith of Christ. It may help to indicate also to the theological student the nature of the problem which he has to consider in the interpretation of Scripture, at once harder and easier than he at first supposed—easier because simpler, harder because beset with artificial difficulties. Were the Epistles bearing the name of St. Paul not ten but thirty in number, a great change would take place in our mode of studying them. Is it not their shortness which provokes microscopic criticism?—the scantiness of materials giving rise to conjectures, the fragmentary thought itself provoking system? Words and phrases such as 'justification by faith without the works of the law' could not have had such a powerful and exclusive influence on the theology of aftertimes had they been found in two only out of thirty Epistles. Theories and constructions soon come to an end when materials are abundant; ingenuity ceases to make an attempt to fill up the blanks of knowledge when the mind is distinctly conscious that it is dealing not with the whole but with a part only.

4. No difference is made by the supposition which has been raised respecting the extant Epistles considered as a rule of life and practice. Almost any one of them is a complete witness to the Author and Finisher of our faith; a complete text-book of the truths of the Gospel. But it is obvious that the supposition, or rather the simple fact, that Epistles have been lost which were written by St. Paul, is inconsistent with the theory of a plan which is sometimes

attributed to the extant ones, which are regarded as a temple having many parts, even as there are many members in one body, and all members have not the same office. A mistaken idea of design is one of the most attractive errors in the interpretation of Scripture no less than of nature. No such plan or unity can be really conceived as existing in the Apostle's own mind; for he could never have distinguished between the Epistles destined to be lost and those which have been allowed to survive. And to attribute such a plan to an overruling Providence would be an arbitrary fancy, involving not inspiration, but the supernatural selection and preservation of particular Epistles, and destructive to all natural ideas of the Gospel. It is a striking illustration of what may be termed the incidental character of Christianity, that (not without a Providence in this as in all other earthly things) some of the Epistles of St. Paul, in the course of nature, as if by chance, are for ever lost to us; while others, as if by chance, are handed down to be the treasures of the Christian world throughout all ages.

5. There is no reason to suppose that those Epistles of St. Paul which have been preserved were more sacred or inspired than those which were lost, or either more so than his discourses in the synagogue at Thessalonica during 'three Sabbath days,' at Athens, at Corinth, at Rome, or the other places in which he preached the Gospel. The supposition of the lost Epistles indefinitely extends itself when we think of lost words. Of these it might be truly said, 'that if they were written every one, even the world itself would not contain the books that should be written.' The writings of the Apostle, like the words of our Saviour, are but a fragment of his life. And they must be restored to their context before they can be truly understood. They do not acquire any real sacredness by isolation from the rest. It would be a loss, not a gain, to deprive the New Testament of its natural human character—instead of receiving a higher and diviner meaning, it would only be

reduced to a level with the sacred writings of the Asiatic religions. 'So Christ and his Apostles went about speaking day after day,' is a truer and more instructive thought than 'these things were formally set down for our instruction.' Nor does it really diminish the power of Scripture to describe it, as it appears to the eye of the critical student, as a collection of fragmentary and occasional pieces. For these fragments are living plants; the germ of eternal life is in them all; the least of all seeds, when compared in bulk with human literature, they have grown up into a tree, the shade of which covers the earth.

THE EPISTLE

TO THE

GALATIANS

INTRODUCTION

Two questions, closely connected with each other, arise in the mind of every reader of the Epistles of St. Paul who is desirous of forming an idea of the state of the Churches to which they were addressed: first, whether the Church was founded by the Apostle himself; secondly, whether it was composed of Jewish or of Gentile Christians. For the answer to these questions, in the case of the Galatians, our chief attention must be directed to the intimations of the Epistle itself; to which a gleam of uncertain information may be added from other writings of the Apostle, and the analogy of other Churches mentioned in them. The Acts of the Apostles supply one or two facts of doubtful import. The latter of the two questions unavoidably runs up into a more general inquiry respecting the original relations of Jew and Gentile before they came together in the Christian Church, which will be more fully discussed in another place.

The indications of the Epistle may be summed up in a few words. On the one hand, the tone of authority which the Apostle adopts, as well as particular expressions, such as iii. 2, 'This only would I learn of you, Received ye the Spirit by the works of the law, or by the hearing of faith?'; or iv. 9-19 in which the Apostle speaks of their having been converted, not to bondage, but to freedom, and of himself as again becoming their spiritual father (comp. 1 Cor. iv. 15; also Acts xvi. 6); as well as the manner in which he mentions the Apostles at Jerusalem in chap. ii would certainly lead us to suppose that the Galatians must have been converted by himself or by his followers. And that they were originally Gentiles, is implied in chap. iv. ver. 8—'When ye knew not God, ye did service unto them which by nature are no gods.' But if they were converts of the Apostle, and also Gentiles, how are we to account for their ready reception of Judaism, to the repulsive rites of which they seem to have been drawn almost by instinct? That would lead rather to the opposite supposition, that they were not Gentiles, but Jews. Naturally, it might be urged, when the Apostle's personal influence was withdrawn from them, Judaism overlaid Christianity, the law prevailed over the Gospel. And this latter opinion is confirmed by the fact, that the Apostle argues with them out of the law and the prophets, and that in none of his Epistles has the cast of the reasoning a more Jewish character.

Thus on a first view we seem to arrive at opposite conclusions, an appearance of inconsistency which will present itself again to our notice in the Epistle to the Romans. One set of presumptions leads to the inference, that the Galatians were Gentiles; or rather the text quoted above (iv. 8) expressly says so. Another set of presumptions (from which we cannot exclude the almost equally explicit statement that they were Jews, chap. iv. 9, and desirous to return to 'the beggarly elements' around which their hearts still lingered) leads to the opposite inference. Out of this dilemma how are we to make our escape? (1) Can we suppose St. Paul himself to have been a teacher of the law (compare Introductory Essays on the Epistles to the Thessalonians and Romans), and to have once taught what he now denounced? Admitting that at no period of his life he wholly ceased to be a Jew (Acts xviii. 18 ; xxi. 26 ; xxiii. 6); that there were threads in his doctrine, which entangled him with the false teachers (Gal. v. 11); that there was a time in which he spoke of himself as 'having known Christ according to the flesh,' and that constant reference to the authority of the Old Testament is difficult to reconcile with his renunciation of the law; still the extreme antagonism in which he places himself to the Judaizers renders it impossible that he could ever have been one of them. The Galatians 'had begun in the Spirit'; it is another Gospel to which they are 'removed'; they had originally received with enthusiasm the same lesson which St. Paul is seeking to revive. (2) But if we cannot suppose St. Paul himself to have been a teacher of the law, whence did the infection of Judaism arise in the Churches of Galatia? It might be suggested that the Galatians were first converted by teachers of the circumcision, and afterwards reconverted by St. Paul. Yet, in Gal. iii. 2 ; iv. 19, the Apostle implies that they were converted by himself, and, as he expresses it in the passage just quoted, 'began in the spirit.' Or, (3) shall we conceive him to be describing, first, the Gentiles, then the Jews in successive verses? Granting that the Galatian Church, like most other Christian communities, may have contained Jewish as well as Gentile Christians, still the context shows that those who 'served them which by nature are no gods,' and those who were ready to relapse into the weak and beggarly elements of the law, were the same persons, iv. 8–10. Nor is there any trace in the Epistle that he distinguished the case of the Jew from that of the Gentile in reference to the obligation of circumcision; to all he says alike, 'if ye be circumcised Christ shall profit you nothing.' Would this have been his language had the Church been divided between Jews and

Gentiles? Yet, (4) once more it might be argued, that Judaism and heathenism were regarded by St. Paul as a single prior dispensation, the two parts of which he is not careful to distinguish, which he seems alike to include elsewhere in the expression 'elements of the world,' Col. ii. 8, 20. But no such common point of view under which he may have regarded the former estate of Jew and Gentile, would have justified him in saying of the Jew: 'Howbeit then, when ye knew not God, ye did service unto them which by nature are no gods.'

The most probable mode of escaping these difficulties is the following:—The Galatians we may suppose to have been a Gentile Church, which was first converted to Christianity by St. Paul, but previous to its conversion had gone through a phase of Judaism. There were three states out of which Gentile converts passed, or might have passed, into the acceptance of the Gospel as preached by St. Paul: first, heathenism; secondly, a more or less strict proselytism; thirdly, Jewish Christianity. The second of these was probably the state of the Galatian converts. Strange as it may seem, it is an undoubted fact that, before the appearance of Christianity the religion of the Jews exercised a great and mysterious influence over the Roman world. It had already bridged the chasm which separated the faith of Jehovah from the wisdom of the Greek philosopher. It was 'a schoolmaster,' bringing men to Christ, not in idea only but in fact. The natural and political force of Judaism, even in its most abject state, its simple faith in the unity of God, the proselytising spirit of the Jews themselves (Matt. xxiii. 15), their dispersion throughout the world, the diffusion of the Greek translation of the Old Testament Scriptures, the absorbing power of the Jewish Alexandrian philosophy, are sufficient to account for the hold which it acquired on the minds of men, standing, as it seemed, erect in the decline of the classical religions and the chaos of Eastern superstitions. The Roman poets in the age of Augustus were perfectly well acquainted with the belief and practices of the Jews, which extended to others as well as to their regular proselytes; a knowledge which is the more remarkable, when contrasted with the slender information about the Christians, which is displayed by every heathen writer, for the first century and a half after the Christian era[1].

Admitting the general fact of the diffusion of Judaism, no people were more likely to have fallen under its power than the inhabitants of Galatia. A half-civilized race of Western origin, in an Eastern land, were peculiarly liable to be influenced by the contagion of the Jewish settlers who dwelt among them (1 Pet. i. 1). Their national religion was already mingled with the gods of the nations among whom they settled. They did not altogether cease to be heathen by becoming Jews, any more than they wholly left their ancient Gallic rites for Greek and Phrygian customs. Nor can we tell how many elements of Christianity, as, for example, the doctrine of a Messiah, may have been included in their Judaizing tenets (compare Heb. vi. 1 : 2 Cor. ii. 5, 16 : John iv. 25). Marked as such distinctions appear in language, there could not have always been a definite line which separated heathenism from proselytism or proselytism from Jewish Christianity, any more than the Gospel of the circumcision from that of the uncircumcision. The more lax of either class must have insensibly faded into the other; and Judaism itself may have taken new forms when coming into contact with semi-barbarous races. Much that we look upon as a corruption of Christianity was, in fact, prior to Christianity, inherent in the magical or philosophical tendencies of the age, and clustering around the name of Christ as a new source of life and power. There was a spiritualized Judaism, as well as a Judaized heathenism. In the case of the Galatians, we can only infer from the language of the

---

[1] See Introduction to Epistle to the Romans.

Epistle that they could not have been so completely Christians as to set aside St. Paul's claim to have converted them ; nor so completely Jews as to have lost all remembrance of that former state in which they did service 'to them that are no gods.'

Supposing then the Galatians to have passed through the gate of Judaism to Christianity, there is no difficulty in explaining their relapse into Judaism. The Jewish teachers were there before St. Paul, and they remained there after his departure : and the language of the Old Testament itself, sanctioned by the authority of St. Paul, though read in a spirit unlike his, would seem to tell of the continued obligation of the law and of the necessity of circumcision. He himself, they insidiously said, had at one time preached that very circumcision which he now denounced (v. 11). By such arguments a half-wavering multitude, who had been once ready to die for the Apostle, now that he was absent, were shaken in their allegiance to his authority.

The slenderness of our materials will not allow us to complete the picture of the Galatian Church. There is not a single figure to fill up the vacant space. It is only a probability that, in ch. v. 10, the Apostle is alluding to an individual opponent. ('He that troubleth you shall bear his judgement, whosoever he be.') We see the levity and inconsistency of the converts ; their confusion of the Gospel with the Law ; the manner in which dislike of the doctrine of the Apostle degenerated into hatred of his person. Fainter traces are also discernible of Judaism mingling with heathenism in ch. iv. 9, as in Col. ii. 18 ; and perhaps in Rom. xiv.

GALATIA.

A NOTICE of the inhabitants of Galatia will throw a remote light on the Epistle to the Galatians. Some have thought to identify them with the barbarous people of Lycaonia who first worshipped the Apostles and afterwards stoned them. But whatever similarity may be traced in the character of the people, Derbe and Lystra were not within the district termed Galatia (comp. Acts xiv. 1, 6), which lay to the north, separated by Paphlagonia and Bithynia from the Euxine Sea. It was bounded on the south by Phrygia and Cappadocia, on the east by Pontus and Cappadocia, on the west by Phrygia and Bithynia, and included in its domain several of the Phrygian cities most celebrated for the worship of the mother of the gods.

The inhabitants of this district were the Gauls of Asia. They were the remnant of the great Celtic and Germanic migrations, which overspread Greece and Asia Minor at the commencement of the third century before the Christian era. Like the Biscayans or Hungarians in Europe, they remained the isolated monument of the deluge which had passed away. At one time they had been the terror of the Greek cities of Asia Minor, and alternately the adversaries or the mercenaries of Alexander's successors. They were reduced by the Roman Consul, C. Manlius Vulso, in the year 189, but retained their separate kings by favour of the Romans, until about eighty years before this time, A.C. 26, when Amyntas, their last king and the favourite successively of Augustus and Antony, was murdered, and the country finally placed under a Roman governor.

In character they are described as a free impetuous race, ever ready to bear arms for themselves or others. For a long time after their settlement in Asia, they retained their national and religious customs, the latter even including that of human sacrifices. St. Jerome (Gal. i. 2) describes them, even in his own day, as having a peculiar dialect, which he compares to the German spoken about Trèves. Their government in early times was a military aristocracy divided into twelve tetrarchies, the respective chiefs of which were not hereditary, but elected. The Gauls themselves were apportioned in three tribes, and two subject peoples existed side by side with them, the Greeks and Phrygians, to whom they stood in the same relation as the Spartans to the Laconians and Messenians. Gradually the language and religion of the conquered made an impression on the conquerors. That they must have understood Greek is proved by the Epistle itself; and their supreme Council of three hundred corresponding to the tetrarchies of which Strabo (xii. 567) speaks, was probably of Greek origin. And long before this time they had adopted or added to their own religion the rites of Cybele, and participated in the worship on Mount Dindymus and the gainful occupation of selling the oracles of the goddess to the rest of Asia.

From the use of the plural ($\tau\alpha\hat{\iota}s$ $\dot{\epsilon}\kappa\kappa\lambda\eta\sigma\acute{\iota}\alpha\iota s$) we may gather that the Churches were scattered throughout the district, in more than one village or town. It is impossible to say what the names of these Churches were, or whether the Epistle is addressed to converts who were Gauls, Phrygians, or Greeks by origin. Only the tone of the Apostle and the fickleness of those who received him 'as an angel of God, even as Christ Jesus' (comp. Acts xiv. 16-19; xxviii. 6), 'and afterwards became his enemies,' may lead us to conjecture that he is addressing a people subject to violent religious impulses, a people such as might have been celebrated for their ancient Phrygian and Bacchic rites, amongst whom in heathen days extravagant superstition most readily found a home; and who, when converted to Christianity, gave birth to Phrygian heretics and to the Montanism of the second century [1].

[1] [For more recent information on this subject see Mr. W. M. Ramsay's writings, especially the Article 'Phrygia' in *Encyc. Brit.* ed. ix.]

SUBJECT OF THE EPISTLE.

It is to the second Epistle to the Corinthians that the Epistle to the Galatians offers the greatest resemblance. In both there is the same sensitiveness in the Apostle to the behaviour of his converts to himself, the same earnestness about the points of difference, the same remembrance of his own 'infirmity' while he was yet with them, the same consciousness of the precarious basis on which his own authority rested in the existing state of the two Churches. Abruptness of style is characteristic of both; the excitement of feeling seems to clog the current of ideas. Both Epistles display a greater emotion than is to be found in any other portion of his writings, a deeper contrast of inward exaltation and outward suffering, more of personal entreaty, a greater readiness to assert himself; all together seeming to tell us what he told the people of Derbe and Lystra, that he 'was a man of like passions with ourselves,' and working through the instrumentality of those passions, yet not the less approved of God in his high calling. In such passages as 'Henceforth let no man trouble me, for I bear in my body the marks of the Lord Jesus,' at the end of the Galatians, or in the similar feeling of the verse of the Corinthians, 'I think that God hath set forth us the Apostles last appointed unto death,' we seem to trace a momentary reaction in the mind of him on whom came 'the care of all the Churches.'

GENUINENESS OF THE EPISTLE.

No one has doubted the genuineness of the Epistle to the Galatians; it is not, therefore, necessary to recapitulate at length the evidence in its favour. That evidence consists of the testimonies of Patristic as well as of heretical writers, from the time of Irenaeus downwards, going back, that is, to within a century of the date of its composition. But here a doubt may be raised respecting the value of the testimonies themselves; for it may be truly urged, that evidence as ancient, and as nearly contemporary, can be quoted in favour of the Gospel of St. James, the Shepherd of Hermas, the Revelation of Peter, and other spurious writings. Why is it, then, that a short epistle like that to the Galatians has been universally acknowledged, even by critics of the most extreme school, as a genuine writing of St. Paul?

The reason of this universal agreement is the internal evidence of its genuineness. Considering the number of forgeries, which we know to have existed in the second century, and the absence either of the spirit or of the faculty of criticism in the early Church, we cannot set a high value on the testimony of the Fathers, except to events which were contemporary with themselves. What they really testify respecting the books of the New Testament is to their use and authority in their own day as the writings of the authors whose names they bear. But if the external testimony to the books of Scripture seems to be in this way weakened, the internal evidence of the genuineness of many of them may be regarded as greatly enhanced. What criticism has restored, though incapable of being put in a definite and tangible form, abundantly compensates for what it has destroyed. If it will not allow us to take our stand upon tradition, it supplies us with many new kinds of proof. It enables us to affirm that a particular writing, from the richness of its style, the mannerisms of thought and language, the minuteness of the detail, the consistency, and, sometimes, the very singularity of the events recorded in it, must be an original, and not a mere imitation. It analyses the character which is proper to an individual writer, and can be in no two writers the same. And it fortunately happens, that the age least capable of affording reliable external testimony, is the age also least capable of feigning the marks of a genuine writing.

CHAPTERS I, II.

The main object of the first portion of the Epistle is to assert the independent authority of the Apostle against the attacks of the Judaizers. The words, 'Paul, an Apostle, not of man, neither by man, but by Jesus Christ,' are the text of the two first chapters; and the narrative which follows is the commentary. He begins by denouncing the treason of the Galatians against himself. After the burst of his indignation has subsided, the Apostle proceeds to state facts illustrative of his Divine mission, and his relation to the Twelve. First, his independence was marked by the manner of his conversion; he did not receive the Gospel through any human instrument, but by immediate revelation. His previous education, and the well-known circumstance that he had been a persecutor of the Church, were a bad preparation for such a call. No one could have expected that the Pharisee or zealot for the law would have become the servant of Christ. Nevertheless, it pleased God to work this change in him. The independence of his mission was further marked by the fact that, after his conversion, he did not go up to Jerusalem to throw himself into the arms of the Apostles, but away from it, and only after long intervals went there at all, and then saw but one or two of them, and only for a few days; so entirely were his teaching and office his own, for so little was he indebted to them. He had never preached to the Jewish Churches; he was unknown to them by face, and only a report had reached them, which they received with joy and thankfulness, that the persecutor of the Gospel had now become its preacher.

In the second chapter, with a like object, he describes the freedom of his conduct at what is termed the Council of Jerusalem. He refused to yield (or, according to another interpretation, declares himself to have yielded only from motives of expediency and fear of treachery) the circumcision of Titus to the demands of the false brethren. He was not overawed by the greatness of the other Apostles, whom he met as their equal; and it was owing to himself rather than to them that a successful resistance was made to the Judaizing Christians. Yet they parted in love and fellowship; the heads of the Church at Jerusalem reminding him of the wants of their poor members, a labour of love in which he was very willing to join. They saw that he himself was among the Gentiles what Peter was to the circumcision, and they agreed to divide the field of labour. Afterwards Peter followed him to Antioch, where, if he did not violate the letter, he at any rate forgot the spirit, of their agreement. On this occasion he openly resisted him, and boldly reasoned with him, as 'building up the things which he had pulled down.' These are the proofs that he was an Apostle, not of men, nor by man, and had an authority at least equal to the other Apostles, to whom the Judaizers made their appeal.

CHAPTERS III, IV.

THE Apostle has concluded his narrative, and the argument to which it gave birth. His thoughts return to the Galatians, whom he once more addresses with the same vehement emotion as at i. 6–10. He schools them like children; he appeals to their experience; he bids them remember the hour of their conversion. Did they mean to invert the order of grace?—beginning with what was inward, to end with what was outward; in the spirit once, and now in the flesh? Those influences of which they had been the subject; those great effects which they had witnessed—did they spring from works of the law, or from the hearing of faith? As elsewhere, the word 'faith' awakens a new strain of argument in the Apostle's mind, which, dropping his previous emotion, he pursues to the end of the chapter. This argument is based on the words of Genesis: 'Abraham had faith in God, and it was counted to him for righteousness.' Like the parallel discourse on the same theme in the Epistle to the Romans (ch. iv), it may be divided into two parts: in the first of which (1) Abraham, the father of the faithful, is identified with his children, and the faith of both contrasted with the works of the law, as blessing is to cursing in the language of the law itself—from which curse of the law, Christ, by becoming a curse (as the law also taught), has made a way of escape, that the blessing of Abraham might reach the Gentiles; (2) the second division of the argument (which commences with verse 15), taking occasion from the words 'unto thy seed,' which the Apostle, in passing, refers to Christ, and dwelling specially on the time at which the promise was made (430 years before the law), thereby showing the mediate, subordinate, intercalary character of the latter.

The feeling which marked the opening of the Epistle, and the address to the Galatians, reappears again at the ninth verse of the fourth chapter. The bearing of the previous passage had been to show that the state of those under the law was a kind of pupilage or slavery, from which Christ had redeemed us by being Himself 'born under the law,' as, in a nearly similar way of speaking, it was said at verse 13 of the previous chapter, that He had 'redeemed us from the curse of the law by being made a curse for us.' Of this truth of redemption from the law, the Apostle proceeds to make a practical application to the Galatians themselves, contrasting their half heathen, half Jewish superstitions with the liberty of the sons of God. Then, for an instant, he pauses to speak of his personal relation to them. He was touched by the thought of their ancient love for him, especially when he remembered his own infirmities, which, instead of being an object of disgust to them, seemed almost to transfigure him into the likeness of Christ Jesus. But how had this passed away! He will not accuse them of a wrong to himself (though he can find no other reason for their change of feeling, but his own plain speaking); he will only beg of them to be at one with him again. He then briefly glances at the false teachers, their reception of whom he seems to attribute to a sort of ignorance of the world, and as if words out of the law must be better rhetoric to them than any that he could employ, once more harping on the instance of Abraham, he repeats the story of Isaac and Ishmael, the child of promise, and the child born after the flesh, and arguing in a manner more convincing and intelligible to his own age than to ours, as above from the letter of the text, so here from the connexion between Hagar and the land in which the law was given, he concludes, as he began, the chapter by associating the idea of bondage with the law.

CHAPTERS V, VI.

IN the Third Section of the Epistle the Apostle proceeds to the application of the argument which has gone before: 'Ye are not the children of the bondwoman, but of the free; with that freedom Christ has made you free; stand, therefore, and be not again entangled in the yoke of bondage to the law.' This is enforced by a personal appeal, in which the Apostle sets forth with great earnestness the contrariety of the law and Christ. He who receives the seal of the law is involved in all its obligations. He is not half Jew and half believer in Christ, but wholly a Jew and no longer a believer. The law and Christ (like the law and the promise) are exclusive of each other. For the life of the Spirit, which is in Christ, has nothing to do with circumcision or uncircumcision; it is different in kind from either (1-6).

The latter portion of nearly all the Epistles of St. Paul is remarkable for abruptness of style. The Apostle passes from one subject to another, dropping the intervening links by which they are associated in his own mind. New thoughts are suddenly introduced; old ones unexpectedly came back again. His manner is that of a person speaking rather than writing; he is full of animation, saying what occurs to him without always expressing the point which he intends. In the verses that follow (7-13), contrary emotions draw him different ways; and he seems almost to lose the power of arranging his words. There was a time, he would say, when you promised well; who has persuaded you to rebel? This persuasion is not of God; it is a delusion of the enemy. The error of a few leavens the mass. Looking forward in faith, I perceive that ye will hereafter be of one mind, and that the troublers of the Church shall themselves be the sufferers. And yet, brethren, when I think of their strange and inconsistent charges against myself, I cannot but feel indignant. Is it likely that they would persecute me if I still preached circumcision? And then, with a momentary feeling of disgust at the whole subject, he adds in irony: Would that they would make themselves eunuchs who trouble you! That would indeed cut off the matter in dispute.

For the Divine call which you received is very different from the call which they teach. It was a calling unto liberty; I do not mean licentiousness, but that liberty which is a service of love to one another. For love is the single word which fulfils the law. How unlike are ye to the servants of that law! the end of whose bickerings and jealousies is mutual destruction (13-15).

All my precepts may be summed up in one: 'Walk in the Spirit and ye shall not fulfil the lust of the flesh.' For there are two ways; the way of the flesh, and the way of the Spirit: and these are contrary the one to the other, and their fruits are like them (16-24). We who are spiritual should walk in the Spirit, humbling our hearts in consideration of others, forgiving their slips and bearing their burdens.

It is mere self-deception to think ourselves above this. Every man who tries himself will find he has a burden of his own. A particular instance of this duty of mutual support is the duty of supporting teachers, in which, as in all other Christian duties, we must be single and indefatigable, ready to do good to all men, and especially to members of the Church (v. 24—vi. 10).

Look, says the Apostle, at the large and misshapen letters which I am tracing with mine own hand. A word more, and I have done. Those who would have you circumcised, act only on motives of expediency; their object is to keep well with the Jewish Christians; their own inconsistency in the observance of the law is a sufficient proof that they desire only to glory in you as their disciples. But God forbid that I should glory in you, or in anything but that which is at the same time the symbol of humiliation, the cross of Christ. The question of circumcision or uncircumcision I count as nothing in comparison with a change of heart. This is my rule. Peace be upon them who walk by it, and are 'Israelites indeed.'

Reverence me henceforth; for I bear the person of Christ, and fill up the measure of His sufferings. The grace of Christ be with your spirit.

THE EPISTLE

TO THE

GALATIANS

1 PAUL, an apostle, (not of men, neither by man, but by Jesus Christ, and God the Father, who raised him 2 from the dead;) and all the brethren which are with 3 me, unto the churches of Galatia; grace be to you and peace from God the Father, and from our Lord 4 Jesus Christ, who gave himself for our sins, that he

1. The Epistle to the Galatians is the only one among St Paul's Epistles, in which he omits all words of compliment or friendship in the opening verses. In other Epistles he begins with commendation, and passes on to reproof when he has gained a hold on the affections of those whom he is addressing. Thus, in the case of the Corinthian Church, though they had grave faults, and ought rather to have mourned for the sin of the incestuous person, and their many divisions and profaneness in celebration of the Lord's Supper, he introduces himself to them with words of conciliation : 'I thank my God always on your behalf for the grace of God which is given you by Jesus Christ, that in every thing ye are enriched by him in all utterance and in all knowledge;' and so passes on to his censure. But in the Epistle to the Galatians he adopts a different course, either because it was more natural to his own feelings, or the actual state of the Church was worse or more likely to be roused by the severity of his tone.

4. ὅπως ἐξέληται ἡμᾶς ἐκ τοῦ αἰῶνος τοῦ ἐνεστῶτος πονηροῦ, *that he may take us out of this evil world present.*] These words contain an allusion to the Jewish distinction of αἰὼν ἐνεστώς, or αἰὼν οὗτος, and the αἰὼν μέλλων, the times before and after the inauguration of Messiah's kingdom. But their

might deliver us from this present evil world, according to the will of God and our Father: to whom be glory for ever and ever. Amen.

6 I marvel that ye are so soon ^a transferred[∥] from Him that called you ^b in[∥] the grace of Christ unto

^a removed   ^b into

meaning may be said to vary as the thing signified by them assumes to the believer a more inward or outward nature, is more past or present. The αἰὼν ἐνεστώς is the world around him, from which the Christian withdraws into communion with God, from which he shall be delivered finally in the world of glory. It is called evil, in the same spirit in which the Apostle says in the Epistle to the Romans, that 'the whole creation groaneth and travaileth together until now;' also as it is the scene of the believer's trials and persecutions, in which he is waiting, too, for the redemption of the body.

To this present world of evil is opposed the future world, of which Christ is the Lord. The one is the creation made subject to bondage, 'full of principalities and powers, and spiritual wickedness in heavenly places;' the other is the glorious liberty of the children of God. A trace of the same thought occurs in the word ἐνεστῶσα in 1 Cor. vii. 26 διὰ τὴν ἐνεστῶσαν ἀνάγκην, 'on account of this present necessity.' The mind of the Apostle is overpowered by the contrast of faith and sight; the bondage and constraint of the world, which might well make a man go out of the world, and the hope of salvation,' which is nearer than when we believed.' There is a tone of suffering and sadness expressed in this verse; it is the feeling of the close of the Epistle: 'I bear in my body the marks of the Lord Jesus.'

The word αἰών passes through the same change of meaning in the New Testament as the Latin word 'saeculum.' First it is used for continuance of time—'Thou shalt not wash my feet εἰς τὸν αἰῶνα,' for ever; or with more emphasis, as in John vi. 51 ζήσεται εἰς τὸν αἰῶνα, 'shall live for ever;' or still more strongly in the plural, of the eternal existence of God, or the everlasting happiness of the blessed, as in the Book of Revelation. In the writers of the New Testament, as in the Jewish writers, ὁ αἰὼν οὗτος Rom. xii. 2, ἐνεστώς as in this place, ὁ νῦν as in 1 Tim. vi. 17, are opposed to ὁ αἰὼν ἐκεῖνος Luke xx. 34, ὁ μέλλων Matt. xii. 32, ἐρχόμενος Luke xviii. 30, as present and future, as evil and good.

The idea of ὁ αἰὼν οὗτος is further illustrated by Eph. ii. 2: 'And you (hath he quickened), being dead in trespasses and sins, wherein in time past ye walked according to the course of this world, according to the prince of the power of the air, the spirit that now worketh in the children of disobedience'—which not only

7 another gospel: which is not another; but there be
some that trouble you, and would pervert the gospel
8 of Christ. But though we, or an angel from heaven,
preach any other gospel unto you than that which
we have preached unto you, let him be accursed.
9 As we said before, so say I now again, If any man
preach any other gospel unto you than ye have
10 received, let him be accursed. For do I now persuade
men, or God? or do I seek to please men? ᶜ⁻⁾ if I yet
pleased men, I should not be the servant of Christ.
11 ¹ But I certify you, brethren, that the gospel which
12 was preached of me is not after man. For I neither

c add *for*

gives the associations implied in ὁ αἰὼν τοῦ κόσμου τούτου, but assists in explaining the change of meaning by which αἰών comes to signify the world without the idea of time; as in Heb. xi. 3, 'The worlds are framed by the word of God;' or in 1 Cor. i. 20, 'The disputer of this world.' Compare also our uses of 'the world,' for the heavens and earth and all things in them; for this present state, as opposed to the life to come; also, in a bad sense, for the world, whether within or without man, as opposed to the kingdom of God; and in a neutral one, irrespective of good or evil, to signify the mass of mankind, or the public opinion of mankind.

7. ὅ οὐκ ἔστιν ἄλλο, *which is not another*.] Either, (1) which turning aside is nothing else but certain troublers seeking to pervert the Gospel of Christ; or, (2) which Gospel is not another Gospel (for there cannot be two Gospels), but only certain troublers who pervert it; ἄλλο being unemphatic in the first way of taking the words, emphatic in the second. The last is the more probable explanation.

10. εἰ ἔτι ἀνθρώποις ἤρεσκον, *if I yet pleased men*.] The Apostle does not mean that before his conversion, or at any other time in his life, 'he had been a pleaser of men.' The expression, which is not free from difficulty, is most probably to be taken in a general sense; 'If at this time, after all that has happened to me, I am, or were still, a pleaser of men, I could not be the servant of God.' Comp. Matt. vi. 24: 'No man can serve two masters;' and for the use of ἔτι, v. 11.

12. Revelation is distinguished from ordinary moral and spiritual influences by its suddenness. It is an anticipation of moral truth and of the course of experience. No reason can be given why amid Canaanitish and Egyptian idolatries, a belief in the unity of God

¹ Reading Γνωρίζω δέ

received it of man, neither was I taught it, but by
13 the revelation of Jesus Christ. For ye have heard
of my conversation in time past in the Jews' religion,
how that beyond measure I persecuted the church of
14 God, and wasted it: and profited in the Jews' religion
above many my equals in mine own nation, being
more exceedingly zealous of the traditions of my
15 fathers. But when it pleased God, who from my
mother's womb separated me, and called me by his

should have sunk into the hearts of men. No reason can be given why truth and justice should have been Divine attributes ages before philosophy became conscious of a moral principle. No reason can be given why our Saviour, Himself living amid the rites of the Temple worship, should yet have taught a religion purely spiritual, which was a contradiction of the maxims of the Scribes and Pharisees, and an inversion of the common religious notions of mankind to the end of time.

It is this anticipation of truth, this communication of truth to particular persons, or at particular times out of the course of nature, in ways unlike the methods of human knowledge, that is termed in the language of theology 'revelation.' It is in this sense that we speak of Christianity as a revelation ; of a Mosaic revelation ; of revelation as opposed to reason or natural religion. The use of the word in the New Testament is more varied and less conventional. It might be explained in the language of the Book of Revelation as a 'being in the spirit at the day of the Lord ;' it may be contrasted with prophecy as universal, and not national only ; it is relative to the 'times of that ignorance which God winked at.' He who was the subject of it might, like St. Paul, 'be caught up into the third heaven ;' he might hear a voice whispering to him, 'My grace is sufficient for thee ;' he might receive 'lively oracles' respecting his own conduct or the government of the Church ; he might have intimations respecting his 'going in and coming out.' We must not suppose that such intimations were mere illusions, because they no longer occur within the range of our own experience. Some faint approximation to them may be found still in the intuitions of the mind respecting matters of conduct, or in the suddenness of thought itself.

15. ἀφορίσας, *who separated*] has a double meaning : first, a literal and physical one; secondly, that of which this is the figure—a spiritual one : 'Who took me out of my mother's womb, and separated me ; or whose separation of me at my birth was the image of my separation unto himself.' ἐκ refers to time.

16 grace, to reveal his Son in me, that I might preach him among the heathen; immediately I conferred not
17 with flesh and blood: neither went[1] I ᵈ⁻ᵍ to Jerusalem to them which were apostles before me; but I went into
18 Arabia, and returned again unto Damascus. Then after three years I went up to Jerusalem to see ᵉCephas,ᵍ and
19 abode with him fifteen days. But other of the apostles

ᵈ add *up* ᵉ *Peter*

Compare Jer. i. 5: 'Before I formed thee in the belly I knew thee; and before thou camest forth out of the womb I sanctified thee, and I ordained thee a prophet unto the nations;' and Is. xliv. 2; also note on Rom. i. 1.

19. The arguments in favour of the position that James the brother of our Lord is the same with James the son of Alpheus the Apostle (not including the words of 1 Cor. xv. 7: 'He was seen of James, then of all the Apostles,' which are equally ambiguous with the present passage) may be summed up as follows:—

(1) The name of 'James the less' implying that there were only two and not three of that name.

(2) The result of the comparison of the three following passages:—

Mark xv. 40: 'There were also women looking on afar off; among whom was Mary Magdalene, and Mary the mother of James the less and of Joses, and Salome.'

John xix. 25: 'There stood by the cross of Jesus his mother, and his mother's sister, Mary the wife of Cleophas, and Mary Magdalene.'

Mark vi. 3: 'Is not this the carpenter, the son of Mary, the brother of James, and Joses, and of Juda, and Simon? and are not his sisters here with us?' Comp. Matt. xiii. 55 [where, instead of Joses, Lachmann and Tischendorf read Joseph, which occurs also as a variation in the text of Matt.].

Here, Mary the mother of James and Joses is identified with Mary the wife of Cleophas; and this identification of the two Marys is confirmed by the third passage, which speaks of her sons as the brethren of Jesus.

Lastly, the name Alpheus is the same as Cleophas; being in the Aramaic חלפי, and the two forms arising only out of the different pronunciations of the ח.

A simpler explanation is also possible. Mary the mother of James the less, and Joses, and Salome, may be the same with Mary the wife of Cleophas; and yet James 'the brother of the Lord' not the same with James the less, who was her son, but the son of the Virgin Mary and of Joseph. In favour of this supposition may be urged:—

(1) The words of Mark vi. 3, which expressly refer to 'the

[1] Reading ἀπῆλθον

20 saw I none, save James the Lord's brother. Now the things which I write unto you, behold, before God, I lie
21 not. Afterwards I came into the regions of Syria and
22 Cilicia; and was unknown by face unto the churches
23 of Judæa which were in Christ: but they had heard only, That he which persecuted us in times past now
24 preacheth the faith which once he destroyed. And they glorified God in me.

carpenter' and Mary the mother of Christ, and can hardly allude to the sons of another Mary in the same verse.

(2) The emphatic use of the term 'brother of the Lord,' which would not have been applied in the sense of a special relation to one who was not a brother. There were many cousins of Christ, but only one who was called His brother. Nor could the designation cousin or kinsman of Christ, even if it were a natural explanation of the word ἀδελφός, have been any claim to extraordinary respect in the early Church.

(3) The obvious meaning of Matt. i. 25: 'And knew her not until she had brought forth her firstborn son,' which has been smothered by the feelings of a later age.

(4) The distinction which is drawn in Acts i. 13, 14, between the twelve Apostles, who are all mentioned by name, and the brethren of the Lord, who are spoken of separately in the following verse 'with the women, and Mary the mother of Jesus.'

(5) The testimony of antiquity. Even if the term ἀδελφός is sometimes used in a vaguer sense when it is the translation of a Hebrew word (as in Gen. xxxi. 23), there can be no doubt of the meaning in which it was understood by Josephus (Ant. xx. 9. 1), or by Hegesippus (quoted by Eusebius ii. 23; iii. 32; iv. 22), who expressly mentions James the just as the brother of our Lord 'together with the Apostles,' and Simeon, his successor in the episcopate, as the son of Cleophas, his uncle, and the cousin of Christ (ἀνεψιός).

The comparison of Mark vi. 3 with xv. 40 suggests the improbability of Mary the mother of Christ and Mary the wife of Cleophas each having two sons the same in name, James and Joses, the latter being specially designated by the names of her sons. The force of this objection is, in a great measure, done away by the reading of Lachmann and Tischendorf ('Ἰάκωβος, Ἰωσήφ), in the parallel passage of Matt. xiii. 55 (comp. Matt. xxvii. 56), and the variation of reading (Ἰωσῆ, Ἰωσῆτος, Ἰωσήφ) even in the text of Mark vi. It might be replied, further, that we are otherwise involved in the greater difficulty of supposing that two persons of the same name were sisters. Such hypotheses or counter-hypotheses are

2 Then fourteen years after I went up again to Jerusalem with Barnabas, and took Titus with me also. And I went up by revelation, and communicated unto them that gospel which I preach among the Gentiles, but privately to them which were of reputation, lest by any means I should run, or had run, in vain. But

not worth drawing out. The natural use of language and the express testimony of the oldest writers are safer grounds of argument than the probability that Mary the wife of Cleophas or Alpheus was sister of Mary the mother of Christ.

2. 2. τοῖς δοκοῦσιν, *to them of reputation*,] is used absolutely, as sometimes in classical Greek, 'to the men of influence, reputation.' There is a degree of irony in the application of the term to the Apostles, who, as St. Paul is about to describe, added nothing to what he had told them. The irony is heightened by the altered form of expression in ver. 6 οἱ δοκοῦντες εἶναί τι, but is lost again in the new turn given to it at ver. 9, οἱ δοκοῦντες στῦλοι εἶναι, the last words marking that he truly recognized the dignity of the other Apostles as heads of the Church at Jerusalem. Compare, as illustrative of the feeling, 2 Cor. xi. 5; xii. 11 οἱ ὑπερλίαν ἀπόστολοι.

3-5. As it is certain that copies existed in the second and third centuries in which the negation in ver. 5 was omitted, the question of the reading cannot be absolutely determined by the weight of MS. authority which is in favour of their insertion. On the one hand, it may be urged that the omission has arisen from the desire to improve the structure of the sentence, which is thus rendered more regular; perhaps, also, the example of Timothy may have led to the inference that the Apostle would have done in one case as he did in the other, and that Titus was circumcised as Timothy was circumcised; a meaning which is more easily obtained if the words οἷς οὐδέ are omitted. On the other hand, it is not unreasonable to maintain the opposite thesis, that the [erroneous omission] of the words is improbable, because it runs counter to the spirit of the passage. The feeling which makes us unwilling to believe that St. Paul yielded a question of principle at a critical moment, would have prevented Fathers and early transcribers from altering the text in such a manner as to render this interpretation of the Apostle's acts possible. And, therefore, it may be argued that the reading which raises the suspicion is probably not the altered but the genuine one. So the canon 'difficilioris lectionis' may be arrayed on either side. Nor will any other argument place either reading beyond doubt.

Was Titus circumcised or not? That is an inquiry the answer to which is not wholly dependent

neither Titus, who was with me, being a Greek, was
4 compelled to be circumcised: ᶠbut*ᵍ* because of the false brethren unawares brought in, who came in privily to spy out our liberty which we have in Christ

ᶠ and that

on the variety of the text. For, supposing the negative in ver. 5 to be retained, still, by laying the emphasis on *compelled*, the sentence may be read in such a manner as to admit the fact that Titus was circumcised: 'Titus, who was with me, was circumcised, though not of compulsion; but I and the other Apostles thought it better that this should be done to prevent the false brethren from going about and saying that we had men uncircumcised among us, not that we gave way to them for an instant in the submission that we showed or that they claimed' (τῇ ὑποταγῇ). The fact was as the opponents of St. Paul stated, but nothing was thereby decided respecting the necessity of circumcision, the question at issue in the Galatian Church.

Such is a possible train of thought in the Apostle's mind, whichever reading we adopt. And the form of the sentence, in which Titus is the principal subject, is in favour of this mode of interpretation: 'Titus was circumcised, though not of compulsion,' is a more natural explanation of the words οὐδὲ Τίτος ἠναγκάσθη περιτμηθῆναι, than 'Titus was not circumcised, though they sought to compel him.' That the Apostle was charged with preaching circumcision (v. 11) is implied by himself; nor is it impossible that the example of Titus may have been brought forward by teachers of the circumcision; in which case the words Ἕλλην ὤν may have formed a part of their statement. It is the profession of the Apostle himself, that 'to the Jews he became a Jew;' an expression which accords with his conduct in taking upon himself a Nazarite's vow on the occasion of his last visit to Jerusalem. Again, the circumcision of Timothy is nearly, if not quite, parallel with that of Titus; for Timothy was the son of a Greek father, and had not been circumcised in infancy; nor was it intended by St. Paul that he should work in any special field of labour among Jewish Christians. Of him, too, it might have been said with equal truth, 'neither Timotheus being a Greek was compelled,' &c. And the reason given in the Acts of the Apostles for the circumcision of Timothy is equally applicable to the case of Titus: 'Because of the Jews that were in those parts.' The time is also observable:—soon after the meeting of the Apostles, which renders the circumcision of Timothy as remarkable a circumstance as the circumcision of Titus at the meeting itself. Lastly, the obscurity of the passage may be thought to arise out of the difficulty that the Apostle felt in defending himself

₅ Jesus, that they might bring us into bondage:—to whom we gave place by subjection, no, not for an hour; that the truth of the gospel might continue

against the true charge that he had waived the question of circumcision in the case of Titus.

The point, however unessential in itself, is of interest as bearing on the character of the Apostle. The reasons already given, though strong, are not conclusive, as they have to be weighed against other reasons, the chief of which is the context of the passage. Is language such as that of ver. 4 and 5 reconcilable with the supposition of an act which is really a contradiction of it? that is the question: 'We gave way to the false brethren, no, not for an hour, except in reference to that which was the chief matter in dispute.' The Apostle was not in the temper of accommodation at the meeting at Jerusalem; it was not the time to be all things to all men, nor the time to tell the Galatians if he had been so. For his whole object is to show how little he yielded to the Jewish Christians, and how independently of the Twelve he maintained his cause. It is only a conjecture, that he has mentioned the case of Titus because the false teachers had brought it forward against him; and, otherwise, there would be no reason for his naming it himself. Why should he of his own accord introduce the mention of a concession which would make him seem inconsistent with himself? How ill these two statements agree together, 'I admit that I yielded in the case of Titus,' and 'Behold, I, Paul, say unto you that if ye be circumcised Christ shall profit you nothing.' There is also a degree of weakness in the words, Ἕλλην ὤν and ἵνα ἡ ἀλήθεια τοῦ εὐαγγελίου διαμείνῃ πρὸς ὑμᾶς, upon the supposition that Titus was circumcised. It is good sense to say: 'For Titus being a Greek was not circumcised, &c., that the truth of the Gospel might remain unto you Gentiles;' but the point is lost if we turn the sentence: 'For Titus being a Greek was not circumcised by compulsion; but merely as a matter of prudence, that the truth of the Gospel to the Gentiles might continue.'

So many points may be pleaded on either side of the question in dispute, it is not necessary, or indeed possible, to arrive at any certain conclusion. The drift of the argument appeared to Tertullian to involve the circumcision of Titus; to us the opposite inference seems, on the whole, most likely to be the truth.

Altogether, three ideas seem to be struggling for expression in these ambiguous clauses:—(1) Titus was not circumcised; (2) though an attempt was made by the false brethren to compel him; (3) which as a matter of principle we thought it so much the more our duty to resist. The ambiguity has arisen from the double connexion in which the clause διὰ τοὺς παρεισάκτους ψευδαδέλφους stands, (1) to ἠναγκάσθη which

6 with you. But of those who seemed to be somewhat,— (whatsoever they were, it maketh no matter to me: God accepteth ᵍnot⁽⁾ man's person:) for they who seemed to be somewhat in conference added nothing 7 to me: but contrariwise, when they saw that the Gospel of the uncircumcision was committed unto me, 8 as the gospel of the circumcision was unto Peter, (for he that wrought effectually in Peter to the apostleship of the circumcision, the same ʰwrought effectually⁽⁾ 9 in me toward the Gentiles:) and when James, Cephas,

ᵍ no ʰ was mighty

precedes, and (2) to οἷς οὐδὲ πρὸς ὥραν εἴξαμεν which follow.

6. ὁποῖοί ποτε ἦσαν.] Some degree of feeling is indicated in these words, as in the similar expression, v. 10 ὅστις ἂν ᾖ, and 2 Cor. xi. 5 οἱ ὑπερλίαν ἀπόστολοι. The Apostle is afraid lest the expression οἱ δοκοῦντες may be interpreted to mean that he gave way to their authority; he therefore hastens to add, that they were as he was in the sight of God; he will not speak of them slightingly, but he wishes it to be remembered that God is no respecter of persons (comp. Rom. ii. 11: 1 Cor. iv. 3), and that as a fact, whatever their dignity and authority might be, those great men left him to himself.

9. ἵνα... περιτομήν, that ... circumcision.] How is this division of labour to be understood? Not, if we may judge from the Acts, as though it were intended that Paul should confine himself to the Gentiles, and Peter to the circumcision; for in every place Paul first preached to the Jews, and in nearly every place the Judaizers followed in his track. It may mean either that St. Paul was not 'to intrude on other men's labours;' or that one Gospel was to be preached to the Gentiles, leaving open the question of circumcision, and another to the Jews, enforcing or encouraging the practice. The sense in which the agreement was made may have been determined, either by the character of the Church, whether composed chiefly of Jewish or heathen Christians; or by its situation, whether in Palestine or elsewhere, or by the Gospel having been preached at a particular place by St. Paul, or by one of the Twelve. That, independently of his own labours, St. Paul found the faith of Christ growing up around him, and the preaching of others coming into contact with his own, is implied in Rom. xv. 20: 2 Cor. x. 13. We can hardly suppose that, in the fluctuating state of the Church, the agreement could have been strictly acted upon, especially in Churches like Antioch and Corinth, in which both parties must have met.

and John, who seemed to be pillars, perceived the grace that was given unto me, they gave to me and Barnabas the right hands of fellowship; that we should go unto the heathen, and they unto the circumcision. Only they would that we should remember the poor; the same which I also was forward to do. But when ⁱCephas ᶦᶦ was come to Antioch, I withstood him to the face, because he was ᵏcondemned.ᶦ For before that certain came from

ⁱ Peter ᵏ to be blamed.

10. It is a presumption of the still unbroken unity of the Church, that the Jewish Christians were willing to receive, or the Gentiles to give alms. This presumption is further strengthened by the manner in which the obligation to contribute is viewed, both in the Epistles to the Romans and the Corinthians, Rom. xv. 27: 'They thought it good, and their debtors they are; for if the Gentiles have participated with them in their spiritual things, they ought also to participate with them in temporal things.' Compare 1 Cor. xvi. 1; ix. 1.

Two collections for the Church at Jerusalem are mentioned; the first (Acts xi. 29), that which was carried up on St. Paul's second journey from Antioch; the second, the collection in Macedonia and Achaia, which he brought with him on his last visit to Jerusalem, in the contributions to which the Galatians had themselves a share (1 Cor. xvi. 1).

12. The obvious meaning of this verse is, that Peter acted under the influence of certain that came from James. In most controversies the followers are less scrupulous than the leaders; in this case it is impossible for us to determine what was the degree of these persons' connexion with the brother of the Lord, or how far they were responsible for the conduct of the Galatian teachers. The words, however, imply that they were actually sent by James. It must be remembered that in Acts xxi. 18 James advises Paul to propitiate 'the multitude zealous for the law,' by performing a vow in the temple. His conduct on the present occasion, whether reconcilable or not with what is related of him in Acts xv, is perfectly in accordance with the narrative just alluded to, as well as with the ecclesiastical tradition respecting him.

The attempts of Origen, Jerome, Chrysostom, and Theophylact, to show that the dispute between Peter and Paul was either a preconcerted controversy for the edification of believers, or that Cephas here mentioned was some obscure disciple, and not the Apostle, are not without interest, as illustrating the history of the interpretation of Scripture.

Besides the antagonism in

James, he did eat with the Gentiles: but when they were come he withdrew and separated himself, fearing 13 them which were of the circumcision. And the other Jews dissembled likewise with him; insomuch that Barnabas also was carried away with their 14 dissimulation. But when I saw that they walked not uprightly according to the truth of the Gospel, I said unto Peter before them all, If thou being a Jew, livest after the manner of Gentiles, and not as do the Jews, ¹how ⁋ compellest thou the Gentiles to live as do the Jews?

15 We who are Jews by nature, and not sinners of 16 the Gentiles, knowing that a man is not justified by the works of the law, but by the faith of Jesus Christ, even we have believed in Jesus Christ, that we might be justified by the faith of Christ, and not by the works of the law: for by the works of the 17 law shall no flesh be justified. But if, while we seek

¹ *why*

which this passage represents the two great Apostles, it throws an important light on the history of the Apostolic Church in the following respects:—(1) As exhibiting Peter's relation to James, and his fear of those who were of the circumcision, whose leader we should have naturally supposed him to have been. (2) Also, as portraying the state of indecision in which all, except St. Paul, even including Barnabas, were in reference to the observance of the Jewish law.

15-21. These words are the substance of a conversation between the two Apostles, of which one side only is narrated, and which soon passes off into the general subject of the Epistle. Verse 14 is the answer of St. Paul to Peter; what follows is more like the Apostle musing or arguing with himself, with an indirect reference to the Galatians. Compare John iii, where the discourses of Christ with Nicodemus, and of John the Baptist, appear in the same way to mingle imperceptibly with the thoughts of the Evangelist; also Rom. iii. 1-8: 1 Cor. xi. 25.

17-20. But if seeking to be justified in Christ, we, too, are found sinners as well as the Gentiles; that is, in other words, if we too fall back under the power of the law, Christ becomes the cause of this we make Him the to be justified in Christ, we ourselves also are found sinners, then is Christ the minister of sin. God forbid. 18 For if I build again the things which I destroyed, 19 I make myself a transgressor. For I through the

minister of that law which is the strength of sin,' which 'reviving, we die.' Not so, it were absurd to think it. It is we, not he, who are the ministers of sin ; we make ourselves transgressors by imposing upon ourselves a law which makes us transgress. We build up what we pulled down. The law was but the negation of itself, the means to its own extinction, and the creation of a new life in us. But now the law that was dead is made alive again.

Had the thought of the law being death been placed first, there would have been no difficulty in understanding the Apostle's meaning, which clears up as we proceed. He is speaking from his own point of view, not from ours, or from that of his opponents. He cannot imagine any justified by works, without falling under the power of sin. 'Whatsoever is not of faith, is sin,' as he says in the Romans. And when men are in this sinful condition, was it Christ that brought them to it? Not Christ, but what they have added to Christ ; for where there is no law, there is no transgression.

First let us consider the words διὰ νόμου ἀπέθανον, 'I through the law was dead that I may live.' The law had wrought in me the infinite consciousness of sin, and the sense that, do what I would, the fulfilment of its requirements was impossible. It was a state of death, but of death unto life. Now, the Apostle adds to this thought, 'through the law I died unto the law, that I may live unto God.' (Compare the parallelism in Rom. iv. 10, 'in that he died he died unto sin once, but in that he liveth he liveth unto God.') In this second relation ἀπέθανον is used in a different sense. For as before it denoted the highest state of discord, the 'paralysis of our moral nature,' here in reference to νόμῳ it rather denotes insensibility to the law which has no more power over a dead man.

It has been objected to the above explanation that too much use is made in it of the Epistle to the Romans, and especially that it supposes the doctrine of the seventh chapter of the Romans to have been everywhere and at all times present to the mind of the Apostle. That it was present in writing this passage, is, I think, shown by the expression, 'I through the law was dead to the law,' which is more abrupt and epigrammatical than the language of the Epistle to the Romans, yet, in substance, the same. When the Apostle says, 'the law came and sin revived, and I died,' and goes on to trace the course of this death, paralysing the soul, which at last, in its agony, casts aside the burden too heavy to be borne, is not this an expansion, or dra-

law am dead to the law, that I might live unto God.
20 I am crucified with Christ: nevertheless I live; yet not I, but Christ liveth in me: and the life which I now live in the flesh, I live by the faith of the Son of God, who loved me, and gave himself for
21 me. I do not frustrate the grace of God; for if righteousness come by the law, then Christ is dead in vain.

3 O foolish Galatians, who hath bewitched you, $^{m-l}$ before whose eyes Jesus Christ hath been evidently set
2 forth crucified among you? This only would I learn of you, Received ye the Spirit by the works of the law,
3 or by the hearing of faith? Are ye so foolish? having

^m add *that ye should not obey the truth*

matic illustration, of the words just quoted?

The truth of an interpretation is sometimes tested by a comparison with other interpretations. What other interpretations of this passage are possible? First, here as in Rom. vi the Apostle may be answering antinomian objections, and with this the general tone of the passage agrees, the fatal flaw being the want of connexion with Peter's speech; or, secondly, verse 17 may be paraphrased as follows:—'If we believers in Christ maintain obedience to the law, and at the same time transgress it, is Christ the cause of this? No, not Christ, but ourselves.' But here, though the sense of the words, εὑρέθημεν καὶ αὐτοὶ ἁμαρτωλοί, be easier, the connexion with ver. 19, 20 again breaks down.

20. The words which follow afford a good example of the manner in which the language of identity, or communion with Christ, passes into that of substitution. First, we are said to die or live with Christ. Then the phrase receives a further development;—not only we live or die with Christ, but Christ lives or dies in us.—First, we are one with Christ, and then Christ is put in our place. So far we are using the same language with the Apostle. At the next stage a difference appears. We begin with figures of speech—sacrifice, ransom, lamb of God; and go on with logical determinations—finite, infinite, satisfaction, necessity in the nature of things. St. Paul also begins with figures of speech—life, death, the flesh; but passes on to the inward experience of the life of faith, and the consciousness of Christ dwelling in us.

3. 3. ἐναρξάμενοι πνεύματι, *having begun, &c.*] Taking up the words of the two previous verses, ἀνόητοι, πνεῦμα, as his manner is, the Apostle adds: 'Having begun in

begun in the spirit are ye now made perfect by the
flesh? have ye suffered so many things in vain? if
ⁿ indeed it be " in vain. HE therefore that ᵒ gave " to
you the Spirit, and ᵖ wrought miracles in you, did " he
it by the works of the law, or by the hearing of faith?
Even as Abraham ᑫ had faith in " God, and it was
accounted to him for righteousness. Know ye therefore that they which are of faith, the same are the
children of Abraham. And the Scripture, foreseeing

ⁿ it be yet   ᵒ ministereth
ᵖ worketh miracles among you, doeth   ᑫ believed

the Spirit, are ye now ending in the flesh?' The opposition is not between holiness and uncleanness, or good and evil generally; but between the Gospel and the law. σάρξ is used in a figure as the symbol of what is outward and visible; also as the seat of the desires which the law stirs into sinful action (Rom. vii. 7, 8). It is applied to the Mosaic dispensation: (1) in the general sense of 'external;' (2) as propagated by fleshly descent; (3) as sealed by the mark of circumcision in the flesh.

4. τοσαῦτα ἐπάθετε εἰκῆ;] (1) 'Did ye suffer all those persecutions in vain?' or (2) 'Had you all those experiences in vain?' The latter is more agreeable to the context and to the general spirit of St. Paul's teaching, as well as to the few facts which we know about the Galatian Church, in which probably as yet no persecution had occurred. Even were this otherwise, it is unlike the noble style of the Apostle to say: 'Have you thrown away the fruits of all those persecutions?' The Apostle adds a qualification: εἴ γε καὶ εἰκῆ, 'Have you had all these experiences in vain? if, indeed, which I cannot bear to think, it be in vain;' not 'if it be only and not worse than in vain,' which gives a good sense, but is not expressed in the words.

8. The words of the quotation, as they occur in the LXX (Gen. xii. 3), are εὐλογηθήσονται ἐν σοὶ πᾶσαι αἱ φυλαὶ τῆς γῆς,—πάντα τὰ ἔθνη being introduced from the repetition of the same promise in Gen. xviii. 18. The promise to Abraham is interpreted by the Apostle as a declaration of the Gospel of the Gentiles. ἐν σοί means 'in thee;'—that is, 'in thee as their type,' or 'in thy faith.' In the original passage it has the sense, 'by thee;'—that is, the form of their blessing shall be, by thy name. 'The Lord bless thee, as he blessed Abraham and his descendants.' ἔθνη has also received a change of meaning, referring in Genesis to the nations of the world in general; but here (compare ver.

that God would justify the heathen through faith, preached before the Gospel unto Abraham, saying, In ⁹thee shall all nations be blessed. So then they which be of faith are blessed with ʳthe " faithful Abraham. ¹⁰For as many as are of the works of the law are under the curse: for it is written, ˢthat every one is cursed who " continueth not in all things which are ¹¹written in the book of the law to do them. But that no man is justified by the law in the sight of God, ¹²it is evident: for, The just shall live by faith. ᵗBut " the law is not of faith: but ᵘhe " that doeth them shall ¹³live in them. Christ hath redeemed us from the curse

ʳ omit the   ˢ *Cursed is every one that*   ᵗ And   ᵘ *the man*

14) confined by St. Paul to the heathen, who are to be saved by faith. The general meaning is as follows:—' It was not a mere accident that it was said, In thee shall all the Gentiles be blessed; but because Abraham was justified by faith, as the Gentiles were to be justified by faith.'

13. χριστὸς ἡμᾶς ἐξηγόρασεν.] A further proof that we cannot be justified by the law is, that the curse of the law is what Christ redeemed us from. We were like captives, and Christ paid the penalty for us.

When the Apostle speaks of 'us,' is he referring to the Jew only, or also to the Gentile? Primarily, to the Jew; in a degree also to the Gentile. By the same act the burden is taken off the Jew, and a way is laid open to the Gentile. But the same figure is not equally applicable to both. The Gentile too has a rule of nature, and a conscience accusing or excusing himself; but he can hardly be described as subject to

ordinances, or tempted by the law to sin. He has no lively sense of responsibility; he is not distracted by any spiritual conflict. The general conception of his previous state is rather expressed by the words : 'Ye were carried away by dumb idols, even as ye were led.' Whether there was any degree of truth in these idolatries—whether in any respects they were akin to the Jewish ceremonial law—was a question which would never have occurred to the thoughts of the Apostle. To him it was a 'mystery kept secret from the foundation of the world' that the Gentile was to have the Gospel revealed to him. The law is the only 'schoolmaster to bring men to Christ,' and the Jew alone is subject to it. Of a single prior dispensation of Judaism and heathenism, such as philosophical writers in modern times have sometimes imagined, there is no trace in the Epistles.

It is true, however, that the

of the law, being made a curse for us; ˣ forasmuch as
it is written, Cursed is every one that hangeth on
14 a tree: that the blessing of Abraham might come
on the Gentiles through Jesus Christ; that we might
receive the promise of the Spirit through faith.

ˣ *for*

Apostle often places Jew and Gentile side by side, and easily passes from one to the other. From his ideal point of view the distinction seems to vanish. The figurative language in which he describes one is readily transferred to the other. As in Rom. i, ii, the same eye of the soul is turned upon both. As in Rom. iii. 19, he places the Gentile within the sphere of the law, that he may condemn him by the words of the law. As in Rom. iv the distinction of Jew and Gentile is lost in the common designation of children of the faith of Abraham. Hence, though in ver. 13 he uses the words 'redeemed us from the curse of the law,' which are only applicable to Jews, he passes on in the latter clause of ver. 14 to include in one both Jew and Gentile. The Jew was a captive, and Christ called him into the liberty of the sons of God. The Gentile is a partaker of the same heritage.

But how, it may be asked, was this effected by 'Christ being a curse for us?' To answer this question we must distinguish between the spirit and the letter, the inward meaning and the figure of the Jewish law.

(1) The inward meaning is that Christ's teaching and life and death drew men to Him, until they were taken out of themselves, and in all their thoughts and actions became one with Him.

(2) That His life seemed naturally to bring upon Him the penalty of the Jewish law: 'We have a law, and by our law he ought to die.'

(3) That at the same time that His death was a fulfilment of the law, it was also the end of the law. He endured the law and did away with the law at once.

(4) Mankind, contrasting the image of His life, and the requirement of the law, feel that they are placed above the law, and so escape with Him from its burden.

To the figure must be assigned the notion of a ransom or sacrifice, by which, as by the victim on the altar, God is satisfied or pleased.

ἐπικατάρατος, *cursed.*] The Apostle again confirms his view by a passage from the Old Testament, which is cited from the LXX with a slight verbal difference, St. Paul reading ἐπικατάρατος πᾶς, instead of κεκατηραμένος ὑπὸ θεοῦ πᾶς Deut. xxi. 23. In its original connexion it refers to the body of the criminal, which was not to be left hanging after the evening, lest the earth should be polluted by the corse. This St. Paul transfers to Christ. The abhorred death of the cross,

15 Brethren, I speak after the manner of men; Though it be but a man's covenant, yet if it be confirmed, 16 no man disannulleth, or addeth thereto. Now to Abraham and his seed were the promises made. He saith not, and to seeds, as of many; but as of one,

which the Romans inflicted on their slaves, recalled to his mind the curse of the Jewish law.

15. Ἀδελφοί, *Brethren.*] The Apostle continues to soften his tone.

κατὰ ἄνθρωπον λέγω, *I speak after the manner of men.*] The expression is used with various shades of meaning; sometimes, as in Rom. iii. 5, as a sort of apology for some supposition about Divine things; sometimes, in the sense of 'It is I who say, and not the Lord;' sometimes simply 'I speak after the manner of men,' or 'I use a human figure.' To which may be added, in this passage, the notion of what we should term an *à fortiori* argument from human to Divine things: 'I speak as a man; if this is true in human things, how much more in Divine?'

A general view of the passage that follows will assist in the explanation of the several verses. As in the Romans, the Apostle has quoted the case of Abraham, who was justified by faith, and received also the universal promise that 'in him all nations of the earth should be blessed.' This is a figure of the Gospel dispensation, or rather it is the very Gospel which Paul preached among the Gentiles. Two thousand years have passed away, and the meaning of the promise to Abraham is just coming to light.

But here the thought arises in the Apostle's mind—'There has been a long interval; the law came between.' To answer this objection, as at the commencement of the seventh chapter of the Romans, he brings forward an illustration: 'Human covenants are binding for ever; you cannot alter them, or add to them. How much more the covenant of Him with whom a thousand years are as one day, and one day as a thousand years?' But the Jew would reply, the covenant was but the beginning of the law, as we might say in a figure, the angel who talked with Abraham was lost in the brightness of Mount Sinai. It is this point of view that the Apostle seeks to invert. According to him the covenant was to remain, the law to pass away. In the very words in which the covenant was given, 'not unto seeds, as of many, but as of one,' was contained an intimation that it referred to Christ. It was in force 430 years. Can we suppose that it was superseded by the law? Rather the law and the promise are opposed to each other, as the law and faith, and it was through the promise that God gave the gift to Abraham. Then what shall we say of the law? It was an accident, an interpolation, an addition, designed not to do men good, but to

17 and to thy seed, which is Christ. And this I say; [y–y] the covenant that was confirmed before of God [z–z] the law which was four hundred and thirty years after cannot disannul, that it should make the promise

---

[y] *add* that   [z] add *in Christ*

---

make them conscious of evil, and in everything showing its transitory and inferior nature. Is it then opposed to the promises? Not so. It had right, if it had had might; it had the idea of righteousness, if it had had the power to give life. But it was a law of condemnation only, the import of which to us is that it made us capable of the promise. While it lasted we were shut up, as it were, in prison, waiting for the coming revelation. 'So that the law was our schoolmaster to bring us to Christ;' and was itself done away when Christ came.

17. μετὰ τετρακόσια καὶ τριάκοντα ἔτη, *four hundred and thirty years after.*] The law, which was given so long after, could not do away with the promise.

There is a well-known chronological difficulty in these words, connected with a similar chronological difficulty in the Old Testament, respecting the sojourn of the Israelites in Egypt. In the books of Genesis and Exodus the period of 430 years (Ex. xii. 40), or in round numbers, 400 years (Gen. xv. 13, quoted in the Acts, vii. 6), is assigned, not to the interval between the promise to Abraham, and the giving of the law; but to the actual sojourn of the children of Israel in Egypt. [Exod. xii. 40: 'Now the sojourning of the children of Israel who dwelt in Egypt was four hundred and thirty years.' Gen. xv. 13: 'And he said, Know of a surety that thy seed shall be a stranger in a land that is not theirs, and shall serve them, and they shall afflict them four hundred years: and also that nation, whom they shall serve, will I judge; and afterward shall they come out with great substance.'] It is found on examination of the genealogies, however, that in some lines, as, for example that of Moses himself, the whole time of 400 years comprises only three generations; and hence it has been argued, that the call of Abraham is the true limit of the period in question; and laborious calculations have been entered into to show that, in the course of two centuries, the children of Israel might possibly have increased from Jacob and his sons to several hundred thousands.

If these and similar difficulties could be removed, we should only have escaped an inaccuracy in the New Testament, by introducing a contradiction into the Old. That St. Paul is not quoting from any independent tradition is plain from his giving the exact number of Exod. xii. 40. It is also clear, that in the narrative of Exodus this number refers to the actual time of servitude, and not to the interval between the promise and the law. But the

18 of none effect. For if the inheritance be of the law, it is no more of promise: but God gave it to Abraham 19 by promise. Wherefore then serveth the law? It

Apostle has so applied it. He takes 430, the years of servitude mentioned in the Old Testament, for a period longer than 430 years — that is, for the whole time from Abraham to Moses.

19. The first impression on reading this verse is, that the Apostle meant to say that the law was added to restrain men from transgressions, in the interval of time between the promise and the coming of Christ. According to this view, the law would be regarded as the principle of order in the world, designed to keep men from utterly corrupting themselves, and giving them a moral preparation for the revelation which was to follow. Such a view may be thought to derive confirmation from ver. 24 : 'The law was our schoolmaster to bring us to Christ;' it agrees with our own ideas of the purposes of law in general, and of the relation of the Mosaic law to the Gospel (comp. Heb. vii. 19) in particular. Yet the words themselves are indefinite, and the comparison of other passages in the Epistles, such as Rom. vii. 7-25 ; iii. 20 ; iv. 15 ; v. 20 : 1 Cor. xv. 56, would lead us to expect a different tone of thought respecting the law. On this, above all other subjects, it is necessary to remember the axiom, 'non nisi ex ipso Paulo Paulum potes interpretari.' And the characteristic mode of thought and speech in the passages just referred to would incline us to suppose that the Apostle's meaning probably was, not that the law was added to restrain transgressions ; but that the law was added to produce transgressions, or at least to give men that consciousness of sin which makes sin to be what it is, 'for where there is no law there is no transgression,' and 'the strength of sin is the law.' The law, it must be remembered, is not with St. Paul an element or principle of good ; but an abstract good. It is not the law of the land which punishes crime ; but an ideal law, the very characteristic of which is, that it cannot be realized in action. It would attribute too much power to the law to suppose that it could restrain men from sin. Then it would not be far from 'a law that might give life.' 'By the deeds of the law,' as the Apostle says in the Epistle to the Romans, 'shall no flesh be justified, *for* by the law is the knowledge of sin.' In other words justification is the very opposite of that knowledge of sin which is by the law. In the language of the Epistle to the Romans (v. 20), it might be said that the law was added to the covenant 'that transgression might abound ;' the other side of this doctrine being given in the latter part of the same verse, 'that grace might yet more abound.'

One further point of view we must not lose sight of in the consideration of this question ; that is, the near connexion of the final cause with the fact in the was added because of transgressions, till the seed should come to whom the promise was made; and

Apostle's mind, in this, as in other instances. The whole doctrine of righteousness by faith may be said to be based in a certain sense on fact, on two great facts especially;—the conversion of the Apostle himself, and the conversion of the Gentiles. So in this case, what St. Paul saw to be the result, he also considered as the purpose of God. 'Known unto God are all his works from the beginning.' It was the fact that the law had increased sin, and therefore he regarded it as given for this purpose τῶν παραβάσεων χάριν. It is hardly probable that an interpretation of Scripture will be generally accepted which runs counter to the superficial meaning of the words. Like the canon, 'Potior lectio difficilior,' potior difficilior interpretatio may also have a truth. In this instance the interpretation given is based solely on the comparison of the Epistle to the Romans, which is the only Epistle from which we are able to gather at all fully St. Paul's view of the nature of the law, and which has a very close connexion with the Epistle to the Galatians.

διαταγεὶς δι' ἀγγέλων, *ordained by angels.*] There is no mention in the Old Testament of the law being given by angels, with the exception of a remote allusion in Deut. xxxiii. 2, 'The Lord came from Sinai; he came with ten thousand of his saints.' It was slowly and gradually, and as many have thought, not until the Babylonish captivity, that the angel of His presence in the Pentateuch, the angel of the Lord in the Books of Kings and Chronicles, and the covering cherubim of the prophets expanded into a multitude of the heavenly host, with distinct names and personalities. The word διαταγείς here, as the word διαταγή in Acts vii. 53, 'Who have received the law by the disposition of angels, and have not kept it,'—refers rather to the administration than to the giving of the law. As in Heb. ii. 2, the law being in the disposition of angels, is contrasted with the Gospel, which is a revelation of a higher kind.

μεσίτου, *of a mediator.*] I. e. Moses or the high priest, or in general the priest or prophet who stood between God and the people.

Before entering on the discussion of this passage, which has received 430 interpretations, it will be well for us to ascertain the drift of the verse before and after, which give almost the sole key we possess to the meaning of the disputed words. To supply the connecting-link will be an easier task than to explain the ambiguous text from itself.

We will first begin by considering an opposite view of the connexion to that implied in the preceding note. The object, it may be urged, of the words διαταγεὶς δι' ἀγγέλων ἐν χειρὶ μεσίτου is, not to depreciate the law in comparison of the Gospel, but rather to express its Divine character as a subordinate and intermediate dispensation. 'The law it was ordained by angels in the hand of a mediator. 20 Now a mediator is not a mediator of one, but God

was given because of transgressions,'—i. e. as now explained, to remove transgressions; and it was kept in the administration of angels, and one was appointed to stand between God and the people. The figure of angels, it might be said, belongs rather to the pomp and array of the law, and could not naturally be urged as an argument of depreciation. This is true; and may be further confirmed by Acts vii. 53, and yet is sufficiently answered by the context and the parallel of Heb. ii. 2.

If we go backwards from ver. 21, 'Is the law then against the promises of God? God forbid:' it is plain from these words, that something has been said which implies a depreciation of the law. It would be neither good sense nor agreeable to the manner of St. Paul to say, Whereunto serveth the law? It was added because of transgressions, and was firmly established and appointed by angels, and in the hands of a mediator, and a mediator we may explain to be, &c. Is the law then against the promises of God? There has been nothing in the previous verse which indicated, or could be imagined to indicate that it was. There would be a want of point in such a way of writing. It would be guarding against an inference that could not possibly arise. The view here taken, that there must have been a previous depreciation, is still further strengthened by a comparison of a parallel passage in Rom. vii. 5, 7, where the Apostle suddenly bursts out with the words, 'What shall we say then, is the law sin? God forbid,' as if to counteract and anticipate the effect of what he had said just before: 'The motions of sins which were by the law, did work in our members.'

Thus far we are led to suppose that the enigmatical verse 20 must form an antithesis to verse 21. Such an interpretation we shall be able to put upon it, if we paraphrase ver. 19 as follows:— 'The law was added not so much for the removal of sin, as to call it into existence, and it was in the appointment of angels, not of God himself, and did not admit of an immediate approach to him.' It has been said that such an interpretation does not agree with the words διαταγεὶς δι'ἀγγέλων, which could not, as was observed above, be intended to depreciate the law, but rather to magnify its pomp and circumstance. Admitting this, which may or may not be so, there is no difficulty in supposing that St. Paul might, in one point of view, intend to depreciate the law, while, in another, he may have glorified it: at any rate so far as to use respecting it an expression familiar to the minds of the Jews; as in 2 Cor. iii. 6 he recognizes the law as the ministration of death, and yet acknowledges its glory. It is characteristic of St. Paul, even where he is making towards a point, to insert clauses which are beside his point.

21 is one. Is the law then against the promises of God? God forbid; for if there had been a law given which could have given life, verily righteousness should 22 have been ¹ by the law. But the scripture hath ᵃ shut up ᵃ all under sin, that the promise by faith of Jesus

ᵃ concluded

We have now to seek for a suitable interpretation of verse 20, of which two principal conditions may be laid down :—(1) that it should agree with the connexion; and (2) that it should admit of the word εἷς being taken in the same sense in both members of the sentence. The following combines both these conditions; if it seem obscure, it must be remembered that, in a writer at once so subtle and abrupt as St. Paul, obscurity is not a strong ground of objection :—

The Apostle is contrasting the law which had a mediator, with the Gospel or the promise of faith (for in this passage they are not distinguished) which has no mediator, but an open access to God. Part of the perplexity of the passage has arisen from the circumstance that the Apostle's mode of speaking is in direct opposition to the ordinary language of later theology, and even of some passages in the New Testament itself. It sounds like a paradox to modern ears, to place the superiority of the Gospel over the law in the fact that the law had a mediator and the Gospel had not. Yet such is the Apostle's reasoning. The law, he says, was in the hands of a mediator. Hereby, as we gather from the context, he seems to mark some imperfection or infirmity in the law. How is this? He proceeds to enlarge his thought in the 20th verse. Now a mediator, he adds, is not a mediator of one, but God is one. That is, a mediator implies two persons—duality, mediation ;—or the principle of a mediator is not unity, but mediation ;—but in God is no mediation—He is one :— 'Hear, O Israel,' as the law said, 'the Lord your God is one God.' He who is interposed between God and man intercepts instead of revealing God; one is better than two; the dispensation of mediation is inferior to the open vision.

21. The powerlessness of the law was the actual fact ; in modern language, it had become effete ; it belonged to a different state of the world ; nothing human or spiritual remained of it. The Apostle, who carried back justification by faith to Abraham, went on to compare also the notion of the law which he gathered from his own age, with its first idea and origin. It was a sort of riddle to him, in the meshes of which he seems to struggle, how the law could be powerless ; the law could be the occasion, the strength, and almost the cause

¹ Reading ἐκ νόμου

3. 28]   EPISTLE TO THE GALATIANS   151

23 Christ might be given to them that believe. But before faith came, we were kept ᵇ in ward ″ under the law, shut up unto the faith which should afterwards 24 be revealed. ᶜ So that ″ the law was our schoolmaster ᵈ⁻″ unto Christ, that we might be justified by faith. 25 But after that faith is come, we are no longer under 26 a schoolmaster. For ye are all the children of God 27 by faith in Christ Jesus. For as many of you as have been baptized into Christ have put on Christ. 28 There is neither Jew nor Greek, there is neither bond

ᵇ *omit* in ward   ᶜ Wherefore   ᵈ *add* to bring us

of sin, and yet bear the stamp of Divine authority. In some sense he is assured that it is holy, just, and good; its very perfection involving its imperfection or negative nature; the conviction of sin which it wrought being the way to a new life.

23. The condition of the Jew and Gentile in reference to the Gospel, may be figured by the image of men within and without a prison; the first with the shining of a candle to give them light, the second wandering in darkness over the whole earth. The sun arises upon both; to the latter disclosing an endless prospect, while the former, with their candle grown dim before the coming day, are still within the curtains of their tabernacle. No longer shut up under the law, they are afraid to come out and look upon the light of heaven. The world is all before them, if they did but know it, and every part full of the Divine presence.

27. The figure of putting on Christ has a reference, first, to the robe in which the newly-baptized person was arrayed on coming up out of the water, and recalls also an idiomatic expression in later Greek, of 'putting on another' to signify close and intimate friendship with him. See on Rom. xiii. 14. In this latter passage, St. Paul exhorts believers 'to put on Christ;' here he implies that they have already attained in baptism the state which is thus described. In one sense the believer is regenerate; in another, not. His whole life is anticipated in the beginning, and still he may be exhorted to begin. Compare Col. iii. 9, 10: 'Putting off the old man with his actions; and putting on the new man which is renewed unto knowledge in the image of him that created him.'

28. It has been often asked whether Christianity has altered the condition of women and slaves; and the answer sometimes given is, that no positive precepts are found in the New Testament forbidding that subjection of either, which seemed natural to the ancient world.

nor free, there is neither male nor female: for ye are all one in Christ Jesus. And if ye be Christ's, then are ye Abraham's seed, ᵉ⁻ᵉ heirs according to the promise.

4 Now I say, That the heir, as long as he is a child, differeth nothing from a servant, though he be lord of all; but is under tutors and governors until the time appointed of the father. Even so we, when we were children, were in bondage under the elements of the

ᵉ add *and*

Some have even thought that the spirit of the Gospel tended rather to slavery than to freedom, in enjoining the forgiveness of injury and discouraging the desire to be free. It is true that no class or sex is encouraged by Christianity to claim its rights; yet not the less surely in the lapse of centuries did the Gospel mould the institutions of mankind. It was a leaven which was hid in three measures of meal, until the whole was leavened. Of the world and the Roman empire, and the institutions of ancient times, no less than of the Jewish religion, the words of Christ hold good: 'Destroy this temple, and in three days I will raise it up again.' And with reference to the present verse, it could not but be a consequence of regarding men and women, bond and free, as one and alike in the presence of God, that their spiritual freedom became also an external and actual one.

4. 3. The expression, 'principles of the world,' is ideal, and it is impossible to say precisely what the Apostle meant by it, any more than what he meant by 'rulers of the darkness of this world.' As to ourselves, so to St. Paul, the world means that portion of evil, or of mankind, with which we come most nearly into contact, and which is most directly opposed to us, as well as all the world which is unknown to us, and which we comprise in the imaginary limit of an abstract term. The heathen world was to him its first and most natural meaning, but the evil of the heathen world was also the figure of the Jewish, just as the Jewish law was a figure of the law written in the heart of the Gentile. Hence the transition was easy from the Gentile to the Jew. By a similar transposition of language, we speak of 'the world' in modern times finding a place in the hearts of religious men, or of Christianity being infected with a worldly spirit, the force of which consists in using against the professing Christian the term which he uses against others; just as St. Paul, here writing to professing Jews, applies to Judaism the language which was ever in the Jew's mouth against the rest of mankind.

₄ world: but when the fulness of the time was come, God sent forth his Son, made of a woman, made under ₅ the law, to redeem them that were under the law, ₆ that we might receive the adoption of sons. And because ye are sons, God hath sent forth the Spirit of his Son into ᶠour*ᶠ* hearts, crying, Abba, father. ₇ Wherefore thou art no more a servant, but a son: and if a son, then an heir ᵍthrough God.*ᵍ*

₈ Howbeit then, when ye knew not God, ye did ₉ service unto them which by nature are no gods. But now, after that ye have known God, or rather are known of God, how turn ye again to the weak and beggarly elements, whereunto ye desire ʰto begin*ʰ* ₁₀ again to be in bondage? Ye observe days, and

^f *your*   ^g *of God through Christ*   ^h *omit to begin*

4. ὅτε δὲ ἦλθε τὸ πλήρωμα τοῦ χρόνου, *but when the fulness of time was come.*] Shall we say that great events arise from antecedents, or without them; in the fullness of time, or out of due time? by sudden crises, or with long purpose and preparation? It is impossible for us to view the great changes of the world under any of these aspects exclusively. The spread of the Roman empire, the fall of the Jewish nation, the decline of the heathen religions— Jewish prophecy, Greek philosophy, these are the natural links which connect the Gospel with the actual state of mankind, the causes, humanly speaking, of its propagation, and the soil in which it grew. But there is something besides of which no account can be given. The external circumstances or conditions of events do not explain history any more than life. Why the Gospel came into the world in a particular form, or at a particular time, is a question which is not reached by any analysis of this sort.

This Providential time is what the Apostle calls 'the fulness of time,' not because in the modern way of reflection the causes and antecedents of the Gospel were already in being, but because it was the time appointed of God, the mysterious hour when the great revelation was to be made. It is when contemplated from within, not from without, that it appears to him to be the fullness of time; standing in the same relation to the world at large, that the moment of conversion does to the individual soul.

10. Ye observe sabbath days, and new moons, and times for feasts, and sabbatical years. That is to say, ye observe all the requirements of the Jewish law.

months, and times, and years. I am afraid of you, lest I have bestowed upon you labour in vain. Brethren, I beseech you, be as I am; for I am as ye are. Ye have not injured me at all. Ye know how ⁱamidⁱ infirmity of the flesh I preached the Gospel unto you at the first, and ᵏyourⁱ temptation which was in my flesh¹. Ye despised not, nor rejected ¹meⁱ; but received me as an angel of God, even as Christ Jesus. Where is then the blessedness ye spake of? for I bear you record, that, if it had been possible, ye would have plucked out your own eyes and have

ⁱ through　　ᵏ my　　ⁱ *omit* me

Compare Col. ii. 16: 'Let no man judge you in meat or in drink, or in respect of an holyday, or of the new moon, or of the sabbath days.'

Our Lord and St. Paul, everywhere, speak against the superstitious observance of the Sabbath; they nowhere enforce the consecration of one day in seven, however right and free from superstition such an institution may be in itself, on Christians. The Christian Sunday rests on another foundation: ancient use, the reason of the thing, the practice of the Christian Church—these grounds are sufficient to make thoughtful men careful of its observance for themselves, and fearful of giving offence to others, in violating the custom of their own or other countries.

12. The Apostle changes his tone. His old affection for the Galatians revives, and he implores them to consider that he is not speaking of any personal wrongs of his own. He is touched by the memory of their attachment to him while he was yet with them. 'I know how weak and feeble I was, how much reason there was for you to despise me; but you did the opposite, you received me as an angel of God. Your affection for me was indeed extravagant; there was nothing which you would not have done for me.'

13. δι'ἀσθένειαν τῆς σαρκός, *through weakness of the flesh.*] In explaining these words, we have to choose between Greek usage and the sense required by the context. Adhering to the ordinary meaning of διά with the accusative, we should translate, 'Ye know that it was on account of an illness that I preached to you at first.' There would be no want of courtesy in this, if we only lay the stress on the latter part of the sentence. 'You saw that it was a mere accident that made me preach to you, yet you showed

¹ Punctuating after ἐν τῇ σαρκί μου.

16 given them to me. Am I therefore become your enemy,
17 because I tell you the truth? They zealously ᵐentreat *ᵈ*
you, but not well; yea, they would exclude you, that
18 ye might affect them. But it is good to be zealously
ⁿentreated *ᵈ* always in a good thing, and not only
19 when I am present with you. My ᵒ⁻*ᵈ* children, of
whom I travail in birth again until Christ be formed
20 in you, I desire to be present with you now, and to
change my voice; for I stand in doubt of you.

21 Tell me, ye that desire to be under the law, do ye

ᵐ affect   ⁿ affected   ᵒ add *little*

no want of care or tenderness to me.' Yet it seems hardly likely that the Apostle would have spoken of mere illness, in the succeeding verse, as 'your temptation in my flesh.' Illness would create sympathy, not, as he seems to imply in the words ἐξουθενήσατε and ἐξεπτύσατε, ridicule and disgust. There is no intimation in the Acts of the Apostles of any peculiar occasion leading him to preach the Gospel in Galatia; nor in an illness, which hindered his journey, a likely or natural one.

It is more probable that the Apostle is alluding to the thorn in the flesh, to that depression of spirit and feebleness of bodily presence which he refers to elsewhere in 2 Corinthians (i. 9; ii. 13; x. 10), and which may have been a form of the same disorder. (Compare 'The messenger of Satan to buffet me,' which seems to denote a half mental, half bodily affliction.) He is speaking of the state in which he preached to them, not of some accidental cause of his mission. Compare again 2 Cor. x. 10, 'bodily presence weak, and speech contemptible;' and the words of 1 Cor. ii. 3, which are still nearer, 'I was with you in weakness, and in fear, and in much trembling.' All these passages give the same idea of the Apostle's personal appearance. Of such an one it might be truly said, 'Ye did not show contempt or dislike.'

15. μακαρισμός,] not 'blessedness;' but, as in Rom. iv. 9, the attribution of blessedness. So here the declaration of how blessed you were — the state described also in Gal. iii. 2.

21 ff. Whether this is an argument or an illustration, is a question that naturally occurs to the mind of the reader. To an Alexandrian writer of the first century (may we say, therefore, to St. Paul himself?) the question itself could hardly have been made intelligible. That very modern distinction between argument and illustration was precisely what his mind wanted, to place it on a level with the modes of thought of our own age. We must, there-

22 not hear the law? For it is written, that Abraham had two sons, the one by a bondmaid, the other by 23 a free woman. But he who was of the bondwoman was born after the flesh; but he of the freewoman 24 was by promise. Which things are an allegory: for these are the two covenants; the one from the mount Sinai, which gendereth to bondage, which is Agar 25 (¹ ᵖ for this mount Sinai is in Arabia ʸ), and answereth to Jerusalem which now is (ᑫ for she is ʸ in bondage 26 with her children). But Jerusalem which is above 27 is free, which is the mother of us all. For it is written, Rejoice, thou barren that bearest not; break

ᵖ *for this Agar is Mount Sinai in Arabia*   ᑫ *and is*

fore, find some other way of characterizing the passage. It is neither an argument nor an illustration, but an interpretation of the Old Testament Scripture after the manner of the age in which St. Paul lived; that is, after the manner of the Jewish and Christian Alexandrian writers. Whatever difference there is between him and them, or between Philo and the Christian fathers as interpreters of Scripture, is not one of kind, but of degree. A truer difference is made by the noble spirit of the Apostle shining through the elements of the law in which he clothes his meaning. The form of allegory, or of mysticism, does not straiten the freedom of the Gospel. Strange as it may at first appear, that his mode of interpreting the Old Testament Scriptures should not conform to our laws of logic or language, it would be far stranger if it had not conformed with the natural modes of thought and association in his own day.

25. τὸ γὰρ Σινᾶ ὄρος ἐστὶν ἐν τῇ Ἀραβίᾳ, *for Sinai is a mountain in Arabia.*] The MS. authority and later editors are nearly divided about the admission of the word Ἄγαρ in this verse. The insertion, however, does little towards supplying the connexion of the 25th and 24th verses; as the old explanations, that Hagar is the Arabic word for a rock, or the Arabic name of mount Sinai (whether we suppose it probable or otherwise, that St. Paul would have quoted Arabic words in writing to the Galatians), are destitute of foundation. On better authority it is stated that there was a town Hagar close to the mountain, the name of which may have been given to Sinai itself; of this latter fact, however, no proof is adduced.

A sufficient sense is obtained by laying the stress on ἐν τῇ Ἀρα-

---

¹ Reading τὸ γὰρ Σινᾶ ὄρος ἐστίν

forth and cry, thou that travailest not: for the desolate hath many more children than she which hath an husband. ¹ʳBut ye,[1] brethren, as Isaac was, are the children of promise. But as then he that was born after the flesh persecuted him that was born after the Spirit, even so it is now. Nevertheless what saith the Scripture? Cast out the bondwoman and her son: for the son of the bondwoman shall not be heir with the son of the freewoman. ˢWherefore, brethren, we are not children of the bondwoman, but of the free.

ʳ *Now we*   ˢ *So then*

βίᾳ. 'For mount Sinai is in Arabia, the land of the children of Hagar;' or 'For this Hagar is mount Sinai in the land of the children of Hagar.' (Comp. Ps. lxxxiii. 7.) I. e. Hagar typifies the law given on mount Sinai, because mount Sinai is in the country of the descendants of Hagar.

31. So in language old yet new, ' in the oldness of the letter itself,' the Apostle tells of the freedom of the Gospel. The child of promise is the figure of the kingdom of heaven which is persecuted on earth, yet in the highest sense free, and the mother of all mankind. The persecutor is the fleshly heir, the image of the covenant of mount Sinai, who is now cast out and not suffered to inherit with the child of promise. The law and the Gospel cannot dwell together; the Gospel must drive out the law.

Such a tale in that age and country, finding its way to the minds of men, gave them a type or symbol, a form of truth and knowledge in which they received a principle not otherwise easy for them to grasp; it might be compared to an earthen vessel, in which the water of life was raised to the lips. Such adaptations or illustrations have ever been the mode in which the past has been interpreted by the present; broken to pieces and put together again; a new temple built out of the old stones—a new life given to the dry bones. Great as has been the influence of the wisdom of former ages, that influence has arisen much more from the idea which posterity have attributed to it, or extracted from it, than from what the critic of modern days now perceives to have been the original meaning of the poet or philosopher. And it is singular, yet true, and a sort of economy in the education of the human race, that these new applications of the sayings of those of old time have

[1] Reading ὑμεῖς ... ἐστέ

5 ᵗ With that freedom Christ hath made us free. Stand fast therefore,⁰ and be not entangled again with the yoke of bondage.

2 Behold, I Paul say unto you, that if ye be circum-
3 cised, Christ shall profit you nothing. ᵘAnd⁰ I testify again to every man that is circumcised, that he is
4 a debtor to do the whole law. Christ is become of no effect unto you, whosoever of you are justified by the
5 law; ye are fallen from grace. For we through the Spirit wait for the hope of righteousness by faith.
6 For in Jesus Christ neither circumcision availeth any thing, nor uncircumcision; but faith which worketh by love.

ᵗ *Stand fast therefore in the liberty wherewith Christ hath made us free*
ᵘ For

derived a part of their authority by an illusion, from the names of those whose meaning they no longer convey.

5. 3. In other passages, the Apostle exhorts men to overlook lesser points of difference, such as the eating of meat or herbs, the observance of days, the eating of meats offered to idols; Rom. xiv: 1 Cor. viii. In such cases, the double rule of faith and charity should operate; it is quite consistent to be free from scruples ourselves, and yet to be tender to those of others. But there are cases in which it is equally important to yield nothing, because the very least concession implies everything. The principle expressed in the words, 'I will eat no meat as long as the world standeth, lest I make my brother to offend,' has to be balanced and modified by the other principle, 'I testify again to every man that is circumcised, that he is a debtor to keep the whole law.' And the Spirit of both must be at last regulated by the words which follow:—'Neither circumcision availeth anything, nor uncircumcision, but faith which worketh by love.'

6. δι' ἀγάπης, *by love.*] There is no trace in the writings of St. Paul of the opposition of faith and love which is found in Luther. Such an opposition did not exist in the language of Christ and His Apostles. It came from the schools; Luther was driven to adopt it by the exigencies of controversy. At some point or other it was necessary to draw a line between the Catholic and Reformed doctrine of justification. Was it to include works as well as faith? but, if not, was love to be a coefficient in the work of justification? Luther felt this difficulty, and tried to preserve the doctrine from the alloy of self-righteousness and

5. 12]   EPISTLE TO THE GALATIANS   159

7 Ye did run well; who did hinder you that ye
8 should not obey the truth? This persuasion cometh
9 not of him that calleth you. A little leaven leaveneth
10 the whole lump. ¹ˣHowbeit ⁰ I have confidence in you
through the Lord, that ye will be none otherwise
minded: but he that troubleth you shall bear his
11 judgment, whosoever he be. But I, brethren, if I
yet preach circumcision, why do I yet suffer persecution? then ʸ has ⁰ the offence of the cross ceased.
12 I would ᶻ that they would even make themselves
eunuchs ⁰ which trouble you.

x omit *Howbeit*   y is   z they were even cut off

external acts by the formula of 'faith only.'

The necessity has passed away, and Christian feeling and the common sense of mankind find a truer reflection in the indefinite language of Scripture itself. Whether we say that we are justified by faith, or by love, or by faith working by love or by grace, or by the indwelling of Christ, or of the Spirit of Christ—the difference is one of words, and not of things. For although these distinctions admit of being defined by logic, and have been made the basis of opposing systems of theology, the point of view in which the writers of Scripture regard them is not that of difference, but of sameness. The words of St. Paul are equally far removed from a protest against Protestant doctrine and against Catholic doctrine; they belong to another world.

11. Similar covert answers to other charges occur in the Epistles to the Corinthians. (1 Cor. ix. 1, 7: 2 Cor. x. 7.) At Corinth, too, he seems to have been accused, amid many other calumnies, of not 'being of Christ' in that special sense in which his opponents claimed to be so. Had we that other Epistle which the Church at Corinth addressed to the Apostle, it would furnish a remarkable commentary on the two Epistles to the Corinthians. Had we the other side of the controversy with the Galatians, the obscurity which rests on several passages of the Epistle would probably be removed.

then has the offence of the cross ceased,] may be read without difference of meaning, either with or without a question. In either case it is most agreeable to the connexion to take the words ironically: 'Then you have nothing more to say against me, I am to infer; or, Am I to infer that the offence of the cross has ceased?' It is observable that, not Christ Himself, but the cross of Christ, is spoken of as the

¹ Reading ἐγὼ δέ

13 For, brethren, ye have been called unto liberty;
only use not ᵃ your ᵈ liberty for an occasion to the
14 flesh, but by love serve one another. For all the law
is fulfilled in one word, even in this; Thou shalt love
15 thy neighbour as thyself. But if ye bite and devour
one another, take heed that ye be not consumed one
of another.

16 ᵇ Now ᵈ I say then, Walk in the Spirit, and ye shall
17 not fulfil the lust of the flesh. For the flesh lusteth
against the Spirit, and the Spirit against the flesh;
ᶜ for ᵈ these are contrary the one to the other: ᵈ in
order that ye may not ᵈ do the things that ye would.
18 But if ye be led of the Spirit, ye are not under the
19 law. Now the works of the flesh are manifest, which
are these; ᵉ⁻ᵈ fornication, uncleanness, lasciviousness,
20 idolatry, witchcraft, hatred, variance, ᶠ emulation,ᴶ
21 wrath, strife, seditions, heresies, envyings, ¹ murders,

ᵃ *omit* your   ᵇ This   ᶜ *and*   ᵈ so that ye cannot
    ᵉ add *adultery*   ᶠ *emulations*

peculiar object of Jewish hatred. The reason seems to be, that it was the symbol of that Gospel which was most opposed to the belief in a Jewish Messiah; that Gospel which was preached by St. Paul among the Gentiles. Even in St. John there are not many allusions to the cross or to the death of Christ, in comparison with the allusions to His birth and life. The Word becoming flesh is the great theme; not the doctrine of the cross, which is spoken of as a sign rather of the exaltation of Christ than of His humiliation. 'As Moses lifted up the serpent;' and 'I, if I be lifted up from the earth, shall draw all men after me.' It is otherwise with St. Paul; that which expresses his innermost feeling respecting the truth, which most perfectly describes the contrast of the Gospel with the world, which is the most complete condemnation of the law, which seems also to be the figure or rather the reality of his own suffering state, is—the cross of Christ.

18. The key to this verse is again given by Rom. vii. The state which the Apostle has been describing is that which he there explains as the state of those under the law. From doing the things they would not men are delivered by the guidance of the Spirit—'the law of the Spirit of life

¹ Reading [φόνοι]

drunkenness, revellings, and such like: of the which I tell you before, as I have also told you in time past, that they which do such things shall not inherit the 22 kingdom of God. But the fruit of the Spirit is love, joy, peace, longsuffering, gentleness, goodness, faith, 23 meekness, temperance: against such there is no law. 24 And they that are Christ's have crucified the flesh 25 with the affections and lusts. If we live in the Spirit, 26 let us also walk in the Spirit. Let us not be desirous of vain glory, provoking one another, envying one another.

6 Brethren, if a man be overtaken in a fault, ye which are spiritual, restore such an one in the spirit of meekness; considering thyself, lest thou also be tempted.

makes them free from the law of sin and death.' The law, sin, death, the struggle of the Spirit against the flesh—all express different aspects of the same condition of human nature, the last extremity of misery and variance with self. From this old man he who is in the Spirit is already free.

22. χαρά, *joy.*] Cp. Rom. xii. 15 χαίρειν μετὰ χαιρόντων. Joy or light-heartedness is, in itself, a Christian duty; it may be regarded as a higher degree of peace, not unconnected with that 'glorying in the Lord' of which the Apostle elsewhere speaks. Gal. vi. 14: 2 Cor. xii, xiii, &c.

εἰρήνη, *peace*] opposed to ἔχθραι, ἔρις, ζῆλος, and therefore primarily signifying peace with man, from which, however, peace towards God is inseparable.

χρηστότης, *gentleness*] is used in the New Testament for goodness, in the sense of kindness or mercy, whether of God or man.

ἀγαθωσύνη, *goodness*] may be distinguished from χρηστότης, as goodness in the sense of probity, from goodness in the sense given in the previous note.

πίστις, *faith.*] As in 1 Cor. xii. 9: 2 Tim. ii. 22, faith is here used, not for the door of all virtues, but for a particular virtue.

6. 1. ὑμεῖς οἱ πνευματικοί,] 'Ye who are spiritual,' opposed to σαρκικοί. Ye who know the truths of the Gospel, and are freed from the law, and live in communion with God and Christ. Spirituality may be described as the unity of moral virtues in God and Christ; it implies a nature in harmony with other men; in harmony with self; judging all men, and judged of no man; above, and also on a level with them. It is not absolutely without parts; like moral virtue in Aristotelian ethics, it admits an idea at least of separation into the several Christian graces, each of which

2 Bear ye one another's burdens, and so ᵍshall ye
3 fulfil ⁋ the law of Christ. For if a man think himself
to be something, when he is nothing, he deceiveth
4 himself. But let every man prove his own work, and
then shall he have rejoicing in himself alone, and not
5 in another. For every man shall bear his own burden.
6 ʰBut ⁋ let him that is taught in the word communicate
7 unto him that teacheth in all good things. Be not
deceived; God is not mocked: for whatsoever a man
8 soweth, that shall he also reap. For he that soweth to
his flesh shall of the flesh reap corruption; but he that
soweth to the Spirit shall of the Spirit reap life ever-
9 lasting. ⁱBut ⁋ let us not be weary in well doing:
10 for in due season we shall reap, if we faint not. As
we have therefore opportunity, let us do good unto
all men, especially unto them who are of the household
of faith.

11 ᵏ See in what large letters ⁋ I have written unto you

<blockquote>
ᵍ <i>fulfil</i>   ʰ <i>omit</i> But   ⁱ And
ᵏ Ye see how large a letter
</blockquote>

implies the whole, as in this passage it is particularized as 'the spirit of meekness.'

6. The obscurity of the precept seems to arise from the delicacy with which the Apostle has stated it. The same thought is in his mind as in the Epistles to the Romans and Corinthians; but in writing to a hostile or alienated communion he does not express himself with equal clearness. Compare 1 Cor. xvi. 3: 2 Cor. viii. 4; also Phil. iv. 17; and for an instance of obscurity arising from a similar cause, 1 Thess. iv. 4, 5. That the duty of making the contribution was urged by him about this time on the Galatian Church,

we know from 1 Cor. xvi. 1: 'As I have given order to the churches of Galatia so do ye.'

11. This curious verse has received several interpretations:—that of the English translation, 'Ye see how large a letter I have written to you with my own hand;' to which it is truly objected that the Greek requires πηλίκα γράμματα ἔγραψα; it may be further added, though the objection is of less weight, that the word γράμματα is not elsewhere used by St. Paul in the sense of a letter. Chrysostom and other Fathers refer the expression to the ill-formed characters which St. Paul had

12 with mine own hand. As many as desire to make
a fair shew in the flesh, they constrain you to be
circumcised; only lest they should suffer persecution
13 for the cross of Christ. For neither they themselves
who are circumcised keep the law; but desire to have
you circumcised, that they may glory in your flesh.
14 But God forbid that I should glory, save in the cross
of our Lord Jesus Christ, by whom the world is
15 crucified unto me, and I unto the world. [1] For in
Christ Jesus neither circumcision [1] is any thing, nor
16 uncircumcision, but a new creature. And as many as

[1] *availeth*

written with his own hand, to attest the genuineness of the Epistle. Such an explanation appears not improbable, although that of Jerome is yet more likely, who takes the aorist for a present. 'See you with what large letters I write with my own hand.' This explanation is put in its most probable point of view, if we suppose the remainder of the Epistle, which stands in no immediate connexion with what has preceded, but is a recapitulation of the whole, to be also written with the Apostle's own hand. He has taken up the pen, and subjoins in a few emphatic sentences the substance of what he had previously dictated. That it was not his usual custom to write himself may be inferred from Rom. xvi. 22, and from the words of 2 Thess. iii. 17 : 'The salutation of me, Paul, *with my own hand,* which is the sign in every Epistle ; so I write.'

13. The precise point of the accusation we do not know ; its general truth is witnessed to by the Church in all ages. Inconsistency rather than consistency is natural to man. He is apt to look with one eye upon this life, even when the other is turned towards God. He finds it hard to be true to himself when the influences of party or interest draw him in different directions. Never, perhaps, since the Gospel came into the world has there been any controversy in which zeal has not at times shaken hands with expediency, or in which some degree of fanaticism has not mingled with some degree of insanity or imposture.

14. κόσμος, *world.*] Cp. above στοιχεῖα τοῦ κόσμου. The reciprocity of the expression is characteristic of the Apostle (comp. 1 Cor. xiii. 12); it implies the completeness of the separation, as we might say, 'He is nothing to me, and I am nothing to him.'

What is meant by being cruci-

[1] Reading ἐν γὰρ χριστῷ Ἰησοῦ οὔτε

ᵐ shall ⁸ walk according to this rule, peace be on them,
17 and mercy, and upon the Israel of God. From henceforth let no man trouble me; for I bear in my body the marks of ⁿ⁻⁸ Jesus.
18 Brethren, the grace of our Lord Jesus Christ be with your spirit. Amen. ᵒ⁻⁸

ᵐ *omit* shall   ⁿ add *the Lord*   ᵒ *Unto the Galatians written from Rome.*

fied to the world? Not certainly being despised by the world, still less despising the world in return, nor yet a mere figure of speech; but whatever is meant by being dead or buried with Christ, or by the life hidden with Christ in God. Language fails to express the contrasted paradoxical notion of the Christian state, which has a truth of feeling even to those who are living in the world.

17. τὰ στίγματα, *the marks.*] The feeling of this verse is anger passing into sorrow. The Apostle rightly thinks that the sufferings which he had endured should give him a kind of sacredness in their eyes. The expression, 'I bear in my body the marks of Jesus,' is of the same kind as 'I am crucified with Christ,' Rom. vi. 6: Gal. ii. 20; or 'I fill up what is behind of the sufferings of Christ in my flesh,' Col. i. 24. Having recently suffered persecution, he felt that this was a new link which bound him to his Lord. The marks which he saw in his flesh, reminded him of the wounds of Christ, perhaps suggesting also the thought that he was His branded slave. There have been those in later ages of the Church, who have by a self-imposed penance borne the marks of the Lord Jesus. In the well-known story of St. Francis of Assisi there is a trace of the influence of these words.

Comp. St. Paul's own record of his sufferings, 2 Cor. xi. 23-33.

ESSAY

ON THE

CHARACTER OF ST. PAUL

Οἴδατε δὲ ὅτι δι' ἀσθένειαν τῆς σαρκὸς εὐηγγελισάμην ὑμῖν τὸ πρότερον, καὶ τὸν πειρασμὸν ὑμῶν ἐν τῇ σαρκί μου οὐκ ἐξουθενήσατε οὐδὲ ἐξεπτύσατε, ἀλλ' ὡς ἄγγελον θεοῦ ἐδέξασθέ με, ὡς χριστὸν Ἰησοῦν.—Gal. iv. 13, 14.

THE narrative of the Gospel gives no full or perfect likeness of the character of the Apostles. Human beings do not admit of being constructed out of a single feature, nor is imagination able to supply details which are really wanting. St. Peter and St. John, the two Apostles whose names are most prominent in the Gospels and early portion of the Acts, both seem to unite two extremes in the same person; the character of St. John combining gentleness with vehemence, almost with fierceness; while in St. Peter we trace rashness and timidity at once, the spirit of freedom at one period of his life, and of narrowness and exclusiveness at another. He is the first to confess, and the first to deny Christ. Himself the captain of the Apostles, and yet wanting in the qualities necessary to constitute a leader. Such extremes may easily meet in the same person; but we do not possess sufficient knowledge to say how they were really reconciled. Each of the twelve Apostles grew up to the fullness of the stature of the perfect man. Even those who to us are little more than names, had individual features as lively as our own contemporaries. But the mention of their sayings or acts on four or five occasions while they followed the footsteps of the Lord on earth, and then on two or three occasions soon after He was taken from them, then once again at an interval of twelve or fourteen years, is not sufficient to enable us to judge of their whole character. We may distinguish Peter from John, or James from either; but we cannot set them up as a study to be compared with each other.

More features appear of the character of St. Paul, yet not sufficient to give a perfect picture. We should lose the individuality which we have, by seeking to idealize and generalize from some more common type of Christian life. It has not been unusual to describe St. Paul as a man of resolute will, of untiring energy, of logical mind, of classic taste. He has been contrasted with the twelve as the educated with the uneducated, the student of Hebrew and Greek learning, brought up in Jerusalem at the feet of Gamaliel, with the fishermen of Galilee 'mending their nets' by the lake. Powers of government have been attributed to him such as were required, and in some instances possessed, by the great leaders of the Church in later ages. He is imagined to have spoken with an accuracy hardly to be found in the systems of philosophers. Not of such an one would the Apostle himself 'have gloried;' he would not have understood the praises of his commentators. It was not the wisdom of this world which he spoke, but 'the hidden wisdom of God in a mystery.' All his life long he felt himself to be one 'whose strength was perfected in weakness;' he was aware of the impression of feebleness which his own appearance and discourse made upon his converts; who was sometimes in weakness and fear and trembling before them, 'having the sentence of death in himself,' and at other times 'in power and the Holy Ghost and in much assurance;' and so far from having one unchanging purpose or insight, that though determined to know one thing only, 'Jesus Christ and Him crucified,' yet in his manner of teaching he wavers between opposite views or precepts in successive verses. He is ever feeling, if haply he may find them, after the hearts of men. He is carried away by sympathy, at times even for his opponents. He is struggling to describe what is in process of revelation to him. 'Rude in speech but not in knowledge,' as he himself says. The life of the Greek language had passed away, and it must have been a matter of effort for him to write in a foreign tongue, perhaps even to write at all; yet he puts together words in his own characteristic way which are full of meaning, though often scattered in confusion over the page. He occasionally lights also on the happiest expressions, stamping old phrases in a new mould, and bringing forth the new out of the treasury of the old. Such are some of the individual traits which he has left in his Epistles; they are traits far more interesting and more like himself than any general image of heroism, or knowledge, or power, or goodness. Whatever other impression he might have made upon us, could we have seen him face to face, there can be little doubt that he would have left the impression of what was remarkable and uncommon.

There are questions which it is interesting to suggest, even when they can never receive a perfect and satisfactory answer. One of these questions may be asked respecting St. Paul: 'What was the relation in which his former life stood to the great fact of his conversion?' He himself, in looking back upon the times in which he persecuted the Church of God, thought of them chiefly as an increasing evidence of the mercy of God, which was afterwards extended to him. It seemed so strange to have been what he had been, and to be what he was. Nor does our own conception of him, in relation to his former self, commonly reach beyond this contrast of the old and new man; the persecutor and the preacher of the Gospel; the young man at whose feet the witnesses against Stephen laid down their clothes, and the same Paul disputing against the Grecians, full of visions and revelations of the Lord, on whom in later life came daily the care of all the Churches.

Yet we cannot but admit also the possibility, or rather

the probable truth of another point of view. It is not unlikely that the struggle which he describes in the seventh chapter of the Romans is the picture of his own heart in the days when he 'verily thought that he ought to do many things contrary to Jesus of Nazareth;' the impression of that earlier state, perhaps the image of the martyr Stephen (Acts xxii. 20), may have remained with him in after-years. For men seem to carry about with them the elements of their former lives; the character or nature which they once were, the circumstance which became a part of them, is not wholly abolished or done away; it remains, 'even in the regenerate,' as a sort of insoluble mass or incumbrance which prevents their freedom of action; in very few, or rather in none, can the old habit have perfect flexure to its new use. Everywhere, in the case of our acquaintance, who may have passed through great changes of opinion or conduct, we see from time to time the old nature which is underneath occasionally coming to the surface. Nor is it irreverent to attribute such remembrances of a former self even to inspired persons. If there were any among the contemporaries of St. Paul who had known him in youth and in age, they would have seen similarities which escape us in the character of the Apostle at different periods of his life. The zealot against the Gospel might have seemed to them transfigured into the opponent of the law; they would have found something in common in the Pharisee of the Pharisees, and the man who had a vow on his last journey to Jerusalem; they would perhaps have observed arguments, or quotations, or modes of speech in his writings which had been familiar to them and him in the school of Gamaliel. And when they heard of his conversion, they might have remarked that to one of his temperament only could such an event have happened, and would have noted many superficial resemblances which showed him to be the same man, while the great inward change which had overspread the world was hid from their eyes.

The gifts of God to man have ever some reference to natural disposition. He who becomes the servant of God does not thereby cease to be himself. Often the transition is greater in appearance than in reality, from the suddenness of its manifestation. There is a kind of rebellion against self and nature and God, which, through the mercy of God to the soul, seems almost necessarily to lead to reaction. Persons have been worse than their fellow-men in outward appearance, and yet there was within them the spirit of a child waiting to return home to their father's house. A change passes upon them which we may figure to ourselves, not only as the new man taking the place of the old, but as the inner man taking the place of the outer. So complex is human nature, that the very opposite to what we are has often an inexpressible power over us. Contrast is not only a law of association; it is also a principle of action. Many run from one extreme to another, from licentiousness to the ecstasy of religious feeling, from religious feeling back to licentiousness, not without a 'fearful looking for of judgment.' If we could trace the hidden workings of good and evil, they would appear far less surprising and more natural than as they are seen by the outward eye. Our spiritual nature is without spring or chasm, but it has a certain play or freedom which leads very often to consequences the opposite of what we expect. It seems in some instances as if the same religious education had tended to contrary results; in one case to a devout life, in another to a reaction against it; sometimes to one form of faith, at other times to another. Many parents have wept to see the early religious training of their children draw them, by a kind of repulsion, to a communion or mode of opinion which is the extreme opposite of that in which they have been brought up. Let them have peace in the thought that it was not always in their power to fulfil the duty in which they seem to themselves to have failed. These latter reflections have but a remote bearing on the character of St. Paul ; but they serve to make us think that all spiritual influences, however antagonistic they may appear, have more in common with each other than they have with the temper of the world ; and that it is easier to pass from one form of faith to another than from leading the life of all men to either. There is more in common between those who anathematize each other than between either and the spirit of toleration which characterizes the ordinary dealings of man and man, or much more the spirit of Christ, for whom they are alike contending.

Perhaps we shall not be far wrong in concluding, that those who have undergone great religious changes have been of a fervid imaginative cast of mind ; looking for more in this world than it was capable of yielding; easily touched by the remembrance of the past, or inspired by some ideal of the future. When with this has been combined a zeal for the good of their fellow-men, they have become the heralds and champions of the religious movements of the world. The change has begun within, but has overflowed without them. 'When thou art converted, strengthen thy brethren,' is the order of nature and of grace. In secret they brood over their own state ; weary and profitless their soul fainteth within them. The religion they profess is a religion not of life to them, but of death ; they lose their interest in the world, and are cut off from the communion of their fellow-creatures. While they are musing, the fire kindles, and at the last—'they speak with their tongue.' Then pours forth irrepressibly the pent-up stream—'unto all and upon all' their fellow-men ; the intense flame of inward enthusiasm warms and lights up the world. First they are the evidence to others ; then, again, others are the evidence to them. All religious leaders cannot be reduced to a single type of character ; yet in all, perhaps, two characteristics may be observed ; the first, great self-reflection ; the second, intense sympathy with other men. They are not the creatures of habit or of circumstances, leading a blind life, unconscious of what they are; their whole effort is to realize their inward nature, and to make it palpable and visible to their fellows. Unlike other men who are confined to the circle of themselves or of their family, their affections are never straitened; they embrace with their love all men who are like-minded with them, almost all men too who are unlike them, in the hope that they may become like.

Such men have generally appeared at favourable conjunctures of circumstances, when the old was about to vanish away, and the new to appear. The world has yearned towards them, and they towards the world. They have uttered what all men were feeling; they have interpreted the age to itself. But for the concurrence of circumstances, they might have been stranded on the solitary shore, they might have died without a follower or convert. But when the world has needed them, and God has intended them for the world, they are endued with power from on high; they use all other men as their instruments, uniting them to themselves.

Often such men have been brought up in the faith which they afterwards oppose, and a part of their power has consisted in their acquaintance with the enemy. They see other men, like themselves formerly, wandering out of the way in the idol's temple, amid a burdensome ceremonial, with prayers and sacrifices unable to free the soul. They lead them by the way themselves came to the home of Christ. Sometimes they represent the new as the truth of the old; at other times as contrasted with it, as life and death, as good and evil, as Christ and anti-Christ. They relax the force of habit, they melt the pride and fanaticism of the soul. They suggest to others their own doubts, they inspire them with their own hopes, they supply their own motives, they draw men to them with cords of sympathy and bonds of love; they themselves seem a sufficient stay to support the world. Such was Luther at the

Reformation; such, in a higher sense, was the Apostle
St. Paul.

There have been heroes in the world, and there have
been prophets in the world. The first may be divided into
two classes; either they have been men of strong will and
character, or of great power and range of intellect; in a few
instances, combining both. They have been the natural
leaders of mankind, compelling others by their acknowledged
superiority as rulers and generals; or in the paths of science
and philosophy, drawing the world after them by a yet
more inevitable necessity. The prophet belongs to another
order of beings: he does not master his thoughts; they
carry him away. He does not see clearly into the laws
of this world or the affairs of this world, but has a light
beyond, which reveals them partially in their relation to
another. Often he seems to be at once both the weakest
and the strongest of men; the first to yield to his own
impulses, the mightiest to arouse them in others. Calmness,
or reason, or philosophy are not the words which describe
the appeals which he makes to the hearts of men. He
sways them to and fro rather than governs or controls them.
He is a poet, and more than a poet, the inspired teacher of
mankind; but the intellectual gifts which he possesses are
independent of knowledge, or learning, or capacity; what
they are much more akin to is the fire and subtlety of
genius. He, too, for a time, has ruled kingdoms and even
led armies; 'an Apostle, not of man, nor by men;' acting,
not by authority or commission of any prince, but by an
immediate inspiration from on high, communicating itself
to the hearts of men.

Saul of Tarsus is called an Apostle rather than a prophet,
because Hebrew prophecy belongs to an age of the world
before Christianity. Now that in the Gospel that which
is perfect is come, that which is in part is done away. Yet,
in a secondary sense, the Apostle St. Paul is also 'among
the prophets.' He, too, has 'visions and revelations of the

Lord,' though he has not written them down 'for our instruction,' in which he would fain glory because they are not his own. Even to the outward eye he has the signs of a prophet. There is in him the same emotion, the same sympathy, the same 'strength made perfect in weakness,' the same absence of human knowledge, the same subtlety in the use of language, the same singleness in the delivery of his message. He speaks more as a man, and less immediately under the impulse of the Spirit of God; more to individuals, and less to the nation at large; he is less of a poet, and more of a teacher or preacher. But these differences do not interfere with the general resemblance. Like Isaiah, he bids us look to 'the man of sorrows;' like Ezekiel, he arouses men to a truer sense of the ways of God in his dealings with them; like Jeremiah, he mourns over his countrymen; like all the prophets who have ever been, he is lifted above this world, and is 'in the Spirit at the day of the Lord.' (Rev. i. 10.)

Reflections of this kind are suggested by the absence of materials such as throw any light on the early life of St. Paul. All that we know of him before his conversion is summed up in two facts, 'that the witnesses laid down their clothes with a young man whose name was Saul,' and that he was brought up at the feet of Gamaliel, one of the few Rabbinical teachers of Greek learning in the city of Jerusalem. We cannot venture to assign to him either the 'choleric' or the 'melancholic' temperament. [Tholuck.] We are unable to determine what were his natural gifts or capacities; or how far, as we often observe to be the case, the gifts which he had were called out by the mission on which he was sent, or the theatre on which he felt himself placed 'a spectacle to the world, to angels, and to men.' Far more interesting is it to trace the simple feelings with which he himself regarded his former life. 'Last of all he was seen of me also, who am the least of the Apostles, that am not worthy to be called an Apostle, because I persecuted the Church of God.' Yet there was a sense also [in which it is true] that he was excusable, and that this was the reason why the mercy of God extended itself to him. 'Yet I obtained mercy because I did it ignorantly in unbelief.' And in one passage he dwells on the fact, not only that he had been an Israelite, but more, that after the strictest sect of the Jews' religion he lived a Pharisee, as though that were an evidence to himself, and should be so to others, that no human power could have changed him ; that he was no half Jew, who had never properly known what the law was, but one who had both known and strictly practised it.

We are apt to judge extraordinary men by our own standard ; that is to say, we often suppose them to possess, in an extraordinary degree, those qualities which we are conscious of in ourselves or others. This is the easiest way of conceiving their characters, but not the truest. They differ in kind rather than in degree. Even to understand them truly seems to require a power analogous to their own. Their natures are more subtle, and yet more simple, than we readily imagine. No one can read the ninth chapter of the First, or the eleventh and twelfth chapters of the Second Epistle to the Corinthians, without feeling how different the Apostle St. Paul must have been from good men among ourselves. We marvel how such various traits of character come together in the same individual. He who was 'full of visions and revelations of the Lord,' who spake with tongues more than they all, was not 'mad, but uttered the words of truth and soberness.' He who was the most enthusiastic of all men, was also the most prudent; the Apostle of freedom, and yet the most moderate. He who was the strongest and most enlightened of all men, was also (would he have himself refrained from saying ?) at times the weakest ; on whom there came the care of all the Churches, yet seeming also to lose the power of acting in the absence of human sympathy.

Qualities so like and unlike are hard to reconcile; perhaps they have never been united in the same degree in any other human being. The contradiction in part arises not only from the Apostle being an extraordinary man, but from his being a man like ourselves in an extraordinary state. Creation was not to him that fixed order of things which it is to us; rather it was an atmosphere of evil just broken by the light beyond. To us the repose of the scene around contrasts with the turmoil of man's own spirit; to the Apostle peace was to be sought only from within, half hidden even from the inner man. There was a veil upon the heart itself which had to be removed. He himself seemed to fall asunder at times into two parts, the flesh and the spirit; and the world to be divided into two hemispheres, the one of the rulers of darkness, the other bright with that inward presence which should one day be revealed. In this twilight he lived. What to us is far off both in time and place, if such an expression may be allowed, to him was near and present, separated by a thin film from the world we see, ever ready to break forth and gather into itself the frame of nature. That sense of the invisible which to most men it is so difficult to impart, was like a second nature to St. Paul. He walked by faith, and not by sight; what was strange to him was the life he now led; which in his own often repeated language was death rather than life, the place of shadows and not of realities. The Greek philosophers spoke of a world of phenomena, of true being, of knowledge and opinion; and we know that what they meant by these distinctions is something different from the tenets of any philosophical school of the present day. But not less different is what St. Paul meant by the life hidden with Christ and God, the communion of the Spirit, the possession of the mind of Christ; only that this was not a mere difference of speculation, but of practice also. Could any one say now— 'the life' not that I live, but that 'Christ liveth in me'?

Such language with St. Paul is no mere phraseology, such as is repeated from habit in prayers, but the original consciousness of the Apostle respecting his own state. Self is banished from him, and has no more place in him, as he goes on his way to fulfil the work of Christ. No figure is too strong to express his humiliation in himself, or his exaltation in Christ.

Could we expect this to be otherwise when we think of the manner of his conversion? Could he have looked upon the world with the same eyes that we do, or heard its many voices with the same ears, who had been caught up into the third heaven, whether in the body or out of the body he could not tell? (2 Cor. xii. 1–5.) Must not his life have seemed to him a revelation, an inspiration, an ecstasy? Once and again he had seen the face of Christ, and heard Him speak from heaven. All that followed in the Apostle's history was the continuation of that first wonder, a stream of light flowing from it, 'planting eyes' in his soul, transfiguring him 'from glory to glory,' clothing him with the elect 'in the exceeding glory.'

Yet this glory was not that of the princes of this world, 'who come to nought;' it is another image which he gives us of himself;—not the figure on Mars' hill, in the cartoons of Raphael, nor the orator with noble mien and eloquent gesture before Festus and Agrippa; but the image of one lowly and cast down, whose 'bodily presence was weak, and speech contemptible;' of one who must have appeared to the rest of mankind like a visionary, pierced by the thorn in the flesh, 'waiting for the redemption of the body.' The saints of the middle ages are in many respects unlike St. Paul, and yet many of them bear a far closer resemblance to him than is to be found in Luther and the Reformers. The points of resemblance which we seem to see in them, are the same withdrawal from the things of earth, the same ecstasy, the same consciousness of the person of Christ. Who would describe Luther by the words 'crucified with

Christ?' It is in another manner that the Reformer was called upon to war, with weapons earthly as well as spiritual, with a strong right hand and a mighty arm.

There have been those who, although deformed by nature, have worn the expression of a calm and heavenly beauty; in whom the flashing eye has attested the presence of thought in the poor withered and palsied frame. There have been others again, who have passed the greater part of their lives in extreme bodily suffering, who have, nevertheless, directed states or led armies, the keenness of whose intellect has not been dulled nor their natural force of mind abated. There have been those also on whose faces men have gazed 'as upon the face of an angel,' while they pierced or stoned them. Of such an one, perhaps, the Apostle himself might have gloried; not of those whom men term great or noble. He who felt the whole creation groaning and travailing together until now was not like the Greek drinking in the life of nature at every pore. He who through Christ was 'crucified to the world, and the world to him,' was not in harmony with nature, nor nature with him. The manly form, the erect step, the fullness of life and beauty, could not have gone along with such a consciousness as this, any more than the taste for literature and art could have consisted with the thought, 'not many wise, not many learned, not many mighty.' Instead of these we have the visage marred more than the sons of men, 'the cross of Christ which was to the Greeks foolishness,' the thorn in the flesh, the marks in the body of the Lord Jesus.

Often the Apostle St. Paul has been described as a person the furthest removed from enthusiasm; incapable of spiritual illusion; by his natural temperament averse to credulity or superstition. By such considerations as these a celebrated author confesses himself to have been converted to the belief in Christianity. And yet, if it is intended to reduce St. Paul to the type of what is termed 'good sense' in the present day, it must be admitted that the view which thus describes him is but partially true. Far nearer the truth is that other quaint notion of a modern writer, 'that St. Paul was the finest gentleman that ever lived;' for no man had nobler forms of courtesy, or a deeper regard for the feelings of others. But 'good sense' is a term not well adapted to express either the individual or the age and country in which he lived. He who wrought miracles, who had handkerchiefs carried to him from the sick, who spake with tongues more than they all, who lived amid visions and revelations of the Lord, who did not appeal to the Gospel as a thing long settled, but himself saw the process of revelation actually going on before his eyes, and communicated it to his fellow-men, could never have been such an one as ourselves. Nor can we pretend to estimate whether, in the modern sense of the term, he was capable of weighing evidence, or how far he would have attempted to sever between the workings of his own mind and the Spirit which was imparted to him.

What has given rise to this conception of the Apostle's character has been the circumstance, that with what the world terms mysticism and enthusiasm are united a singular prudence and moderation, and a perfect humanity, searching the feelings and knowing the hearts of all men. 'I became all things to all men that I might win some;' not only, we may believe, as a sort of accommodation, but as the expression of the natural compassion and love which he felt for them. There is no reason to suppose that the Apostle took any interest in the daily life of men, in the great events which were befalling the Roman Empire, or in the temporal fortunes of the Jewish people. But when they came before him as sinners, lying in darkness and the shadow of God's wrath, ignorant of the mystery that was being revealed before their eyes, then his love was quickened for them, then they seemed to him as his kindred and brethren; there was no sacrifice too great for him to make; he was willing to die with Christ, yea, even to be accursed from Him that he might 'save some of them.'

Mysticism, or enthusiasm, or intense benevolence and philanthropy, seem to us, as they commonly are, at variance with worldly prudence and moderation. But in the Apostle these different and contrasted qualities are mingled and harmonized. The mother watching over the life of her child, has all her faculties aroused and stimulated; she knows almost by instinct how to say or do the right thing at the right time; she regards his faults with mingled love and sorrow. So, in the Apostle, we seem to trace a sort of refinement or nicety of feeling, when he is dealing with the souls of men. All his knowledge of mankind shows itself for their sakes; and yet not that knowledge of mankind which comes from without, revealing itself by experience of men and manners, by taking a part in events, by the insensible course of years making us learn from what we have seen and suffered. There is another experience that comes from within, which begins with the knowledge of self, with the consciousness of our own weakness and infirmities; which is continued in love to others and in works of good to them; which grows by singleness and simplicity of heart. Love becomes the interpreter of how men think, and feel, and act; and supplies the place of, or passes into a worldly prudence wiser than, the prudence of this world. Such is the worldly prudence of St. Paul.

Once more; there is in the Apostle, not only prudence and knowledge of the human heart, but a kind of subtlety of moderation, which considers every conceivable case, and balances one with another; in the last resort giving no rule, but allowing all to be superseded by a more general principle. An instance of this subtle moderation is his determination, or rather omission to determine the question of meats and drinks, which he first regards as indifferent, secondly, as depending on men's own conscience, and this again as limited by the consciences of others, and lastly resolves all these finer precepts into the general principle, 'Whatever ye do, do all to the glory of God.' The same qualification of one principle by another recurs again in his rules respecting marriage. First, 'do not marry unbelievers,' and 'let not the wife depart from her husband.' But if you are married and the unbeliever is willing to remain, then the spirit of the second precept must prevail over the first. Only in an extreme case, where both parties are willing to dissolve the tie, the first principle in turn may again supersede the second. It may be said in the one case, 'your children are holy;' in the other, 'What knowest thou, O wife, if thou shalt save thy husband?' In a similar spirit he withdraws his censure on the Corinthian offender, lest such an one, criminal as he was, should be swallowed up with overmuch sorrow. There is a religious aspect of either course of conduct, and either may be right under given circumstances. So the kingdoms of this world admit of being regarded almost as the kingdom of God, in reference to our duties towards their rulers; and yet touching the going to law before unbelievers, we are to think rather of that other kingdom in which we shall judge angels.

The Gospel, it has been often remarked, lays down principles rather than rules. The passages in the Epistles of St. Paul which seem to be exceptions to this statement, are exceptions in appearance rather than in reality. They are relative to the circumstances of those whom he is addressing. He who became 'all things to all men,' would have been the last to insist on temporary regulations for his converts being made the rule of Christian life in all ages. His manner of Church government is so unlike a rule or law, that we can hardly imagine how the Apostle, if he could return to earth, would combine the freedom of the Gospel with the requirements of Christianity as an established institution. He is not a bishop administering a regular system, but a person dealing immediately with other persons out of the fullness of his own mind and nature. His writings are like spoken words, temporary, occasional, adapted to other men's thoughts and feelings, yet not without an eternal meaning. In sending his instructions to the Churches he is ever with them, and seems to follow in his mind's eye their working and effect ; whither his Epistles go he goes in thought, absent, in his own language, 'in the body, but present in spirit.' What he says to the Churches, he seems to make them say : what he directs them to do, they are to do in that common spirit in which they are united with him ; if they live he lives ; time and distance never snap the cord of sympathy. His government of them is a sort of communion with them ; a receiving of their feelings and a pouring forth of his own : he is the heart or pulse which beats through the Christian world.

And with this communion of himself and his converts, this care of daily life, there mingles the vision of 'the great family in heaven and earth,' 'the Church which is his body,' in which the meaner reality is enfolded or wrapt up, 'sphered in a radiant cloud,' even in its low estate. The language of the Epistles often exercises an illusion on our minds when thinking of the primitive Church ; individuals perhaps there were who truly partook of that light with which the Apostle encircled them ; there may have been those in the Churches of Corinth, or Ephesus, or Galatia, who were living on earth the life of heaven. But the ideal which fills the Apostle's mind has not, necessarily, a corresponding fact in the actual state of his converts. The beloved family of the Apostle, the Church of which such 'glorious things are told,' is often in tumult and disorder. His love is constantly a source of pain to him : he watches over them 'with a godly jealousy,' and finds them 'affecting others rather than himself.' They are always liable to be 'spoiled' by some vanity of philosophy, some remembrance of Judaism, which, like an epidemic, carries off whole Churches at once, and seems to exercise a fatal power over them. He is a father harrowed and agonized in his feelings; he loves more and suffers more than other men; he will not think, he cannot help thinking, of the ingratitude and insolence of his children; he tries to believe, he is persuaded, that all is well; he denounces, he forgives; he defends himself, he is ashamed of defending himself; he is the herald of his own deeds when others neglect or injure him; he is ashamed of this too, and retires into himself, to be at peace with Christ and God. So we seem to read the course of the Apostle's thoughts in more than one passage of his writings, beginning with the heavenly ideal, and descending to the painful realities of actual life, especially at the close of the Second Epistle to the Corinthians — altogether, perhaps, the most characteristic picture of the Apostle's mind; and in the last words to the Galatians, 'Henceforth let no man trouble me, for I bear in my body the marks of the Lord Jesus.'

Great men (those, at least, who present to us the type of earthly greatness) are sometimes said to possess the power of command, but not the power of entering into the feelings of others. They have no fear of their fellows, they are not affected by their opinions or prejudices, but neither are they always capable of immediately impressing them, or of perceiving the impression which their words or actions make upon them. Often they live in a kind of solitude on which other men do not venture to intrude; putting forth their strength on particular occasions, careless or abstracted about the daily concerns of life. Such was not the greatness of the Apostle St. Paul; not only in the sense in which he says that 'he could do all things through Christ,' but in a more earthly and human one, was it true, that his strength was his weakness and his weakness his strength. His dependence on others was also the source of his influence over them. His natural character was the type of that communion of the Spirit which he preached; the meanness of appearance which he attributes to himself, the image of that contrast which the Gospel presents to human greatness. Glorying and humiliation ; life and death ; a vision of angels strengthening him, the 'thorn in the flesh' rebuking him ; the greatest tenderness, not without sternness ; sorrows above measure, consolations above measure ; are some of the contradictions which were reconciled in the same man. It is not a long life of ministerial success on which he is looking back a little before his death, where he says, 'I have fought the good fight, I have finished my course, I have kept the faith.' These words are sadly illustrated by another verse of the same Epistle, 'This thou knowest, that all they which are in Asia be turned away from me.' (2 Tim. i. 15.) So when the contrast was at its height, he passed away, rejoicing in persecution also, and 'filling up that which was behind of the afflictions of Christ for his body's sake.' Many, if not most, of his followers had forsaken him, and there is no certain memorial of the manner of his death.

Let us look once more a little closer at that 'visage marred' in his Master's service, as it appeared about three years before on a well-known scene. A poor aged man, worn by some bodily or mental disorder, who had been often scourged, and bore on his face the traces of indignity and sorrow in every form--such an one, led out of prison between Roman soldiers, probably at times faltering in his utterance, the creature, as he seemed to spectators, of nervous sensibility ; yearning, almost with a sort of fondness, to save the souls of those whom he saw around him[1]—spoke a few eloquent words in the cause of Christian truth, at which kings were awed, telling the tale of his own conversion with such simple pathos, that after-ages have hardly heard the like.

Such is the image, not which Christian art has delighted to consecrate, but which the Apostle has left in his own

[1] Gal. ii. 20; iv. 14; vi. 17: 1 Cor. xv. 32: 2 Cor. i. 9; vi. 12 ; x. 10; xi. 23-27 ; xii. 7-10 : Philem. ver. 9.

writings of himself; an image of true wisdom, and nobleness, and affection, but of a wisdom unlike the wisdom of this world; of a nobleness which must not be transformed into that of the heroes of the world; an affection which seemed to be as strong and as individual towards all mankind, as other men are capable of feeling towards a single person.

ON THE QUOTATIONS

FROM

THE OLD TESTAMENT IN THE WRITINGS OF ST. PAUL

———••———

THE New Testament 'is ever old, and the Old is ever entwined with the New.' Not only are the types of the Old Testament shadows of good things to come; not only are the narratives of events and lives of persons in Jewish history 'written for our instruction;' not only is there a deep-rooted identity of the Old and New Testament in the revelation of one God of perfect justice and truth; not only is 'the law fulfilled in Christ to all them that believe;' not only are the spiritual Israel the true people of God, and the taking of Jerusalem a figure of the end of the world: a nearer though more superficial connexion is formed by the volume of the Old Testament itself, which, like some closely-fitting vesture, enfolds the new as well as the old dispensation in its language and imagery, the words themselves, as well as the thoughts contained in them, becoming instinct with a new life, and seeming to interpenetrate with the Gospel.

This verbal connexion of new and old is not peculiar to Christianity. All nations who have ancient writings have endeavoured to read in them the riddle of the past. The Brahmin, repeating his Vedic hymns, sees them pervaded by a thousand meanings, which have been handed down by tradition: the one of which he is ignorant is that which we perceive to be the true one. Without more reason, and almost with equal disregard or neglect of its natural import, the Jewish Alexandrian and Rabbinical writers analysed the Old Testament; in a similar spirit Gnostics and Neoplatonists cited lines of Homer or Pindar. Not unlike is the way in which the Fathers cite both the Old and New Testament; and the manner in which the writers of the New Testament quote from the Old has more in common with this last than with modern critical interpretations of either. That is to say, the quotations are made almost without reference to the connexion in which they originally occur, and in a different sense from that in which the prophet or psalmist intended them. They are fragments culled out and brought into some new combination; jewels, and precious stones, and corner-stones disposed after a new pattern, to be the ornaments of another temple. It is their place in the new temple, not their relation to the old, which gives them their effect and meaning.

Such tessellated work was after the manner of the age: it was no invention or introduction of the sacred writers. Closely as it is wrought into the New Testament, it belongs to its externals rather than to its true life. All religions which are possessed of sacred books, and many which are without them, have passed through a like secondary stage, although the relation of the earlier to the later form of the same religions may have been quite different from that in which the Gospel stands to the Old Testament. In heathenism, as well as Christianity, language has played a great part in connecting the old and the new. There seem to be times in which human nature yearns towards the past, though it has lost the power of interpreting it. Overlooking the chasm of a thousand years, it seeks to extract from ancient writings food for daily life. The mystery of a former world lies heavy upon it, hardly less than of the future, and it lightens this burden by attributing to 'them of old time' the thoughts and feelings of contemporaries. It feels the unity of God and man in all ages, and attempts to prove this unity by reading the same thoughts in every word which has been uttered from the beginning. A new spirit takes possession of the words, and imperceptibly alters them into accordance with itself.

The Gnostic and Alexandrian writings furnish a meeting-point between the past and future in which the present is lost sight of, and ideas supersede facts. But something analogous is observable in the New Testament itself; which may be described also as the confluence of past and future on the ground of the present, the person of Christ and 'the Church which is his body' being the centre in which they meet. Some Divine heat or force welds together the old and new. The scattered rays of prophecy are collected in one focus. Language becomes plastic and refashions itself on a new type. Gradually and naturally, as it were a soul entering into a body that had been prepared for it, the new takes the form of the old. The truth and moral power of the Gospel prevent this new formation from resembling the fantastic process of Eastern heresy. The writers of the New Testament use the modes of speech of their contemporaries, but they also ennoble and enlighten them. That traces of their age should appear in them is the necessary condition of their speaking to the men of their age. 'The water of life' was not to be strained through the sieve of grammar and logic; nor is it conceivable how a Gospel could have been 'preached to the poor' which was founded on a critical interpretation of the Old Testament.

But although the quotations from the Old Testament in the New conform to the manner of the age, and have a superficial similarity with the use of Homer or Pindar in later classical authors, essential differences lie beneath. First, the connexion is not, as in the case of heathen authors, merely accidental; the Old Testament looks forward to the New, as the New Testament looks backward on the Old. Reading the psalmists or prophets, we feel that they were pilgrims and strangers, hoping for more than was on the earth, whose sadness was not yet turned into joy. There are passages in which the Old Testament goes beyond itself, in which it almost seems to renounce itself; 'lively oracles' of which it might be said, either in Christian or heathen language, 'that it speaks not of itself;' or, that 'its voice reaches to a thousand years.' It is otherwise with heathen literature. There is no future to which Homer or Hesiod looked forward; no moral truth beyond themselves which they dimly see. The life of the world was not to awaken in their song. They were poetry only, out of which came statues of gods and heroes. The deeper reverence for the 'volume of the book' may be in part the reason why the half-understood words of the Old Testament exercise a greater power over the mind. But the mere application of them is also a new creation. They are not dead and withered fragments of the wisdom of ancient times; the force of the new truth which they express reanimates and reillumines them. Secondly, if we admit that the superficial connexion between the Old and New Testament is arbitrary, or, more properly speaking, after the manner of the age, there is a deeper connexion also which is founded on reason and conscience. The language of the Psalms and prophets is the natural voice of Christian feeling. In the hour of sorrow, or joy, or repentance, or triumph, we turn to the Old Testament quite as readily as to the New. Thirdly, a difference in kind is observable between the use which is made of quotations by the Alexandrian writers and in the New Testament. In the one they are the form of thought; in the other the mode of expression. That is to say, while in the one they exercise an influence on the thought; in the other they are controlled by it, and are but a sort of incrustation on it, or ornament of it; in some cases the illustration or allegory through which it is conveyed. The writings of St. Paul are not the less one in feeling and spirit, because the language in which he continually clothes his thoughts is either avowedly or unconsciously taken from the Old Testament.

It is remarkable that the Old Testament in many places is built up out of its own materials, in the same way as the New out of the Old. Later Psalms repeat the language of earlier ones; successive prophets use the same words and images, and deliver the same precepts. For example, Jeremiah and the later Isaiah both speak of 'the Lamb led to the slaughter;' and Jeremiah and Ezekiel alike revoke the old 'proverb in the house of Israel.' The Book of Deuteronomy, especially, is full of prophetic elements, either received from or communicated to the later prophets. Instead of the repetition being wearisome or unmeaning, it adds to the depth and power of the words that they are not used for the first time. No happy combination of new language could have imparted to them the weight which they derive from associations of the past. In like manner the portions of the New Testament in which the verbal connexion with the Old is most striking, such as the Epistle to the Hebrews, and the fifteenth chapter of 1 Corinthians, are also those which are most awful and impressive to us. It is a circumstance not always attended to by commentators on the Apocalypse (at any rate by English ones), that this wonderful book is a mosaic of Old Testament thoughts and words, the pieces of which are put together on a new and glorious pattern. A glance at the marginal references is sufficient to show in how subtle a manner they are interlaced. The inspired author is not merely narrating a new vision which he had seen and heard, to be added to the former visions of Ezekiel or Daniel; but he is collecting and bringing together the scattered elements of prophecy and sacred imagery in one last vision or revelation of the day of the Lord. The kingdom of God is not at a distance; it already exists; it has gathered to itself the figures and glories of the Old Testament. Many of the apocryphal writings exhibit signs of the same imitation; they borrow the imagery of the elder prophets. But none of them are inspired with the faith or power which conceives the glorious things that have been said as a living reality.

Perhaps it may be thought paradoxical that the words of the Old Testament should receive a new meaning in the Epistles, and also retain their original power and sacredness; yet in our own use of quotations a similar inconsistency may be observed. For, not only in ancient but in modern times, a certain waywardness is discernible in the application of the words of others. Quotation, with ourselves, is an ingenious device for expressing our meaning in a pointed or forcible manner; it implies also an appeal to an authority. And its point frequently consists in a slight, or even a great, deviation from the sense in which the words quoted were uttered by their author. Its aptness lies in being at once old and new; often in bringing into juxtaposition things so remote, that we should not have imagined they were connected; sometimes in a word rather than in a sentence, or in the substitution of one word for another; nor is its force diminished if it lead to a logical inference not strictly warranted. In like manner the quotations of the New Testament are at once new and old. They unite a kind of authority and antiquity with a new interpretation of the passage quoted. Sometimes the application of them is a sort of argument from their exact rhetorical or even grammatical form. Their connexion often hangs upon a word, and there are passages in which the word on which the connexion turns is itself inserted. There are citations too, which are a composition of more than one passage, in which the spirit is taken from one and the words from another. There are other citations in which a similarity of spirit, rather than of language, is caught up and made use of by the Apostle. There are passages which are altered to suit the meaning given to them; or in which the spirit of the New Testament is substituted for that of the Old; or the spirit of the Old Testament expands into that of the New. Lastly, there are a few passages which have one sense in the Old Testament, and have an entirely different or opposite one in the New. Almost all gradations occur between exact verbal correspondence with the Greek of the LXX and discrepancy in which resemblance is all but lost; between the greatest similarity and difference, even opposition, of spirit in the original passage and its application. The first connexion is nearly always lost sight of; only in Rom. iv. 10 it is referred to generally, and in Rom. xi. 4 imperfectly remembered.

The quotations in the writings of St. Paul may be classified under the following heads:—

i. Passages in which the meaning or the words of the Old Testament are altered, or both; the alterations sometimes arising from a composition of passages; in other instances from an adaptation of the text quoted to its new context. In one case a verse of the Old Testament is repeated with variations in two places. See Rom. xi. 34: 1 Cor. ii. 16.

ii. Passages in which the spirit or the language of the Old Testament is exactly retained, or with no greater variation of words than may be supposed to arise out of difference of texts, and no greater diversity of spirit than necessarily arises from the transfer of any passage in the Old Testament into another connexion in the New. To which may be added—

iii. Passages which contain latent or unacknowledged quotations.

iv. Allegorical passages.

i. (1) An instance in which the meaning of the quotation has been altered, and also in which the new meaning given to it is derived from another passage, occurs in Rom. ii. 24

τὸ γὰρ ὄνομα τοῦ θεοῦ δι' ὑμᾶς βλασφημεῖται ἐν τοῖς ἔθνεσιν, where the Apostle is speaking of the scandal caused by the violence and hypocrisy of the Jews. The words are taken from Isa. lii. 5 δι' ὑμᾶς διαπαντὸς τὸ ὄνομά μου βλασφημεῖται ἐν τοῖς ἔθνεσι; where, however, they refer not to the sins of the house of Israel, but to their sufferings at the hand of their enemies. The turn which the Apostle has given the passage is gathered from Ezek. xxxvi. 21–23 καὶ ἐφεισάμην αὐτῶν διὰ τὸ ὄνομά μου τὸ ἅγιον, ὃ ἐβεβήλωσαν οἶκος Ἰσραὴλ ἐν τοῖς ἔθνεσιν οὗ εἰσήλθοσαν ἐκεῖ, κ.τ.λ.

A composition of passages occurs also in Rom. xi. 8, which appears to be a union of Isa. vi. 9, 10 and xxix. 10. The twenty-sixth and twenty-seventh verses of the same chapter also furnish a singular instance of combination. (Isa. lix. 21 καὶ αὕτη αὐτοῖς ἡ παρ' ἐμοῦ διαθήκη, to which the clause, ὅταν ἀφέλωμαι τὰς ἁμαρτίας αὐτῶν, is added from Isa. xxvii. 9.) The play upon the word ἔθνη (nations = Gentiles) is repeated in Rom. iv. 17 (Gen. xvii. 5): Gal. iii. 8 (Gen. xii. 3): Rom. xv. 11 (Ps. cxvi. 1).

(2) Another instance in which the general tone of a quotation is from one passage, and a few words are added from another, is to be found in Rom. ix. 33 ἰδοὺ τίθημι ἐν Σιὼν λίθον προσκόμματος καὶ πέτραν σκανδάλου καὶ ὁ πιστεύων ἐπ' αὐτῷ οὐ καταισχυνθήσεται. The greater part of this passage occurs in Isa. xxviii. 16 ἰδοὺ ἐγὼ ἐμβάλλω εἰς τὰ θεμέλια Σιὼν λίθον πολυτελῆ ἐκλεκτὸν ἀκρογωνιαῖον, ἔντιμον εἰς τὰ θεμέλια αὐτῆς καὶ ὁ πιστεύων οὐ μὴ καταισχυνθῇ. But the words λίθον προσκόμματος are introduced from Isa. viii. 14. And the remainder of the passage (καὶ ... καταισχυνθήσεται) is really inconsistent with these words, though both parts are harmonized in Him who is in one sense a stumbling-stone and rock of offence; in another a foundation-stone and chief corner-stone.

(3) A slighter example of alteration occurs 1 Cor. iii. 19, where the Apostle quotes from Ps. xciv. 11 κύριος γινώσκει

τοὺς διαλογισμοὺς τῶν σοφῶν ὅτι εἰσὶ μάταιοι. Here the words τῶν σοφῶν are substituted for τῶν ἀνθρώπων in the LXX, which in this passage agrees with the Hebrew. They are required to connect the quotation in the Epistle with the previous verses. A similar instance of the introduction of a word (πᾶς) on which the point of an argument turns, occurs in Rom. x. 11 λέγει γὰρ ἡ γραφή, πᾶς ὁ πιστεύων ἐπ᾽ αὐτῷ οὐ καταισχυνθήσεται, where the addition is the more remarkable, as the Apostle had quoted the verse without πᾶς in the preceding passage (ix. 33). The insertion seems to be suggested by the words of Joel which follow.

(4) Another instance of addition and adaptation is furnished by 1 Cor. xiv. 21 ἐν τῷ νόμῳ γέγραπται ὅτι ἐν ἑτερογλώσσοις καὶ ἐν χείλεσιν ἑτέρων λαλήσω τῷ λαῷ τούτῳ, καὶ οὐδ᾽ οὕτως εἰσακούσονταί μου, λέγει κύριος. This quotation, which is said to be 'written in the law' (comp. John x. 34; xii. 34; xv. 25), is from Isa. xxviii. 11, 12, where the words in the LXX are, διὰ φαυλισμὸν χειλέων, διὰ γλώσσης ἑτέρας, ὅτι λαλήσουσι τῷ λαῷ τούτῳ, and in the English translation, 'with stammering lips and another tongue will he speak unto this people.' But the last words, οὐδ᾽ οὕτως εἰσακούσονται, are taken from the following verse, where a clause nearly similar occurs in a different connexion : λέγοντες αὐτοῖς, τοῦτο τὸ ἀνάπαυμα τῷ πεινῶντι καὶ τοῦτο τὸ σύντριμμα, καὶ οὐκ ἠθέλησαν ἀκούειν v. 12. The whole is referred by the Apostle to the gift of tongues, which he infers from this passage 'to be a sign to unbelievers.'

(5) An adaptation, which has led to an alteration of words, occurs in Rom. x. 6–9 ἡ δὲ ἐκ πίστεως δικαιοσύνη οὕτω λέγει· μὴ εἴπῃς ἐν τῇ καρδίᾳ σου· τίς ἀναβήσεται εἰς τὸν οὐρανόν; τοῦτ᾽ ἔστι χριστὸν καταγαγεῖν; ἢ τίς καταβήσεται εἰς τὴν ἄβυσσον; τοῦτ᾽ ἔστι χριστὸν ἐκ νεκρῶν ἀναγαγεῖν. ἀλλὰ τί λέγει; ἐγγύς σου τὸ ῥῆμά ἐστιν, ἐν τῷ στόματί σου καὶ ἐν τῇ καρδίᾳ σου· τοῦτ᾽ ἔστι τὸ ῥῆμα τῆς πίστεως, ὃ κηρύσσομεν· ὅτι ἐὰν ὁμολογήσῃς ἐν τῷ στόματί σου κύριον

Ἰησοῦν, καὶ πιστεύσῃς ἐν τῇ καρδίᾳ σου ὅτι ὁ θεὸς αὐτὸν ἤγειρεν ἐκ νεκρῶν, σωθήσῃ. The introductory formula in this passage, μὴ εἴπῃς ἐν τῇ καρδίᾳ σου, is taken from Deut. viii. 17; the substance of the remainder is abridged from Deut. xxx. 11-14 ὅτι ἡ ἐντολὴ αὕτη ἣν ἐγὼ ἐντέλλομαί σοι σήμερον οὐχ ὑπέρογκός ἐστιν, οὐδὲ μακρὰν ἀπό σού ἐστιν· οὐκ ἐν τῷ οὐρανῷ ἄνω ἐστί, λέγων, τίς ἀναβήσεται ἡμῖν εἰς τὸν οὐρανόν, καὶ λήψεται ἡμῖν αὐτὴν καὶ ἀκούσαντες αὐτὴν ποιήσομεν; οὐδὲ πέραν τῆς θαλάσσης ἐστί, λέγων, τίς διαπεράσει ἡμῖν εἰς τὸ πέραν τῆς θαλάσσης, καὶ λάβῃ ἡμῖν αὐτήν, καὶ ἀκουστὴν ἡμῖν ποιήσῃ αὐτήν, καὶ ποιήσομεν; ἐγγύς σού ἐστι τὸ ῥῆμα σφόδρα, ἐν τῷ στόματί σου καὶ ἐν τῇ καρδίᾳ σου καὶ ἐν ταῖς χερσί σου ποιεῖν αὐτό. To these verses the Apostle has added what may be termed a running commentary, applying them to Christ. To make the words πέραν τῆς θαλάσσης thus applicable, the Apostle has altered them to εἰς τὴν ἄβυσσον, a change which we should hesitate to attribute to him, but for the other examples which have been already quoted of similar changes. (Compare also Rom. xi. 8; xii. 19: Eph. iv. 8, quoted from Ps. lxvii. 18: Eph. v. 14. The latter passage, in which as here the name of Christ is introduced, is probably an adaptation of Isa. lx. 1.) He has also omitted ἐν ταῖς χερσί, which was not suited to his purpose. Considering the frequency of such changes, it would be contrary to the rules of sound criticism to attribute the introduction of the words to a difference of text in the Old Testament.

(6) An example of a new turn given to a passage from the Old Testament occurs in Rom. xi. 2, 3, where the Apostle has put together in one connexion two verses which are disconnected in the original. In the Book of Kings (1 Kings ix. 15-18), the words, 'I have left to myself seven thousand men who have not bowed the knee to Baal,' are a continuation of the instruction to anoint Jehu and Hazael. But, in the application which the Apostle makes of them, they are quoted as the answer of God to the

complaint of Elijah. The misplacement seems to have arisen from the words, 'I am *left* alone,' and the allusion to the worshippers of Baal. Compare Jus. *Dial.* c. 39, n. 2, 3 ; 46, n. 18.

(7) The words of 1 Cor. xv. 45 οὕτως καὶ γέγραπται· Ἐγένετο ὁ πρῶτος ἄνθρωπος Ἀδὰμ εἰς ψυχὴν ζῶσαν, ὁ ἔσχατος Ἀδὰμ εἰς πνεῦμα ζωοποιοῦν, afford a remarkable instance of discrepancy, both in expression and meaning, from Gen. ii. 7 ἐνεφύσησεν εἰς τὸ πρόσωπον αὐτοῦ πνοὴν ζωῆς καὶ ἐγένετο ὁ ἄνθρωπος εἰς ψυχὴν ζῶσαν ; to the two clauses of which the Apostle appears to have applied a distinction analogous to that which Philo draws (*De Legum Alleg.* i. 12 ; *De Creat. Mun.* 24. 46) between the earthly and the heavenly man (Gen. ii. 7 and i. 27). The words are apparently inconsistent with the twenty-second verse of the same chapter: 'As in Adam all die, even so in Christ shall all be made alive ;' which, in the sense sometimes given them, are also inconsistent with the forty-seventh verse: 'The first man is of the earth, earthy ; the second man is the Lord from heaven.' An instructive parallel to both inconsistencies is offered by the application of the expression of Genesis, 'the image of God,' not only to the regenerate man and to Christ (Col. iii. 10 : 2 Cor. iv. 4), but also to the natural man, or to man in general, without any such allusion, as in 1 Cor. xi. 7. Compare Jas. iii. 9.

(8) A curious instance of a subtle and at the same time strained application of a passage occurs in Gal. iii. 16–19, to which (τῷ σπέρματι) attention has been drawn in the notes. Compare Heb. vii. 1 : 1 Tim. ii. 13, 14.

(9) Cases occur in which the words of the Old Testament are quoted in contrast to the Gospel ; as, for example, the words of Lev. xviii. 5 ἃ ποιήσας αὐτὰ ἄνθρωπος, ζήσεται ἐν αὐτοῖς, repeated in Rom. x. 5 : Gal. iii. 12 : so Deut. xxvii. 26 : in Gal. iii. 10. The first of the two examples affords an instance of a minor peculiarity, viz. disorder introduced into the grammatical construction by quotations.

ii. A good example of the second class of quotations is the passage from Hab. ii. 4 quoted in Rom. i. 17 ὁ δὲ δίκαιος ἐκ πίστεως ζήσεται; which occurs also in two other places, Heb. x. 38 : Gal. iii. 11, which the LXX read, ὁ δὲ δίκαιος ἐκ πίστεώς μου ζήσεται, and the English version translates from the Hebrew, 'but the just shall live by *his* faith.' It is remarkable, that in Rom. i. 17 : Gal. iii. 11, the verse should be quoted in the same manner, and that slightly different, either from the LXX or the Hebrew; in Heb. x. 38 it agrees precisely with the LXX. Like the other great text of the Apostle, 'Abraham believed God, and it was counted to him for righteousness,' which is also repeated three times in the New Testament (Rom. iv. 3 : Gal. iii. 6 : Jas. ii. 23), it offers an example of the way in which the language of the Old Testament is enlarged and universalized in the New; the particular faith of Abraham or of the Israelite becoming the type of faith as opposed to the law. The wider sphere of Messianic prophecy, which extends the promise of the root of Jesse to the Gentiles (Isa. xi. 10), is also appropriated as of right by St. Paul. Here too the meaning is enlarged, as in the application of the words of Isaiah : 'I was found of them that sought me not' (lxv. 1), Rom. x. 20. It is less characteristic of the Apostle, that the predestinarian language of the Old Testament is in some instances transferred by him to the New, as in Rom. ix. 13 after Mal. i. 2, 3 ('Jacob have I loved ; Esau have I hated'), and in Rom. ix. 20 after Isa. xxix. 16. Some of the passages which speak of the vanity of human wisdom are taken from the Old Testament (1 Cor. i. 19, 20 after Isa. xxix. 16 ; xlv. 9).

Other examples of the second class of quotations are such places as the following : 'Blessed is the man whose iniquity is forgiven, and whose sin is pardoned ; blessed is the man to whom the Lord doth not impute sin ;' Rom. iv. 7, from Ps. xxxii. 1, 2. 'The reproaches of them that reproached thee fell on me ;' Rom. xv. 3, from Ps. lxix. 9. 'Who hath believed our report?' Rom. x. 16, from Isa. liii. 1. 'For thy sake we are killed all the day long, we are accounted as sheep for the slaughter,' Ps. xliii. 22, quoted in Rom. viii. 36; in which the instinct of the Apostle has caught the common feeling or spirit of the Old and New Testament, though the texts quoted contain no word which is a symbol of his doctrine.

Passages which might be placed under either head are Rom. x. 13: 'Jacob have I loved, and Esau have I hated,' the words of which exactly agree with the LXX, although their original meaning in Mal. i. 2, 3, whence they are taken, has to do, not with the individuals Jacob and Esau, but with the natives of Edom and Israel: the cento of quotations in Rom. iii. descriptive of the wickedness of the Psalmist's enemies, or of those who were the subjects of the prophetical denunciations, which are transferred by the Apostle to the world in general (compare Justin, *Dial.* c. 27, n. 6, where several of the quotations occur in the same order); Rom. xii. 20: 'Therefore if thine enemy hunger, feed him; if he thirst, give him drink; for in so doing thou shalt heap coals of fire on his head,' the words of which are exactly quoted from the LXX (Prov. xxv. 21, 22), though the meaning given to them is ironical; for which reason the succeeding clause, 'But the Lord shall reward thee,' which would have destroyed the irony, is omitted.

iii. What may be termed latent or unacknowledged quotations vary in extent from whole verses down to single words; there are instances in which mere resemblances of form may be traced, with no word the same. A remarkable example of an entire verse which is thus quoted is furnished by the application of Prov. xxv. 21, 22 (Rom. xii. 20, 'Therefore if thine enemy,' &c.), already referred to. A few words are traceable in Eph. v. 30, also affording a good instance of what may be termed the spiritualization of the natural or physical language of the Old Testament. Gen. ii. 23; xxix. 14 τοῦτο νῦν ὀστοῦν ἐκ τῶν ὀστέων μου, καὶ σὰρξ ἐκ τῆς σαρκός μου; so of Christians, μέλη ἐσμεν τοῦ σώματος αὐτοῦ, ἐκ τῆς σαρκὸς αὐτοῦ καὶ ἐκ τῶν ὀστέων αὐτοῦ. So 1 Cor. x. 20, after Deut. xxxii. 17 : Eph. i. 22 (compare 1 Cor. xv. 27, 28), taken from Ps. viii. 6 ; and without any change of meaning, Eph. iv. 26, from Ps. iv. 4. In like manner, Eph. ii. 13–17 contains a remembrance of Isa. lvii. 19; Eph. vi. 14, 17 of Isa. lix. 17. A single word, ὁ ὄφις ἠπάτησέ με Gen. iii. 13 (which is also quoted 2 Cor. xi. 3), has probably left a trace of itself in the personification of sin, Rom. vii. 11 ἡ ἁμαρτία ἐξηπάτησέ με . . . καὶ ἀπέκτεινε. The verses 2 Cor. vi. 9, 11 contain two examples of verbal allusion. The slightest thread is enough to form a connexion. In 2 Cor. xiii. 1 ἐπὶ στόματος δύο μαρτύρων καὶ τριῶν σταθήσεται πᾶν ῥῆμα, the association which leads the Apostle's mind to the quotation (from Deut. xix. 15 : compare Matt. xviii. 16 : John viii. 17) seems to be only the word τρεῖς, arising out of the circumstance that he has mentioned just before that he is coming to them for the third time. 1 Cor. v. 13 offers another example of the use of the language of the LXX (Deut. xxii. 24), in which the Apostle clothes a command to the Church. The verse 1 Cor. xv. 32, 'Let us eat and drink, for to-morrow we die,' is taken word for word from Isa. xxii. 13 ; and in the same chapter the words, 'O death, where is thy sting? O grave, where is thy victory?' (vers. 55, 56), with almost verbal exactness, from Hos. xiii. 14.

iv. Once more. In a few passages the Apostle, after the manner of his time, has recourse to allegory. These are :—
(1) the allegory of the woman who had lost her husband, in Rom. vii. (compare Gal. iv. 1–3, which is supported by Isa. liv. 1); (2) Of the children of Israel in the wilderness, in 1 Cor. x ; (3) Of Hagar and Sarah, in Gal. iii ; (4) Of the veil on the face of Moses, in 2 Cor. iii ; (5) Abraham himself, who is a kind of centre of allegory, the actions of whose life, as well as the promises of God to him, are symbols of the coming dispensation ; (6) The history of the

patriarchs, and cutting short of the house of Israel, in Rom. ix, x. Of these examples, the first, third, and fourth are what we should term illustrations; while the second, fifth, and sixth have not merely an analogous or metaphorical meaning, but a real inward connexion with the life and state of the first believers.

A few general results of an examination of the quotations from the Old Testament in St. Paul's Epistles may be summed as follows:—

1. The number of direct quotations in which reference is made to the original is about eighty-seven, of which about fifty-three are found in the Epistle to the Romans, fifteen in 1 Corinthians, six in 2 Corinthians, ten in Galatians, two in Ephesians, one in 1 Timothy. Of these nearly half show a precise verbal agreement with the LXX; while, of the remaining passages, at least two thirds exhibit a degree of verbal similarity which can only be accounted for by an acquaintance with the LXX. Minuter traces of the Old Testament language are far more numerous.

2. None of these passages offer any certain proof that the Apostle was acquainted with the Hebrew text [1]. That he must have been so can hardly be doubted; yet it seems improbable that he could have had a familiar knowledge of the original without straying into parallelisms with the Hebrew, in those passages in which it varies from the LXX. His acquaintance with the Hebrew was probably of such a kind as we might acquire of a version of the Scriptures not in the vernacular. No Englishman incidentally quoting the English version from memory would adapt it to the Greek, though he might very probably adapt the Greek to the English. The inference is, that the Greek and not the Hebrew text must have been to the Apostle what the English version is to ourselves.

---

[1] Compare Rom. ix. 7; x. 15: 1 Cor. ii. 9, as the best instances on the other side; they do not, however, disprove the truth of the remark.

3. While many of these quotations are introduced, as we have already seen, without any acknowledgement in the New Testament, a few others, as for example, Rom. xii. 19 : 1 Cor. xv. 45, are hardly, if at all, discernible in the text of the Old. The familiarity with the Old Testament which has led to the first of these two phenomena is probably also the cause of the second. As the words suggest themselves unconsciously, so the spirit without the words occasionally comes into the Apostle's mind ; or the language and spirit of different passages blend in one.

4. There is no evidence that the Apostle remembered the verbal connexion in which any of the passages quoted by him originally occurred. He isolates them wholly from their context ; he reasons from them as he might from statements of his own, 'going off upon a word,' as it has been called, in one instance almost upon a letter (Gal. iii. 16), drawing inferences which in strict logic can hardly be allowed, often extending the meaning of words beyond their first and natural sense. There is nothing to distinguish his use of quotations from that of his age, except greater power and life ; he clings more than his contemporaries to the spirit and less to the letter, his inaccuracy about the latter arising in some instances from his feeling for the spirit.

5. There is no reason to think that the Apostle ever quotes from apocryphal writings, nor could it be gathered from the language of his Epistles that he was acquainted with the works of classical authors. Similarities are found with apocryphal writings ; but they are all explainable on the supposition of a common source. Three or four verses from Greek poets also occur in the Acts and Epistles ; these, however, are common and proverbial expressions, which the Apostle might very well have known without having been read in the works of Aratus, Epimenides, Euripides, or Menander.

6. Vestiges of Old Testament language are so numerous, as to admit of an argument from their occurrence to the

genuineness of the Epistles. If the same interpenetration of new and old phraseology occurs in the Epistle to the Ephesians that we find in the Epistles to the Romans, Corinthians, and the Galatians, here is considerable reason for supposing that they are writings of the same author, or at any rate of the same date. A new argument from coincidence arises, for no one would imagine that it could have occurred to a forger of a later age to imitate the manner in which St. Paul used the language of the LXX. The argument is only suggested; it requires careful consideration to enable an estimate to be formed of its exact value. It certainly applies, however, with some force, to the Epistle to the Ephesians, in which there are very few traces of direct citation, but many of verbal resemblances.

7. The study of the quotations from the Old Testament draws attention to the knowledge which the Apostle must have had of the Greek Scriptures. It is hardly possible to exaggerate the minuteness of this acquaintance. In the greater number of quotations he is verbally accurate. Hence, we may also infer that it is not from want of memory that he disregards the connexion. His writings teem with the phraseology of the Psalms and the Prophets. They suggest his thoughts, they are his weapons of controversy, they supply him with words and expressions as well as with a 'form of truth.' The Greek Old Testament Scriptures are not only sacred books to him, they are also his language and literature. What are often termed the Hebraisms of the Apostle are, for the most part, if not always, Hellenisms; that is to say, Hebraisms contracted through the influence of the LXX.

Lastly, It may be asked whether St. Paul regarded these texts of Scripture as prophecies or accommodations, as illustrations or arguments, as types or figures of speech, as designed or undesigned coincidences? The answer is, that such distinctions had no place in his mind; to attribute them to him is a logical anachronism. He did not say to himself: This was designed, that undesigned; this is an illustration, that an argument. He adopted what appeared to his own mind a natural form of expression, what he conceived would convey his meaning to others. His own language and that of the psalmists and prophets are bound together by him in various ways:

(1) Often (as we have already seen) whole verses of the Old Testament are latent in the Epistle, without note or sign.

(2) In other passages they are preceded by καθὼς γέγραπται: τί λέγει ἡ γραφή; λέγει ἡ γραφή: καθάπερ Μωσῆς λέγει. David, Isaiah, Elijah, Hosea, are also cited by name.

(3) A stronger formula is found in Gal. iii. 8 προϊδοῦσα δὲ ἡ γραφή, and one more emphatic still in 1 Cor. x. 11 ταῦτα δὲ πάντα τυπικῶς συνέβαινον ἐκείνοις, ἐγράφη δὲ πρὸς νουθεσίαν ἡμῶν, εἰς οὓς τὰ τέλη τῶν αἰώνων κατήντηκε.

THE

EPISTLE TO THE ROMANS

INTRODUCTION.

THE Epistle to the Romans has ever been regarded as first in importance among the Epistles of St. Paul, the cornerstone of that Gospel which he preached among the Gentiles. Not only does it present more completely than other parts of Scripture the doctrine of righteousness by faith, but it connects this doctrine with the state of mankind in general, embracing Jew and Gentile at once in its view, alternating them with each other in the counsels of Providence. It looks into the world within, without losing sight of the world which is without. It is less than the other Epistles concerned with the disputes or wants of a particular Church, and more with the greater needs of human nature itself. It turns an eye backward on the times of past ignorance both in the individual and mankind, and again looks forward to the restoration of the Jews and to the manifestation of the sons of God. It speaks of the law itself in language which even now 'that the law is dead to us and we to the law,' still pierces to the dividing asunder of the flesh and spirit. No other portion of the New Testament gives a similarly connected view of the ways of God to man; no other is spread over truths so far from us and yet so near to us.

It is not, however, this higher and more universal aspect of the Epistle to the Romans with which we are at present immediately concerned. Our first question is a critical and historical one: What was the Roman Church, and in what relation did it stand to the Apostle? The difficulty in answering this question partly arises from the very universality of the subject of the Epistle. The great argument takes us out of the accidents of time and place. We cannot distinctly recognize what we but remotely see, the particular and individual features of which are lost in the width of the prospect. Could the Apostle himself have had, and therefore is it to be expected that he could communicate to us, the same vivid personal conception of the Church at Rome as of Churches whose members were individually known to him, whom, in his own language, he had himself begotten in the Gospel? In an Epistle written from a distance to converts unknown to him by face, it is not to be supposed that there will be found even the materials for conjecture which are supplied by the Epistles to the Galatians and Corinthians. Naturally the personality of the writer, and still more of those whom he is addressing, falls into the background. He writes upon general topics which are equally applicable to almost all Churches, which fail, therefore, to throw any light on the particular Church to which the Epistle is addressed. Nor can this dimness of the critical eye receive any assistance from external sources. With the exception of the well-known command of Claudius to the Jews to depart from Rome about fifteen years previously, to which we may add the faint traces of a Christian Church which was apparently distinct from the Jews, in Acts xxviii. 15, and the separate mention of Christians in Tacitus and Suetonius, nothing has come down to us which throws any light, however uncertain, on the beginnings of the Roman Church.

The old belief was, that the Roman Church consisted partly of Jews and partly of Gentiles, and that the Epistle was written with the intention of adjusting the disputes that had arisen between them. The latter part of this statement finds no support from the Epistle itself, and appears to be nothing more than an arbitrary assumption suggested by the analogy of the Corinthians and the Galatians. The former part need not be wholly denied : for in every Christian Church there were probably some Jews and some Gentiles. Yet it does not follow from this that the community was divided between them, or that both were numerous enough to form separate parties. The Epistle affords no intimation of such parties existing side by side, whether peaceably or otherwise, in the Roman communion. St. Paul never speaks of Jew and Gentile as in actual contact, disputing about circumcision, or purification, or meats and drinks, or sabbath days. The relation which he supposes between them is wholly ideal ; that is, in the purposes of God, not in their assemblies or daily life. They divide the world and time ; they have nothing to do with each other as individuals. Nor does the theory that the Roman Church was a half Jewish, half Gentile community agree with either of the facts stated above—the fact that the name Gentiles is applied to all, while the tone and style of the Epistle are wholly Jewish.

It is more reasonable, as well as far more in accordance with the indications of the Epistles, to regard the Churches planted by the Apostle, not as divided into two sections of Jew and Gentile, circumcision and uncircumcision, but as always in a state of transition between the two, dropping gradually their Jewish customs, and opening the door wider and wider to their Gentile brethren, slowly, but at length entirely, convinced that it was not ' at this time the kingdom was to be restored to Israel.' Such must, at any rate, have been the case with the Churches not founded by St. Paul. It was long ere the curtains of the tabernacle were drawn aside, or the veil rent in twain, or the earthly and visible temple exchanged for that building in the heavens, the house not made with hands. Disputes about the outward rite of circumcision would be succeeded by another stage of controversy respecting the inward obligation of the Law on the conscience, and the authority of St. Paul and the Twelve. There were cases, also, in which an idealized or Alexandrianized Judaism had been the soil in which the Gospel was originally planted. Here the transition would be more rapid; the faith of the earliest believers would linger less around the weak and beggarly elements; they would more easily harmonize the old and new; they would more readily comprehend the length and breadth of the purposes of God. The change required of them would be in their ways of thought rather than in their habits of life; and the latitude which such converts allowed themselves would react on the stricter Jewish communities.

Changes like these may be supposed to have been passing over the Roman Church. At the time St. Paul wrote to them, there was no question of circumcision; that, if it had ever been, was now left behind. But in a more general way the same difficulty still pressed upon them. What was the obligation of the Law? And, as they looked upon the passing scene, and saw the chosen race becoming a spectacle to the world, to angels, and to men, they could not but ask also, 'What God intended respecting it?' Whether were they to melt away among the Gentiles, or to preserve their name and heritage? While men were pondering such thoughts in their hearts, of the Law and its sabbaths, and ceremonies, and sacrifices, of the consolation of Israel, and the restoration of the kingdom, we may conceive the Apostle to have written this Epistle with a view of meeting their doubts, and adjusting their thoughts, and vindicating the ways of God to man, and revealing the way of salvation. He gave them the full truth for the half-truth, the day for the twilight, and established their faith in Christ, not by drawing back, but by going further than they had imagined, and resting the Gospel on an immutable moral foundation (Rom. ii. 11; iii. 29).

Such we conceive to have been the state of feeling in the

Roman Church, because such is the state of feeling to which the words of the Apostle are appropriate. Neither the earlier one, in which men said, 'except ye be circumcised ye cannot be saved,' and an Apostle himself withdrew and refused to eat with the Gentiles; nor the later one, in which it was clearly understood that all such differences were done away in Christ, are suitable to the argument of the Epistle to the Romans. The Apostle was still seeking to teach a Jewish Church the great lesson of the admission of the Gentiles more perfectly. So far the hypothesis of Baur affords a good key to the interpretation of the Epistle. But still the expression in the fifth verse of the first chapter has not been disposed of. In what sense could they be said to be Gentiles? For supposing the Roman Church to have consisted of Jews gradually passing into the state of Gentiles, we have an explanation of the frequent dwelling on the Law, and the relation of Jew and Gentile, but none of the term 'other Gentiles,' under which the Apostle comprehends them. No gradual change in their opinions and circumstances could have justified him in calling those Gentiles who were originally Jews. Nor, however much he might 'magnify his office,' would he have included the chosen people under the common name, which he everywhere opposed to them. The very meaning of the Apostle of the Gentiles would have been lost had the term 'nations' extended itself to them.

The attempt to solve this difficulty runs up into the general question of the state and circumstances of the early Church: our inquiry respecting which must, however, be restricted to the single point which bears upon the present subject; viz. how far the Gentile Churches were originally in feeling Jewish—whether to the Gentiles also the gate of the New Testament was through the Old? For if it could be shown that Jewish and Gentile Christianity were not so much opposed as successive—that the Gospel of the Jewish Apostles was the first, and that of St. Paul the sub-

sequent, stage in the history of the Apostolic Church—
then the difficulty of itself disappears, and the double aspect
of the Epistle to the Romans is what we should expect.

Our conception of the Apostolical age is necessarily based
on the Acts of the Apostles and the Epistles of St. Paul.
It is in vain to search ecclesiastical writings for further
information; the pages of Justin and Irenaeus supply only
the evidence of their own deficiency. Confining ourselves,
then, to the original sources, we cannot but be struck by
the fact, that of the first eighteen years after the day of
Pentecost, hardly any account is preserved to us in the
Acts, and that to this scanty record no addition can be made
from the Epistles of St. Paul. Isolated facts are narrated,
but not events in their order and sequence: there is no
general prospect of the Christian world. Churches are
growing up everywhere: some the result of missions from
Jerusalem, others of unknown origin; yet none of them
standing in any definite relation to the Apostles of the
circumcision. It seems as if we had already reached the
second stage in the history of the Apostolic Church, without
any precise knowledge of the first. That second period, if
we terminate it with the supposed date of the Apostle's
death, extends over about fourteen or fifteen years—years
full of life, and growth, and vicissitude. Could the preceding period have been less so, or does it only appear
to be so from the silence of history? Is it according to
the analogy of human things, or of the workings of Divine
power in the soul of man, that during the first part of its
existence, Christianity should have slumbered, and after
fifteen years of inaction have suddenly gone forth to conquer
the world? Or, are we falling under that common historical
illusion, that little happened in a time of which we know
little?

And yet how are we to supply this lost history out of
the single verse of the Acts (xi. 19), 'They which were
scattered abroad upon the persecution that arose about

Stephen travelled as far as Phenice and Cyprus and Antioch, preaching the word to none but unto the Jews only.' What reply is to be made to the inquiry respecting the origin of the Christian Church in the two cities which in after-ages were to exercise the greatest influence on its history, Alexandria and Rome? We cannot tell. Our slender materials only admit of being eked out by some general facts which do not fill up the void of details, but are of the greatest importance in illustrating the spirit and character of the earliest Christian communities. Foremost among these facts is the dispersion of the Jews. The remark has been often made that the universality of the Roman Empire was itself a preparation for the universality of the Gospel, its very organization throughout the world being the image, as it may have been the model, of the external form of the Christian Church. But not less striking as an image of the external state of the earliest Christian communion is the dispersion of the ten tribes throughout the world, and not less worthy of observation as it was an inward preparation for Christianity is the universal diffusion of that religion, the spirit of which seemed at the time to be most narrow and contracted within itself, and at first sight most hostile to the whole human race. Of all religions in the world it was probably the only one capable of making proselytes—which had the force, as it had the will, to draw men within its circle. Literally, and not only in idea, 'the Law was a schoolmaster to bring men to Christ.' The compassing sea and land 'to make one proselyte' was not without its results. Seneca, who did not know, or at least has not told anything of the Christians, says of the Jews, 'Victoribus victi leges dederunt.' The Roman satirists were aware of their festivals, and speak of them in a way which implies not only converts to Judaism, but a degree of regard for their opinions. They had passed into a proverb in Horace's time for their zeal in bringing men over to their opinions. (1 *Sat.* iv. 143.) Philo mentions the suburb beyond the Tiber in which they were domiciled by Augustus, the greater number of the inhabitants of which are said to have been freedmen. (*Leg. ad Caium*, 23.) Tacitus's account of their origin is perhaps an unique attempt in a Roman writer to investigate the religious antiquities of an Eastern people, implying of itself, what it also explicitly states, the tendency towards them. No other religion had been sustained for centuries by contributions from the most remote parts of the empire to a common centre; contributions the very magnitude of which is ascribed to the zeal of numerous converts. (Tacitus, *Hist.* v. 5; Cicero *pro Flacco*, c. 28.) According to Josephus, whole tribes in the neighbourhood of Judea had submitted to the rite of circumcision. (*Ant.* xiii. 9, 1; 11, 3; 15, 4.) The women of Damascus in particular are mentioned as not trusted by their husbands in a massacre of the Jews, because they were 'favourable to the Jews' religion.' The Jews in Alexandria occupied two of the five quarters into which the city was divided: and the whole Jewish population of Egypt was rated by Philo at a million. Facts like these speak volumes for the importance and influence of the Jews.

In one sense it is true that the Jewish religion seemed already about to expire. To us, looking back from the vantage ground of the Gospel, nothing is clearer than that it contained within itself the seeds of its own destruction. 'The Law and the Prophets were until John, and now the kingdom of heaven suffereth violence, and the violent take it by force.' Before Christ—after Christ—this is the great landmark that divides Judaism from Christianity, while for a few years longer the devoted nation, already within the coils of its own destiny, lingers about its ancient seat. It was otherwise to its contemporaries. To them the Jewish people were not declining, but growing. There seemed to be no end to its wealth and influence. The least of all peoples in itself, it was a nation within a nation in every city.

In the wreck of the heathen religions, Judaism alone remained unchanged. Nor is there anything strange in its retaining undiminished this power over the human mind, when its own national glory had already departed. Its objects of faith were not lessened, but magnified by distance. It contained in itself that inward life which other religions were seeking for, and for the want of which they expired. It could not but communicate to others the belief in the unity of God, which had sunk for ages into the heart of the race;—to the educated Greek 'one guess among many,'— to the Israelite a necessary truth. It formed a sort of meeting-point of East and West, which in the movement of either towards the other naturally exercised a singular influence. Many elements of Greek cultivation had insensibly passed into the mind of the Jewish people, as of other Asiatic nations, before the reaction of the Maccabean wars; cities with Greek names covered the land: even after that time the rugged Hebrew feeling was confined within narrow limits. The Gospel as it passed from the lips of our Lord and the Twelve had not far to go in Palestine itself before it came in contact with the Greek world. In other countries the diffusion of the Greek Version of the Old Testament is a proof that a Hellenized Judaism was growing up everywhere. The Alexandrian philosophy offered a link with heathen literature and mythology. Judaism was no longer isolated but wandering far and wide. Clinging to its belief in Jehovah and abating nothing of its national pride, it was nevertheless capable of assuming to itself new phases without losing its essential character, of dropping its more repulsive features and entering into and penetrating the better heathen mind both of East and West.

The heads of many subjects of inquiry are summed up in these reflections, which lead us round to the question from which we started, 'Whether to the Gentiles also the gate of the New Testament was through the Old?' And they suggest the answer to the question, that 'so it was,' not because the minds of the first teachers were unable to rise above the 'rudiments of the Law,' but because the soil for Christianity among the Gentiles was itself prepared in Judaism. It was the natural growth of the Gospel in the world as it then was. The better life of the Jewish people passed into the earliest Christian Church; the meaning of prophecy was lost to the Jew and found to the believer in Christ. And the facts recorded in the Acts of the Apostles represent the outward side of this inward tendency: it was the Jewish proselyte who commonly became the Christian convert. Such were Cornelius and the Ethiopian eunuch, and the deputy Sergius Paulus, who 'of his own accord desired to hear the word of God.' The teachers themselves wore the habit of Jews, and they came appealing to the authority of the Old Testament. That garb and form and manner which we insensibly drop in thinking of the early teachers of Christianity, could not have failed to impress its Jewish character on their first hearers. It would be their first conception of the Gospel, that it was a kind of Judaism to which they were predisposed by the same kind of feelings which led them towards Judaism itself.

Now if the history of Judaism in the Augustan age, no less than the indications of the New Testament itself, leads to the inference that the first disciples, even in Gentile cities, were commonly Jewish converts, or, at any rate, such as were acquainted with the Law and the Prophets, and were disposed to receive with reverence Jewish teachers, the difficulty in the Epistle to the Romans is solved, at the same time that the fact of its solution is an additional confirmation of the view which has been just taken. The Roman Church appeared to be at once Jewish and Gentile; Jewish in feeling, Gentile in origin. Jewish, because the Apostle everywhere argues with them as Jews; Gentile, because he expressly addresses them by name as such. In this double fact there is now seen to be nothing strange or anomalous: it typifies the general condition of Christian

Churches, whether Jewish or Gentile ; whether founded by St. Paul, or by the Apostles of the circumcision. It was not only in idea that the Old Testament prepared the way for the New, by holding up the truth of the unity of God ; but the spread of that truth among the Gentiles, and the influence of the Jewish Scriptures, were themselves actual preparatives for the Gospel.

To those who were Gentiles by birth, but had received the Gospel originally from Jewish teachers, the subject of the Epistle to the Romans would have a peculiar interest. It expressed the truth on the verge of which they stood, which seemed to be peculiarly required by their own circumstances, which explained their position to themselves. It purged the film from their eyes, which prevented them from seeing the way of God perfectly. Hitherto they had acquiesced in the position which public opinion among the heathen assigned to them, that they were a Jewish sect : and they had implicitly followed the lives as well as the lessons of their first instructors in Christ. But a nobler truth was now to break upon them. God was not the God of the Jews only, but of the Gentiles also. And this wider range of vision involved a new principle, not the Law, but faith. If nations of every language and tongue were to be included in the Gospel dispensation—barbarian, Scythian, bond and free—the principle that was to unite them must be superior to the differences that separated them. In other words, it could not be an institution or a Church, but an inward principle, which might belong alike to all mankind. This principle was faith, the view of which in St. Paul's mind is never separated from the redemption of mankind at large.

SUBJECT OF THE EPISTLE.

The Gentile origin and Jewish character of the Roman Church are a sufficient explanation of the style and subject of the Epistle to the Romans. The condemnation of the Jew first, and afterwards of the Gentile—the justification of the Jew first, and afterwards of the Gentile—the actual fact of the rejection of the Jews, and the hope of their restoration—are all of them topics appropriate to what we may conceive to have been the feeling of the Roman converts, in whom a Jewish education had not obliterated a Gentile origin, and whom a Gentile origin did not deprive of the hope of Jewish promises. The Apostle no longer appears to be speaking to the winds of heaven, what, after being borne to and fro upon the earth, might return to the profit of the Church after many days, but what had an immediate interest for it, and arose naturally out of its actual state.

Assuming the results of the preceding essay, we may consider the structure of the Epistle, with the view of tracing the relation of the parts to each other and to the whole. What was primary, what secondary, in the Apostle's thoughts? Is the order of the composition the same as the order of ideas? Do we proceed from without inwards— that is, from the admission of the Gentiles to the justification of the individual believer? or from within outwards— that is, from the individual believer to the world at large? Is the episode of the restoration of the Jews subordinate or principal—a correction of the first part of the Epistle, or, as Baur supposes, the kernel of the whole? These are subtle and delicate inquiries, respecting which it is not possible to attain absolute certainty, and in the prosecution of which we are always in danger of attributing to the Apostle more of method and plan than he really had. Such inquiries can only be made by a comparison of other writings of the Apostle, and an accurate examination of the Epistle itself.

SUBJECT OF THE EPISTLE

We may begin by asking, 'Whether there is any subject which the Epistle to the Romans has in common with the other Epistles, which is specially identified with the life and working of the Apostle?' There is. While the doctrine of righteousness by faith without the deeds of the Law is but slightly referred to in the other Epistles of St. Paul, and is but once mentioned in the Acts of the Apostles, there is another truth, which is everywhere and at all times insisted upon by him, and everywhere connected with his name, which recurs in almost every one of his Epistles, and is everywhere dwelt upon in the Acts as the result of his Apostleship—the admission of the Gentiles. He speaks of himself, and is always spoken of, as the Apostle of the Gentiles; his conversion itself is bound up with this labour of universal love; in 'the beginning of the Gospel' he stands up for their rights, among 'the Apostles that were before him;' all through his life he is proclaiming in a more or less spiritual manner, 'God hath made of one blood all nations of the earth.' (Acts xvii. 26.) 'Is he the God of the Jews only, is he not also of the Gentiles?' (Rom. iii. 29.) All are one in Christ, in whom 'neither circumcision nor uncircumcision avail anything, but a new creature' (Gal. iii. 28; vi. 15); or, according to another form of expression, 'in whose circumcision the Gentiles also are circumcised.' (Col. ii. 11.) Compare 1 Cor. xii. 13: Eph. i. 10; iii. 3–6.

Such repeated reference to the same subject justifies our regarding it as the leading thought of the Apostle's mind, the great truth which the power of God had inspired him to teach. Yet, itself had a twofold aspect, for the differences of Jew and Gentile were done away with, not on the ground of any abstract equality of the human race in the sight of God, but as they became one in Christ. It is a union with Christ which breaks through all other ties of race and language, and knits men together into a new body which is His Church. So while looking at the external world we seem almost at once to pass inward, and to blend the assertion of the general principle with the experience of the individual soul. The cord of love which encircles all men has its beginning too in the believer's heart. 'There is neither barbarian nor Scythian, bond nor free,' not on any speculative grounds of morality, but because his own spiritual instinct tells him that all these differences are done away in Christ.

But with this outward aspect of Christianity is connected also another thought, which follows it as the shadow does the light, 'the times of that ignorance which God winked at,' 'the passing by of past sins' (Rom. iii. 25), 'which was kept secret since the world began' (Rom. xvi. 25), 'which in other ages was not made known . . . that the Gentiles should be fellow-heirs, and of the same body' (Eph. iii. 6). It was strange to look at the world around, and see the Gentiles also pressing into the Kingdom of Heaven. But it was not less, but perhaps even more strange, to think of the Gentiles in past times who seemed to have so little relation to the God who made them; in the world of darkness and silence, on which the eye could rest, but which it could not pierce. Nor was the same thought inapplicable to those who were under the Law. They too, though with many 'advantages,' were still subject to ordinances, shut up in prison until the time appointed. The prior states of Jew and Gentile were not wholly dissimilar: the Law was the glass which might be held up to both to convict them of sin; in which, world within world, mirror within mirror, the Jew was first seen, afterwards the Gentile. Jew and Gentile, the times before and the times after, are the outlines or divisions of the book in the volume of which are contained the purposes of God.

Such is the external aspect of the Apostle's teaching so far as it can be separated from the inward life, which penetrates the individual and the Church alike. But there is a world within as well as a world without, nor can we view one except through the medium of the other. The knowledge which the Apostle himself has of the works of God, is transferred to the heathen; the consciousness which he feels of his own union with Christ is the living proof of the acceptance of all mankind; the remembrance of his struggle under the Law, is the image of the state of those under the Law. Though the thought comes upon him daily of his mission to the Gentiles everywhere, he does not look upon them as they appear in the pages of ancient authors, or on their modes of worship, as they present themselves to the student of mythology. He is not writing a philosophy of history, but a religion of history. He does not, in modern phraseology, put himself in the position of the heathen, or even of the Jew, but retains his own. Nor must we, in our interpretation of the Epistle, endeavour to force his words, from this simple and natural point of view, into one more in accordance with our tastes and feelings.

An illustration from heathen philosophy may serve to indicate the peculiar nature of this transition from the individual mind to the world at large. All modern commentators on Plato admit that in the Republic the individual and the state pass into one another. The virtues, duties, distinctions of one are also those of the other; the consideration of the one seems to lead the philosopher on to the deeper and more enlarged consideration of the other. Not altogether unlike this is the manner in which the individual conscience in the Epistles of St. Paul is the reflection not only of itself, but of the world at large; and in which the thought of the world at large, and the Church, of which he is a member, re-acts upon the inmost feelings of the believer. The kingdom of God is not yet separated into outward and visible, and inward and spiritual; nor election into that of nations and individuals.

As the Apostle looks upon the face of the world, he sees all men, by the light of revelation in himself, returning, through Christ, into union with the God who made them.

There is no distinction of Jew or Gentile, circumcision or uncircumcision. Soon he passes over into another point of view, 'setting the world in their hearts.' Two dispensations are in the bosom of every man who comes to the knowledge of the truth; these are symbolized by two words, the Law and Faith. The one is slavery, the other freedom; the one death, the other life; the one strife, the other peace; the one alienation from God, the other reconciliation with Him. Not at once does the one dispensation take the place of the other. There is a period of natural life first; the Law enters and plants the seeds of mortal disease. Will and knowledge, the common sources of human action, begin to decompose, the will to evil struggling with the knowledge of good. The creature is made powerless to act by his consciousness of sin; the Law only terrifies—he dies at the very sight of it; it is a dry 'eye' turning every way upon his misery. The soul, hanging between good and evil, is in a state of paralysis, doing what it would not, and hating itself for what it does. But, again, the soul is persuaded by many arguments that 'the Law is dead;' it throws away the 'worser' half, and clings to its risen Lord. Faith is the hand by which it is united to Him—the instrument whereby it is accepted, renewed, sanctified—the sense through which it looks up to God, revealing Himself in man, and around on creation.

These two, the Law and Faith, are so inseparable, that they seem each to derive their meaning from the other. Faith is not the Law; the Law is not Faith. Whatever is not Faith is the Law; whatever is not the Law is Faith. The Law, no less than Faith, is an inward feeling—a tablet of stone, yet written also on fleshly tables of the heart. Yet the Apostle's manner of speaking of both is such as, at first sight, prevents our perception of this. Through a great portion of the Epistle he drops their subjective character, and represents them to us as powers, almost as persons—the symbols of the past and present—of the followers of Moses and Christ, arrayed against each other in the battlefield of the world and the human heart; blended in the example of Abraham; typified in the first and second Adam; the figures of two kinds of death, in sin and to sin.

In the course of the Epistle we pass more and more inward to the dividing asunder of the flesh and spirit, until darkness takes the place of light, and death of life. More than once the shadow of peace rests upon us in passing, but we must first enter into the depths of human nature, and take part in the struggle, ere we can attain finally to that rest which is in Christ Jesus. At length the body of death slips from us: the law of the spirit of life prevails over the law of sin. And yet the fleshly body, though dead to sin, still cleaves to us: it has ceased to strive against the spirit, but is not yet adopted into the fellowship of Christ. But, though groaning within ourselves, we have the inward witness of the Spirit; we know that all things are working together for good: we ask in triumph, 'If God be for us, who can be against us?'

Thus far we have proceeded from without inwards—that is to say, from the relation of the Gospel to Jew and Gentile, and its place in the history of the world, to its influence on the heart and conscience. At this point the former aspect of the Epistle re-appears. The question of salvation is no longer personal, but national. All mankind have been included under sin; all mankind, even as Abraham, are righteous by faith: 'As in Adam all die, even so in Christ shall all be made alive.' Thence the Apostle digressed to guard against practical inferences; to describe the inward need of pardon as before the outward. But still there was one exception to the offer of universal salvation. All the world was included; but the favoured nation seemed by its own act to exclude itself from the gracious circle. As a nation the Jews had rejected the Gospel; and to them the Apostle returns, first, to justify their rejection, secondly, to prophesy their restoration.

The remainder of the Epistle is a practical exhortation to Christian graces and moral virtues; commencing with a general invitation to a holy life, or, as the Apostle expresses it in language borrowed from the Law, to present the body a living sacrifice. The ground of this invitation is the mercy of God, as set forth in the scheme of Providence:— 'So then God concluded all under sin that he might have mercy upon all;' 'I beseech you, therefore.' Thence the Apostle passes onwards, as towards the conclusion of several Epistles, to a series of practical precepts, some of which have a peculiar reference to the state and circumstances of the early Church. Here the connexion with the main subject of the Epistle appears to drop, and the very want of connexion leads us to remark that the separate duties are not regarded by the Apostle as absorbed in the single truth of righteousness by faith, but are stated by him independently of it. Throughout the twelfth, thirteenth, and fourteenth chapters there is scarcely the least reference to the preceding portions of the Epistle. Thence the Apostle digresses still further to a personal narrative, in which, as towards the conclusion of the Epistle to the Galatians, in a few pregnant verses, the main subject of the Epistle is again introduced; whence he returns once more to himself and his intended visit, and his mission to Jerusalem, and concludes with salutations of the brethren.

TIME AND PLACE.

THE time and place of writing the Epistle to the Romans are distinctly marked in the fifteenth chapter. The Apostle is on his way to Jerusalem, 'ministering to the saints,' xv. 25, in accordance with his half-expressed intention in

1 Cor. xvi. 4. He is carrying up the contributions of Macedonia and Achaia, for the poor at Jerusalem, ver. 26. Having completed his labours in Asia Minor and Greece, xv. 23 (compare 2 Cor. x. 13), when his mission to Jerusalem is accomplished, ver. 28, he hopes to visit the Roman converts on his way to Spain, ver. 22; a purpose which he has often entertained, xv. 22, but never fulfilled, i. 12. (Compare Acts xix. 21.) The mention of Cenchrea, the port of Corinth, in xvi. 1, agrees with the other circumstances, in indicating his second visit to Corinth as the time and place of writing the Epistle. In reference to these allusions it may be remarked :—(1) That the Apostle, though on his way to Rome, has no intention of making Rome the resting-place from his labours. He is the Apostle of the whole world, hastening onward, ere his sun sets, 'to the extreme west' of Clement. His preference of Spain above other countries might be suggested by the circumstance that the Gospel had not yet spread there, and that he went to plant it. Or, more probably, considering the definite manner in which he speaks of his intention, he was led to choose Spain rather than Africa or Italy, from some acquaintance with, or invitation from, Jews or Christians already settled there. As there is no reason to suppose that the journey was ever accomplished, it is useless to speculate further on the motive of it. (2) It is observable also that he wrote the Epistle to the Romans from Corinth, or its neighbourhood, and therefore after the second Epistle to the Corinthians, which already indicates that a reaction had taken place in the Corinthian Church in favour of the Apostle; a change of feeling which might probably be confirmed by the Apostle's visit. Supposing this to have been the case, the Apostle, though in the midst of that city of factions, was writing the Epistle to the Romans at a time when their violence was abated. This agrees with the conciliatory tone of the Epistle, as pointed out in the two preceding essays, which also harmonizes

with the immediate occasion of his journey to Jerusalem. For (3) at the very time of writing, the Gentile Apostle was engaged in carrying up alms to the Jewish Church at Jerusalem, much after the manner that other Jewish pilgrims brought gifts from distant parts of the Empire for the service of the Temple. He was fearful of the violence of his countrymen in Judea, and not without apprehension of the feeling with which the Church might regard him, xv. 31. Yet 'his heart's desire towards Israel' was not dead within him, notwithstanding his fears and sufferings. He had been for a long time previously gathering the alms in Asia, 1 Cor. xvi. 1, as well as in Greece, according to an agreement which he had entered into with the Apostles at Jerusalem on a previous visit, Gal. ii. 10. Speaking after the manner of men, may we not say that no one could be long employed in such mission of charity, without feeling his soul melt towards those who were its objects? What had never been personal hostility to the Church at Jerusalem, must soon have given way, in a mind so sensitive as St. Paul's, to the liveliest sympathy with them. In his own words to the Corinthians it might be said :—'His heart is enlarged towards them ; they are not straitened in him, but in themselves.' Nor could this insensible change have occurred, without drawing his thoughts to their place in the scheme of Providence. The feelings of his own mind would inevitably cast a distant light and shade on the Jewish and Gentile world.

The Epistle to the Romans is naturally compared with the Epistle to the Galatians; the subjects are the same, or nearly so, the illustrations often similar, and minute resemblances of language surprisingly numerous. Yet the Epistle to the Galatians would have been in great measure unintelligible to us, but for the larger growth and fuller development of the same truths in the Epistle to the Romans. The first mentioned Epistle is personal and occasional ; it has much of passion and sadness ; it bears the impress everywhere of the struggle which agitated the Galatian converts, and could only have been written to a Church which was known by face to the Apostle. On the other hand, the Epistle to the Romans, except in one or two passages, has a tone of calmness and deliberation: it is spiritual and ideal; the distance at which the Apostle places himself from the strifes of the Church, enabling him to take a more extended survey of the purposes of God. The difference between the two Epistles is further analogous to the difference between proselytes of the gate, and the so-called proselytes of righteousness. The question in the one case is 'circumcision,' the outward symbol of the Jewish law, which affected the minds of the converts much, we may suppose, as that of caste would occupy the minds of the Hindoos at the present day, or as some ritual or legal question might prevail over the better religious feeling among ourselves. The other Epistle never touches on the subject of circumcision, as an obligation to be enforced, or not enforced; but only as the seal of God's mercy to all mankind, in the instance of the Father of the faithful, Rom. iv. The mind of the writer is absorbed in the contemplation of the world as divided into Jew and Gentile, past and present, the Law and Faith. The beginnings of this contemplation are discernible in the Epistle to the Galatians; but more as a feeling or spiritual instinct, less as a system or scheme of Providence. 'In Christ Jesus neither circumcision availeth anything, nor uncircumcision, but a new creature.' But there is a height not yet attained to, at which every obstacle disappears, and the ways of God are justified finally, the circumcision accepted through faith, and the uncircumcision; the circumcision again returning to God in Christ, and the length and breadth of Divine love made manifest. This is only reached in the Epistle to the Romans.

No certain inference respecting the length of time by which the Epistle to the Romans is separated from the Epistle to the Galatians can be drawn from these considerations. It is of more importance to remark, that in reading the Epistle to the Romans, we have already advanced in the series of Epistles a step onward towards the Epistles of the Imprisonment.

CHAPTER II.

THE second chapter of the Romans has often been regarded as containing the exclusive condemnation of the Jew for hypocrisy, as the first chapter contains the condemnation of the Gentile for sins below nature. This statement, however, is not quite exact. That the Apostle intended to include both Jew and Gentile under sin, may be inferred from chap. iii. 9 ; the two heads of the proof do not, however, precisely correspond to the divisions of the chapters. The course of his thought may be traced as follows :—He has been speaking of the inhuman and unnatural vices of the Gentiles, and now passes on to another class of sins—hypocrisy and deceit—in which he loses sight of the Gentiles, and addresses man in the abstract. Assuming that all mankind are guilty before God, the judgement of others is a condemnation of self. But whence is this assumption? Not strictly deducible from the preceding chapter, in which the Apostle has been speaking only, or chiefly, of the Gentiles, yet in spirit agreeing with it ; for the judgement of others is a higher degree of that knowledge of God which 'hinders the truth in unrighteousness.' Still there is a link wanting. We must allow the Apostle to make a silent transition from the Gentile to mankind in general, just as in chap. iii. 19 he has included the Gentile under the condemnation of the Jew. Full of the general idea of the universal sinfulness of man, he follows his own thought without looking back at the connexion. There would have been no difficulty had he spoken first of the sinfulness of the Gentile and then of the sinfulness of the Jew; and, thirdly, of the additional guilt incurred by either in hypocrisy and judgement of others. But the sinfulness of the Jew being greatly increased by or mainly consisting in this last, he has sunk the mention of other sins, leaving them to be inferred or suggested from the general description that preceded.

With the first verse of the second chapter the style changes; the contemplation of the heathen world is ended, and the Apostle proceeds to reason with an imaginary opponent, whom he draws within the circle of human evil and will not allow him to escape, under the pretence of judging others, which does but aggravate his guilt. Such a one is trying to deceive God, but only deceives himself. Gradually we approach the Jew. In the third verse there is a glimpse of the notion that God would judge the heathen but spare the sons of Abraham; in the fourth and fifth verses is presented to us a picture, like those in the Old Testament, of the rebellious spirit of the Jew, and the long-suffering of God towards him; in the tenth and eleventh verses occurs a declaration of God's equal justice to all; in the twelfth and thirteenth the spirit of the law is opposed to the letter, and the believing Gentile to the unbelieving Jew; until at last, in ver. 17, the Apostle turns to make the direct attack on the Jew, for which, in the previous verses, he has been indirectly preparing: 'But if thou art called a Jew, and restest in the law and gloriest in God.'

Throughout this paragraph, as elsewhere, the connexion is in a great measure formed by the repetition of words in the successive verses and clauses. Thus $\pi\rho\acute{a}\sigma\sigma o\nu\tau as$ and $\kappa\rho\hat{\iota}\mu a$ connect verses 1 and 2; $\tau o\grave{\upsilon}s$ $\tau\grave{a}$ $\tau o\iota a\hat{\upsilon}\tau a$ $\pi\rho\acute{a}\sigma\sigma o\nu\tau as$ is taken up from ver. 2 in ver. 3; in the latter part of ver. 4 $\tau\grave{o}$ $\chi\rho\eta\sigma\tau\grave{o}\nu$ $\tau o\hat{\upsilon}$ $\theta\epsilon o\hat{\upsilon}$ is a repetition of $\tau o\hat{\upsilon}$ $\pi\lambda o\acute{\upsilon}\tau o\upsilon$ $\tau\hat{\eta}s$ $\chi\rho\eta\sigma\tau\acute{o}\tau\eta\tau os$ in the former part of the verse; $\grave{o}s$ $\grave{a}\pi o\delta\acute{\omega}\sigma\epsilon\iota$, $\kappa.\tau.\lambda.$, in ver. 6 is an expansion of the word $\delta\iota\kappa a\iota o\kappa\rho\iota\sigma\acute{\iota}as$ in ver. 5; $\delta\acute{o}\xi a$ $\delta\grave{\epsilon}$ $\kappa a\grave{\iota}$ $\tau\iota\mu\acute{\eta}$, in the tenth verse, is a resumption of the same words in the seventh.

CHAPTER III.

The force of the Apostle's argument in the first verses of the following chapter, may be illustrated by a parallel which comes home to ourselves. We may suppose a person enlarging, in a sermon or in conversation, on the comparative state of the heathen and Christian world, dwelling first of all on the enormities and unnatural vices of India or China, and then on the formalism and hypocrisy and conventionality of Christians throughout the world, until at last he concludes by saying that many heathen are better than most Christians, and that at the last day the heathen may judge us; and that as God is no respecter of persons, it matters little whether we are called Christians or not, if we follow Christ. Christian or heathen, 'he can't be wrong,' it might be said, 'whose life is in the right.' Then would arise the question, What profit was there in being a Christian if, as with the Jews of old, many should come from the East and the West, and sit down with Christ and His Apostles in the kingdom of heaven, while those bearing the name of Christians were cast out? To which there would be many answers; first, that of St. Paul respecting the Jews, 'because that unto us are committed the oracles of God;' and above all, that we have a new truth and a new power imparted to us. Still difficulties would occur as we passed beyond the limits of the Christian world. Passages of Scripture would be quoted, which seemed to place the heathen also within the circle of God's mercies; and again, other passages which seemed to exclude them. It might be doubted whether in any proper sense there was a Christian world; so little did there seem to be anything resembling the first company of believers; so faint was the bond of communion which the name of Christian made amongst men; so slender the line of demarcation which mere Christianity afforded, compared with civilization and other influences. Suppose, now, a person, struggling with these and similar difficulties, to carry the question a stage further back, and to urge that Christianity, failing of its end, this is of itself an impeachment of the truth and goodness of God. For if there were any who did not accept the Gospel, then it could not be said that an Omnipotent Being who had the power, and an Omniscient Being who knew the way, had also the will that all mankind should be saved. Why should the Unchangeable punish men for sins that could not affect Himself? Why should He execute a vengeance which He was incapable of feeling? And so he would lead us on to the origin of evil and the eternal decrees, and the everlasting penalty. Speaking as a philosopher, he might say, that we must change our notion of a Divine Being, in the face of such facts. Those who were arguing with him, might be unable or unwilling to discuss speculative difficulties, and might prefer to rest their belief on two simple foundations: first, the truth and justice and holiness of God; and, secondly, the moral consequences of the doctrine of their opponents. It makes no difference whether we suppose the argument carried on between disputants, or whether we suppose a religious sceptic arguing with himself on the opposite aspects of those great questions, which in every age, from that of Job and Ecclesiastes, have been more or less clearly seen in various forms, Jewish as well as Christian, as problems of natural or of revealed religion, common alike to the Greeks and to ourselves, and which have revived again and again in the course of human thought.

The train of reflection which has been thus briefly sketched, is not unlike that with which St. Paul opens the third chapter. The Jew and the Gentile have been reduced to a level by the requirements of the moral law. The circumcision of the heart and the uncircumcision of the letter take the place of the circumcision of the letter and uncircumcision of the heart. Such a revolution naturally leads the Jew to ask what his own position is in the dispensations of Providence. What profit is there in being sons of Abraham, if of these stones God was raising up children unto Abraham? To which the Apostle replies, first, that they had the Scriptures. But it might be said, 'they believed not.' Such an objection is suggested by the Apostle himself, who draws it out of the secret soul of the Jew, that he may answer it more fully. 'Shall their unbelief make the promise of God of none effect.' Such promises are 'yea and amen;' but they are also conditional. God forbid that they should be called in question, because man breaks their conditions. Imagine all men faithless, yet does God remain true.

Still the objector or the objection returns, in the fifth verse, from another point of view, which is suggested by the quotation which immediately precedes, 'that thou mayest be justified in thy sayings, and mayest overcome when thou art judged.' In any case then God is justified; why doth He yet punish? If we do no harm to Him, why does He do harm to us? We are speaking as one man does of another; but is not God unjust? To which the Apostle replies (according to different explanations of τὸν κόσμον), either, 'shall not the Judge of all the earth do rightly?' or, how can you, who are a Jew, suppose that the God whose attribute it is 'to judge among the heathen' is one who may be called unjust? In this question is contained the answer to those who say, 'My unrighteousness commends the righteousness of God, and therefore God has no right to take vengeance on me.' Still the objection is repeated in a slightly altered form, not now, 'If my unrighteousness commends the righteousness of God;' but, 'If my falsehood abounds to the glory of His truth, why am I still judged as a sinner?' To which St. Paul replies, not by dwelling further on the truth or justice of God, but by ironically stating the consequence of the doctrine, 'Let us do evil that good may come, let us sin to the glory of God, let us lie to prove his truth;' and, then dropping the strain of irony, he adds seriously in his natural style, 'whose damnation is just.'

The chief difference between this argument and the one which, for the sake of illustration, is prefixed to it, is that the great questions which are suggested in the first, are here narrowed to the Jewish point of view. The objector does not find any general difficulty in justifying the ways of God to man, but in harmonizing the rejection of the Jews with the privileges of the chosen race. What seemed to him injustice, was justice to all mankind. He is animated by a sort of moral indignation at being reduced to the same level as the rest of the world.

CHAPTER IV.

AT the end of the second chapter the Apostle had almost declared that Jew and Gentile were both alike; of this he stopped short and spoke in a figure of the spiritual Israelite. In the same way in the fourth chapter, he answers the question which he himself raises, by putting the spiritual in the place of the fleshly Abraham. 'What shall we say that Abraham found, our progenitor according to the flesh? or what shall we say, that Abraham our progenitor found according to the flesh?' The intended answer according to either way of reading the question is 'nothing;' for what he found was not an advantage of that kind for which the Israelite hoped; it was an advantage not according to the flesh, but according to the spirit. But St. Paul avoids the harshness of this inference by a digression in which he points out that the blessedness of Abraham was not of works, but of faith. In this digression he takes up a thread of the argument at the conclusion of the last chapter in which glorying is excluded. 'If Abraham were justified by works, he would have whereof to glory:' this, however, is impossible, and expressly contradicted by the words of Scripture, which says, 'Abraham believed God, and it was counted to him for righteousness.' This is the indirect answer to the question, 'What shall we say that Abraham found, our progenitor according to the flesh?'

Subordinate to this assertion of the general principle in the person of Abraham, is the minor question respecting the time of which the words were spoken 'not in circumcision, but in uncircumcision,' in which little fact the Apostle read their universal import. Circumcision came afterwards; it had nothing to do with the faith or with the promise that had preceded; it only conveyed through Abraham the privileges of which it was the seal to the faithful everywhere. (Compare Gal. iii. 17.) The sign of circumcision was but the accident of that higher relation in which the Patriarch stood already to God and man. As in the last chapter the words, 'a man is justified by faith without the deeds of the law' (verse 28), were quickly followed by the declaration (verse 29), that 'God was the God of the Gentiles also;' so here the statement that Abraham 'believed God, and it was counted to him for righteousness,' leads the Apostle instantly to think of him as the 'heir of the world,' a title with which the pride of the Israelite delighted to invest him. Is he the father of the Jews only, is he not also of the Gentiles? Yes; both aspects of the Gospel are seen in him. And the narrative of the birth of Isaac—the calling of the living out of the dead—is repeated by the Apostle with a kind of triumph as a lesson of new and universal interest.

CHAPTER V.

EVERY pause in the Epistle may be made the occasion for taking a glance backward, and surveying the whole. In the construction of the work we observe that the same threads again and again reappear, tangling the web of discourse, and are never finished and worked off. Thus the commencement of the fifth chapter is but the anticipation of the eighth:—

Therefore being justified by faith, we have peace with God through our Lord Jesus Christ.

There is therefore now no condemnation to them which are in Christ Jesus.

Compare again the following:—
(1) ch. iii. 1. What advantage then hath the Jew?
9. What then are we better than they?
27. Where then is boasting?
iv. 1. What shall we say then that Abraham hath found, our progenitor according to the flesh?
(2) ch. vi. 1. What shall we say then? are we to continue in sin that grace may abound?
15. What then? shall we sin, because we are not under the law, but under grace?
vii. 7. What shall we say then? is the law sin?
(3) Also the first verse of ch. ix, x, xi.
ix. 1. I say the truth in Christ, that I have great sorrow for Israel.
x. 1. Brethren, my heart's desire and prayer to God for Israel is, that they might be saved.
xi. 1. I say then, hath God cast aside his people?
where the Apostle thrice returns to the same point in his argument, and begins again with the same theme.

Similarities of form and repetitions of thought may also be noted in successive verses.

Compare:—
v. 8-10: 'But God commended his love to us in that, while we were yet sinners, Christ died for the ungodly. Much more then, being now justified by his blood, we shall be saved from wrath through him. For if, when we were enemies, we were reconciled to God by the death of his Son; much more, being reconciled, we shall be saved

by his life.' These words are followed by the favourite 'not only so,' which has already occurred at the beginning of verse 3.

Compare also verses 15, 17, 18, 19, and i. 24, 26, 28; vii. 15, 19; 17, 22; as instances of a structure in which the same ideas are repeated rather than developed, and in some of which the form of the first sentence prescribes the form of the second.

Many slight inaccuracies appear on the surface when we look at the Epistle to the Romans through a microscope. It will be often found that the successive clauses are not logically connected, or that qualifications are introduced which are not duly subordinated to the principal thought; or the latter end of a sentence may seem to forget the beginning of it, or for an instant the Apostle may hesitate between two alternatives. But flaws of this kind disappear when we remove to a little distance; the irregularity of the details is lost in the general effect. It might be said of the Apostle in his own language, that he is not speaking with 'the persuasive words of man's wisdom, but with demonstration of the spirit and with power.' It does not impair the force of what he says that he repeats a word, or that he uses a particle where it is not needed, or that he has so framed a particular clause that its bearing on the next clause is doubtful. It does not interfere with the unity of his writings that they have not the symmetrical character of a modern composition. We often speak of his style; according to modern notions he can hardly be said to have a style. He uses the rhetorical forms of his age because he cannot help doing so: they are his only way of expressing himself. He is not free to mould language with the hand of a master. Yet, in general, his meaning is perfectly clear. If, following Locke's rule, we read the Epistle through at a single sitting, the broken thoughts come together, and a new kind of unity begins to arise; the unity not of a whole with many parts aptly disposed, but of a single idea, appearing and reappearing everywhere. The stream is one, though parting into two branches—the universality of salvation, and the doctrine of righteousness by faith. To the end of the eleventh chapter there is nothing irrelevant, nothing that does not bear on one or other of these two aspects of the great truth. Imagine the writer full of these two thoughts, yet incapable of mastering the language in which he wrote, encumbered with formulas and modes of speech; eager to declare the whole counsel of God, yet conscious of the way in which men might wrest it to their own destruction; seeking 'to entwine the new with the old, and to make the old ever new;' and you would expect a composition similar in texture to the Epistle to the Romans.

The Epistle is full of repetitions, yet the repetitions carry us onward. The revelation of righteousness by faith is first made in the seventeenth verse of the first chapter. Then, after the necessity for it has been shown from the self-condemnation of the world, it is repeated at the twenty-first verse of the third chapter. Here it might seem as if the Apostle's task was over. But another link has yet to be wrought into the chain. Is it the Apostle only who is saying these things? Saith not the law the same also? Yes; the doctrine of justification and forgiveness is contained in the book of the law. Abraham as well as ourselves was justified by faith, and not by works. Then the Apostle states his doctrine once more in the form of a conclusion to an argument, and proceeds to display it as embodied in the type and antitype, the first and second Adam. Still he has to guard against inferences that might be deduced from it, such as the antinomianism at which he had before hinted, 'Let us continue in sin that grace may abound, let us do evil that good may come.' Then he returns to the same note which he had struck before, the confirmation of his doctrine from the book of the law. Lastly, he fights the battle over again; not now in the world at large, but in the narrower sphere of the individual soul; he describes the last state of paralysis and death, until at length the agony is at its height and the victory is won; and, having now turned to view the scheme of redemption in every aspect—in reference to the former state of the world, divided between Jew and Gentile, in reference to the patriarchs, in reference to human nature itself, in reference to possible consequences as well as the inward experience of the soul,—he repeats the conclusion which in chap. v had been already anticipated, chanting, as it were, the hymn of peace after victory, 'There is, therefore, now no condemnation to them which are in Christ Jesus.'

CHAPTER VI.

THERE are some errors in religion which are ever attendant on the truths connected with them. Not only have men blessed with the grace of God greater powers and responsibilities than others, but they have also dangers, if not greater, yet peculiar to them, and seeming from the very constitution of the human mind itself to be inseparable from their religious state. There are faults, delusions, prejudices, tendencies to evil, to which they are liable, and which religion itself seems to foster in the weakness of human nature. One of these tendencies is antinomianism, or the tendency to rest in feeling, without knowledge of action. It is a corruption not peculiar to Christianity, but common to all religions which have had anything of spiritual life or power; in the case of individuals often exercising a subtle influence among those who disavow it in words. It already existed among the Jews in the time of St. Paul, as we may gather from the Epistle of St. James, and are informed by Philo, *De Migr. Abrah.* (Mangey, i. 450).

Against this corruption the Apostle sets himself in the

present chapter. There was nothing more natural if grace abounded, than that men should continue in sin, that it might yet more abound. Experience sadly proves that there is a faith without works, hope of forgiveness without repentance, final assurance without moral goodness. There are religious states in which the eye of the soul seems to lose its clear insight into right and truth, and even obscures with the consolations of the Gospel its sterner sense of the holiness of God. In the hour of death especially, nature herself seems to assist in the delusion. In the first ages, as in all other times of religious excitement, such a delusion was more than ordinarily likely to prevail. It was a charge made against the Apostle himself that he said: 'Let us do evil that good may come.'

At this point, therefore, in his great argument, when the abundance of Divine grace has been already developed, the Apostle pauses to guard against the dangerous inference. His manner of doing so is characteristic of his view of the doctrine itself. He does not seek to test the Christian state by external acts, but to exalt our inward notion of it. He does not say, a true faith is that which brings forth good works, or that which is known like a tree by its fruits. To him, the very idea of Christian life is death to sin, and death with Christ. In the previous chapter no language seemed too strong to express the fullness and freedom of the grace of God. That might tempt us to continue in sin. But no, we are dead to sin. The state of grace itself is a state of union with Christ, in which we follow Him through the various stages of His life. When we think of it as death, sin dies within us; when we think of it as life, we are risen with Him.

CHAPTER VII.

According to the similitude which the Apostle here uses, the relation of the Jew to the law is likened to the case of a wife who has lost her husband. As a widow the law, of course, said that she might marry again; her husband had no claim on her. Even so the law itself was dead, and the Jew was free to marry again to Christ, who was not dead, but risen from the dead.

There is, however, a difficulty in the application of the similitude in verses 4, 5, 6. This arises from the believer being regarded in two points of view. In the figure he is compared to the wife, while in the application he seems to change places, and become identified with the husband, who, in a certain sense, as well as the wife, is freed from the law; for 'he that is dead, has been freed from sin.' For this change there seem to be two reasons:—First, In working out the figure, the resemblance of the Christian to the husband as well as to the wife, strikes the Apostle; for as the husband is dead, so also is the Christian dead to the law. Secondly, The change may be regarded as a sort of euphemism to Jewish ears. The Apostle avoids the harshness of saying that 'the law is dead,' by substituting 'ye are dead to the law.'

In the previous chapter the believer had been described as dead unto sin, but alive unto righteousness. 'Sin,' said the Apostle, 'shall have no more dominion over you; for ye are not under the law, but under grace.' This thought he carries out further in the present passage, illustrating it by the particular case of the woman and the husband, which, in the language of the Epistle to the Galatians, shows, in a figure, 'that the law is dead to us, and we to the law.' The only difference is that in the last chapter what the Apostle was speaking of was a 'death unto sin;' here rather of what in his view is so closely connected as to be almost identical with it, 'a death unto the law.' It is the close connexion between them that leads him to guard, in verse 7, against the possible inference that 'the law is sin.'

Nothing but the exigencies of controversy would have induced Augustine, against his better mind and the authority of the earlier Fathers, to refer this passage to the condition of the regenerate man. He was led to this interpretation, as others have been, by the equal, if not greater, difficulty of referring the description of the Apostle to the unregenerate.

The latter interpretation is plainly repugnant to the spirit of the passage; for whom shall we conceive the Apostle to be describing? or, rather, which is the same thing, whom do we ourselves mean by the term unregenerate? Is it the Jew, or the heathen, or the hypocrite, or the sensualist? To none of these characters will such a description refer. They know of no struggle between the things they would and would not; they live in no twilight between good and evil; their state is a lower and less conscious one. Who would speak of the unregenerate heart of Caesar or of Achilles? Language itself teaches us the impropriety of such expressions. And the reason of the impropriety is, that we feel with the Apostle, though our point of view may be somewhat different, that the guilt of sin is inseparable from the knowledge of sin. Those who never heard the name of Christ, who never admit the thought of Christ, cannot be brought within the circle of Christian feelings and associations.

There have been few more frequent sources of difficulty in theology, than the common fallacy of summing up inquiries under two alternatives, neither of which corresponds to the true nature of the case. We may admit the logical proposition that all things are animal or not animal, vegetable or not vegetable, mineral or not mineral. But we cannot say that all men are civilized or uncivilized, Christian or unchristian, regenerate or unregenerate. Such a mode of division is essentially erroneous. It exercises a false influence on the mind, by tending to confuse fixed states and transitions, differences in degree with differences in kind. All things may be passing out of one class into another, and may therefore belong to both or neither. The very attempt to classify or divide them may itself be the source of an illusion.

Obvious as such a fallacy is, it is only by the light of experience that theology can be freed from it. From 'the oppositions of knowledge falsely so called,' we turn to the human heart itself. Reading this passage by what we know of ourselves and other men, we no longer ask the question:—'Whether the Apostle is speaking of the regenerate or unregenerate man?' That is an 'after-thought,' which has nothing to correspond to it in the world, and nothing to justify it in the language of the Apostle. Mankind are not divided into regenerate and unregenerate, but are in a state of transition from one to the other, or too dead and unconscious to be included in either. What we want to know is the meaning of the Apostle, not in the terms of a theological problem, but in the simpler manner in which it presented itself to his own mind.

He is speaking of a conflict in the soul of man, the course of which, notwithstanding its sudden and fitful character, is nevertheless marked by a certain progress. It commences in childish and unconscious ignorance ('I was alive without the law once'), which is succeeded by the deep consciousness of sin, which the law awakens, and so hovering between death and life, passes on to the last agony and final deliverance. The stages of this contest are not exactly defined. In the earliest of them is an element of reason and of good; in the latest, we seem only to arrive at a more intense conviction of human misery. The progress is not a progress from works to faith, or from the law to grace, but a growing separation and division, in which the soul is cut in two— into the better and the worse mind, the inner and the outer man, the flesh and the Spirit. The law is the dividing principle, 'sharper than any two-edged sword,' which will not allow them to unite. On the one side remains the flesh, as it were, a decomposing body of death; on the other, the mind and spirit flutter in lawless aspirations after good which they have no means or instruments to attain. The extremity of the conflict is the moment of deliverance; when completely in the power of sin, we are already at the gate of heaven.

The use of the first person is not merely rhetorical. It seems as though the Apostle were speaking partly from recollections of his former state, partly from the emotions of sin, which he still perceived in his members, now indeed pacified and kept under control, yet sufficiently sensible to give a liveliness to the remembrance, and make him feel his dependence on Christ. So much of the struggle continued in him as he himself describes in such passages as 2 Cor. i. 9, 10, or xii. 7. He who says, 'without were fightings, within fears' (2 Cor. v. 7), who had 'the sentence of death in himself,' and 'a messenger of Satan to buffet him,' could not have lived always in an unbroken calm of mind, any more than we can imagine him to have been constantly repeating, 'O wretched man that I am!' Further, we may remark, that the combat, as it deepens, becomes more ideal—that is, removes further away from the actual consciousness of mankind; the Apostle is describing tendencies in the heart of man which go beyond the experience of individuals.

CHAPTER VIII.

THE struggle has passed away, and the conqueror and the conquered are side by side. The two laws mentioned in the last chapter have changed places, the one becoming mighty from being powerless, the other powerless from being mighty. The helplessness of the law has been done away in Christ, that its righteous requirement may be fulfilled in us, who walk not after the flesh but after the spirit. The Apostle returns upon his former track that he may contrast the two elements, not, as in the previous chapter, in conflict with each other, hopelessly entangled by 'occasion of the commandment,' but in entire separation and opposition. These two, the flesh and the spirit, stand over against one another, as life and death, as peace and enmity with God. Do what it will, the flesh can never be subjected to the law of God. And this antagonism is not an antagonism of ideas only, but of persons also. It is another mode of expressing the same thought, to say that they that are in the flesh cannot please God. 'But ye,' the Apostle adds, 'are not in the flesh, but in the Spirit, which is the Spirit of God and Christ, and have the body dead, and the Spirit that is in you life; and as God raised up Christ from the dead, he will raise you up, because you have his Spirit dwelling in you. Are we not debtors then to live according to the Spirit, which is the only source of life and immortality, under the guidance of which, too, we are no longer the servants but the sons of God?'

CHAPTERS IX—XI.

THE chapters that have preceded have been connected with each other by a sort of network, some of the threads of which have never ceased or been intermitted. At this point we come to a break in the Epistle. What follows has no connexion with what immediately precedes. The sublime emotion with which chapter viii concludes is in another strain from that with which chapter ix opens. We might almost imagine that the Apostle had here made a pause, and only after a while resumed his work of dictating to 'Tertius who wrote this Epistle.' It is on a more extended survey of the whole that order begins to reappear, and we see that the subject now introduced, which was faintly anticipated at the commencement of the third chapter, has also an almost necessary place in the Apostle's scheme.

The three chapters ix—xi have been regarded by an eminent critic as containing the true germ and first thought of the Epistle. Such a view may be supported by various arguments. It may be said that a letter must arise out of circumstances, and that this portion of the Epistle only has an appropriate subject; that we can imagine the Apostle, though unknown by face to the Church which was at Rome, writing to Jewish Christians on a topic in which they, as well as he, were so deeply interested as the restoration of their countrymen; but that we cannot imagine him sitting down to compose a treatise on justification by faith; that to explain the dealings of God with his people, it was necessary for him to go back to the first principles of the Gospel of Christ, and that this mode of overlaying and transposing what to us would seem the natural order of thought is quite in accordance with his usual manner. (Compare, e. g. the structure of 1 Cor. x.) It may be urged, that in several passages, as, for example, at the commencement of the third and fourth chapters, he has already hinted at the maintenance of the privileges of the Jews. All such arguments, ably as they have been stated by Baur, yet fail to convince us that what is apparently prominent and on the surface, and also occupies the greater part of the Epistle, is really subordinate, and that what is apparently subordinate and supplementary, held the first place in the Apostle's thoughts. (See Introduction.)

The theory of Baur is, however, so far true, as it tends to bring into prominence, as a main subject of the Epistle, the admission of the Gentiles. To the Apostle himself and his contemporaries, this was half, or more than half, the whole truth, not less striking or absorbing than the other half, of 'righteousness by faith only.' It is with this aspect of the doctrine of St. Paul that the portion of the Epistle on which we are now entering is to be connected. 'Is he the God of the Jews only? is he not also of the Gentiles? Yes, of the Gentiles also.' But granting this, innumerable difficulties and perplexities arose in the mind of the Israelite or of the reader of the Old Testament. What is the meaning of a chosen people? What advantage hath the Jew? and above all, what is to be his final end? When the circle of God's mercy is extended to the whole world, is he to be the only exception? Thrice the Apostle essays to answer this question; thrice he turns aside, rather to justify God's present dealings in casting away His chosen, than to hold out the hope with which he concludes, that all Israel shall be saved.

We have seen elsewhere (chaps. iii. 1-8; v. 12-21; vii. 7-11) that in many passages the Apostle wavers between the opposite sides of a question, before he arrives at a final and permanent conclusion. The argument in such passages may be described as a sort of struggle in his own thoughts, an alternation of natural feelings, a momentary conflict of emotions. The stream of discourse flows onward in two channels, occasionally mingling or contending with each other, which meet at the last. There are particular instances of this peculiarity of style in the chapters which follow, ix. 19; x. 14. But the most striking illustration of it is the general character of the whole three chapters, in which the Apostle himself seems for a time in doubt between contending feelings, in which he first prays for the restoration of Israel, and then reasons for their rejection, and then finally shows that in a more extended view of the purposes of God their salvation is included. He hears the echo of many voices in the Old Testament, by which the Spirit spoke to the Fathers, and in all of them there is a kind of unity, though but half expressed, which is not less the unity of his own inmost feelings towards his kinsmen according to the flesh. He is like one of the old prophets himself, abating nothing of the rebellions of the house of Israel, yet still unable to forget that they are the people of God. As an Israelite and a believer in Christ, he is full of sorrow first, of consolation afterwards; two opposite feelings struggle together in his mind, both finally giving way to a clearer insight into the purposes of God towards the chosen nation.

When the first burst of his emotion has subsided, he proceeds to show that the rejection of Israel was not total, but partial, and that this partial rejection is in accordance with the analogy of God's dealings with their fathers. The circle of God's mercy to them had ever been narrowing. First, the seed of Abraham was chosen; then Isaac only; then Jacob before Esau, and this last quite irrespective of any good or evil that either of them had done. There was a preference in each case of the spiritual over the fleshly heir. Shall we say that here is any ground for imputing unrighteousness to God? He Himself had proclaimed this as His mode of dealing with mankind. The words of the law are an end of controversy. He does it, therefore it is just; He tells it us, therefore it is true. Who are we that we should call in question His justice, or challenge His ways? The clay might as well reason with the potter, as man argue against God. And, after all, this election of some to wrath, others to mercy, is but justice in mercy delayed, or an alternation of mercy and justice. The rejection of the Jews is the admission of the Gentiles. And to this truth the prophets themselves bear witness. They speak of 'a remnant,' of 'another people,' of 'a cutting short upon the earth,' of 'a rock of offence.' The work that God has done is nothing unjust or unexpected, but a work of justice and mercy upon the house of Israel, of which their own prophets witness; of which they are themselves the authors, as they sought to establish their own righteousness, and rejected the righteousness that is of faith.

But the subject of God's dealings with the Jews is not yet finished; it is, indeed, scarcely begun. The first verses of the ninth chapter gave an intimation that this would not be the final course of the Apostle's thought. Israel had sought to establish their own righteousness, and rejected the righteousness that was of faith. But this very rejection, which was their condemnation, was not without excuse, in that it arose from a mistaken zeal for God. That mistake consisted in their not perceiving the difference between the righteousness of the law and the righteousness of faith ; the one a straight and unbending rule; the other, 'very nigh, even in thy mouth and thy heart,' and extending to all mankind. 'But,' we expect the Apostle to say at the end of the contrast, 'notwithstanding this, Israel may yet be saved.' The time for this is not yet come. In what follows, to the end of the chapter, he digresses more and more ; first, as at vers. 14–19 of the previous one, to state the objections of the Jew ; secondly, to show that those objections are of no weight, and are disproved by the words of their own prophets.

Nowhere does the logical control over language, that is, the power of aptly disposing sentences so as to exhibit them in their precise relation to each other, so fail the Apostle as at the conclusion of the tenth chapter. We see his meaning, but his emotions prevent him from expressing it. At the commencement of the eleventh chapter, finding that he is so far away from his original subject, he makes an effort to regain it. 'Hath God then cast away his people ?' The Apostle is himself a living proof that this is not so. Though Israel 'hath not obtained it,' the elect, who are part of Israel, who are the true Israel, have obtained it. The fall of the rest is but for a time, and is itself an argument for their final restoration. The rejection of the Jews is the admission of the Gentiles, and the admission of the Gentiles comes round in the end to be the restoration of the Jews. And besides, and beneath all this, amid these alternations of thought and vicissitudes of human things, there is an immutable foundation on which we rest in the promises of

God to Israel. The friend of the patriarchs cannot forget their children; the Unchangeable cannot desert the work of His hands.

CHAPTER X.

THE commencement of this chapter, as well as of the one which follows, affords a remarkable instance of a sudden transition of feeling in the mind of the Apostle. At the end of the previous chapter, he had passed out of the sorrowful tone in which he began, to prove that very truth over which he sorrowed—the rejection of Israel. But at this point he drops the argument, and resumes the strain which he had laid aside. The character of the passage may be illustrated by the parallel passage in chap. iii. 1–8. There he had been arguing that the Gentiles were better than the Jews, or at least as good; because they, not having the law, were a law unto themselves. Then to correct the impression that might have arisen from what he had been saying, he goes on to point out that the Jew too had advantages. Now, a similar contrast is working in his mind. There was something that the Jew had, though not the righteousness of faith. He was not a sinner of the Gentiles, he had a zeal for God, he had the mark of distinction which it has been said made Jacob to be preferred to Esau; 'he was a religious man.' But almost before the thought of his heart is fully uttered, the Apostle returns to his former subject—'the righteousness of faith, Christ the end of the law to every one that believeth;' and gathers fresh proof from the prophecies that the rejection of Israel was but according to the will of God.

CHAPTER XI.

The whole of the three chapters viii, ix, x may be regarded as the passionate struggle of conflicting emotions in the Apostle's mind—πότε μὲν νυνὶ δέ—of his present and former self. Are Israel saved, or not? They must be, for I also am one of them. At last, the purpose of God respecting them clears before his eyes. That they are rejected is a fact; but it is only for a time, that the Gentiles may be received. Hitherto he has been occupied with laying the broad foundation of a universal Gospel. Is He the God of the Jews only? is He not also of the Gentiles? Yes; of the Gentiles also; and of the Gentiles exclusively it seemed, but for the remnant who are saved. Such was the impression to which his own reception would naturally have led the Apostle, as he went from city to city, finding no hearers of the word, but Gentiles only. Of the two divisions of mankind, he seemed to lose one, and gain the other. The meditation of this fact had revealed to him a new page in God's dealings with mankind. But now a further insight into the purposes of God breaks upon him. In the order of Providence came the Jew first, and afterwards the Gentile; and the Jew last returning to the inheritance of his fathers. The erring branch that has twined with the briars of the wilderness, is brought back to its own olive, and the tree covers the whole earth.

CHAPTERS XII—XVI.

The last five chapters may be considered as a third section of the Epistle to the Romans, in which, as in the latter portion of the Galatians, Colossians, Ephesians, Thessalonians, exhortation takes the place of doctrinal statement, and the imperative mood becomes the prevailing form of sentence. There is less of plan than in what has preceded, and more that throws light on the state of the Church. At first sight, it seems as if the Apostle were dictating to an amanuensis unconnected precepts, which his experience, not of the Roman converts, to whom he was unknown by face, but of the Church and the world in general, led him to think useful or necessary.

Yet these fragments, including in them chaps. xii. 1—xv. 7, at which point the Apostle returns briefly to his main theme, and concludes with a personal narrative, are not wholly deficient in order, especially that recurring order which was remarked in the introduction to the fifth chapter, and which consists in the repetition, at certain intervals, of a particular subject. The great argument is now ended; what follows is its practical application: 'For God concluded all under sin, that he might have mercy upon all;' the inference from which is not 'Let us continue in sin that grace may abound,' but rather, 'How shall we, who are dead to sin, live any longer therein?' which the Apostle expresses once more in language borrowed from the law: 'I beseech you, therefore, brethren, by the mercies of God, to present your bodies a living sacrifice.' Leaving this thought, he passes on at ver. 3 to another, which can hardly be said to be connected with it in any other than that general way in which all the different portions of Christian truth or practice are connected with each other, or in which the part may be always regarded as related to the whole. This new thought is Christian unity, which is introduced here much in the same manner as love of the brethren in the Epistle to the Thessalonians. The ground of this unity is humility, each one retiring into his own duties, that the whole may be harmonious, remembering that he is a member of the body of Christ, in which there are diversities of gifts, which the members of that body are severally to use. Thence the Apostle goes on to the mention of Christian graces, apparently unconnected with each other, among which, at ver. 16, the first thought of humility, which is the true source of sympathy, reappears, with which peace and forgiveness of injuries meet in one. At the commencement of chap. xiii what may be termed the key-note of this portion of the Epistle returns—the order of the Church, not now considered in reference to the members of the same body, but to those that are without the Church— the heathen rulers with whom they came into contact, whom they were to obey as to the Lord and not to men. The remainder of this chapter stands in the same relation to the former part as the latter portion of chap. xii to the commencement; that is to say, it consists of precepts which arise out of the principal subject; here honesty in general, out of the duty of paying tribute, which leads, by a play of words, to the endless debt of love, which is the fulfilment of the law; all which is enforced by the near approach of the day of the Lord, corresponding to the argument of the preacher from the shortness of life among ourselves.

The remaining section of the Epistle, from chap. xiv to xv. 6, is taken up with a single subject—the treatment of weak brethren, who doubt about meats and drinks and the observance of days. This subject is distinct from what has preceded, and forms a whole by itself; yet, in the mode of handling it, vestiges of former topics reappear. It is a counsel of peace, to show consideration to the doubters; and for the doubters themselves, it is a proper humility not to judge others, chap. ii. 1: and in our conduct towards the weak brethren, it must be remembered how awful a thing is the conscience of sin, which is inseparable from doubt, 'for whatever is not of faith, is sin.' And here we come back once more to our original text, 'Be of the same mind one with another.'

At this point, the Apostle returns from his digression to the main subject of the Epistle, which he briefly sums up under the figure of Jesus Christ a minister of the circumcision to the Gentiles, and once more clothes in the language of the prophets. Yet a certain degree of difference is discernible between his treatment of it in this and in the earlier portions of the Epistle. It is less abstract and more personal. He seems to think of the truths which he taught more in connexion with his own labours as Apostle of the Gentiles. A similar image to that of Christ the minister of the circumcision he applies to himself—the minister of Christ, the offerer up of the sacrifice of the Gentiles. Still, Apostle of the Gentiles as he is, he is careful not to intrude on another man's labours. He has fulfilled his mission where he is, and does but follow the dictates of natural feeling in going first to Jerusalem, and then to the Christians of the West; for the success of which new mission he desires their prayers, that it may be acceptable to his friends and without danger from enemies, and may end in his coming to them with joy.

The last chapter consists almost entirely of salutations. Among these are interspersed a few of the former topics, some of which occur also at the end of other Epistles, such as peace and joy at the success of the Gospel. There are names of servants of God, among whom are Aquila and Priscilla, and others of whom no record has been elsewhere preserved. One expression raises without satisfying our curiosity, 'distinguished among those who were Apostles before me.' The Epistle, as it began with a summary of the Gospel, concludes with a thanksgiving—in which the subject of the Epistle is once more interwoven—to God the author of the Gospel, which was once hidden, but now revealed that the Gentiles also might be obedient to the faith.

CHAPTER XIII.

In the previous chapter the Apostle had spoken of the unity of the Church, and of the offices of its members. He had gone on to scatter admonitions, following each other in order sometimes of sound, sometimes of meaning, which, like the precepts of the sermon on the Mount, went beyond the maxims of heathen virtue, or the sayings of 'them of old time.' Men were to think humbly of themselves, to return good for evil, to feed their enemies, to live peaceably with all. Continuing in the same spirit, he adds, 'they are to be obedient to the powers that be.' This is a part of the Christian's duty, which he will more easily fulfil if he regards the magistrate as he truly is, as 'the minister of God for good.'

The earnestness with which St. Paul dwells upon his theme, as well as the allusions to the same subject in other passages of the New Testament (Titus iii. 1 : 1 Pet. ii. 13-18), are proofs that he is guarding against a tendency to which he knew the first believers to be subject. He is speaking to the Christians at Rome, as a bishop of the fourth or fifth century might have addressed the multitudes of Alexandria; preaching counsels of moderation to 'the fifth monarchy men' of that day. They were more in the eye of the Christian world than believers elsewhere, more likely to come into conflict with the imperial power, perhaps in greater danger of being led away with the dream of another kingdom. The spirit of rebellion, against which the Apostle is warning them, was not a mere misconception of the teaching of the Gospel; it lay deep in the circumstances of the age and in the temper of the Jewish people. It is impossible to forget, however slight may be their historical groundwork, the well-known words of Suetonius, *Claud.* c. 25, 'Judaeos impulsore Chresto assiduè tumultuantes Romà expulit.' (Acts xviii. 2.) The narrative of Scripture itself affords indications of similar agitations, so far as they can be expected to cross the peaceful path of our Saviour and His disciples. The words of the prophecy, as it is termed, of Caiaphas respecting our Lord, however unfounded, imply a political fear more than a religious enmity. The question of the Pharisees, 'Is it lawful to give tribute to Caesar?' and the argument with which the Jews wrought on the fears of Pilate, are also not without significance. The account of Judas the Gaulonite, in Josephus, 'who rose up about the time of the taxing,' and whom Josephus terms 'the founder of the fourth philosophy of the Jews' (*Ant.* xviii. c. 1, §§ 1, 6), is a more explicit evidence of the spirit of insubordination. That 'philosophy' consisted in an inviolable attachment to liberty, and 'in calling no man Lord' but God Himself (§ 6), a principle which was maintained by its adherents with indescribable constancy. The author of the movement was no ordinary man, and the movement itself so far from being a transient one, that it continued through above half a century, and is regarded by Josephus, as 'laying the foundation of the miseries' of the Jewish war (xvii. c. 1, § 1).

The account of Josephus himself, unwilling as he is to do them justice, shows that in their first commencement the Zealots were animated by noble thoughts, their testimony to which they were ready to seal by tortures and death. Many of these 'Galileans' (for in this country they were chiefly found) were probably among the first converts. Like the Essenes, they stood in some relation that we are unable to trace to the followers of John the Baptist and of Christ. We cannot suppose that in all cases the temper of the Zealot had died away in the bosom of the Christian. A very slight misunderstanding of the manner in which 'the kingdom was to be restored to Israel' might suffice to rekindle the flame. If our Lord Himself had said, Peace I leave with you, He had also said, I come not to bring peace on earth, but a sword; if He had commanded Peter to put up his sword into the sheath, He had also commanded them each to sell his garment and buy one; if He had paid tribute, He had also declared that the children of the kingdom were free from the tribute. We could hardly wonder if those who heard His words sometimes mistook the result for the object, or confused the Jewish belief of the kingdom of heaven upon earth with the kingdom of God that is within. The after-history of the Church teaches how near such a confusion lay to the truth itself. Not once only, nor during our Lord's lifetime only, there have been those who have 'taken him by force to make him a king.'

The words 'the powers that be are ordained of God' have been made the foundation of many doctrines of passive obedience and non-resistance. Out of the Apostle's 'counsels of moderation' have developed themselves the Divine right of government, however exercised and under all circumstances, and even of particular forms of government. The party feelings of an age have been clothed in the language of Scripture, and established on the ground of antiquity. If the first Christians were to obey the heathen emperors, how can we ever be justified in shaking off the yoke of a Christian sovereign? If St. Paul said this under Nero, how much more is it true of the subjects of King Charles I?

Such arguments are two-edged? for as many passages may be quoted from Scripture which indirectly tend to the subversion, as can be adduced for the maintenance, of order or of property. The words of the psalmist, 'to bind their kings in chains, their nobles in fetters of iron,' are in the mouth of one class; 'shall I lift up my hand to slay the Lord's anointed?' of another; and in peace and prosperity men turn to the one, in the hour of revolution to the other. Many are the texts which we either silently drop or insensibly modify, with which the spirit of modern society seems almost unavoidably to be at variance. The blessing on the poor, and the 'hard sayings' respecting rich men, are not absolutely in accordance even with the better mind of the present age. We cannot follow the simple precept, 'Swear not at all,' without making an exception for the custom of our courts of law. We dare not quote the words, 'Go sell all thou hast and give to the poor,' without adding the caution, 'Beware, lest in making the copy thou break the pattern.' We are not so often exhorted 'to obey God rather than man,' as warned against the misapplication of the words.

These instances are sufficient to teach us how moderate we should be in reasoning from particular precepts, even where they agree with our preconceived opinions. The truth seems to be that the Scripture lays down no rule applicable to individual cases, or separable from the circumstances under which it is given. Still less does it furnish a political or philosophical system—'My kingdom is not of this world,' which it scarcely seems to touch. No one can infer from the passage that we are considering that St. Paul believed it wrong to rise against wicked rulers in any case, because they were the appointment of God, any more than from his speaking of wrestling against principalities and powers we can conclude that he supposed, with some of the Ebionitish sects, that all power was of the devil. It never occurred to him that the hidden life which he thought of only as to be absorbed in the glory of the sons of God, was one day to be the governing principle of the civilized world. Though 'he has written this in an epistle,' he would not have us use it 'altogether' without regard to the state of this world. Only in reference to the time at which he is writing, looking at the infant community in relation to the heathen world, he exhorts them to suffer rather than oppose; and if ever the thought rises in their minds that those whom they obey are the oppressors of God and His Church, to remember that without His appointment they could not have been, and that, after all, it is for their own faults they themselves are most likely to endure evil even at the hands of Gentile magistrates.

CHAPTER XIV.

It has been already stated, that we hardly know anything of the Roman Church. Hence the illustrations of the present chapter must rather consist in references to the floating opinions of the time than to precise facts. Even in regard to what we may seem to gather from the Epistle itself, it is not quite certain whether St. Paul is speaking from a knowledge of the circumstances of a Church which he had never visited, or from what he knew of the state of other Churches and of general tendencies in the mind of the first believers, or in the age generally. He may have had among his numerous acquaintances (xvi) some who, like the household of Chloe at Corinth, brought him news of what passed among the Christians at Rome. On the other hand, it may be remarked that a mention of similar observances to those here spoken of, recurs in the Epistle to the Colossians; and that a like scrupulosity of temper appears to have existed among the converts at Corinth.

The practices about which the first believers had scruples and on which the Apostle here touches, were—the use of animal food, and the observance of special days. The most probable guess at the nature of these scruples is that they were of half-Jewish, half-Oriental origin; similar practices existed among Jewish Essenes or Gentile Pythagoreans. Abstinence from animal food may be regarded as one among many indications of the ever-increasing influence of the East upon the West; unnatural as it seems to us, like circumcision it had become a second nature to a great portion of mankind. Fancy represented the eating of flesh as a species of cannibalism, and the Ebionites declared the practice to be an invention of evil demons (Clem. *Hom.* viii. 10-16). And with those who were far from superstitions of this kind, the fear of eating things offered to idols, or forbidden by the Mosaic law, operated so as to make them abstain where there was a danger of contact with Gentiles. Instances of such scruples occur in the book of Daniel and the Apocrypha. It was the glory of Daniel and the three holy children that they would 'not defile themselves with the portion of the king's food;' Dan. i. 8. So Tobit 'kept himself from eating the bread of the Gentiles;' i. 10, 11. Judas Maccabeus and nine others, living 'in the mountains after the manner of beasts, fed on herbs continually, lest they should become partakers of the pollution ;' 2 Macc. v. 27. Such examples show what the Jews had learned to practise or admire in the centuries immediately preceding the Christian era. So John the Baptist, in the narrative of the Gospels, 'fed on locusts and wild honey.' A later age delighted to attribute a similar abstinence to James the brother of the Lord (Heges. apud Euseb. *H. E.* ii. 23); and to Matthew (Clem. Alex. *Paed.* ii. 1, p. 174) : heretical writers added Peter to the list of these encratites (Epiph. *Her.* xxx. 2 ; Clem. *Hom.* xii. 6). The Apostolical canons (li, liii) admit an ascetic abstinence, but denounce those who abstain from any sense of the impurity of matter. See passages quoted in Fritsche, vol. iii. pp. 151, 152.

Jewish, as well as Alexandrian and Oriental influences, combined to maintain the practice of abstinence from animal food in the first centuries. Long after it had ceased to be a Jewish scruple, it remained as a counsel of perfection. In earlier ages, it was the former more than the latter. Those for whom the Apostle is urging consideration are the weak, rather than the strong ; not the ascetic, delighting to make physical purity the outward sign of holiness of life— against him it might have been necessary to contend for the freedom of the Gospel—but 'the babe in Christ,' feeble in heart and confused in head, who could not disengage himself from opinions or practices which he saw around him ; for whom, nevertheless, Christ died.

Respecting the second point of the observance of days, we know no more than may be gathered from Gal. iv. 9, 10, 17, 'How turn ye again to the weak and beggarly elements whereunto ye again desire to be in bondage? ye observe days, and months, and times, and years ;' where the Apostle is writing to a Church entangled in Judaism, which he therefore thinks it necessary to denounce: and Col. ii. 16, 'Let no man therefore judge you in respect of an holyday or a new moon, or of the sabbath days :' where the Apostle also reproves the same spirit as inconsistent with the close connexion or rather identity of the believer with his Lord. Whether in the Epistle to the Romans he is alluding to the Jewish observance of the Sabbath is uncertain; his main point is that the matter, whatever it was, should be left indifferent, and not determined by any decision of the Church. Superstitions of another kind may have also found their way among the Roman as well as the Colossian and Galatian converts. Astrology was practised both by Jew and Gentile; nor is it improbable that something of a heathen mingled with what was mainly of a Jewish character; the context of the two passages just quoted (Col. ii. 18, 20: Gal. iv. 9), would lead us to think so. It is true that the words, ὃς μὲν κρίνει ἡμέραν παρ' ἡμέραν, ὃς δὲ κρίνει πᾶσαν ἡμέραν (ver. 5), probably mean only that 'one man fasts on alternate days, another fasts every day.' But the expression ὁ φρονῶν τὴν ἡμέραν, in ver. 6, implies also the observance of particular days.

It has been already intimated, that this chapter furnishes no sure criterion that the Roman converts were either Jews or Gentiles. If it be admitted that it has any bearing at all on the state of the Roman converts, it tends to show that they were, not simply Gentiles converted from the ancient religion of Rome to Judaism or Christianity, but persons into whose minds Oriental notions had previously insinuated themselves, who with or before Christianity had received distinctions of days, and of meats and drinks, which in St. Paul's view were the very opposite of it. If, on the other hand, we suppose St. Paul to have written without any precise knowledge of the state of the Roman Church, we may regard this chapter, and part of that which follows, as characteristic of the general feeling in the Churches to which the Apostle preached.

The subject recurs in the eighth and tenth chapters of the First Epistle to the Corinthians. Here, as there, the Apostle knows but one way of treating these scruples and distinctions which were so alien to his own mind. It may be shortly described as absorbing the letter in the Spirit. When you see the weak brother doubting about his paltry observances, remember that the strength of God is sufficient for him ; when you feel disposed to judge him, consider that he is another's servant, and that God will judge both him and you ; when you rejoice in your own liberty, do not forget that this liberty may be to him 'an occasion of stumbling.' Place yourself above his weaknesses by placing yourself below them, remembering that your very strength gives him a claim on you for support.

THE
EPISTLE TO THE ROMANS

1 PAUL, a servant of Jesus Christ, called ^{a–*f*} an apostle,
2 separated unto the gospel of God, which he had promised afore by his prophets in the Holy Scriptures,
3 concerning his Son, ^b who came ^{*f*} of the seed of David
4 according to the flesh; ^c appointed ^{*f*} to be the Son of God with power, according to the spirit of holiness, by ^d resurrection of ^{*f*} the dead, ^e Jesus Christ our Lord ^{*f*};
5 by whom we ^{f–*f*} received grace and apostleship, for obedience to the faith among all the Gentiles for his
6 name: among whom are ye also the called of Jesus
7 Christ: to all that be in Rome, beloved of God, called ^{g–*f*} saints: Grace to you and peace from God our Father, and the Lord Jesus Christ.
8 First, I thank my God through Jesus Christ for you

^a *add* to be   ^b Jesus Christ our Lord, which was made   ^c and declared
^d the resurrection from   ^e *omit* Jesus Christ our Lord
^f *add* have   ^g *add* to be

1. 4. We may paraphrase the passage thus:—'Concerning Christ who belonged to two worlds, a former and a latter one: the first, earthly, human, Jewish; the other, spiritual and invisible: the Son of David appointed to be the Son of God, as He was holy, and had the Spirit of God dwelling in Him.' All this is not fully or definitely expressed in this passage; but is yet so closely connected with it, that the attempt to explain the several words becomes almost unmeaning without such a prolongation of them.

8, 9. It is characteristic of the Apostle, that all his Epistles, with all, that your faith is spoken of ʰ in all the *ˡ* world. 9 For God is my witness, whom I serve with my spirit in the gospel of his Son; how without ceasing I make 10 mention of you, always in my prayers making request,

ʰ throughout the whole

the exception of the Galatians, begin with language of conciliation. As in ordinary life we first address one another with courteous salutation, so does the Apostle introduce himself to his readers, with the words of Christian charity. He lingers for an instant around that pleasant impression of a Church without spot, such as it never will be in this world, before he passes onward to reprove and exhort those whom he is addressing. It is an ideal Church that he contemplates, elect, spiritual, heavenly, going on to perfection, the image of which seems ever to blend with, and to overshadow those who bear its glorious titles.

In the introductions to the Epistles the language of common life is idealized and spiritualized. The manner is Eastern, a circumstance which, from our familiarity with the New Testament, we often fail to recognize; it is also that of the Apostle and his time. Were we to translate verses 8-10 into common words, they might be expressed as follows:—'I rejoice to hear of your faith everywhere, for I solemnly declare that I never forget you; it is one of my first prayers to come to you.' But, partly from the intensity of his feelings, partly from the style of the age and country in which he wrote, most of all from the circumstance that the ordinary events of life come to him with a Divine power, and seem, as it were, to be occurring in a spiritual world, his words fall into a different mould. He employs language, according to our sober colours of expression, too strong for the occasion; as where he says that their faith is spoken of throughout the whole world; or where he calls God to witness of his desire to come to them, though there was no reason for them to doubt this. So again in 1 Thess. i. 8: 'For from you sounded out the word of the Lord, not only in Macedonia and Achaia, but also in every place your faith to Godward is spread abroad; so that we need not speak any thing.' Yet, at the time of writing these words, the Apostle could hardly have travelled beyond the limits of Macedonia and Achaia.

Comp. Phil. i. 8, as an instance of the same affection towards those 'unknown to him by face;' and, as an example of the same intensity of language, Gal. i. 20, where he calls God to witness that 'he lies not' about the details of his visits to Jerusalem.

ὅτι ἡ πίστις ὑμῶν, *that your faith.*] No commentary could throw half as much light on the Epistle as a knowledge of the state of those whose faith is thus described. Had the Roman Church long ago or recently been converted to the Gospel? May we suppose that the

if by any means now at length I may have a prosperous
11 journey by the will of God to come unto you. For
I long to see you, that I may impart unto you some
12 spiritual gift, to the end ye may be established; that
is, that I may be ⁱ together comforted in ⁱ you by the
13 mutual faith both of you and me. Now I would not
have you ignorant, brethren, that oftentimes I purposed
to come unto you, ᵏ and ⁱ was let hitherto, that I might
have some fruit among you also, even as among other
14 Gentiles. I am debtor both to the Greeks, and to the
Barbarians; both to the wise, and to the unwise.

ⁱ comforted together with   ᵏ but

news of it was carried thither by the 'strangers of Rome' who about twenty-five years previously had been present at the day of Pentecost? Is it possible that the name of Christ Himself had reached the metropolis of the world during His lifetime? Had Priscilla and Aquila any acquaintance with the Gospel before they met with St. Paul at Corinth? Who were those brethren whom the prisoner Paul found at Puteoli, or who came to meet him at Appii forum? No answer can be given to these questions, yet the statement of them is not without interest. There were many in the Roman Church whose names were known to the Apostle; some whom he describes as of note among the Apostles who were before him. Comp. Acts xxviii. 15-31: Rom. xvi.

12. The meaning of the word παρακαλεῖν, as of παράκλητος, wavers between consolation and exhortation, or includes both. In the LXX the former sense is the prevailing one; here both are combined. What the progress of language and the analysis of Christian feelings have separated into two, was, in the age of the Apostles, one idea and one word, with a scarcely perceptible diversity of meaning. The idea of 'consolation' implied in it does not, however, refer to comfort or sympathy in any particular sorrow, but rather to the conscious communion of Christians in this present evil world. Nor is there implied in the notion of exhortation the bringing forward of statements or precepts respecting the Christian faith, but the imparting of a new spirit or temper of mind. If, allowing for the great difference between our own and the Apostolic times, we could imagine a person who had listened to a preacher, or received the counsel of a friend, who exactly touched the chords of his soul, such a one might express himself in one word as comforted and instructed; that word would be παρακαλεῖσθαι. For a similar connexion of παρακαλεῖν

1. 18] THE EPISTLE TO THE ROMANS 261

15 So, as much as in me is, I am ready to preach the
16 gospel to you that are at Rome also. For I am not
ashamed of the gospel [1]; for it is the power of God
unto salvation to every one that believeth; to the
17 Jew first, and also to the Greek; for therein is the
righteousness of God revealed from faith to faith: as
it is written, [m] But the just shall live by faith.
18 For the wrath of God is revealed from heaven
against all ungodliness and unrighteousness of men,

[1] add *of Christ*   [m] omit But

and στηρίζειν, compare 1 Thess. iii. 2 : 2 Thess. ii. 17.

17. Passing onward to the height of his great argument, the Apostle involves reason within reason, four times in three successive verses. Such is the overlogical form of Hellenistic Greek. 'I preach the Gospel, *for* I glory in it; *for* it is not weak but strong, a power to save to him that has faith, *for* it is a revelation of the righteousness of God through faith; *for* the times of that ignorance God no longer winks at,' &c. The repetition of γάρ does but represent the different stages and aspects of the Apostle's thought.

The point of view in which the Apostle regards the heathen, is partly inward and partly outward; that is to say, based on the contemplation of the actual facts of human evil which he saw around, but at the same time blending with this, the sense and consciousness of sin which he felt within him. The Apostle himself had been awakened suddenly to the perception of his own state: in the language of this chapter, 'the wrath of God from heaven' had been revealed in him; 'the righteousness of God, which is by faith' in Jesus Christ, had been also revealed in him. Alive without the law once, he had become conscious of sin and finally sensible of deliverance. And now transferring the thoughts of his own heart to an evil world, he tries it in like manner by the law of God and nature : it seems to him to be in the first stage of the great change, to have knowledge and to be self-condemned. The knowledge of God it always had latent in the works of creation; and now it has fallen below itself and is convicted by itself. It is true that the Apostle, like all other teachers, supplies from within what did not consciously exist in the mind of man. What he sees before him, might have seemed to another as nothing more than a dead inert mass of heathenism and licentiousness. But there are two lights by which he regards it : first, the light of his own experience, which seems to stir and quicken it into life; secondly, the light of God's law, by which, when brought

19 who hinder the truth in unrighteousness; because that which ⁿis ᵈ known of God is manifest in them; 20 for God °manifests ᵈ it unto them. For the invisible

ⁿ may be °hath shewed

near to it, it is condemned, and thus enters, as it were, on a new epoch, condemned and forgiven at once.

19. The heathen knew the truth, and did not know it. They had the elements of knowledge, but not knowledge itself. As the laws of nature, though unknown to man, existed from the first; so did the God of nature, though unknown to man, exist before the worlds. Yet how can that be termed knowledge which was ignorance?

The Apostle is speaking, not from within the circle of the heathen world, but from without. He is describing what he felt respecting them, not what the heathen felt respecting themselves. Yet the strain which he adopts, might have received confirmation from the writings of 'their own prophets,' and have found an echo in the better mind of the age itself. He brings them into the presence of nature, 'the heavens declaring his glory, and the firmament shewing his handiwork,' and condemns them before it. There was a witness in the world, that might have taught them, and seemed intended to teach them, which contrasted with the human idols of Greece, and with the winged and creeping things of Egypt and the East. It does not follow, that individuals among them could separate themselves from the ties of habit and education, and read the lesson spread before them. Yet even thus, it was a condemnation of the existing polytheism.

20. The sense in which they knew and did not know, admits of another illustration from the workings of conscience, which may further remind the student of Aristotle's Ethics, of the discussion which is entered upon by the great master, of another form of the Socratic opinion. There are moral as well as spiritual truths, which we know and we do not know; know at one moment and forget the next; know and do not know at the same instant; for our ignorance of which we cannot help blaming ourselves, even though it were impossible that we should know them; and which, when presented to us, work conviction and sorrow for the past. And so if St. Paul be judging the heathen from his own point of view rather than theirs, he is also holding up before them a picture, the truth of which, as they became Christians, they would themselves recognize.

It is natural to ask of whom St. Paul is speaking in this description? What class among the heathen had he in his thoughts when he said, they knew God, and worshipped Him not as God? He is not speaking of the vulgar certainly, nor yet of the educated in the highest sense; that is, not of the true wisdom of heathen antiquity, but of the sophist, the things of him from the creation of the world are clearly seen, being understood by the things that are made, even his eternal power and Godhead; so 21 that they are without excuse: because that, when they

mystic, the Athenian ever desirous to hear some new thing; the Greek in the cities of Asia; the Alexandrian Jew mingling all opinions, human and divine, in his system of knowledge, falsely so called; the half-educated, on whom the speculations of Stoics or Epicureans exercised a kind of secondary influence; the traditional lore of Egypt, enhanced, doubtless by the fame of its new learning, which seemed so strangely to contrast with the meanness and grotesqueness of its superstition. These were the forms of heathen life and philosophy with which the Apostle must generally have come in contact, which it is, therefore, reasonable to suppose that he had in view in this description.

It is a further question, how far St. Paul was acquainted with those masterpieces of heathen learning which have exerted so great power on the thoughts of men. Had he read Plato, or Aristotle, or the writings of the Stoics? Can we suppose him to have heard of Seneca, with whom his name is connected by an ancient and widely received forgery? Is it of these that he says: 'affirming they were wise, they became fools?' There is no reason to suppose that St. Paul was skilled in any Greek learning but the Alexandrian philosophy, and that rather as a current mode of thought of his time than as a system which he had especially cultivated. But as little reason is there to suppose that unless he had ceased to be himself, he would have viewed these great classical works in any other way than he regarded heathen literature in general, or have received them in the spirit of the later Fathers, as semi-inspired works, or have recognized in them the simplicity or grand moral lesson which has preserved them to our time. Sacred and profane literature fly from the touch of each other; they belong to two different worlds. Nor is it likely that the first teachers of Christianity would have sought to connect them, nor conceivable to us how the Gospel could have converted mankind, if, in its infancy, it had to come into collision with the dialectics of Plato, or the severe self-control of the Stoic. It must gain a form and substance of its own, ere it could leaven the world. Afterwards it might gather into itself the elements of good in all things. Nor is there reason to think that it could have drawn to itself the nobler spirits of heathen antiquity, any more than it could have taken from them. Had Tacitus known ever so much of that 'exitiabilis superstitio,' is it natural, humanly speaking, to suppose that he would have bowed at the foot of the cross?

21. The senselessness of the hea-

knew God; they glorified him not as God, neither were thankful; but became vain in their imaginations, 22 and their foolish heart was darkened. Professing ᵖ⁻ᵖ 23 to be wise, they became fools, and changed the glory of the uncorruptible God into an image made like to corruptible man, and to birds, and four-footed beasts, 24 and creeping things. Wherefore God ᵠ⁻ᵠ gave them up to uncleanness ʳ in ˢ the lusts of their own hearts, to dishonour their own bodies between themselves: 25 who changed the truth of God into a lie, and worshipped and served the creature ˢ rather ˢ than the Creator, 26 who is blessed for ever. Amen. For this cause God gave them up unto vile affections: for ᵗ⁻ᵗ their women did change the natural use into that which is against 27 nature: and likewise also the men, leaving the natural use of the woman, burned in their lust one toward another; men with men working that which is unseemly and receiving in themselves that recompence

ᵖ *add* themselves   ᵠ *add also*   ʳ through   ˢ more   ᵗ *add* even

then religions and their worshippers, was an aspect of them far more striking to contemporary Jews or Christians than to ourselves. We gaze upon the fragments of Phidias and Praxiteles, and fancy human nature almost ennobled by the 'form divine.' Our first notions of patriotism are derived from Marathon and Thermopylae. The very antiquity of heathenism gives it a kind of sacredness to us. The charms of classical literature add a grace. It was otherwise with the Jews and first believers. They saw only 'cities wholly given to idolatry,' whose gods were but stocks and stones, described in the sarcasm of the prophet, 'The workman maketh a graven image.'

24. παρέδωκεν, *gave them up.*] Origen and several of the Fathers soften the meaning of the word, παρέδωκεν, by interpreting εἴασεν, permitted to be given over, rather than delivered over. Such explanations are not interpretations of Scripture, but only adaptations of it to an altered state of feeling and opinion. They are 'afterthoughts of theology,' as much as the discussions and definitions alluded to above, designed, when the question has begun to occupy the mind of man, to guard against the faintest supposition of a connexion between God and evil. So in modern times we say God is not the cause of evil: He only allows it; it is a part of His moral government, incidental to

28 of their error which was meet. And ^{u-ǁ} as they did not like to retain God in their knowledge, God gave them over to a reprobate mind, to do those 29 things which are not convenient; being filled with all unrighteousness, ^{x-ǁ y} evil, wickedness, villany, covetousness^ǁ; full of envy, murder, debate, deceit, 30 malignity; whisperers, backbiters, ^z hated^ǁ of God, despiteful, proud, boasters, inventors of evil things, 31 disobedient to parents, without understanding, covenant-breakers, without natural affection,^{a-ǁ} unmerciful: 32 who knowing the judgment of God, that they which commit such things are worthy of death, not only do the same, but have pleasure in them that do them.

^u *add* even   ^x add *fornication*
^y wickedness, covetousness, maliciousness   ^z haters   ^a add *implacable*

His general laws. Without considering the intimate union of good and evil in the heart of man, or the manner in which moral evil itself connects with physical, we seek only to remove it, as far as possible, in our language and modes of conception, from the Author of good. The Gospel knows nothing of these modern philosophical distinctions, though revolting, as impious, from the notion that God can tempt man. The mode of thought of the Apostle is still the same as that implied in the aphorism: 'Quem Deus vult perdere, prius dementat.' To preserve this is essential, or we shall confuse what the Epistles do say, and what we suppose that they ought to have said; the words used to express the operation of the Divine Being, and the general impression of Divine goodness which we gather from Scripture as a whole.

While we reject the distinction of God causing and permitting evil as unsuited to Scripture, a great difference must, nevertheless, be admitted between sin as the penalty of sin, or, as we should say, the natural consequence of sin, and sin in its first origin. In the latter sense the authorship of evil is nowhere attributed to God; in the former, it is. God makes man to sin, in the language of Scripture, only when he has already sinned, when, to the eye of man, he is hopelessly hardened. In this point of view, the metaphysical difficulty, which is not here entered upon, still remains; but the practical one is in a great degree removed.

32. It has been already remarked, that the form of St. Paul's writings is often more artificial and rhetorical than the thought. May not this be the explanation of the passage which we are con-

2 Therefore thou art inexcusable, O man, whosoever thou art that judgest: for wherein thou judgest another, thou condemnest thyself; for thou that judgest doest the same things. But we are sure that the judgment of God is according to truth against them which commit such things. And thinkest thou this, O man, that judgest them which do such things,

sidering? The opposition is really one of particles, not of ideas. The Apostle does not mean to say 'who do them, and, more than that, have pleasure in those that do them,' but simply 'who do them, and assent to those who do them.' (Compare 2 Cor. viii. 10 οἵτινες οὐ μόνον τὸ ποιῆσαι, ἀλλὰ καὶ τὸ θέλειν προενήρξασθε ἀπὸ πέρυσι, which is probably to be explained in the same way, and where the commentators have recourse to similar forced interpretations.) He is aggravating the picture by another, but not necessarily a deeper shade of guilt.

2. 3. Hypocrisy is almost always unconscious; it draws the veil over its own evil deeds, while it condemns its neighbours; it deceives others, but begins by deceiving the hypocrite himself. It is popularly described as 'pretending to be one thing, and doing, thinking, or feeling another;' in fact, it is very different. Nobody really leads this sort of unnatural and divided existence. A man does wrong, but he forgets it again; he sees the same fault in another, and condemns it; but no arrow of conscience reaches him, no law of association suggests to him that he has sinned too. Human character is weak and plastic, and soon reforms itself into a deceitful whole. Indignation may be honestly felt at others by men who do the same things themselves; they may often be said to relieve their own conscience, perhaps, even to strengthen the moral sentiments of mankind by their expression of it. The worst hypocrites are bad as we can imagine, but they are not such as we imagine. The Scribes and Pharisees, 'hypocrites,' were unlike what they seem to us ; much more would they have regarded their own lives in another light from that in which our Lord has pictured them. Their hypocrisy, too, might be described as weakness and self-deception, only heightened and made more intense by the time and country in which they lived. It was the hypocrisy of an age and of a state of society blinder, perhaps, and more fatal for this very reason, but less culpable in the individuals who were guilty of it. Those who said, 'we have a law, and by our law he ought to die,' were not without 'a zeal for God,' though seeking to take away Him in whom only the law was fulfilled.

But although experience of ourselves and others seems to show that hypocrisy is almost always unconscious, such is not the idea

and doest the same, that thou shalt escape the judg-
4 ment of God? Or despisest thou the riches of his
goodness and forbearance and longsuffering; not
knowing that the goodness of God leadeth thee to
5 repentance? But after thy hardness and impenitent
heart treasurest up unto thyself wrath in the day of
wrath and revelation of the righteous judgment
6 of God; who will render to every man according to
7 his deeds: ᵇ to those who patiently endure in a good

ᵇ to them who by patient continuance in well doing seek for glory and honour and immortality, eternal life

that we ordinarily attach to the word 'hypocrite.' This singular psychological phenomenon is worth our observing. The reason is, first, that the strong contrast we observe between the seeming and the reality, between the acts and words of the hypocrite, leads us to speak as though the contrast was present and conscious to himself. We cannot follow the subtle mazes through which he leads himself; we see only the palpable outward effect. Secondly, the notion that hypocrisy is self-deception or weakness, is inadequate to express our abhorrence of it. Thirdly, our use of language is adapted to the common opinions of mankind, and often fails of expressing the finer shades of human nature.

5. It has been asked, what does the Apostle mean by saying that we shall be judged by our works, when the whole tenor of the Epistle goes to prove that we are to be justified by faith?

Many answers may be given to this question: First, the Apostle has not yet taught the doctrine of righteousness by faith, and therefore cannot properly adopt what in modern times might be termed the language of Pauline theology. He is speaking exoterically, it might be said, in words borrowed from the Old Testament, on the level of Jews, or heathens, not of Christians, from the same point of view as in 9, 10. Secondly, the words τὰ ἔργα in this passage are not opposed to faith, but to pretensions, self-deceptions, and may be paraphrased in the expression that follows ὑπομονὴν ἔργου ἀγαθοῦ. But thirdly, the Apostle needs these excuses to make him consistent, not with himself, but with some of his interpreters. He says, indeed: 'We are justified by faith without the deeds of the law.' But he uses other language also: 'Now abideth faith, hope, love; and the greatest of these is love.' Nor does the expression 'righteousness by faith' occur at all in several of his Epistles. We may not 'straiten' the Apostle where he is not 'straitened' in his own writings. There are occasions on which we can conceive him using the language of St.

work, seeking for eternal life, glory and honour and
8 immortality⁹: but unto them that are contentious,
and do not obey the truth, but obey unrighteousness,
9 indignation, and wrath. Tribulation and anguish,
upon every soul of man that doeth evil, of the Jew
10 first, and also of the Gentile; but glory, honour, and
peace, to every man that worketh good, to the Jew
first, and also to the Gentile.

11
12 For there is no respect of persons with God. For

James as a corrective to the abuse of his own. A subject so vast and various as the salvation of man, cannot be bound within the withs of logic. As with our Lord, so with His Apostles the message is, first, 'Believe, and thou mayest be saved;' but secondly, 'The hour is coming, and now is, when they that are in the graves shall hear his voice.'

It is the strongest presumption that the difficulty is not a real one, that the Apostle himself is wholly unconscious of it: we cannot imagine him discussing whether faith in Christ, or the love of Christ, or the inward life of Christ are the sources of justification. Is it irreverent to say, that disputes of this kind would hardly have been intelligible to him? No more can we conceive him regarding the case of the heathen, after, as well as before, Christianity, in any other spirit than 'God is no respecter of persons.'

8. ἀπειθοῦσι τῇ ἀληθείᾳ.] By the truth is meant the law of right, and the will of God generally. The ideas of truth and right are not separated in Scripture, as they are in our way of speaking, or in the forms of thought of the Greek Philosophy. There is no 'division of the soul,' in Aristotle's language, into moral and intellectual. Hence, knowledge in Scripture is often spoken of as a moral quality, and with the word 'truth' are associated expressions denoting acts and states of the will rather than of the intellect. See chap. i. 20.

11. It was one of the first ideas that the Israelite had of God, that He was no respecter of persons; Deut. x. 17: 2 Chron. xix. 7: Job xxxiv. 19. But this disregard of persons was only in His dealings with individuals of the chosen people. St. Paul used the expression in the wider sense of not making a difference of persons between Jew and Gentile, circumcision or uncircumcision, bond or free, just as he adapted the words 'there is one God' to the meaning of God one and the same to all mankind, in iii. 30 and elsewhere. Nothing could be less like the spirit of his countrymen than this sense of the universal justice of God. Still it might be asked of the Apostle himself, how the fact of their ever having been a privileged people,

as many as ^{c—ǁ} sinned without law shall also perish without law: and as many as ^{d—ǁ} sinned in the law
13 shall be judged by the law; for not the hearers of the law are just before God, but the doers of the
14 law shall be justified; for when the Gentiles, which have not the law, do by nature the things contained in the law, these, having not the law, are a law unto
15 themselves: which shew the work of the law written in their hearts, their conscience also bearing witness, and ^ethoughts accusing or else excusing them one
16 with another^ǁ; in the day when God shall judge the secrets of men by Jesus Christ according to my gospel.

^c *add* have   ^d *add* have
^e their thoughts the meanwhile accusing or else excusing one another

was consistent with the belief of this equal justice to all mankind. Like many other difficulties, we can answer this by parallel difficulties among ourselves. Though living in the full light of the Gospel, there are many things which to us also 'God hath put in his own power,' and which we believe rather than know to be reconcilable with His justice. What to us the heathen are still, standing apparently on the outskirts of God's moral government, that to St. Paul and the believers of the first age were 'the times of that ignorance that God winked at.' Are we not brought by time to a later stage of the same difficulty?

15. The 14th and 15th verses contain an analysis of the natural feeling of right and wrong, in three states or stages. First, the unconscious stage, in which the Gentiles not having the law, show its real though latent existence in their own hearts; of which, secondly, they have a faint though instinctive perception in the witness of conscience; which, thirdly, grows by reflection into distinct approval or disapproval of their own acts and those of others.

16. A difficulty occurs in the construction of this verse, the future ᾗ κρινεῖ being joined with the present ἐνδείκνυνται, or as some interpreters think with κατηγορούντων and ἀπολογουμένων. The English version has enclosed vers. 13-15 in a parenthesis, to escape the difficulty; an expedient which it has frequently adopted, as at ch. v. 13-18: Eph. iv. 9, 10, but which is peculiarly unsuited to the unravelling of the tangle of discourse, in such a writer as St. Paul. The thread of any broken construction may in this way be resumed; yet unless the parenthesis really had a place in the author's mind, our supposed explanation will be a mere gram-

17 *But if* thou art called a Jew, and restest in the
18 law, and gloriest in God, and knowest his will, and
approvest the things that are more excellent, being
19 instructed out of the law; and art confident that thou
thyself art a guide of the blind, a light of them which
20 are in darkness, an instructor of the foolish, a teacher
of babes, which hast the form of knowledge and of

add Behold

matical figment like the 'word understood,' in explanation of a difficult construction. A real parenthesis is the insertion of a clause, or of a thought, between two points of a sentence, the meaning of which should be clearly broken off at its beginning, and clearly resumed at its conclusion. The parenthetical thought, as it is hurried over in discourse, should be really an afterthought, yet necessary to the comprehension of the sentence. The present passage does not come within this rule, and therefore a parenthesis has no place here. It is far more probable that, as elsewhere, St. Paul wrote without perfect sequence, than that he suspended his meaning through several verses, and resumed it unimpaired.

We will take the words, therefore, in their plain but ungrammatical construction with ἐνδείκνυνται, 'which shew the work of the law ... in the day which is to come.' The day which is to come is not only future, but present; anticipated in the heart and conscience of every man, as well as in the history of the world. It is 'the day that is coming and now is,' John v. 25, the presence (παρουσία) of Christ.

And the Apostle passes from one tense to the other, unconscious of the solecism.

For a parallel union of dissimilar times compare above θησαυρίζεις σεαυτῷ ὀργὴν ἐν ἡμέρᾳ ὀργῆς. 2 Cor. i. 14 καθὼς καὶ ἐπέγνωτε ἡμᾶς ἀπὸ μέρους, ὅτι καύχημα ὑμῶν ἐσμὲν καθάπερ καὶ ὑμεῖς ἡμῶν ἐν τῇ ἡμέρᾳ τοῦ κυρίου Ἰησοῦ. Eph. i. 3 Εὐλογητὸς ὁ θεὸς καὶ πατὴρ τοῦ κυρίου ἡμῶν Ἰησοῦ χριστοῦ, ὁ εὐλογήσας ἡμᾶς ἐν πάσῃ εὐλογίᾳ πνευματικῇ ἐν τοῖς ἐπουρανίοις ἐν χριστῷ.

17–29. From this point to the end of the chapter, the Apostle exerts all the force of his eloquence to unmask the Jew. All the imaginations with which he flatters himself, all the titles that he delights to heap upon himself, are suggestive of the contrast between what he is and what he seems, which is further heightened by the previous mention of the Gentile who knew not the law and did by nature the things contained in the law, and pointed at the conclusion by a verse from the Old Testament. At ver. 26 the Gentile reappears and the order is finally inverted, uncircumcision which fulfils the law taking the place of circumcision which transgresses the law, and

21 the truth in the law—thou therefore which teachest
another, teachest thou not thyself? thou that preachest
22 a man should not steal, dost thou steal? thou that
sayest a man should not commit adultery, dost thou
commit adultery? thou that abhorrest idols, dost
23 thou ᵍrob temples"? thou that makest thy boast of
the law, through breaking the law dishonourest thou
24 God? For the name of God is blasphemed among
25 the Gentiles through you, as it is written. For
circumcision verily profiteth, if thou keep the law: but
if thou be a breaker of the law, thy circumcision is

ᵍ commit sacrilege

the idea of the Jew in spirit forming a middle term between Jew and Gentile.

21. At length the Apostle turns to strike : the thought for which throughout the chapter he had been preparing, is now uttered with its full force. He cuts short the apodosis with a question, which is also an inference : Is the result of all this that thou who judgest doest the same thing? 'Dost thou,' we might repeat in the language of the Gospels, 'who art paying tithe of mint, of rue, and of cumin, devour widows' houses? Art thou, who castest stones at others, free from the sin of adultery thyself?'

22. ὁ βδελυσσόμενος, *thou who abhorrest.*] The most literal mode of taking the words is also the freest from objections : 'Dost thou who abhorrest idols, rob the idol's temple?' Such an offence might be very possibly committed by a Jew, whom no 'religio loci' would restrain ; and it would occur to St. Paul, as an inhabitant of a Gentile city, to mention it. This explanation is confirmed by the use of the word ἱεροσύλους in Acts xix. 37, curiously translated in the English Version 'robbers of churches' (compare 2 Macc. iv. 42, where it is similarly translated, though referring to the Jewish temple), and by the remarkable interpretation of Exod. xxii. 28, in Josephus, *Ant.* iv. 8, § 10 'Let no one blaspheme those gods whom other cities esteem such, nor any one steal what belongs to strange temples ; nor take away the gifts that are dedicated to any God.'

25. περιτομὴ μὲν γὰρ ὠφελεῖ, *for circumcision profiteth.*] This is one of that class of questions which, in ancient as well as modern times, is seldom brought to the distinct issue of the Apostle. The Rabbi would have hesitated to say that a wicked Jew had a part in Messiah's kingdom, or that the virtuous heathen was necessarily excluded from it. The Christian, in modern times at least, would shrink from affirming that an unbaptized infant is 'a child of

26 made uncircumcision. Therefore if the uncircumcision keep the ʰjudgments ⁱ of the law, shall not his
27 uncircumcision be counted for circumcision? And shall not uncircumcision which is by nature, if it fulfil the law, judge thee, who ⁱ with ⁱ the letter and
28 circumcision dost transgress the law? For he is not a Jew, which is one outwardly; neither is that
29 circumcision, which is outward in the flesh: but he is a Jew, which is one inwardly; and circumcision is that of the heart, in the spirit, and not in the letter; whose praise is not of men, but of God.

3 What advantage then hath the Jew? or what profit
2 is there of circumcision? Much every way: chiefly, because ᵏthey were entrusted with ⁱ the oracles of God.
3 For what if some did not believe? ¹ whether ⁱ shall

ʰ righteousness   ⁱ by   ᵏ that unto them were committed
¹ *omit* whether

wrath,' or that the baptized could hardly, if in any case, fail of salvation at the last. But many even among Christians would gladly, if possible, turn away from the inquiry: they would wish to be allowed to hold premises without pushing them to their conclusions; to take issue upon a word, and not to determine the point of morality or justice.

This is what the Apostle has not done. With him circumcision becomes uncircumcision, if it transgress the law. Uncircumcision becomes circumcision, if it keep the law.

It is true that the spiritual meaning of circumcision was implied in the law itself, and occasionally taught by the doctors of the law. (Deut. x. 16: Philo, ii. 258.) But the habitual feeling of the Jew was the other way. To him circumcision was the seal of the covenant; the charm which protected him from the wrath of God; the sign which had once been characteristic of the nation, and was still appropriated to the individuals who composed it. Like the old prophets in spirit, though in form logical and antithetical, the Apostle answers him by asserting the superiority of the moral to the ceremonial law; he repeats the universal lesson which the whole current of Jewish history tended to obliterate, the same which was once heard in other words from the Saviour's lips, 'Think not to say with yourselves we have Abraham to our Father.'

3. 3. τὴν πίστιν τοῦ θεοῦ, *the faith of God,*] like δικαιοσύνη θεοῦ above. The play of words is hardly

THE EPISTLE TO THE ROMANS

their unbelief make the faith of God without effect?
4 God forbid: yea, let God be true, but every man a liar;
as it is written, That thou mightest be justified in thy
sayings, and mightest overcome when thou art judged.
5 But if our unrighteousness commend the righteousness
of God, what shall we say? Is God unrighteous who
6 taketh vengeance? (I speak as a man) God forbid, for
7 then how shall God judge the world? ¹ For if the
truth of God hath more abounded through my lie unto
his glory; why ᵐ notwithstanding ⁸ am I ⁿ still ⁸ judged
8 as a sinner? and not rather, (as we be slanderously
reported, and as some affirm that we say,) Let us do
evil, that good may come? whose damnation is just.

9 What then? are we better than they? No, in no

ᵐ yet   ⁿ also

translatable in English. 'Shall their want of faith make of none effect the good faith of God.' From the sense of 'the faith' which men have in God, πίστις passes into the meaning of the faith which God exercises towards men. (Compare ἀγάπη θεοῦ.)

Thus we leave the first stage of the objection. May not the unbelief of man mar the faithfulness of God? The second being — But if their unbelief established the righteousness of God, ver. 5. The third — But if their untruth reflected the glory of God.

9-27. At this point the Apostle leaves the digression into which he had been drawn, and returns to the main subject; describing, in the language of the Old Testament, the evil of those who are under the law, that is, of the whole former world; and revealing the new world in which God manifests forth His righteousness in Christ Jesus. In the previous chapter, he had not distinctly denied the privileges of the Jew; or had, at least, veiled the purely moral principle for which he was contending, under the figure of 'the Jew inwardly,' and 'circumcision of the heart.' At the commencement of the third chapter, he brought forward the other side of the argument, from which he is driven by the extravagance of the Jew. At length, dropping his imperfect enumeration of the advantages of the Jew, he boldly affirms the result, that the Jew is no better than the Gentile, and that all need the salvation, which all may have.

9. *are we better than they?*] The Apostle had previously spoken

¹ Reading εἰ γάρ

wise: for we have before proved both Jews and
10 Gentiles, that they are all under sin; as it is written,
11 There is none righteous, no, not one: there is none
that understandeth, there is none that seeketh after
12 God. They are all gone out of the way, they are
together become unprofitable; there is none that
13 doeth good, no, not one. Their throat is an open
sepulchre; with their tongues they have used deceit;
14 the poison of asps is under their lips: whose mouth
15 is full of cursing and bitterness. Their feet are
16 swift to shed blood, °affliction" and misery are in
17 their ways, and the way of peace have they not
18 known. There is no fear of God before their eyes.

º destruction

of the Jews in the third person. Now he is about to utter an unpalatable truth. Is it an over-refinement to suppose that he changes the person to soften the expression by identifying himself with them? Compare 1 Cor. iv. 6 'These things I have transferred in a figure to myself and Apollos, for your sakes.'

18. From the LXX of Psalm xxxvi. 1. What does the Apostle intend to prove by these quotations? That at various times mankind have gone astray, and done evil; that in particular cases the prophets and psalmists energetically denounced the wickedness of the Jews, or of their enemies. This is all that can be strictly gathered from them, and yet not enough to support what is termed the Apostle's argument. From the fact that the enemies of David were perfidious and deceitful, that the children of Israel, in the time of the prophet Isaiah, were swift to shed blood, we can draw no conclusions respecting mankind in general. Because Englishmen were cruel in the times of the civil wars, or because Charles the First had bitter and crafty enemies, we could not argue that the present generation, not to say the whole world, fell under the charge of the same sin. Not wholly unlike this, however, is the adaptation which the Apostle makes of the texts which he has quoted from the Old Testament. He brings them together from various places to express the thought which is passing through his mind; and he quotes them with a kind of authority, as we might use better language than our own to enforce our meaning. In modern phraseology, they are not arguments, but illustrations. The use of them is exactly similar to our own use of Scripture in sermons, where the universal is often inferred from

19 Now we know that what things soever the law saith, it saith to them who are under the law : that every mouth may be stopped, and all the world come into judgment 20 before God. ᵖ Because ‖ by the deeds of the law there shall no flesh be justified in his sight; for by the law 21 is the knowledge of sin. But now the righteousness of God without the law ᑫ has been ‖ manifested, being 22 witnessed by the law and the prophets; even the righteousness of God which is by faith of ʳ⁻‖ Christ

ᵖ Therefore   ᑫ is   ʳ add *Jesus*

the particular, and precepts or events divested of the particular circumstances which accompany them, or the occasions on which they arose, are made to teach a general lesson. It was after the manner of the Apostle's age, and hardly less after the manner of our own.

19. οἴδαμεν δὲ ὅτι, *but we know.*] Either (1) we may suppose that the Apostle, having already concluded the Gentiles under sin in the first chapter, is using these texts against the Jews, to complete the proof against men in general. 'We know that whomsoever these words out of the law touch, they must touch the Jew, who is under the law, so that he forms no exception, and the whole world, including the Jew, come under the judgment of God.' Or, (2) The Jew is regarded by him as the type of the Gentile; and having convicted the one, he assumes, *à fortiori*, the conviction of the other. The Apostle has found words in the law which describe the sinfulness of man, who, from this very circumstance, may be said to be under or in the law.

He does not mean to say that the law speaks to those who are under the law, but that those to whom the law speaks are under the law. All those who are thus described are drawn within the law, and belong to the prior dispensation. Or, more simply : The law in saying these things speaks to persons over whom it has authority (comp. vii. 1 ὁ νόμος κυριεύει τοῦ ἀνθρώπου); it is not a mere abstraction.

20. The object of Arminian and Romanist divines has ever been to confine the 'works of the law' to the ceremonial law, thereby gaining a supposed immunity for the doctrine of justification by works in another sense. Calvinists and Lutherans, with a truer perception of the Apostle's purpose, have affirmed that the moral law could, as little as the ceremonial, be made the groundwork of acceptance with God. They have truly urged, that there is no indication in the writings of St. Paul of the existence of such a distinction. The law is to him one law, the whole law, the figure, indeed, of many things, but never separated into the portion that

unto all ⁸⁻ˡˡ them that believe: for there is no
23 difference: for all have sinned, and come short of the
24 glory of God; being justified freely by his grace
25 through the redemption that is in Christ Jesus: whom
God hath set forth to be a propitiation through faith,

ˢ add *and upon all*

relates to ceremonies, and the portion that relates to moral precepts.

It may be further maintained, not only that there is no such distinction in the mind of the Apostle, but that, consistently with the modes of thought of his age, there could not have been such. It is what has been termed before an afterthought of theology, which would naturally arise when the ceremonial law had died away—a sort of separation of body and soul when life is extinct. Not that to St. Paul, or the Jews who were his contemporaries, all the precepts of the law seemed of equal importance. The prophets had constantly opposed the blood of bulls and goats 'to the doing justice, and loving mercy, and walking humbly with God.' But it does not follow from this, that the moral and ceremonial law were separated from each other in such a sense, that the Scribes and Pharisees placed some precepts under the one head and others under the other. Rather, they were blended together in one, like Ethics and Politics in the early Greek philosophy. When a Jew spoke of the law, it never occurred to him to ask whether he meant the moral or ceremonial law; or when he spoke of sin, to distinguish whether he intended moral evil or ceremonial impurity.

25. ἱλαστήριον] has three senses given it by commentators on this passage: First, as in Heb. ix. 5, 'mercy-seat,' a meaning of the word supposed to have arisen from a misconception of the LXX respecting the Hebrew בַּפֹּרֶת, the covering of the ark, which they wrongly connected with בָּפֶר, to expiate or cover sin. This interpretation is too obscure and peculiar for the present passage: (1) it would require the article; (2) it is inappropriate, because St. Paul is not here speaking of the mercy, but of the righteousness of God; (3) the image, if used, should be assisted by the surrounding phraseology. Two other explanations offer themselves: either (1) ἱλαστήριον may be a masculine adjective in apposition with ὅν, 'whom God set forth as propitiatory,' or better, (2) a neuter adjective, which has passed into a substantive—whom God has set forth as a 'propitiation,' like σωτήριον Exod. xx. 24; cf. xxix. 28.

through faith, by his blood.] No such expression occurs in Scripture as faith in the blood, or even in the death of Christ. Nor is πίστις followed by ἐν in the New Testament, though faith, like all other Christian states, is often

3. 30]   THE EPISTLE TO THE ROMANS   277

^t by " his blood, to declare his righteousness ^u because of the letting go " of sins that are past through the
26 forbearance of God, ^x for the declaration of his righteousness at this time ": that he might be just, and the justifier of him which believeth in Jesus.
27 Where is boasting then? It ^y has been " excluded. By what law? of works? Nay: but by the law of
28 faith. ^z For " we conclude that a man is justified by
29 faith without the deeds of the law. Is he the God of the Jews only? is he not also of the Gentiles?
30 Yes, of the Gentiles also: seeing it is one God,* which

^t in   ^u for the remission
^x to declare, I say, at this time his righteousness   ^y is   ^z *Therefore*

spoken of as existing in Christ. (Gal. iii. 26.) The two clauses should therefore be separated, 'through faith—by his blood.'

διὰ τὴν πάρεσιν τῶν προγεγονότων ἁμαρτημάτων, *because of the letting go of sins that are past.*] The natural translation of the words is : ' Because of the letting go or omission of past sins.' That is the reason why God manifests forth His righteousness, because formerly He had hidden Himself, and seemed not to observe sin. 'The times of that ignorance God winked at, but now commands all men everywhere to repent.' There was a moral necessity which made the old dispensation the cause of the new one. God was not willing that men should be for ever ignorant of His true nature.

26. πρὸς τὴν ἔνδειξιν τῆς δικαιοσύνης αὐτοῦ, *for declaration of his righteousness.*] Not, as in the English Version, a mere resumption of the previous εἰς ἔνδειξιν, ' for the

manifestation, I say, of his righteousness at this time.' The words πρὸς τὴν ἔνδειξιν τῆς δικαιοσύνης are in juxtaposition with ἐν τῇ ἀνοχῇ τοῦ θεοῦ, and closely connected with διὰ τὴν πάρεσιν, as ἐν τῷ νῦν καιρῷ corresponds to προγεγονότων ἁμαρτημάτων. It was partly owing to the long suffering of God, that He 'winked at' past sins; but there was likewise a further object, that He should set forth His righteousness at the time appointed. He hid Himself that He might be revealed. The manifestation of His righteousness was the counterpart of His neglect and long suffering. When the ἔνδειξις was first mentioned this point of view was not touched upon; it is now indicated by the article. Comp. for a similar mode of connecting the two halves of the dispensation, ver. 20 'The law came in that sin might abound, but where sin abounded, grace did much more abound.'

* εἷς ὁ θεὸς ὃς δικαιώσει, iii. 30.—Let us turn aside for a moment to consider how great this thought was in that age and country; a thought which

shall justify the circumcision by faith, and uncircum-
31 cision through faith. Do we then make void the law
through faith? God forbid: yea, we establish the
law.

4 What shall we then say that Abraham ᵃhath found[1],

ᵃ *our father as pertaining to the flesh hath found*

the wisest of men had never before uttered, which at the present hour we imperfectly realize, which is still leavening the world, and shall do so until the whole is leavened, and the differences of races, of nations, of castes, of religions, of languages, are finally done away. Nothing could seem a less natural or obvious lesson in the then state of the world, nothing could be more at variance with experience, or more difficult to carry out into practice. Even to us it is hard to imagine that the islander of the South Seas, the pariah of India, the African in his worst estate, is equally with ourselves God's creature. But in the age of St. Paul how great must have been the difficulty of conceiving barbarian and Scythian, bond and free, all colours, forms, races, and languages alike and equal in the presence of God who made them! The origin of the human race was veiled in a deeper mystery to the ancient world, and the lines which separated mankind were harder and stronger; yet the 'love of Christ constraining' bound together in its cords, those most separated by time or distance, those who were the types of the most extreme differences of which the human form is capable.

The idea of this brotherhood of all mankind, the great family on earth, implies that all men have certain ties with us, and certain rights at our hands. The truest way in which we can regard them is as they appear in the sight of God, from whom they can never suffer wrong; nor from us, while we think of them as His creatures equally with ourselves. There is yet a closer bond with them as our brethren in the Gospel. No one can interpose impediments of rank or fortune, or colour or religious opinion, between those who are one in Christ. Beyond and above such transitory differences is the work of Christ, 'making all things kin.' Moreover, the remembrance of this brotherhood is a rest to us when our 'light is low,' and the world and its distinctions are passing from our sight, and our thoughts are of the dark valley and the solitary way. For it leads us to trust in God, not as selecting us, because He had a favour unto us, but as infinitely just to all mankind. It links our fortunes with those of men in general, and gives us the same support in reference to our eternal destiny, that we receive from each other in a narrow sphere in the concerns of daily life. To think of ourselves, or our church, or our country, or our age, as the particular exceptions which a Divine mercy makes, whether in this life or another, is not a thought of comfort, but of perplexity. Lastly:—It relieves us from anxiety about the condition of other men, of friends departed, of those ignorant of the Gospel, of those of a different form of faith from our own; knowing that God who has thus far lifted up the veil, 'will justify the circumcision through faith, and the uncircumcision by faith;' the Jew who fulfils the law, and the Gentile who does by nature the things contained in the law.

[1] Reading τί οὖν ἐροῦμεν εὑρηκέναι

2 our progenitor according to the flesh? " For if Abraham were justified by works, he hath whereof to glory;
3 but not before God. For what saith the scripture?
ᵇ But " Abraham believed God, and it was counted
4 unto him for righteousness. Now to him that worketh is the reward not reckoned of grace, but of
5 debt. But to him that worketh not, but believeth on him that justifieth the ungodly, his faith is counted
6 for righteousness. Even as David also describeth the blessedness of the man, unto whom God imputeth
7 righteousness without works, saying, Blessed are they whose iniquities are forgiven, and whose sins are
8 covered; blessed is the man to whom the Lord will
9 not impute sin. ᶜ This declaration of blessing is it to the circumcision only that it is spoken, or to " the uncircumcision also? for we say that faith was
10 reckoned to Abraham for righteousness. How was it then reckoned? when he was in circumcision, or in uncircumcision? Not in circumcision, but in un-
11 circumcision. And he received the ᵈmark " of circum-

ᵇ *omit* But   ᶜ Cometh this blessedness then upon the circumcision only, or upon   ᵈ sign

4. 11, 12. And circumcision came afterwards, as the effect not the cause, the seal not the instrument, of the faith which Abraham had had in a previous state. The object of this was that he might be the spiritual parent of all those who like him have faith, yet being uncircumcised, that the righteousness that was sealed in him might be counted to them. There was a further object, that he might link together in one circumcision and uncircumcision, and be a father of circumcision to those who walk in the footsteps of the faith, which he had in his prior state. $\sigma\eta\mu\epsilon\hat{\iota}o\nu$, like $\sigma\phi\rho\alpha\gamma\hat{\iota}s$, refers to the outward mark of circumcision, which is also a sign of the promise. $\epsilon\hat{\iota}s$ $\tau\grave{o}$ $\epsilon\hat{\iota}\nu\alpha\iota$ ... $\epsilon\hat{\iota}s$ $\tau\grave{o}$ $\lambda o\gamma\iota\sigma$., not in the thoughts of Abraham, but in the purpose of God.

It is not quite clear whether the words $\grave{a}\lambda\lambda\grave{a}$ $\kappa\alpha\grave{\iota}$ $\tauo\hat{\iota}s$ $\sigma\tauo\iota\chi o\hat{\upsilon}\sigma\iota\nu$ refer to believing Jews, or to believers in general, whether Jew or Gentile. If the first, they are a limitation on the preceding clause: 'A father of circumcision to those who are not only circumcised but believing, who, like Abraham, have the sign in the

cision, a seal of the righteousness of the faith which he had ᵉ in his uncircumcision ᵍ: that he might be the father of all them that believe, though they be not circumcised, that ᶠthe ᵍ righteousness might be imputed
12 unto them ᵍ⁻ᵍ, and the father of circumcision ʰ not to them who are of the circumcision only, but to them also who ᵍ walk in the steps of that faith of our father Abraham, which he had being yet uncircumcised.
13 For the promise, that he should be the heir of the world, was not to Abraham, or to his seed, through
14 the law, but through the righteousness of faith. For if they which are of the law be heirs, faith is made

ᵉ yet being uncircumcised   ᶠ omit the   ᵍ add also
ʰ to them who are not of the circumcision only, but who also

flesh, and also walk in the footsteps of the faith which he had when uncircumcised' [cp. ch. ii. vv. 28, 29]. This mode of taking the passage has the advantage of retaining the words τοῖς οὐκ in their natural order. A want of point, however, is felt in the clause 'which he had when uncircumcised.' For although the faith of Abraham might be generally regarded as a source of blessing equally to Jew or Gentile, 'the faith which he had when uncircumcised' had no peculiar significance for the Jew. The τοῖς before στοιχοῦσιν is also against this way of explaining the clause. And, notwithstanding the inaccuracy of expression, the form of the first clause, τοῖς οὐκ ἐκ περιτομῆς μόνον, is so similar as to lead to the inference that it must have the same meaning with οὐ τῷ ἐκ τοῦ νόμου μόνον, in ver. 16.

It is simpler and better to refer ἀλλὰ καὶ τοῖς στοιχοῦσιν to the Gentiles. The meaning of the latter part of vers. 11, 12 will then be as follows : That he might as he had faith himself be the father of those who had faith; and as he was circumcised himself, be a father conveying the benefits of circumcision to those who walk in the footsteps of the faith which he had when uncircumcised. Or, in other words, that he might be the father of the faithful, whether Jew or Gentile, and convey to them the privileges of Jews.

13. *the heir of the world.*] The Apostle is alluding to Gen. xv. 7 ἐγὼ ὁ θεὸς ὁ ἐξαγαγών σε ἐκ χώρας Χαλδαίων, ὥστε δοῦναί σοι τὴν γῆν ταύτην κληρονομῆσαι. Compare also Gen. xvii. 5 πατέρα πολλῶν ἐθνῶν τέθεικά σε; and xiii. 15 ὅτι πᾶσαν τὴν γῆν ἣν σὺ ὁρᾷς σοὶ δώσω αὐτὴν καὶ τῷ σπέρματί σου ἕως αἰῶνος. The Rabbis extended this promise to the whole earth. So Mechilta, upon Exod. xiv. 31, quoted by Tholuck, 'Our father Abraham possesses the world

15 void, and the promise made of none effect: ⁱ for ᵏ the law worketh wrath: ᵏ and ᵏ where no law is, there
16 is no transgression. Therefore it is of faith, that it might be by grace; to the end the promise might be sure to all the seed; not to that only which is of the law, but to that also which is of the faith of Abraham;
17 who is the father of us all, (as it is written, I have made thee a father of many nations,) before him whom he believed, even God, who quickeneth the dead, and calleth those things which be not as though they were.
18 Who against hope believed in hope, that he might become the father of many nations, according to that

ⁱ because   ᵏ *for*

that now is, and that which is to come, not by inheritance, but by faith.' In this passage the Apostle has similarly enlarged it. The expression may be regarded either: (1) as a hyperbole, as Jerusalem is said in the Psalms to be 'the joy of the whole earth,' or as darkness is said to have 'come over the whole earth' at the Crucifixion; or (2) the promised land may be taken as the type of the world. On the one hand, it must not be forgotten, in the explanation of this and similar expressions, that the world did not present to the ancients the same distinct idea and conception as to ourselves; nor, on the other hand, that the thought of the promised land was inseparable to the true Israelite from the thought of a world to come. The words of the book of Genesis themselves might seem to the Apostle to promise more than had been or could be fulfilled in this world.

He was fixing his mind on something higher than the occupation of the promised land by the Israelites. It was this which gave the promise to Abraham a new meaning.

15. For the law is the very opposite of grace and faith and the promise; it works wrath not mercy; it takes men away from God instead of drawing them to Him; it makes transgressions where they were not before.

For a fuller explanation of these passages, the reader is referred to the Essay on the Strength of Sin is the Law. The real difficulty respecting them arises from the state without law being an imaginary one. We readily admit that, if anywhere there is no knowledge and no conscience, as in the case of a child, a savage, or a madman, there it is impossible there can be transgression. Of such we should say that they were not to be judged by our standard; that

19 which was spoken, So shall thy seed be. ¹ And not as one weak in faith he considered ᵗ his own body now dead when he was about an hundred years old, and 20 the deadness of Sarah's womb: he staggered not at the promise of God through unbelief; but was strong 21 in faith, giving glory to God; and being fully persuaded that, what he ᵐ has ᵍ promised, he ⁿ is ᵍ able 22 also to perform. And therefore it was imputed to 23 him for righteousness. But it was not written for 24 his sake alone, that it was imputed to him; but for

¹ *And being not weak in faith he considered not*   ᵐ had   ⁿ was

what to our moral notions was an offence was no offence to them; that in their case the laws of civilized countries did not apply. Our difficulty is to conceive the same absence of responsibility in rational beings. The truth is, that there is no absence of responsibility, except in that imaginary state of which the Apostle is speaking; a state without knowledge and without law, and, therefore, conceived of, as without evil and without crime.

23. *not written for his sake alone.*] Cp. Midrash Bereshit Rabba, chap. 40, *ad fin.* (on Genesis xii. 16), 'what is written of Abraham is written also of his children.'

24. A difficulty arises in reference to this verse, from the division of the clauses. There would be nothing to require explanation in such a form of expression as 'Who died and rose again for our sins and our justification.' But why 'died for our sins and rose again for our justification?' May not our justification equally with our sins be regarded as the object or cause of Christ's death?

We might answer that St. Paul often employs an antithesis of words, where there is no antithesis of meaning. Compare, for example, Rom. x. 9, 10 'If thou shalt confess with thy mouth the Lord Jesus, and believe in thy heart that God raised him from the dead, thou shalt be saved. For with the heart it is believed unto righteousness, and with the mouth confession is made unto salvation.' In this passage, were we to transpose the words righteousness and salvation, the meaning would be unaltered. There is no real opposition between them.

Yet there is a certain analogy on which the Apostle proceeds in the last-mentioned expression. The Christian is one with his Lord, and his life, like that of Christ, falls asunder into two divisions, death and life, condemnation and justification. Comp. Rom. vi. 5, 6 'For if we have been planted in the likeness of his death, we shall be also in the likeness of his resurrection: knowing this, that our old man is crucified with him, that the body of sin might be done away.'

us also, to whom it shall be imputed, who believe on him that raised up Jesus our Lord from the dead; 25 who was delivered for our offences and was raised again for our justification.

5 Therefore being justified by faith, [1] we have peace 2 with God through our Lord Jesus Christ: by whom also we have °had the ⁋ access by faith into this grace wherein we stand, and rejoice in hope of the glory of 3 God. And not only so, but we ᵖrejoice ⁋ in tribulations

° *omit* had the   ᵖ glory

So in vers. 10, 11 'For in that he died, he died unto sin once : but in that he liveth, he liveth unto God. Likewise reckon ye also yourselves to be dead indeed unto sin, but alive unto God through Jesus Christ our Lord.' A still nearer parallel is afforded by viii. 10 'But if Christ be in you, the body is dead because of sin; but the spirit is life because of righteousness. But if the spirit of him that raised up Christ from the dead dwell in you,' &c. Comp. also a more subtle trace of the same thought, in Rom. viii. 34, where κατακρίνων is opposed to ἐγερθείς. It would not be in accordance with St. Paul's usual language to invert the order of these terms, or to say, 'who died for our justification and rose again for our sins.' Sin and death, justification and renewal or resurrection, whether in the believer or Christ, are the parallel or cognate ideas.

Had the Apostle said, 'Who by his death was one with us in our sins, by his resurrection one with us in our renewal,' in such a mode of expression there would have been nothing contrary to his usual language. But, as has been already remarked, in describing the work of salvation, forms of thought are fluctuating, because they are inadequate; that which is sometimes the cause being equally, from another point of view, the effect, as in the present instance, the cause is not a cause, but a mode of expressing a more general connexion between two ideas. (See note on i. 4.) We should err in defining exactly that which is in its nature inexact; better to lose sight of the precise terms in the general meaning. It is a slight transition in the language of St. Paul from the form 'who rose again for our justification,' to the other form, 'who was one with us in his resurrection.' This slight change is the source of our difficulty.

5. 3. In the life of Christ, as well as of His followers, is traceable the double character of sorrow and joy, humiliation and exaltation, not divided from each other by time, but existing together, and drawn out alternately by the

[1] Reading ἔχομεν

4 also: knowing that tribulation worketh patience; and
5 patience, experience; and experience, hope: and hope
maketh not ashamed; because the love of God is shed
abroad in our hearts by the Holy Ghost which is
6 given unto us. For when we were yet without
strength, [1] ᑫyetᑫ in due time Christ died for the
7 ungodly. For scarcely for a righteous man will one

ᑫ omit *yet*

external circumstances of their lives. Christ Himself said, 'I, if I be lifted up from the earth, shall draw all men after me.' And just before He suffered, 'The hour is come that the Son of man should be glorified.' So He told His disciples, Matt. v. 12 'In the day of persecution rejoice and be exceeding glad.' And St. Paul, at the commencement of the second Epistle to the Corinthians, speaks as if sorrow brought its own joy and consolation with it; you can hardly tell whether he is sorrowful or joyful, so quickly is his sorrow turned into joy. There is the same mixed feeling of triumph in affliction in the remarkable words, 1 Cor. iv. 9 'I think that God hath set forth us the apostles last, as it were appointed unto death: for we are made a spectacle to the world, to angels, and to men.' And even where external afflictions are wanting, the mere consciousness of this 'present evil world,' 'the whole creation groaning together until now,' the remembrance of having once felt the sentence of death in himself, will make the believer rejoice with trembling for what he feels within or witnesses in others. Compare the aphorism of Lord Bacon, 'Prosperity is the blessing of the Old Testament, adversity of the New.'

7. This verse has been taken in four ways:—

(1) Christ died for the ungodly: this was a great instance of love; for hardly for a just man will one die; yet peradventure, for that exalted character, the good man, some one may even dare to die; or,

(2) Yet, peradventure, for the beneficent man, some would even dare to die; or,

(3) Yet, peradventure, for the good in the abstract, some would even dare to die.

The distinctions between $\delta\iota\kappa\alpha\iota\sigma s$, *good*, and $\dot{\alpha}\gamma\alpha\theta\acute{o}s$, *just*, which are required by the first two modes of explanation, are really assumed to avoid the difficulty. It is singular that the word $\dot{\alpha}\gamma\alpha\theta\acute{o}s$ used of a person occurs nowhere else in the writings of St. Paul. To the third explanation there are many objections: (1) the Apostle could hardly have used $\delta\iota\kappa\alpha\acute{\iota}ov$ of a person, and $\tau o\hat{v}\ \dot{\alpha}\gamma\alpha\theta o\hat{v}$ of a thing; (2) it is doubtful whether the

[1] Reading $\H{\epsilon}\tau\iota\ \gamma\dot{\alpha}\rho\ \chi\rho\iota\sigma\tau\acute{o}s$

die: yet peradventure for ʳ the ⸗ good man some would
even dare to die. But God ˢ establishes ⸗ his love
toward us, in that, while we were yet sinners, Christ
died for us. Much more then, being now justified by
his blood, we shall be saved from wrath through him.
For if, when we were enemies, we were reconciled to
God by the death of his Son, much more, being

ʳ a   ˢ commendeth

neuter τὸ ἀγαθόν would have been used in the sense of moral good; (3) the notion of dying for an abstract idea is entirely unlike the language of the New Testament, or of the age in which the New Testament was written, nor does it give the opposition which the Apostle requires.

(4) The remaining explanation of δικαίου and τοῦ ἀγαθοῦ makes them synonymous. The Apostle corrects his former expression— 'For Christ died, when we had no power to help ourselves, for the ungodly.' But this is unlike what men do for one another; for hardly will one die for a righteous man. Admitting that this statement requires correction (which the word μόλις already seems to imply), say, that for the good man some one may even dare to die, still the case is different, for it was while we were yet sinners that Christ died for us. It is not necessary to suppose any opposition between δικαίου and τοῦ ἀγαθοῦ; the clause ὑπὲρ γὰρ τοῦ ἀγαθοῦ may be regarded, not as subordinate to the previous clause, but as parallel with it, and dependent on the preceding verse. The use of a different word, though without a distinction in meaning, may arise either from a slight sense of the awkwardness of retracting what had just gone before, or from the wish to avoid tautology. Compare John xvi. 21 ἡ γυνὴ ὅταν τίκτῃ, λύπην ἔχει ... ὅταν δὲ γεννήσῃ τὸ παιδίον οὐκ ἔτι μνημονεύει τῆς θλίψεως, for a similar repetition, and for the thought, Rom. ix. 3, where the Apostle offers himself to be accursed from Christ for his brethren's sake.

10. 'We are reconciled to God' (here and 2 Cor. v. 20), or (2 Cor. v. 18) 'God reconciling us to himself through Jesus Christ,' or 'God in Christ reconciling the world to himself' (2 Cor. v. 19), are the modes of expression in Scripture used to describe the work of redemption. God is unchangeable; it is we who are reconciled to Him, not He to us. (Compare the use of καταλλάσσεσθαι, applied to the woman who is reconciled to her husband in 1 Cor. vii. 11.) But, on the other hand, the first spring and motive of redemption comes not from ourselves but from Him.

Much stress, it is true, cannot be laid on the precise use of language; for the Apostle might have spoken in a figure of God being angry with us and of us as hated by Him. And this may

11 reconciled, we shall be saved by his life. And not only so, but we also joy in God through our Lord Jesus Christ, by whom we have now received the †reconciliation.∥

† atonement

seem to be implied in the word ἐχθρός in the present passage. But the comparison of Col. i. 21 ἀπηλλοτριωμένους καὶ ἐχθροὺς τῇ διανοίᾳ ... παραστῆσαι, shows that ἐχθρός may have an active, as well as passive meaning.

12–21. Various expedients have been proposed for completing the construction: First, The device of a parenthesis extending from ver. 13 to ver. 18: the last expedient which should be resorted to in a writer so irregular in his syntax as the Apostle. Secondly, The missing apodosis has been sought for in ver. 12 itself, either in the words διὰ τῆς ἁμαρτίας ὁ θάνατος, or in the clause which follows, either:—

'As by one man sin entered into the world;'

'Death also came by sin:' or,

'As by one man sin entered into the world, and death by sin;'

'Even so death came upon all men.'

Both these explanations, however, do violence to the language in the meaning which they give to καὶ — καὶ οὕτως, and are also inconsistent with the general drift of the passage, which is not to show that 'as sin came into the world,' death followed in its train, but that 'as in Adam all died, even so in Christ shall all be made alive.'

If, disregarding the grammar, we look only to the sense, the missing apodosis is easily supplied both from what has preceded, and from what follows: 'Therefore we receive reconciliation by Jesus Christ, as by one man sin entered into the world.' Comp. δι' οὗ and δι' ἑνὸς ἀνθρώπου, in the 11th and 12th verses. It is further hinted at in the words ὅς ἐστι τύπος τοῦ μέλλοντος at the end of the 14th verse; it is indirectly supplied in ver. 15 and involved in the whole remainder of the chapter.

Admitting the irregularity of the construction, let us dismiss the grammar to follow the thought. The Apostle is about to speak of Adam, the type of sin, as Christ is the type of righteousness. The sin of Adam is the sin of man, as the righteousness of Christ is the righteousness of man. But how is the fact of sin reconcilable with the previous statements of the Apostle: 'Where there is no law there is no transgression'? Such is the doubt which seems to cross the Apostle's mind, which he answers; first, by saying, that there 'was sin in the world before the giving of the law' (though he had said before, 'where there is no law there is no transgression'), and then, as if aware of his apparent inconsistency, he softens his former expression into — 'sin is not imputed where there is no law.' An indirect answer is also sup-

12 Wherefore, as by one man sin entered into the world, and death by sin; and so death passed upon

plied by the verse that follows:
—'Howbeit death reigned from Adam to Moses,' i. e. men died before the time of Moses, and therefore they must have sinned.

The difficulty of this as of some other passages (Rom. iii. 1-8; ix. 19-23) arises out of the conflict of opposite thoughts in the Apostle's mind. Suppose him to have said, 'As by one man sin entered into the world and death by sin (for this is possible though there was no law—when I said, *where no law is, there is no transgression*. I meant that sin is not imputed, but that it exists is proved by the fact of death reigning over all before the time of Moses). But long before we have arrived at this point the thread of the main sentence has been lost. The Apostle makes an attempt to recover it in the words in v. 14 ὅς ἐστι τύπος τοῦ μέλλοντος, and more regularly repeats the parallel in vers. 15, 17.

12. *καὶ διὰ τῆς ἁμαρτίας ὁ θάνατος, and death by sin*.] That the sin of Adam was the cause of the death of Adam was the common belief of the Jews in St. Paul's time. The oldest trace of this belief is found in the Book of Wisdom, ii. 24: 'For God created man without corruption, and made him after the image of his own likeness. Nevertheless, through envy of the devil, came death into the world, and they that hold of his side prove it.' The death of Adam, and of all mankind in him, is again referred to by the Apostle in 1 Cor. xv. 21;

respecting which latter passage two things are observable: first, that the Apostle makes no allusion to the sin of Adam as the cause of his death—rather this is a consequence of his and of other men's earthly nature, 1 Cor. xv. 48, 50; and, secondly, that the death spoken of is plainly, from the contrast, not spiritual, but physical.

And such it is commonly supposed to be in the present passage. Such an interpretation is clear and definite, and one with which most readers will be satisfied. Yet it may be doubted whether, from the mere difference of modes of thought in his time and our own, we do not give it a greater degree of definiteness than it possessed to the Apostle himself. To us sin and death have no natural connexion. So far as they are united, we regard them as united by an act of God. But the Apostle joins them together in the same way that we might join together disease and death, or life and health. The flesh and the body are to him the natural seats both of physical and moral corruption.

It must be allowed that in other passages St. Paul as distinctly speaks of death for spiritual death, as he is here supposed to do for physical death. Compare vii. 9, 10 'Sin revived, and I died;' and ver. 13 'Was it then that which was good that became death unto me?' In other passages, again, θάνατος has an equally distinct meaning of spi-

13 all men, for that all have sinned—for until the law sin was in the world: but sin is not imputed where 14 there is no law. Nevertheless death reigned from Adam to Moses, even over them that had not sinned

ritual and physical death at once. For example, in Rom. vi. 21, the word appears, at first sight, to refer only to spiritual evil; but the parallel of eternal life in the next clause shows that physical death is not excluded. In like manner it may be fairly argued that St. Paul does not connect sin and death in this chapter in any other sense than he connects life and righteousness. But as he could not have meant that the continuance of existence after death depended on the righteousness of Christ, so neither can he mean that temporal death depended on Adam's sin.

Nor can it be left out of sight that in the 15th chapter of the 1 Cor. the Apostle makes no reference to a prior state of innocence from which Adam fell. 'The first man is of the earth, earthy: the second man is the Lord from heaven. As is the earthy so are they that are earthy; as is the heavenly so are they also that are heavenly.' Adam and Christ are here contrasted, not in reference to any act performed by Adam, but to their own nature. It would surely be an error to lay stress on the precise points of view taken by the Apostle in this chapter, considering that a different view occurs in the parallel passage.

These considerations lead us to doubt how far St. Paul distinctly recognized the interpretations which later ages have given to his words. Could the consequences which have been drawn from them have been present to his mind, he might have told us that 'these things are an allegory,' like the bondwoman and the freewoman, or the baptism of the Fathers unto Moses in the cloud and in the sea.

The two clauses that follow are parallel to the two preceding ones, though the order is inverted:—

'As by one man sin entered into the world, and death by sin,'
'And in like manner, as all men sinned, so all men died.'

13. ἄχρι γὰρ νόμου, *for until the law.*] But sin is inseparable from the law, as has been repeated above, 'where there is no law there is no transgression.' How was it, then, that in the interval between Adam and Moses men could have sinned? We answer this difficulty by changing the form of our expression without materially altering its meaning; not, 'where there is no law there is no transgression,' but, 'sin is not imputed where there is no law.' Sin, in other words, was not exceeding sinful; it did not abound or show itself in its true nature, yet it existed still. Comp. ver. 20.

14. ἐπὶ τοὺς μὴ ἁμαρτήσαντας, *over them that had not sinned,*] is commonly interpreted, according as what may be termed the Augustinian or Pelagian view of the pas-

after the similitude of Adam's transgression, who is
15 the figure of him that was to come. But not as the
offence, so also is the free gift. For if through the
offence of one many ᵘ died,ⁿ much more the grace of
God, and the gift by grace, which is by one man,
16 Jesus Christ, hath abounded unto many. And not
as it was by one that sinned, so is the gift: for the
judgment was by one to condemnation, but the free
17 gift is of many offences unto justification. For if by
one ˣ⁻ⁿ offence¹ death reigned ʸ through ⁿ one: much
more they which receive ᶻ the ⁿ abundance of grace
and of the gift of righteousness shall reign in life
18 ᵃ through ⁿ one, Jesus Christ. Therefore as by ᵇ one
offence judgment came upon all men to condemnation; even so by one act of righteousness ⁿ the free
19 gift came upon all men unto justification of life. For
as by one man's disobedience many were made sinners,
so by the obedience of one shall many be made

ᵘ be dead   ˣ *add* man's   ʸ by   ᶻ *omit* the   ᵃ by
ᵇ the offence of one judgement came upon all men to condemnation; even
so by the righteousness of one

sage is preferred, either, who did
not commit actual sin like Adam,
but only inherited Adam's imputed sin ; or, who did commit
actual sin, but not like Adam
against a positive law or commandment.

A third way of explaining the
words, though it necessitates what
may be termed the Augustinian
interpretation, is worthy of attention. ἐπὶ τῷ ὁμοιώματι may be
connected with ἐβασίλευσεν, as
a further explanation of ἐπὶ τοὺς
μὴ ἁμαρτήσαντας. 'But death
reigned from Adam to Moses
upon those who had not sinned,

because of the likeness of the sin
of Adam'—the 'likeness' only,
if, where no law is, there is no
direct imputation of sin. Comp.
ch. vi. 5 εἰ γὰρ σύμφυτοι γεγόναμεν
τῷ ὁμοιώματι τοῦ θανάτου αὐτοῦ,
ἀλλὰ καὶ τῆς ἀναστάσεως ἐσόμεθα.
All men are thus identified with
the sin of Adam, as they are to be
identified with the righteousness
of Him that was to come. Better
than any of these subtle modes it
is to take the passage in a more
general sense : 'But death reigned
from Adam to Moses even upon
those who had not sinned expressly and consciously, to whom

¹ Reading [ἐν τῷ] ἑνὶ παραπτώματι

20 righteous. ᶜBut the law came in besides,ᵍ that the offence might abound. But where sin abounded, grace
21 did much more abound: that as sin ᵈreigned inᵍ death, even so might grace reign through righteousness unto eternal life by Jesus Christ our Lord.

6 WHAT shall we say then? ᵉAre we toᵍ continue
2 in sin, that grace may abound? God forbid. How shall we, that are dead to sin, live any longer therein?
3 Know ye not, that so many of us as were baptized into ᶠChrist Jesusᵍ were baptized into his death?

ᶜ Moreover the law entered   ᵈ hath reigned unto   ᵉ *Shall we*
ᶠ *Jesus Christ*

sin therefore could not be imputed in the same sense as it was to Adam.' Compare verse 13.

21. The leading thought of the preceding section has been, 'As in Adam all die, even so in Christ shall all be made alive.' But there is a great difference between the act of sin and the act of justification. If many died through the first, much more shall they be redeemed by the second; if there was one offence to condemn, there are many offences to be forgiven: where death and condemnation are, much more there are life and grace; as one comes to all men through one, so likewise the other. The five verses from 15–19 consist almost wholly of a repetition of the same thought, in the form either of a parallel between the act of Adam and of Christ, or of a climax in which the grace of Christ is contrasted in its effects with Adam's sin. The law came to increase the sum of transgressions, but grace still exceeded. The law came in with this very object, that as sin had triumphed, grace might triumph also.

6. 3. To be baptized into Christ is to be baptized so as to be one with Christ, or to become a member of Christ by baptism. Compare 1 Cor. xii. 13 εἰς ἓν σῶμα ἐβαπτίσθημεν, between which and the present passage a connecting-link is formed by Rom. vii. 4 ἐθανατώθητε τῷ νόμῳ διὰ τοῦ σώματος τοῦ χριστοῦ. So the Apostle says: 'By being baptized into Christ we were baptized into a common death.'

Philosophy, as Plato says in the Phaedo, is death; so the Apostle says that Christian life is death. It is a state in which we are dead to the temptations of the world, dead to all those things which penetrate through the avenues of sense, dead to the terrors of the law, withdrawn from our own nature itself, shrunk and contracted, as it were, within a narrow space, hidden with Christ and God. It is death and life at once—death in relation to earth, and life in relation to God.

THE EPISTLE TO THE ROMANS

4 Therefore we ^g were *"* buried with him by baptism into death: that like as Christ was raised up from the dead by the glory of the Father, even so we also 5 should walk in newness of life. For if we have been ^h united with him by *"* the likeness of his death, we shall be also ⁱ by *"* the likeness of his resurrection: 6 knowing this, that our old man is crucified with him, that the body of sin might be destroyed, that hence-7 forth we should not serve sin. For he that is dead 8 ^k has been justified *"* from sin. ^l But *"* if we be dead with Christ, we believe that we shall also live with 9 him: knowing that Christ being raised from the dead dieth no more; death hath no more dominion over

^g are   ^h planted together in   ⁱ in   ^k is freed   ^l Now

4. The meaning of this verse will be more clearly brought out if we recall the picture of Baptism in the apostolic age, when the rite was performed by immersion, and Christians might be said to be buried with Christ; and the passing of the Israelites through the cloud and the sea (1 Cor. x. 1, 2), and even the Deluge itself (1 Pet. iii. 21), seemed no inappropriate types of its waters. Imagine not infants, but crowds of grown-up persons already changed in heart and feelings; their 'life hidden with Christ and God,' losing their personal consciousness in the laver of regeneration; rising again from its depths into the light of heaven, in communion with God and nature; met as they rose from the bath with the white raiment, which is 'the righteousness of the saints,' and ever after looking back on that moment as the instant of their new birth, of the putting off of the old man, and the putting on of Christ. Baptism was to them the figure of death, burial, and resurrection all in one, the most apt expression of the greatest change that can pass upon man, like the sudden change into another life when we leave the body.

7. It is not quite clear whether these words refer only to Christ, or to the believer who is in His image also. The latter is most agreeable to the context. The nerve of the Apostle's argument was: 'How shall we who are dead to sin live any longer therein?' Continuing this thought, he says: 'We are dead and buried with Christ, and therefore should rise with him to newness of life. We have left the old man on the cross with Him, that the body of sin may be done away. For death is the quittance of sin.' 'How then shall we any longer live in it?' —is still the Apostle's inference;

10 him. For in that he died, he died unto sin once: 11 but in that he liveth, he liveth unto God. Likewise reckon ye also yourselves ᵐ⁻ᵈ dead indeed unto sin, 12 but alive unto God through Jesus Christ. ⁿ⁻ᵈ Let not sin therefore reign in your mortal body, that ye 13 should obey ᵒ⁻ᵈ the lusts thereof. Neither yield ye your members as instruments of unrighteousness unto sin: but yield yourselves unto God, as those that are alive from the dead, and your members as instruments 14 of righteousness unto God. For sin shall not have dominion over you: for ye are not under the law, but under grace.

15 What then? ᵖ are we to sin,ᵈ because we are not 16 under the law, but under grace? God forbid. Know ye not, that to whom ye yield yourselves servants to obey, his servants ye are to whom ye obey; whether of sin unto death, or of obedience unto righteousness?

ᵐ add *to be*   ⁿ add *our Lord*   ᵒ add *it in*   ᵖ *shall we sin*

not only 'how shall we who are dead to sin,' but, 'how shall we who are justified by death.'

10. Throughout this passage the Apostle is identifying Christ and the believers; and conceptions, primarily applicable or more intelligible in reference to the one, are transferred to the other. We shall better apprehend his meaning, by beginning in a different order. 'For in that we die, we die unto sin; in that we live, we live unto God.' Our death with Christ is the renunciation of sin once for all, and the opening of a new life unto God. Under this figure of what the believer feels in himself, the Apostle describes the work of Christ. Death and life are one but yet two in the individual soul—the negative and positive side of the change which the Gospel makes in him—so they are also in Christ.

14. It might seem, at first sight, tautology to say, 'Let not sin reign over you, for sin shall not reign over you.' A slightly different turn restores the meaning. Do it, as we might say, for you are able to do it. Present yourselves to God as those who are alive from the dead; who were dead once, but now alive; under the law once, but under grace now. Instead of the outward and positive rule, you have the inward union with Christ; for the strength of sin, the consciousness of forgiveness; for fear, love; for bondage, freedom; for slavery,

17 But God be thanked, that ye were the servants of sin,
but ye have obeyed from the heart that form of
18 doctrine ^q whereto ye were delivered; and being⫽
made free from sin, ye became the servants of
19 righteousness. I speak after the manner of men
because of the infirmity of your flesh. For as ye
have yielded your members servants to uncleanness
and to iniquity unto iniquity; even so now yield
your members servants to righteousness unto ʳ sancti-
20 fication.⫽ For when ye were the servants of sin, ye
21 were free ˢ as touching⫽ righteousness. What fruit
had ye then [1]? things whereof ye are now ashamed;
22 for the end of those things is death. But now being
made free from sin, and become servants to God, ye
have your fruit unto ᵗ sanctification,⫽ and the end
23 everlasting life. For the wages of sin is death; but
the gift of God is eternal life ᵘ in⫽ Jesus Christ our
Lord.

7 Know ye not, brethren, (for I speak to them that
know the law,) how that the law hath dominion over
2 a man as long as he liveth? For the woman which
hath an husband is bound by the law to her husband

^q which was delivered you; being then   ʳ holiness   ˢ from
    ᵗ holiness   ᵘ through

sonship; for weakness, power. Such an enlargement of the words of the Apostle may be gathered from other places. The γάρ expresses the ground of motive and encouragement.

23. The evil that we receive at the hand of God is deserved, but the good undeserved. Sin has its wages, and yet eternal life is a free gift. How can we maintain this paradox, which is, moreover, a form of expression natural to us?

It is quite true that the good and evil which we receive at the hands of God is exactly proportioned by His justice and wisdom to our deserts. But what we intend to express by such forms of speech is: (1) Our feeling that He is, in a special sense, the Author of our salvation as well as of all good; (2) That whatever

[1] Placing the point of interrogation after εἴχετε τότε

294   THE EPISTLE TO THE ROMANS   [7. 2

^x that " liveth; but if the husband be dead, she is
3 loosed from the law of her husband. So then if,
while her husband liveth, she be married to another
man, she shall be called an adulteress: but if her
husband be dead, she is free from that law; so that
she is no adulteress, though she be married to another
4 man. Wherefore, my brethren, ye also are become
dead to the law by the body of Christ; that ye should
be married to another, to him who is raised from the
5 dead, that we should bring forth fruit unto God. For
when we were in the flesh, the motions of sins, which
were by the law, did work in our members to bring
6 forth fruit unto death. But now, ^y being dead," we
are delivered from the law ^{z—"} wherein we were held;
^a and so we " serve in newness of spirit, and not in the
oldness of the letter.

7 What shall we say then? Is the law sin? God

^x so long as he   ^y omit *being dead*   ^z add *that being dead*
                                 ^a that we should

may be our deserts in his eye, they would lose their very nature if we regarded them as deserts.

7. 4. ὥστε ὑμεῖς ἐθανατώθητε.] The Apostle changes the figure. The words ἐθανατώθητε and ἀποθανόντες are too strong to allow us to suppose that he is still describing the death of the believer to the law under the image of the wife; who is not dead, but only freed by death. This latter image, however, reappears in the next words, εἰς τὸ γενέσθαι ὑμᾶς ἑτέρῳ. For a similar change, comp. ch. vi. 5, 6, 7: 1 Thess. v. 2, 4.

7. Τί οὖν ἐροῦμεν; *What shall we say then?*] If the law was the instrument whereby the motions of sins worked in our members (ver. 5), if we are freed from sin by being dead to the law (ver. 6), what shall we say? 'Is the law sin?' It has been nearly identified in what precedes, it is all but sin in what follows. There is reason for us to pause before going further.

ὁ νόμος, *the law*.] But what law? the Mosaic, or the law written on the heart? We can only gather from the passage itself, which leads us rather to think of a terrible consciousness of sin, than of questions of new moons, and sabbaths. 'What shall we say then,' we might paraphrase, 'is conscience sin?'

To shift the meaning of νόμος, or to assign remote and different significations to the word in successive verses, may seem like forbid. Nay, I had not known sin, but by the law: for I had not known lust, except the law had said, 8 Thou shalt not ᵇ lust." But sin, taking occasion by the commandment, wrought in me all manner of ᶜ lust." 9 For without the law sin was dead, ᵈ and " I was alive without the law once: but when the commandment 10 came, sin revived, and I died. And the commandment, which was to life, I found to be unto death. 11 For sin, taking occasion by the commandment, de-12 ceived me, and by it slew me. Wherefore the law is holy, and the commandment holy, and just, and good; 13 was then that which is good made death unto me?

ᵇ covet   ᶜ concupiscence   ᵈ for

a trick of the interpreter. Whether it really be so or not, must depend on the fact of how St. Paul uses the word, and on the general use of language in his age. Compare Col. ii. 16-23 for three distinct uses of the word $\sigma\hat{\omega}\mu\alpha$; also vii. 21—viii. 4 for several changes in the sense of $\nu\acute{o}\mu os$, and viii. 19-22 for similar changes in the sense of $\kappa\tau\acute{\iota}\sigma\iota s$.

8. It may be asked, How can the law increase the temptation to sin? It may not make men better; how does it make them worse? Human nature errs from passion and desire; (1) By sin the Apostle means the consciousness of sin, not any mere external act. (2) The state which he describes is partly imaginary. It begins with absolute ignorance (I was alive without the law once) and ends with the utter disruption of the soul between will and knowledge.

12. After balancing the two sides of this question, the conclusion at which the Apostle arrives is, that the law is 'holy, just, and good.' It was the law that made sin to be what it was, and it is true that this comes very near to the law being itself sin. But the other side has also to be put forward. Sin is the active cause, the law only the occasion, the deceiver being human nature itself, and the law forbidding sin at the moment it seems to create it. So that the law, in itself, is no more polluted than the sun in the heavens by the corruption on which it looks. The obscurity in this, as in many other passages, arises from the Apostle, in the alternation of thought, dwelling too long on that side of the argument, which, for the sake of clearness, should have been subordinate. In this instance, he has said so much of the commandment being found unto death and the occasion of sin, that he is obliged to make a violent resumption of the thought with which he commenced.

13. We can imagine a state of

God forbid. But sin, that it might appear sin, working death ᵉ to ᵉ me by that which is good; that sin by the 14 commandment might become exceeding sinful. For we know that the law is spiritual: but I am carnal, 15 sold under sin. ᶠ For what I do I know not ᶠ: for what I would, that do I not; but what I hate, that do 16 I. If then I do that which I would not, I consent

ᵉ in   ᶠ For that which I do I allow not

mind in an individual, or a condition in society, in which vice loses 'half its grossness,' and some of its real evil, either by the veil of refinement beneath which it is concealed, or by the very naturalness to the human mind of vice itself. Suppose the person or society here spoken of, to wake up on a sudden to a consciousness of the holiness of God and the requirements of His law; suppose further, they were made aware of the contrast between their own life and the Divine rule, yet were powerless to change, knowing everything, yet able to accomplish nothing, sensitive to the pangs of conscience, yet 'unequal to the performance of any duty;' of such it might be said, in a figure—'Sin became death that it might appear sin, working death to us through that which is good, that sin might become exceeding sinful.'

The progress of which St. Paul is speaking may be arranged in six stages:—

(1) The state of nature: 'I was alive without the law once.' Ver. 9.

(2) The awakening of nature to the requirements of the law, and the death of sin. Vers. 9-11.

(3) The growing consciousness of right and severance of the soul into two parts, as the sense of right prevails. Vers. 15-23.

(4) Sin, which was originally a mere perversion, strengthening into a law which opposes itself to the law of God. Vers. 23, 24.

(5) Laying aside of the worse half of the soul, that is, justification. Ver. 25.

(6) Peace and glory. Ch. viii. 1.

It would be unlike the manner of St. Paul to draw out these stages in perfectly regular order. Here, as elsewhere, he goes to and fro, and returns upon his former thought. In chapter viii, for example, when the soul has already entered into its rest, he again casts his eye upon the believer's state from his earthly side, 'groaning within himself, waiting for the redemption of the body.'

14. The language of the New Testament does not conform to any received views of psychology. It is the language partly of the Old Testament, but still more of the Alexandrian philosophy, which is defined neither by popular nor by scientific use. In modern times we do not divide the soul into its better and worse half, but into will, reason, consciousness, and other faculties

THE EPISTLE TO THE ROMANS

17 unto the law that it is good: ᵍ and now ″ it is no more
18 I that do it, but sin that dwelleth in me. For I know
that in me (that is, in my flesh) dwelleth no good
thing: for to will is present with me; but how to
19 perform that which is good, ʰ⁻″ not. For the good that
I would I do not: but the evil which I would not,
20 that I do. Now if I do that I would not, it is no
21 more I that do it, but sin that dwelleth in me. I find
then ⁱ the ″ law, that, when I would do good, evil is
22 present with me. For I delight in the law of God
23 after the inward man: but I see another law in my
members, warring against the law of my mind, and
bringing me into captivity to the law of sin which is

ᵍ now then   ʰ add *I find*   ⁱ a

which, for the most part, belong equally to good and bad. Such is, however, the fundamental division of the Apostle. There is a heavenly and earthly, a higher and a lower principle; the first, whereby we hold communion with God Himself, the Spirit; the second, the flesh, or corrupt soil of sin, scarcely distinguishable from sin itself. These two do not correspond to mind and body, which are only the figures under which they are expressed.

17. In this passage, between vers. 14 and 25, the Apostle may be said three times to change his identity: First of all, he is one with his worse nature, which, as having the power to turn the balance of his actions, claims to be the whole man; secondly, with his better nature, which makes a perceptible though ineffectual struggle against the power of evil; and, thirdly, he separates himself from both, and overlooks the strife between them, vers. 21-23.

18. Here is a further change in the personality of the speaker: 'I know that in me,' which is explained to mean 'in my flesh,' there is, as it were standing by my side, the wish for the good, but not the accomplishment of the good. οὐχ εὑρίσκω, the reading of the Text. Recep. and of Δ. G. f. g. v, if genuine, is a continuation of the figure of παράκειται; cp. ver. 21.

23. In the short space between the twenty-first and the twenty-third verses there occur five modifications of the word νόμος: (1) The play of words alluded to above, 'the law that evil is present with him.' (2) The law of God, that is, the law of Moses 'in the Spirit,' not 'in the letter;' or, as we might express it, 'idealized.' (3) The same law presented under a different aspect, as νόμος τοῦ νοός, or conscience.

24 in my members. O wretched man that I am! who
25 shall deliver me from the body of this death? ᵏThanks
be to God ⁰ through Jesus Christ our Lord. So then
with the mind I myself serve the law of God; howbeit
with the flesh the law of sin.

8 There is therefore now no condemnation to them
2 which are in Christ Jesus. ¹⁻⁰ For the law of the
Spirit of life in Christ Jesus hath made ¹me free from

ᵏ *I thank God* ¹ add *who walk not after the flesh but after the Spirit*

(4) νόμος ἐν τοῖς μέλεσιν. (5) νόμος τῆς ἁμαρτίας. Borrowing the language of philosophical distinctions, we may arrange them as follows:—

Subject.
νόμος τοῦ νοός.
νόμος ἐν τοῖς μέλεσιν

Object.
νόμος τοῦ θεοῦ.
νόμος τῆς ἁμαρτίας.

The 23rd verse describes a further progress in the conflict. At first the two 'laws' are opposed to each other; but at length the worse 'law' gets the better, and the soul passes on to consider evil as a sort of internal necessity to which it is by nature liable. The ἕτερος νόμος is only distinguished from the νόμος τῆς ἁμαρτίας, as the wavering emotion of the will from the settled inward principle. The first is the temptation of the natural desires; the second, the law of despair.

The Gospel is often opposed to the law, as the inward to the outward. Here the law of sin is equally figured as internal; though within, that is, in the flesh and the members, it is still incapable of harmonizing with our better life. We might illustrate its relation to the soul, by the example of those poisons whose introduction into the body is said to destroy life because they never become a part of the human frame.

8. 2. The Gospel has been sometimes represented as a law, sometimes as a spirit; as a rule to which we must conform, and also as a power with which we are endowed. Both aspects are united in the expression, 'the law of the Spirit of life,' which is a kind of paradox, and may be compared with 'the law of faith,' at the end of the third chapter. Strictly speaking, in the language of St. Paul, sin stands on the one side, and the Spirit of God on the other; they answer respectively to the worse and the better element of human nature; while, between the two is placed the straight and unbending rule of the law. But the law is used in two other senses also, first, for the rule of sin to which man has subjected himself, and, secondly,

¹ Reading με

3 the law of sin and death. For what the law could not do, in that it was weak through the flesh, God sending his own Son in the likeness of sinful flesh, 4 and for sin, condemned sin in the flesh: that the righteousness of the law might be fulfilled in us, who

for the growth of the higher life, the spirit which becomes a law, the habit which strengthens into a second and better nature. Law, in the first of these two senses, is but a figure to express the strength and uniformity of the power of evil; in the second, it is the harmony of human things in communion with God and Christ: the first is the law under which the first Adam fell: the second, the law, by the fulfilment of which the second Adam redeemed mankind.

νόμου τῆς ἁμαρτίας καὶ τοῦ θανάτου, *the law of sin and death.*] The strength of the language would not be a positive proof that the Apostle is not here speaking of the law of Moses, if we may take the expressions in Gal. iii and iv. 3, and 1 Cor. xv. 56, where he seems to speak of the law as synonymous with 'elements of the world,' and even as 'the strength of sin,' as a measure of his words. Such a view of the words would also agree with the following verse, which speaks of the powerlessness of 'the law through the flesh,' an expression hardly suitable to the 'law in the members' that preceded, which was not powerless, but simply evil. Nor can we suppose that in the 'law of sin and death,' no allusion is implied to the law of Moses, even if the two be not absolutely identical. Still it is less liable to objection, to take the law of sin and death in the same general sense in which the law of sin and the body of death were spoken of in the preceding chapter. It is the law of Moses, and what the law of Moses in its influence on the heart and conscience has grown up into and become, the law which is the strength of sin, which is almost sin, which was made death.

3. κατέκρινε τὴν ἁμαρτίαν ἐν τῇ σαρκί, *condemned sin in the flesh.*] The meaning of the clause derives some light from the words that follow. In Scripture Christ is often said to be in all points like ourselves; and all that we are, and are not, and might have been, is transferred to Him, either to be done away with in us, or imparted to us. Thus, in the language of St. Paul, He died that we might be saved from death; He became a curse to free us from the curse of the law; He condemned sin in the flesh that to us there might be no condemnation. Also He condemned sin that we might condemn it too; or in other words that the righteousness of the law might be fulfilled in us, who walk not after the flesh, but after the spirit.

4. ἵνα τὸ δικαίωμα τοῦ νόμου.] 'That the righteous requirement of the law may be fulfilled in us, who walk not after the flesh but after the spirit.' These words

5 walk not after the flesh, but after the Spirit. For
they that are after the flesh do mind the things of the
flesh; but they that are after the Spirit the things of
6 the Spirit. For ᵐthe mind of the flesh " is death;
7 but ⁿthe mind of the Spirit " is life and peace. Because
the °mind of the flesh " is enmity against God: for it
is not subject to the law of God, neither indeed can
8 be; ᵖand " they that are in the flesh cannot please
9 God. But ye are not in the flesh, but in the Spirit, if

ᵐ to be carnally minded
° carnal mind
ⁿ to be spiritually minded
ᵖ so then

have received three interpretations. They may be supposed to
refer: (1) to Christ's fulfilment
of the law, which is transferred
to us; or, (2) to our participation
in His fulfilment of the law by
union with Him; or, (3) to our
fulfilment of the law by the holiness which He imparts to us.
In other words, they may relate:
(1) to an external righteousness;
or, (2) to a righteousness, external, but imparted; or, (3) to inherent righteousness. Instead of
selecting one of these interpretations, the meaning of any of
which is defined by its antagonism to the other two, we must
go back to the predoctrinal age
of the Apostle himself, ere such
distinctions existed. The whole
Christian life flows with him
from union with Christ. Whether this union is conscious or
unconscious, whether it gives or
merely imputes the righteousness
of Christ, is a question which he
does not analyse. But in thinking of it, he perceives a sort of
balance and contrast between the
humiliation of Christ and the
exaltation of the Christian. The
believer seems to gain what his
master has lost. He throws on
Christ the worse half of self, that
the better half may be endued
with the spirit of life.

6. φρόνημα τῆς σαρκός.] 'Which
some do expound the wisdom,
some sensuality, some the affection, some the desire of the
flesh.' Art. ix.

'The mind' in the sense of
'will, intention,' more nearly
answers to the Greek than any
of these.

In this and the following verses
the Apostle, as in vii. 8, returns
upon the track of the preceding
chapter. He is speaking of the
struggle which is now past, the
elements of which no longer exist
together in the same human soul,
but are the types of classes of men
living in two different worlds.
In ver. 6 we have what may be
termed a further epexegesis of
ver. 5, as ver. 5 was of ver. 4,
both being connected by the
favourite γάρ. As in ver. 5 he
took up the words σάρξ and πνεῦμα
from ver. 4, so here he takes up
the word φρονεῖν from ver. 5.

9. εἴ περ . . . ὑμῖν.] The spirit

so be that the Spirit of God dwell in you. Now if
any man have not the Spirit of Christ, he is none of
10 his. ᑫBut⁺ if Christ be in you, the body is dead
because of sin; but the Spirit is life because of
11 righteousness. But if the Spirit of him that raised
up Jesus from the dead dwell in you, he that raised
up Christ ʳJesus⁺ from the dead shall also quicken
your mortal bodies by his Spirit that dwelleth in you.
12 Therefore, brethren, we are debtors, not to the flesh,
13 to live after the flesh. For if ye live after the flesh,
ye shall die: but if ye through the Spirit do mortify
14 the deeds of the body, ye shall live. For as many as
are led by the Spirit of God, they are the sons of God.
15 For ye have not received the spirit of bondage again
to fear; but ye have received the Spirit of adoption,
whereby we cry, Abba, Father.

16 The Spirit itself beareth witness with our spirit,
17 that we are the children of God: and if children, then
heirs; heirs of God, and joint-heirs with Christ;

ᑫ And   ʳ omit *Jesus*

is spoken of in Scripture indifferently as the Spirit of God or of Christ, Phil. i. 19; or of the Son, Gal. iv. 6; sometimes under the more general term of the Spirit of the Lord, as in 2 Cor. iii. 17, 18. Here the Apostle makes a sudden transition from the Spirit of God to that of Christ, and returns again in the eleventh verse to speak of 'the Spirit of Him that raised up Christ from the dead.'

11. The spiritual resurrection suggests the thought of the actual resurrection, as in John v. 25. In this world the quickening Spirit and the mortal body exist separate from each other; but hereafter the Spirit shall reanimate the body, as it is the Spirit of Him who raised up Christ from the dead; who will do as much for us as he did for Christ. τὰ θνητὰ σώματα, your bodies that would die were it not for His quickening Spirit. Compare vi. 12.

14. This new relation between God and man is introduced by the Gospel. It is not literally true that, in the Old Testament, the children of Israel are not spoken of as the sons of God, but only as His subjects and servants; but it is true that in their essential character the law and the Gospel are thus opposed, as the spirit of bondage again to fear, and the

302 THE EPISTLE TO THE ROMANS [8. 17

^s since ^f we suffer with him, that we may be also
18 glorified together. For I reckon that the sufferings
of this present time are not worthy to be compared
with the glory which shall be revealed ^t unto ^u us.
19 For the earnest expectation of the creature waiteth
20 for the manifestation of the sons of God. For the
creature was made subject to vanity, not willingly,
but by reason of him who hath subjected the same in

^s if so be that   ^t in

Spirit of adoption, whereby we acknowledge God as a father.

18. λογίζομαι γάρ, *for I reckon.*] In Scripture, the glory of the saints is sometimes spoken of as future, sometimes as present; sometimes as at a distance, at other times upon the earth; sometimes as an external state or condition; at other times as an inward and spiritual change, to be revealed in them as they are transformed from glory to glóry. In the writings of St. Paul it is the spiritual sense of a future life which chiefly prevails, as in this passage. He does not paint scenes of the world to come: he is lost in it; 'whether in the body or out of the body he cannot tell.'

19. ἀποκαραδοκία, *expectation.*] As we turn from ourselves to the world around us, the prospect on which we cast our eyes seems to reflect the colours of our own minds, and to share our joy and sorrow. To the religious mind it seems also to reflect our sins. We cannot, indeed, speak of the misery of the brute creation, of whose constitution we know so little; nor do we pretend to discover in the loveliest spots of earth, indications of a fallen world. But when we look at the vices and diseases of mankind, at their life of labour in which the animals are our partners, at the aspect in modern times of our large towns, as in ancient of a world given to idolatry, we see enough to give a meaning to the words of the Apostle. The evil in the world bears witness with the evil and sorrow in our own hearts. And the hope of another life springs up unbidden in our thoughts, for the sake of ourselves and of our fellow-creatures.

20. The Apostle is speaking here, as elsewhere, of the double character of the scheme of Providence, consisting, as it did, of two parts, one of which had a reference to the other. As afterwards he says (xi. 32): 'God concluded all under sin that he might have mercy upon all;' so here— The creature was made subject to evil against its will, and with the hope of restoration, because of him who subjected the same; or the creature was made subject because of him who subjected the same, in hope that, &c. Connecting ἐπ' ἐλπίδι with the following

8. 25]   THE EPISTLE TO THE ROMANS   303

21 hope, because the creature itself also shall be delivered from the bondage of corruption into the ᵘ liberty of
22 the glory ⁋ of the children of God. For we know that the whole creation groaneth and travaileth in pain
23 together until now. And not only they, but ourselves also which have the first-fruits of the Spirit, even we ourselves groan within ourselves, waiting for
24 the adoption, to wit, the redemption of our body. For we are saved by hope: but hope that is seen is not hope: ¹ for what a man seeth, why doth he ˣ⁻⁋ hope
25 for? But if we hope for that we see not, we with patience wait for it.

ᵘ glorious liberty   ˣ add *yet*

clause, 'the creature,' we might paraphrase, 'had no love for this helpless state. He was subjected to it because of Him that subjected him, in the hope that grace might yet more abound.' But who is 'he who subjected?' First, Christ, on account of whose special work the creature was made subject to vanity. (The preposition διά has no proper meaning, if the word ὑποτάξας is referred exclusively to God.) He subjected the creature as He condemned sin in the flesh in His own person, by subjecting Himself. And yet though the work of redemption be attributed to Him, it seems inappropriate to regard Him also as the author of the fallen condition of man. There is the same impropriety in such a mode of expression as there would be in saying, '*Christ* concluded all under sin that he might have mercy upon all.' In the language of St. Paul, He is the instrument of our redemption, not its first author. More truly, in the word ὑποτάξαντα God and Christ seem to meet. 'God in Christ reconciling the world to Himself:' as the Creator considered as the Author and Appointer of all His creatures; as the Redeemer, the final cause and end of their sinful state. In defence of this twofold meaning of ὑποτάξας, compare the transition from God to Christ in vers. 9, 11; also Col. i. 15.

23-30. The connexion of these verses may be traced as follows:—

(1) We walk feebly by hope and not by sight, waiting for the redemption of the body (23-25).

(2) But this feebleness the Spirit helps, and ever makes earnest intercession for us (26, 27).

(3) And there is another side to this view of creation groaning together; viz. that in all things God is working together for good

¹ Reading ὃ γὰρ βλέπει τις, τί ἐλπίζει;

26 Likewise the Spirit also helpeth our ʸinfirmity:⸗
for we know not what we should pray for as we
ought: but the Spirit itself maketh intercession ᶻ—⸗
27 with groanings which cannot be uttered. And he
that searcheth the hearts knoweth what is the mind
of the Spirit, ᵃthat it⸗ maketh intercession for the
28 saints according to the will of God. And we know
that ᵇin all things God works⸗ together for good to
them that love God, to them who are the called
29 according to his purpose. For whom he did fore-

ʸ *infirmities*   ᶻ add *for us.*   ᵃ *because he*   ᵇ *all things work*

to them that love Him; there are
many steps in the ladder of God's
Providence—foreknowledge, predestination, vocation, justification, glory.

26. Ὡσαύτως, *likewise.*] 'We are
saved by hope, not by sight, and
with this our imperfect condition
it agrees well that we have the
Spirit for our help.' For in our
very prayers we know not what
to ask as we ought; but when
language fails, the Spirit utters
for us a cry inexpressible: comp.
Eph. vi. 18: 'Praying always
with all prayer and supplication
in the Spirit;' and 1 Cor. ii. 11
quoted above.

ἀλαλήτοις, *unutterable.*] It sounds
strangely to us at first, that the
Spirit should be spoken of as
'uttering cries.' But the Spirit
of God bearing witness with our
spirits takes part in all our acts.
It is we who cry aloud for help to
God, and God knows this is the
cry of those who are moved by
His Spirit.

28. Not only have we hope,
and patience, and the gift of the
Spirit; but we know that in all
things God works together for
good with them that love Him;
or, according to the reading of
the Textus Receptus (the authority for which is nearly evenly
balanced), 'but we know that
all things work together for good
to them that love God;' who
moreover are chosen according
to His purpose. In these latter
words the Apostle indicates a
further ground of hope and comfort.

29. ὅτι οὓς προέγνω καὶ προώ-
ρισεν, *whom he did foreknow.*] In
most passages of the New Testament where προγινώσκειν and
cognate words occur, as Rom.
xi. 2 : 1 Pet. i. 2, 20 : Acts ii. 23,
the meaning of 'predetermined,
fore-appointed,' is the more natural. 'God hath not cast off his
people whom he fore-appointed'
(οὓς προέγνω). 'By the determinate
counsel and fore-appointment of
God' (τῇ ὡρισμένῃ βουλῇ καὶ προ-
γνώσει). Yet, on the other hand,
Acts xxvi. 5 : 2 Pet. iii. 17, admit
only of the meaning of 'know
beforehand,' but not in reference
to the Divine or prophetic fore-
knowledge, and have, therefore,
no bearing on the present passage.

know, he also did predestinate to be conformed to
the image of his Son, that he might be the firstborn
30 among many brethren. Moreover whom he did predestinate, them he also called: and whom he called,
them he also justified: and whom he justified, them
he also glorified.

31 What shall we then say to these things? If God
32 be for us, who can be against us? He that spared
not his own Son, but delivered him up for us all,
how shall he not with him also freely give us all
33 things? Who shall lay any thing to the charge of

The idea of fore-knowledge, it may be observed, as distinct from predestination, is scarcely discernible in Scripture, unless, perhaps, a trace of it be found in Acts xv. 18 'Known unto God are all his works from the beginning.' The Israelite believed that all things were according to the counsel and appointment of God. Whether this was dependent on his previous knowledge of the intentions of man, was a question which, in that stage of human thought, would hardly have occurred to him. The theories of predestination, which have been built upon the words in the Latin or English version of them, 'whom he did fore-know, them he did predestinate,' are an after-thought of later criticism.

We are thus led to consider the interpretation of fore-appointed, fore-acknowledged, as the true one. We might still translate fore-knoweth in the sense in which God is said to 'know' them that are His. There might be a degree of difference in meaning between $\pi\rhoοέγνω$, 'fore-knew,' as the internal purpose of God, if such a figure of speech may be allowed, and 'predestined,' as the solemn external act by which He, as it were, set apart His chosen ones.

The Apostle is overflowing with the sense of the work of God: what he chiefly means to say is, that all its acts and stages are His, now and hereafter, on earth and in heaven.

31-39. All creation is groaning together; but the Spirit helps us, and God has chosen us according to His purpose, and in all things God is working with us for good. The Lord is on our side; and as He has given us His Son, will give us all else as well. Is it God that justifies who will accuse? Is it Christ who intercedes that will condemn? On the one side are ranged persecution, and famine, and sword, and nakedness; on the other, the love of Christ, from which nothing in heaven or earth, or the changes of life or death, can us part.

33. Who shall lay anything to the charge of God's elect? Is

34 God's elect? ¹ᶜ Shall ⁰ God that justifieth? Who is he that ᵈ will condemn? ⁰ Will Christ that died, ᵉ⁻⁰ rather, that is risen again, who is also at the right hand of God, who also maketh intercession² for us? 35 Who shall separate us from the love of Christ? shall tribulation, or distress, or persecution, or famine, or 36 nakedness, or peril, or sword? As it is written, For thy sake we are killed all the day long: we are 37 accounted as sheep for the slaughter. Nay, in all these things we are more than conquerors through 38 him that loved us. For I am persuaded, that neither death, nor life, nor angels, nor principalities, nor 39 things present, nor things to come, nor powers, nor height, nor depth, nor any other creature, shall be able to separate us from the love of God, which is in Christ Jesus our Lord.

ᶜ It is   ᵈ *condemneth*   ᵉ add *yea*

God who justifies, their accuser? Does He justify and accuse at once? It were a contradiction to suppose this.

34. Who is he that condemneth? Is the condemner Christ who ever lives to intercede for us? Comp. Heb. vii. 25 'Who ever liveth to make intercession for us;' and 1 John ii. 1 'We have an advocate with the Father.'

ὁ ἀποθανών, who died, or more truly rose again, of whom we now speak rather as of one passed into the heavens. The words μᾶλλον δέ, or μᾶλλον δὲ καί, further intimate the inconsistency of Christ condemning us, not only because He died for us, but also, which is an additional reason, because He rose again 'for our justification,' iv. 25; and what is a yet further reason, because He is our advocate.

38. To ask the exact meaning of each of these words, would be like asking the precise meaning of single expressions in the line of Milton:—

'Thrones, dominations, princedoms, virtues, powers.'

The leading thought in the Apostle's mind is that 'nothing ever at any time or place can separate us from the love of Christ.' Of the signification of the particular words we can only form a notion, by attempting to conceive the invisible world, as it revealed itself by the eye of faith to the Apostle's mind, as

¹ Reading θεὸς ὁ δικαιῶν;   ² Reading ὑπὲρ ἡμῶν;

9 I SAY the truth in Christ, I lie not, my conscience
2 also bearing me witness in the Holy Ghost, that
I have great heaviness and continual sorrow in my
3 heart. For I could wish that myself were accursed
from Christ for my brethren, my kinsmen according
4 to the flesh: who are Israelites; *f* whose is *f* the
adoption, and the glory, and ¹ the *g* covenant,*ǁ* and the
giving of the law, and the service of God, and the
5 promises; whose are the fathers, and of whom ² as

---

f to whom pertaineth   *g* *covenants*

---

inward, and yet outward; as present, and yet future; as earthly, and yet heavenly. Compare 1 Pet. iii. 22 ὅς ἐστιν ἐν δεξιᾷ τοῦ θεοῦ, πορευθεὶς εἰς οὐρανόν, ὑποταγέντων αὐτῷ ἀγγέλων καὶ ἐξουσιῶν καὶ δυνάμεων.

9. 1. συμμαρτυρούσης μοι τῆς συνειδήσεως, *my conscience witnesses that I speak the truth.*] It may be asked why should St. Paul asseverate with such warmth what no one would doubt or deny. Such is his manner in other passages, as in Gal. i. 20 'Now the things which I write unto you, behold, before God, I lie not;' although the things that he wrote merely related to his journeys to Jerusalem. But there was a matter behind, which was of vital importance to himself and the Church, viz. his claim to independence of the other Apostles. Hence the strong feeling which he shows. Compare also 2 Cor. xi. 31 'The God and Father of our Lord Jesus Christ knoweth that I lie not;' viz. in the narrative of his sufferings. So here the intensity of his language expresses only the strength of his feelings, not the suspicion that any one would doubt his words. In the first part of the Epistle it might perhaps have been argued that he had lost sight of his own people; he returns to them with a burst of affection.

2. No such ties ever bound together any other nation of the world, as united the Jews. Patriotism is a word too weak to express the feeling with which they clung to their country, to their law and their God. And St. Paul himself, although, to use his own words, 'his bowels had been enlarged' to include the Gentiles, comes back to the feelings of his youth, as with the vehemence of a first love. He sorrows over his people, like the prophets of old, not without an example in the Saviour Himself, Luke xix. 42 'If thou hadst known, even thou, at least in this thy day, the things which belong unto thy peace! but now they are hid from thine eyes.'

5. ὁ ὢν ἐπὶ πάντων, *who is over all.*] It is a question to which

---

¹ Reading ἡ διαθήκη   ² Reading τὸ κατὰ σάρκα. ὁ ὢν ἐπὶ πάντων θεός

concerning the flesh Christ came. ʰ God, who is over all, is ʰ blessed for ever. Amen. Not as though the word of God hath ⁱ failed.ⁱ For they are not all Israel, which are of Israel: neither, because they are the seed of Abraham, are they all children: but, In Isaac shall thy seed be called. That is, They which are the children of the flesh, these are not the children of God: but the children of the promise are counted

ʰ who is over all, God

ⁱ taken none effect.

we can hardly expect to get an answer unbiassed by the interests of controversy, whether the clause, ὁ ὢν ἐπὶ πάντων θεὸς εὐλογητὸς εἰς τοὺς αἰῶνας, is to be referred to Christ, 'of whom is Christ according to the flesh, who is God over all blessed for ever;' or, as in Lachmann, to be separated from the preceding words and regarded as a doxology to God the Father, uttered by the Apostle, on a review of God's mercy to the Jewish people.

Patristic authority is in favour of referring the words in dispute to Christ. Wetstein has led himself and others into error, by assuming that the fathers who denied that the predicate ὁ ἐπὶ πάντων θεός could be applied to Christ, would have refused to apply to Him the modified form, ὁ ὢν ἐπὶ πάντων θεός. The evidence of Iren. Adv. Haer. iii. 16. 3; Tertull. Adv. Prax. 13; Origen and Theodoret on this passage; Athanasius, Hilary, and Cyril (Chrysostom is uncertain), shows clearly the manner of reading the words in the third or fourth century. But the testimony of the third century cannot be set against that of the first, that is,

of parallel passages in St. Paul himself.

According to a third way of taking the passage, the words ὁ ὢν ἐπὶ πάντων are separated from the remainder of the clause, 'of whom came Christ, according to the flesh, who is over all;' upon which follows the doxology as the conclusion of the whole: 'God is blessed for ever.'

8. τουτέστιν, *that is.*] In the passage which follows the Apostle is speaking, according to the Calvinist interpreter, of absolute, according to his opponents, of conditional predestination. The first urges that he is referring to individuals; the second, to nations; the first dwells on the case of Pharaoh, as stated by the Apostle; the second returns to the language of the Old Testament, which says not only 'the Lord hardened Pharaoh's heart,' but 'Pharaoh hardened his own heart.'

What we aim at in modern times in the consideration of such questions is 'consistency;' and the test which we propose to ourselves of the truth of their solution, is whether they involve a contradiction in terms.

9 for ᵏ a " seed. For this is the word of promise, At this
10 time will I come, and Sarah shall have a son. And
not only this; but when Rebecca also had conceived
11 by one, even by our father Isaac; for the children
being not yet born, neither having done any good or
evil, that the purpose of God according to election
might stand, not of works, but of him that calleth:
12 it was said unto her, ¹that " the elder shall serve the
13 younger. As it is written, Jacob ᵐ⁻" I loved, but
Esau ⁿ⁻" I hated.

14 What shall we say then? Is there unrighteous-
15 ness with God? God forbid. For he saith to Moses,
I will have mercy on whom I will have mercy, and

  ᵏ the   ¹ *omit* that   ᵐ *add* have
         ⁿ *add* have

Nothing can be more unlike the mode in which the Apostle conceives them, which is not logical at all. Sometimes he is overpowered by the goodness and mercy of God; at other times he is filled with a sense of the deservedness of man's lot; now, as we should say, for predestination, now for freewill; at one time only forbidding man to arraign the justice of God, and at another time asserting it. Logically considered, such opposing aspects of things are inconsistent. But they are true practically; they are what we have all of us felt at different times, and are not more contradictory than the different phases of thought and feeling which we express in conversation. There are two views of these subjects, a philosophical and a religious one: the first balancing and systematizing them and seeking to form a whole of speculative truth; the latter partial and fragmentary, speaking to the heart and feelings of man. The latter is that of the Apostle.

13. These words are exactly quoted from the LXX, with a very slight alteration in their order. Their meaning must be gathered from the connexion of the Apostle's argument, not from any preconceived notion of the attributes of God. In the prophet (Mal. i. 2, 3) God is introduced as reproaching Israel for their ingratitude to Him, though He had 'loved Jacob and hated Esau.' Here no stress is to be laid on the words 'loved' and 'hated,' which are poetical figures, the thought expressed by them being subordinate to the prophet's main purpose. It is otherwise in the quotation; there the point is that God preferred one, and rejected another of His own free will. As of old, He preferred Jacob, so now

310   THE EPISTLE TO THE ROMANS   [9. 15

I will have compassion on whom I will have com-
16 passion. So then it is not of him that willeth, nor of
him that runneth, but of God that sheweth mercy.
17 For the scripture saith unto Pharaoh, ᵒthat ⁰ for this
same purpose I have raised thee up, that I might shew
my power in thee, and that my name might be declared
18 throughout all the earth. ᵖSo then he hath mercy ⁰ on
19 whom he will, ᑫ⁻⁰ and whom he will he hardeneth. Thou
wilt say then unto me, Why ʳthen ⁰ doth he yet find
20 fault? For who hath resisted his will? Nay rather,
O man, who art thou that repliest against God? Shall
the thing formed say to him that formed it, Why hast
21 thou made me thus? Hath not the potter power over
the clay, of the same lump to make one vessel unto
22 honour, and another unto dishonour? ˢAnd ⁰ if God,

ᵒ even   ᵖ Therefore hath he mercy   ᑫ add have mercy
          ʳ omit *then*   ˢ What

He may reject him. Any further
inference from the unconditional
predestination of nations to that of
individuals, does not come within
the Apostle's range of view.

18. Can we avoid the fatal
consequence that God is here
regarded as the author of evil?
It may be replied that throughout
the passage St. Paul is speaking,
not of himself, but in the language of the Old Testament, the
line drawn in which is not precisely the same with that of the
New, though we cannot separate
them with philosophical exactness. It was not always a proverb
in the house of Israel, that 'God
tempted no man.' In the over-
powering sense of the Creator's
being, the free agency of the
creature was lost, and it seemed
to the external spectator as if the
evil that men did, was but the

just punishment that He inflicted
on them for their sins. Comp.
Ezek. xiv. 9.

The portions of the New Testament which borrow the language
or the Spirit of the Old must not
be isolated from other passages,
which take a more comprehensive
view of the dealings of God with
man. God tempts no man to evil
who has not first tempted himself.
This is the uniform language of
both Old and New Testament;
the difference seems to lie in
the circumstance that in the Old
Testament, God leaves or gives
a man to evil who already works
evil, while the prevailing tone of
the New Testament is that evil
in all its stages is the work of
man himself.

22. The construction of this
passage involves an anacoluthon.
As in ii. 17 εἰ δὲ σὺ 'Ιουδαῖος

willing to shew his wrath, and to make his power known, endured with much long-suffering ᵗ⁻ᵘ vessels of
23 wrath fitted to destruction : ¹ and that he might make known the riches of his glory on the vessels of mercy,
24 which he had afore prepared unto glory ? Even us, whom he hath called, not of the Jews only, but also of
25 the Gentiles, as he saith also in Osee, I will call them my people, which were not my people ; and her beloved,
26 which was not beloved. And it shall come to pass, that in the place where it was said unto them, Ye are not my people ; there shall they be called the children of the
27 living God. Esaias also crieth concerning Israel, Though the number of the children of Israel be as the sand of
28 the sea, a remnant shall be saved. ᵘ For the Lord will

ᵗ *add the* ᵘ *For he is finishing the work, and cutting it short in righteousness; because a short work will the Lord make upon the earth.*

ἐπονομάζῃ, there is no apodosis to εἰ δέ. The thread of the sentence is lost in the digression of verses 23, 24, 25. The corresponding clause should have been, What is that to thee? or, Who art thou who hast an answer to God? There is, however, a further complexity in the passage. The simple thought would have been as follows : But if God shews forth His righteous vengeance on men, what is that to thee? But side by side with this creeps in another feeling, that even in justice He remembers mercy. 'He punishes, and you have no right to find fault with Him for anything which He does.' Still it is implied that He only punishes those who ought to have been punished long before. There would have been no difficulty in the passage had the Apostle said :

'He punishes some and spares others.' But he has given a different turn to the thought, 'He spares those whom He punishes.' 'May not God,' he would say, 'be like the potter dashing in pieces one vessel, and showing his mercy to another ; merciful even in the first, which he puts off as long as he can, and only executes with a further purpose of mercy to others.'

27, 28. It was not only in accordance with the prophecies of the Old Testament that Israel should be rejected. They spoke yet more precisely of a remnant being saved. If any one marvelled at the small number of believers of Jewish race, it was 'written for their instruction' that 'a remnant should be saved.'

28. The passage of Isaiah taken in the sense in which it was

¹ Reading καὶ ἵνα γνωρίσῃ

accomplish his word finishing and cutting it short
29 upon the earth.⁹ And as Esaias said before, Except the Lord of Sabaoth had left us a seed, we had been as Sodoma, and been made like unto Gomorrha.

30 What shall we say then? That the Gentiles, which followed not after righteousness, have attained to righteousness, ˣ but ⁹ the righteousness which is of
31 faith. But Israel, which followed after the law of righteousness, hath not attained to the law. ʸ⁻⁹
32 Wherefore? Because ᶻ not of ⁹ faith, but as it were of works ᵃ⁻⁹ they stumbled at ᵇ the ⁹ stumblingstone;
33 as it is written, Behold, I lay in Sion a stumbling-

  ˣ even   ʸ add *of righteousness*   ᶻ they sought it not by
                  ᵃ add *of the law. For*   ᵇ that

understood by the Apostle, may be paraphrased as follows: Isaiah lifts up his voice in regard to Israel, and says, 'Though the house of Israel be as the sand of the sea, the remnant only shall be saved. For God is accomplishing and cutting short his work, for a short work will God make upon the earth,' or (according to Lachmann's reading), 'For God will perform his work, accomplishing and cutting it short upon the earth.' The application of this to the present circumstances of the house of Israel is, that few out of many Israelites should be saved, for that God was judging them as of old He had judged their fathers. They were living in the latter days, and the time was short.

30. What then is the conclusion? That the Gentile who sought not after righteousness, attained righteousness, but the righteousness that is of faith. But Israel, who did seek after it, attained not to it. What was the reason of this? because they sought it not of faith, but ὡς ἐξ ἔργων, under the idea that it might be gained by works of the law they stumbled at the rock of offence. We are again upon the track of chap. iii.

32. The expression λίθῳ προσκόμματος is taken from Isa. viii. 14 (in the LXX λίθου προσκόμματι). The remainder of the passage is from Isa. xxviii. 16, the words of which are as follows: ἰδοὺ ἐγὼ ἐμβάλλω εἰς τὰ θεμέλια Σιὼν λίθον πολυτελῆ, ἐκλεκτόν, ἀκρογωνιαῖον, ἔντιμον εἰς τὰ θεμέλια αὐτῆς, καὶ ὁ πιστεύων οὐ μὴ καταισχυνθῇ.

While following the spirit of this latter passage, the Apostle has inserted the words λίθον προσκόμματος, so as to give a double notion of the Rock, which is at once a stone of stumbling and rock of offence, and a foundation stone on which he who rests shall not be made ashamed. Compare Luke xx. 17, 18 for a similar stone and rock of offence: and ^c he who " believeth on him shall not be ashamed.

10 Brethren, my heart's desire and prayer to God for
2 ^d them " is, that they might be saved. For I bear them record that they have a zeal of God, but not
3 according to knowledge. For they being ignorant of God's righteousness, and going about to establish their own righteousness, ^e are not subject " unto the right-
4 eousness of God. For Christ is the end of the law
5 for righteousness to every one that believeth. For Moses describeth the righteousness which is of the law, That the man which doeth those things shall
6 live ^f in it." But the righteousness which is of faith

^c *whosoever*   ^d *Israel*   ^e have not submitted themselves   ^f *by them*

double meaning: λίθον ὃν ἀπεδοκίμασαν οἱ οἰκοδομοῦντες, οὗτος ἐγενήθη εἰς κεφαλὴν γωνίας. πᾶς ὁ πεσὼν ἐπ' ἐκεῖνον τὸν λίθον συνθλασθήσεται· ἐφ' ὃν δ' ἂν πέσῃ λικμήσει αὐτόν.

10. 3. Three questions arise on this verse: (1) What is meant by the righteousness of God? The righteousness of God plainly means the righteousness of faith, the new revelation of which the Apostle spoke, Rom. i. 17, which is the power of God unto salvation to every one that believeth. (2) What is meant by their own righteousness? Either the word ἴδιος may simply indicate opposition to θεοῦ, 'their own' as opposed to God's; or it may have a further meaning of private individual righteousness, consisting only in a selfish isolated obedience to the law, not in communion with God or their fellow-creatures. But, (3) what is meant by οὐχ ὑπετάγησαν? Not something entirely different from ἀγνοοῦντες in the first clause; only as that expressed their wilful blindness in not recognizing the Gospel, this indicates the effect on their life and conduct. The expression is analogous to ὑπακοὴ πίστεως, χριστοῦ, ἀληθείας.

4. It was Christ to whom the law pointed, or seemed to point, who was its fulfilment and also its destruction. It was of Him 'Moses in the law, and the prophets spoke;' it was He who was the body of those things of which the law was the shadow. It was He who was to 'destroy this temple, and raise up another temple, not made with hands.' It was He who came to fulfil the law, in all the senses in which it could be fulfilled.

6-8. The language of Deut. xxx. 13 (the book which has been regarded almost as an evangelization of the law, and as standing in the same relation to the other speaketh on this wise, Say not in thine heart, Who shall ascend into heaven? (that is, to bring Christ 7 down from above:) or, Who shall descend into the deep? (that is, to bring up Christ again from the 8 dead). But what saith it? The word is nigh thee, in thy mouth, and in thy heart: that is, the word of 9 faith, which we preach; that [1] if thou shalt confess with thy mouth the Lord Jesus, and shalt believe in thine heart that God hath raised him from the dead, 10 thou shalt be saved. For with the heart man believeth unto righteousness; and with the mouth 11 confession is made unto salvation. For the scripture saith, Whosoever believeth on him shall not be 12 ashamed. For there is no difference between the

books of Moses as the Gospel of St. John to the first three Gospels), is far different. There our duty to God is not spoken of, as outward obedience or laborious service. There the word is described as 'very nigh to us, even in our mouth and in our heart.' Surely this is the righteousness that is of faith.

The Apostle quotes this passage in a manner which is in several ways remarkable: (1) As there is no word in the passage itself which exactly suits the meaning which he requires; it is the spirit, not the letter, which he is quoting, as in Rom. iv. 6. (2) To each clause he adds an explanation, 'Who shall ascend up into heaven? (that is, to bring down Christ from above:) or, Who shall descend into the deep? (that is, to bring up Christ from below.)' Comp. ix. 8: Gal. iv. 25: 2 Cor. iii. 17. (3) He has altered the words, so as to suit them to the application which he makes of them. Compare ix. 17; infra, ver. 11. Lastly, he puts them into the mouth of righteousness by faith, who speaks as a person in the words of Moses; cf. ver. 5.

The principal difference between the passage as quoted by St. Paul, and as it occurs in the LXX, from which the Hebrew very slightly varies, is, that in ver. 7 we have τίς καταβήσεται εἰς τὴν ἄβυσσον; instead of τίς διαπεράσει ἡμῖν εἰς τὸ πέραν τῆς θαλάσσης in the LXX.

The parallel required in the words, 'to bring up Christ from the dead,' has led the Apostle to alter the text in Deuteronomy, so as to admit of his introducing them. The general meaning of ver. 6 to 8 is as follows: 'The righteousness of faith uses a different language. It says, " Deem

[1] Reading ἐὰν ὁμολογήσῃς ἐν τῷ στόματί σου κύριον Ἰησοῦν

Jew and the Greek: for the same Lord ^g is over all,^{*l*}
13 rich unto all that call upon him. For whosoever shall
14 call upon the name of the Lord shall be saved. How
then ^h are they to ^{*l*} call on him in whom they have
not believed? and how ^h are they to ^{*l*} believe in him ^{i—*l*}
whom they have not heard? and how ^k are they to ^{*l*}
15 hear without a preacher? and how ^k are they to ^{*l*}
preach, except they be sent? as it is written, How
beautiful are the feet of them that ^{l—*l*} bring glad
16 tidings of good things! But they have not all
obeyed the gospel. For Esaias saith, Lord, who hath
17 believed our report? So then faith cometh by hearing,

^g over all is   ^h *shall they*   ⁱ *add of*   ^k *shall they*
^l add *preach the gospel of peace and*

it not impossible; do not ask the unbeliever's question: who shall go up into heaven, by which I mean to bring down Christ from above; or who shall descend into hell, by which I mean to bring up Christ from below?" But what saith it? the word is nigh unto thee, even in thy mouth and in thy heart. And by the word I mean, the word of faith which we preach.'

It was doubtless the last verse which induced the Apostle to quote the whole passage: 'The word is within thee, ready to come to thy lips.' Here is a description of faith. To the words which precede the Apostle has given a new tone. In the book of Deuteronomy they mean: 'The commandment which I give you is not difficult or afar off; it is not in the heaven above, nor beyond the sea.' Here they refer, not to action, but to belief. They might be paraphrased in the language of modern times:

'Do not raise sceptical doubts about Christ having come on earth, or being risen from the dead: there is a Christ within whom you have not far to seek for.'

Compare Eph. iv. 9, 10 'Now that he ascended, what is it but that he also descended first into the lower parts of the earth? He that descended is the same also that ascended;' which is in like manner based on Ps. lxviii. 18 'Thou hast ascended on high, thou hast led captivity captive, and received gifts for men.'

14-21. The passage which follows is, in style, one of the most obscure portions of the Epistle. The obscurity arises from the argument being founded on passages of the Old Testament. The structure becomes disjointed and unmanageable from the number of the quotations. Some trains of thought are carried on too far for the Apostle's purpose, while others are so briefly hinted at

18 and hearing by the word of ᵐ Christ.ᵍ But I say, Have they not heard? ⁿ Nay rather,ᵍ their sound went into all the earth, and their words unto the ends of 19 the world. But I say, Did not Israel know? First Moses saith, I will provoke you to jealousy by them that are no people, and by a foolish nation I will 20 anger you. But Esaias is very bold, and saith, I was

ᵐ *God*   ⁿ Yes verily

as to be hardly intelligible. Yet if, instead of entangling ourselves in the meshes of the successive clauses, we place ourselves at a distance and survey the whole at a glance, there is no difficulty in understanding the general meaning. No one can doubt that the Apostle intends to say that the prophets had already foretold the rejection of the Jews and the acceptance of the Gentiles. But the texts by which he seeks to prove or to express this, are interspersed, partly with difficulties which he himself felt; partly, also, with general statements about the mode in which the Gospel was given.

Going off from the word ἐπικαλουμένους and ἐπικαλέσηται, he touches first on an objection which might naturally be urged: 'No one has preached the Gospel to them.' His mode of raising the objection is such that we are left in uncertainty whether this is said by him in the person of an objector, or in his own (cf. iii. 1-8; v. 13, 14; ix. 20, 21). From one step in the rhetorical climax he passes on to another, until the words of the prophet are brought by association into his mind. 'How beautiful are the feet of those who preach good tidings!'

He is now far away from his original point. At ver. 16 he returns to it, and answers the question, 'How are they to call?' &c., by saying that there had been a hearing of the Gospel, but some had not obeyed what they heard. This was implied in the words of the prophet, 'who believed our report?' the inference from which is 'that faith cometh by hearing;' and (we may add) hearing by the word of God. After this interpretation the Apostle returns to his first thought: 'How shall they believe on him whom they have not heard?' The answer is: 'Nay, but they have heard.' All the world has heard. I repeat the question that it may be again answered, 'Did not Israel know?' Moses and the prophets told them in the plainest terms that the Israelites should be rejected, and another nation made partakers of the mercies of God.

19. But I say (to put the case more precisely), Did not Israel know? Did not know, what?— the Gospel, or the word of God in general, or the rejection of the Jews in particular? The latter agrees best with the words which follow: 'First, Moses prophesies of the Jews being provoked to

found ¹ ᵒin ‖ them that sought me not; I was made
21 manifest ᵒin ‖ them that asked not after me. But to
Israel he saith, All day long I have stretched forth my
hands unto a disobedient and gainsaying people.

11 I say then, Hath God cast away his people ² [ᵖwhich
he foreordained ‖]? God forbid. For I also am an
Israelite, of the seed of Abraham, of the tribe of
2 Benjamin. God hath not cast away his people which

ᵒ *unto*   ᵖ omit *which he foreordained*

anger by the Gentiles.' But, on the other hand, what the previous context requires is, not the rejection of the Jews, but the Gospel or the Word of God in general; nor would the laws of language allow us to anticipate what follows as the subject of ἔγνω. 'But I say, did not Israel know of the rejection of the Jews, of which I am about to speak?' The truth seems to be, that what was to be supplied after ἔγνω, was not precisely in the Apostle's mind. He was thinking of the Gospel; but with the Gospel the rejection of the Jews was so closely connected, that he easily makes the transition from one to the other.

21. Such is the mode in which the Apostle clothes his thoughts. The language of the Old Testament is not the proof of the doctrine which he is teaching, but the expression of it. He sees the great fact before him of the acceptance of the Gentiles and the rejection of the Jews, and reads the prophecies by the light of that fact. The page of the Old Testament sparkles before his eyes with intimations of the purposes of God. There is an analogy between the circumstances of Israel, now and formerly, dimly visible. To the mind of the Apostle this analogy does not present itself as to the mind of the author of the Hebrews, as embodied in the whole constitution and history of the Jewish people, but in particular events or separate expressions. Hence, when passing from the law to the Gospel, he is like one declaring dark sayings of old. And his language appears to us fragmentary and unconnected, because he takes his citations in unusual senses, and places them in a new connexion.

11. 1. καὶ γὰρ ἐγώ, *For I also*.] The Apostle feels that the future of his countrymen is bound up with his own; as if he said, 'They cannot be cast off, for then I should be rejected; and they will be accepted, because I am accepted.' He recoils from the one consequence, and is assured of the other. He whom God chose to be the Apostle to the Gentiles could not be a castaway. This is one way of drawing out his thought. More simply, and perhaps truly, it may be said, that he is expressing the feeling

¹ Reading [ἐν] τοῖς   ² Reading [ὃν προέγνω]

he q foreordained.‖ Wot ye not what the scripture saith of Elias? how he maketh intercession to God 3 against Israel,r−‖ Lord, they have killed thy prophets,s−‖ digged down thine altars; and I am left alone, and 4 they seek my life. But what saith the answer of God unto him? I have reserved to myself seven thousand 5 men, who have not bowed the knee to Baal. Even so then at this present time also there is a remnant 6 according to the election of grace. And if by grace, then is it no more of works: otherwise grace is no 7 more grace. t−‖ What then? uhath not Israel‖ obtained that which he seeketh for? But the election hath 8 obtained it, and the rest were blinded (according as it is written, God hath given them the spirit of x torpor,‖ eyes that they should not see, and ears that

---

q foreknew   r add *saying*,   s add *and*
t add *But if it be of works, then is it no more grace: otherwise work is no more work.*   u *Israel hath not*   x slumber

---

as of a parent over a prodigal son, that 'he cannot be lost,' the true ground of which is the affection which will not bear to be separated from him.

For a similar particularity of statement respecting his own claim as an Israelite, compare Phil. iii. 5.

5. So now, at the present time, God has chosen a remnant. In the days of Elias there were more worshippers of the true God than any one could have imagined, in Israel. Even so now, from the Jews themselves, there are a great company of believers.

6. As in many other passages, the Apostle is led back by the association of words to the great antithesis. Compare chap. iv. 4 τῷ δὲ ἐργαζομένῳ ὁ μισθὸς οὐ λο-γίζεται κατὰ χάριν, κ. τ. λ.; Eph. ii. 9 οὐκ ἐξ ἔργων, ἵνα μή τις καυχήσηται. 'But if of grace, not as the Jews suppose by obedience to the law; for grace ceases to be grace, when we bring in works.' In these words the Apostle is already taking up the other side of the argument, that is, he is showing why Israel was rejected, not why a remnant was spared.

In the Textus Receptus is added the parallel clause, resting on very inferior though ancient MS. authority, and even thus requiring help from emendation, εἰ δὲ ἐξ ἔργων, οὐκ ἔτι ἐστὶ χάρις, ἐπεὶ τὸ ἔργον οὐκέτι ἐστὶν ἔργον. It is not necessary to argue whether or not this clause is in character with the style of St. Paul, on which ground probably no fair

9 they should not hear;) unto this day. And David
saith, Let their table be made a snare, and a trap, and
10 a stumblingblock, and a recompense unto them: let
their eyes be darkened, that they may not see, and
bow down their back alway.
11 I say then, Have they stumbled that they should

objection could be raised to it, when the want of external evidence sufficiently condemns it.

9, 10. And David (in Ps. lxix. 23) uses the same language: 'Let their table be made a snare unto them, and a gin and an offence and a retribution. Let them have the evils of old age, blindness and bent limbs.'

St. Paul quotes this passage, not in its original sense of a malediction against the enemies of God, but as a proof of the rejection of the Jews. The original passage is one of those which in all ages have been a stumblingblock to the readers of Scripture, in which the spirit of the Old Testament appears most unlike the spirit of the New. With the view of escaping from what is revolting to Christian feelings, it has not been uncommon to construe the imperative moods as future tenses. The Psalmist or prophet is supposed to be predicting, not imprecating, the destruction of his enemies. But the spirit of these passages cannot be altered by a change of tense or mood; neither is it consistent, in such a psalm, for example, as the lxviii, to read the first portion of the psalm as a prayer or wish, and refuse to consider the remainder as an imprecation. It is better to admit, what the words of the passage will not allow us to deny, that the Psalmist is imprecating God's wrath against his own enemies. But first his enemies are God's enemies, so that his bitter words against them lose the character of merely private enmity. Secondly, the state of life in which such a prayer could be uttered by a 'man after God's own heart,' is altogether different from our own. It was a state in which good and evil worked with greater power in the same individual, and in which a greater mixture of good and evil, of gentleness and fierceness, existed together than we can easily imagine. The Spirit of God was working 'in the untamed chaos of the affections,' but also leaving them often in their original strength and lawlessness. David curses his enemies, believing them to be the enemies of God. The Christian cannot curse even the enemies of God, still less his own. This contrast we need not hesitate to admit; if the writers of the Old Testament did not scruple to disown 'the visitation of the sins of the fathers upon the children;' neither need we refuse to say with Grotius, 'Eis ex spiritu legis optat Davides paria.'

11. Language like this would seem to imply that Israel has

fall? God forbid: but rather through their fall is
salvation unto the Gentiles come, for to provoke them
12 to jealousy. Now if the fall of them be the riches of
the world, and the diminishing of them the riches of
13 the Gentiles; how much more their fulness? ʸ But ᵘ
to you Gentiles I speak, ᶻ nay rather,ᵘ inasmuch as
I am the apostle of the Gentiles, I magnify mine
14 office: if by any means I may provoke to emulation
them which are my flesh, and ᵃ may ᵘ save some of
15 them. For if the casting away of them be the reconciling of the world, what shall the receiving of

    ʸ *For*   ᶻ omit *nay rather*   ᵃ might

fallen. The cup of God's wrath must be full against those of whom such things are said. But the Apostle has not forgotten the other side of his argument, from which he digressed for a moment. Is their stumble a fall? he asks (the very word ἔπταισαν prepares the way for the conclusion at which he is aiming); or (if we take the words ἔπταισαν and πέσωσιν in a metaphorical sense), have they erred so as utterly to fall away from grace? The Apostle, with the words of Moses, which he had quoted in the previous chapter, still in his mind, replies: 'Not so;' their fall was but a Divine economy, in which the Gentiles alternated with the Jews. The temporary precedence of the Gentiles was intended to have, and may have, the effect of arousing them to jealousy. As in other passages, the Apostle recovers the lost theme by repeating the same formula with which he commenced—Λέγω οὖν.

15. Neither is it a merely visionary hope that some of them shall be saved. 'For as I said above, so say I now again; if the casting away of them be the reconcilement of the world, what shall the receiving of them be but life from the dead.' In more senses than one, it might be said, that the casting away of the Jews was the reconciliation of the world, (1) as they were simultaneous; (2) as without the doing away of the law of Moses, the Gentiles could not have been admitted.

The words ζωὴ ἐκ νεκρῶν have had more than one meaning assigned to them: (1) Life out of death; the house of Israel who are dead, shall be alive again. Compare chap. iv. 17-20. But the connexion requires that the benefit should be one in which Gentiles as well as Jews are partakers. There would be a want of point in saying, 'If their casting away be reconcilement to the world, what shall their acceptance be, but the quickening of the Jews into life?' (2) It is better, therefore, to take ζωὴ ἐκ νεκρῶν

16 them be, but life from the dead? ᵇ And ⁂ if the firstfruit be holy, the lump is also holy: and if the
17 root be holy, so are the branches. ᶜ But ⁂ if some of the branches be broken off, and thou, being a wild olive tree, wert graffed in among them, and with them ᵈ becamest partaker ⁂ of the root and fatness of the
18 olive tree; boast not against the branches. But if thou boast, thou bearest not the root, but the root
19 thee. Thou wilt say then, The branches were broken
20 off, that I might be graffed in. Well; because of unbelief they were broken off, and thou standest by
21 faith. Be not highminded, but fear: for if God spared not the natural branches, take heed lest he also spare

ᵇ For ᶜ And ᵈ partakest

of some undefined spiritual good, of which Gentile and Jew alike have a share, and which, in comparison of their former state may be regarded as resurrection; the thought, however, of their prior state, is subordinate. Least of all in a climax, should the meaning of each word which the Apostle uses be exactly analysed. Words fail him, and he employs the strongest that he can find, thinking rather of their general force than of their precise meaning.

16. Ἀπαρχή = the firstfruits of the Gospel; φύραμα, the mass from which the firstfruits are taken, and which is consecrated by their oblation (Num. xv. 21). The image is a favourite one with St. Paul, occurring in 1 Cor. v. 6: Gal. v. 9, as well as here. Stripped of its figure, the meaning of the clause will be: As some Jews are believers, all Jews shall one day become so; the

'firstfruits' of the Gospel consecrate the nation to God. The word ῥίζα, on the other hand, may have several associations. It may either mean the patriarchs (cf. below, verse 28: 'beloved for the fathers' sakes'); or the Jewish dispensation generally; the ideal Israel of the prophets; the stock from which the branches had been broken off. This last interpretation best preserves the parallelism of the clauses, and is most in keeping with verse 18.

17. The olive tree, like the vine, is used in the Old Testament (Jer. xi. 16) as a figure of the house of Israel. No image could be more natural to an inhabitant of Palestine. The relative dignity rather than the fruitfulness of the cultivated and wild olive is here the point of similarity.

21. Let us cast a look over the connexion of the last ten verses. At ver. 12 the Apostle had spoken

22 not thee. Behold therefore the goodness and severity of God: on them which fell, severity; but toward thee, goodness, ᵉ the goodness of God ⁼ if thou continue in his goodness: otherwise thou also shalt be cut off.
23 And they also, if they abide not in unbelief, shall be graffed in: for God is able to graff them in again.
24 For if thou wert cut out of the olive tree which is wild by nature, and wert graffed contrary to nature into a good olive tree: how much more shall these, which be the natural branches, be graffed into their own
25 olive tree? For I would not, brethren, that ye should

ᵉ omit *the goodness of God*

of the 'diminishing of the Israelite' being the 'enrichment of the Gentile.' This led to the thought of the still greater gain which was to accrue to the Gentile from the restoration of the Israelite. Therefore also the restoration of Israel naturally formed a part of that Gospel which he preached among the Gentiles. And that Gospel he would make much of and thrust forward, if only that it might react upon his countrymen. For that Israel would be restored was as true as that the firstfruits consecrated the lump, or that the root implied the tree. And the Gentile should remember that he was not the original stock, but the branch which was afterwards grafted in. Still the Apostle observes a loophole in the argument through which Gentile pretensions may creep in. He may say, Granted; I am not the root, only the branch, but it was they who gave place to me; they were cut off that I might be grafted in. Good, says the Apostle, learn of them but another lesson. Not 'they were cut off that I might be grafted in;' but 'I may be cut off too.'

22. Behold, a twofold lesson: mercy and severity; mercy to you, severity to them. And yet this lesson is one that may make you rejoice with trembling; for you may yet change places.

Ver. 24 is an amplification of 23, 'God is able to graft them in again.' It is an easier and more natural thing to restore them to their own olive, than to graft you into it. It is uncertain, and is of no great importance, whether οἱ is the article or the relative; whether, that is, the last clause is to be translated, 'How much more shall these who are the natural branches be engrafted in their own olive?' or, 'How much more shall these (i.e. be engrafted), who will be engrafted according to nature in their own olive?'

25. μυστήριον, in reference to the heathen mysteries, is a revealed secret, a secret into which a person is admitted, not one

be ignorant of this mystery, lest ye should be wise in
your own conceits; that blindness in part is happened
to Israel, until the fulness of the Gentiles be come in.
26 And so all Israel shall be saved: as it is written, There
shall come out of Sion the Deliverer; ᶠhe ᶠ shall turn
27 away ᵍ ungodlinesses ᶠ from Jacob: ʰ and ᶠ this is my
covenant unto them, when I shall take away their

ᶠ *and*   ᵍ ungodliness   ʰ for

from which they are excluded. Analogous to this is the use of μυστήριον in the New Testament. It is applied to a secret which God has revealed, known to some and not to others, manifested in the latter days, but hidden previously. Thus the Gospel is spoken of in Matt. xiii. 11 as the mystery of the kingdom of God. So Rom. xvi. 25: 'Now to him that is able to stablish you according to my Gospel, and the preaching of Jesus Christ, according to the revelation of the mystery, which hath been kept silent through endless ages.' In Eph. v. 2 the rite of marriage is spoken of as a great mystery, typifying Christ and the Church. So 'the mystery of godliness,' 1 Tim. iii. 16; the mystery of iniquity, 2 Thess. ii. 7; 'the mystery of the seven stars,' Rev. i. 20; 'Mystery, Babylon the great,' xvii. 5. In all these passages reference is made: (1) to what is wonderful; or, (2) to what is veiled under a figure; or, (3) to what has been long concealed or is so still to the multitude of mankind; and in all there is the correlative idea of revelation. The use of the word μυστήριον in Scripture, affords no grounds for the popular application of the term 'mystery' to the truths of the Christian religion. It means not what is, but what was a secret, into which, if we may use heathen language, the believer has become initiated, which there is no purpose to conceal from mankind; rather which he 'would not have other men ignorant of:' so far as it remains a secret it is so because it is spiritually discerned, and some Christians, or those who are not Christians, have not the power of discernment.

26. *all Israel.*] It is evident, by the opposition to the Gentiles that St. Paul is here speaking, not of the spiritual, but of the literal Israel. His words should not, however, be so pressed as to imply universal salvation, which was not in his thoughts. The language of prophecy, and the feelings of his own heart, alike told him that Israel should be saved. But he is thinking of the nation which is to be accepted as a whole, not of the individuals who composed it. It may be said that even in this modified sense the words of the prophecy or aspiration have not been fulfilled.

28 sins. As concerning the gospel, they are enemies for your sakes: but as touching the election, they are be-
29 loved for the fathers' sakes. For the gifts and calling
30 of God are without repentance. For as ye in times past have ⁱ disobeyed ^{*g*} God, yet have now obtained
31 mercy through their ^k disobedience: ^{*g*} even so have these also now not believed ^l through mercy to you,
32 that ^{*f*} they also ^m now ^{*g*} may obtain mercy. For God ⁿ shut up all together ^{*g*} in unbelief, that he ^o may ^{*g*} have mercy upon all.

33 O the depth of the riches ^p and ^{*g*} the wisdom and knowledge of God! how unsearchable are his judg-
34 ments, and his ways past finding out! For who hath known the mind of the Lord? or who hath been his
35 counsellor? or who hath first given to him, and it shall

ⁱ not believed	^k unbelief	that through your mercy
^m omit *now*	ⁿ hath concluded them all	^o might
	^p both of	

We must answer, no more has the Apostle's belief in the immediate coming of Christ; it was the near wish and prayer of his heart, but in its accomplishment far off, and to be realized only in the final victory of good over evil.

Modern criticism detaches the meaning of the Apostle from the event of the prophecy. It has no need to pervert his words, from a determination as it may be called, such as Luther expresses, that the Jews shall not be saved, or with Calvin to transfer them to the Israel of God, because the time seems to have passed for their literal fulfilment. Happy would it have been for the fortunes of the Jewish race and the honour of the Christian name had they never been wrongly applied!

29. *the gifts and calling of God are without repentance.*] In the same spirit in which the Apostle says, 'He that hath begun a good work in you, will continue it to the end;' he says, also, in reference not to individuals, but to nations, 'God is unchangeable, what He has once given, He cannot take back; those whom He has once called, He will not cast out.' We know what the Apostle teaches elsewhere, that the gifts and calling of God are not irrespective of our acceptance and obedience. But in this passage he makes abstraction of the condition; he thinks only of the purpose of God, who is not a man that He should change His will arbitrarily, and be one thing one day, and another thing another, to the

36 be recompensed unto him again? For of him, and through him, and to him, are all things: to ⁱ him ⁿ be glory for ever. Amen.

12 I ʳ EXHORT ⁿ you therefore, brethren, ˢ through ⁿ the mercies of God, ᵗ to ⁿ present your bodies a living sacrifice, holy, acceptable unto God, which is your

<ul style="list-style:none"><li>ᵠ whom   ʳ beseech   ˢ by   ᵗ that ye</li></ul>

objects of His favour. He feels that God cannot desert the work of His hands. Neither need we stop to reason whether or in what way this is reconcilable with the Divine justice. The whole relations of man to God and nature can never be perceived at once: we see them 'in part' 'through a glass,' under many aspects, of which this is one.

12. 1. The last chapter ended with a doxology. All the world was reconciled to God, and Jew as well as Gentile included in the circle of His grace. Therefore the Apostle did not refrain himself from uttering a song of triumph at the end 'of his great argument.' Now he proceeds to draw the cords of divine love closer about the hearts and consciences of individual men.

'Seeing, then, all these things, what manner of persons ought we to be?' This connexion is indicated in the word οἰκτιρμῶν, which refers to ver. 32 of the preceding chapter: 'I exhort you through the mercies of that God who has mercy upon Jew and Gentile alike, who concluded all under sin that he might have mercy upon all.'

The latter part of the chapter is remarkable for the irregularity of its construction and the want of connexion in its clauses. It would be a mistaken ingenuity to invent a system where no system is intended. Precepts occur to the Apostle's mind without any regular sequence, or with none that we can trace. In some instances he appears to go off upon a word, without even remembering the sense of it. Thus, in ver. 13 of this chapter, he passes from τὴν φιλοξενίαν διώκοντες, to εὐλογεῖτε τοὺς διώκοντας ὑμᾶς, which we might have been disposed to regard as an accidental coincidence, were it not that a nearly similar instance occurs in vers. 7, 8 of the following chapter: 'Ἀπόδοτε οὖν πᾶσι τὰς ὀφειλάς, and μηδενὶ μηδὲν ὀφείλετε εἰ μὴ τὸ ἀγαπᾶν ἀλλήλους, κ.τ.λ. Such passages are instructive, as showing how little the style of St. Paul can be reduced to the ordinary laws of thought and language, how entirely we must learn to know him from himself.

τὰ σώματα ὑμῶν,] not 'yourselves,' but 'your bodies,' as opposed to the mind. Compare ver. 2 τῇ ἀνακαινώσει τοῦ νοός. In ch. viii. 10 the body was described as 'dead because of sin,' but the spirit 'life because of righteousness;' and in ver. 23 the believer was said to be 'waiting for the redemption of the

2 ᵘworship in thought.ʲ And ˣnot to be ʲ¹ conformed to this world: but ʸto be ᵗ transformed by the renewing of ᶻ the ᵍ mind, that ye may prove what is that 3 good, and acceptable, and perfect will of God. For I say, through the grace given unto me, to every man that is among you, not to think of himself more highly than he ought to think; but to think ᵃunto sobriety,ʲ according as God hath dealt to every man the measure

ᵘ reasonable service   ˣ be ye not   ʸ be ye   ᶻ your   ᵃ soberly

body.' Here the image is different: the body though offered to God is still alive. And yet the Apostle would have us add in the language of Gal. ii. 20: 'It is not I that live but Christ liveth in me; and the life that I now live in the flesh I live in faith of the Son of God.'

θυσίαν ζῶσαν, *a living sacrifice.*] Comp. for a similar play of words, 1 Cor. xv. 44 σῶμα πνευματικόν; 1 Pet. ii. 5 πνευματικὴ θυσία; and λογικὴ λατρεία below. The sacrifice is dead, but the believer is alive, like his Lord suffering on the cross; the image is yet stronger in Gal. ii. 20 'I am crucified with Christ.' The body of the Christian is called a sacrifice, first, because in one sense it is dead, as the Apostle says in the expression just now quoted; and, secondly, as it is wholly dedicated to God. As he is one with Christ in His crucifixion, death, burial, resurrection, he is also like Him in being a sacrifice, not because of the sins of others, but to put an end to sin in himself, Eph. v. 2.

τὴν λογικὴν λατρείαν ὑμῶν, *which is your worship in thought,*] in apposition with the preceding sentence, as in the well-known classical instance, Ἑλένην κτάνωμεν Μενέλεῳ λύπην πικράν: that is to say, the reasonable service is not the living sacrifice, but the offering up of the body as a living sacrifice. The translation, 'reasonable service,' in the English version, is not an accurate explanation of λογικὴ λατρεία, which is an oxymoron or paradoxical expression, meaning 'an ideal service, a ceremonial of thought and mind.' The word λατρεία signifies a service which consists of outward rites, which in this case is λογικῆ, that is, not outward, but in the mind, the symbol of a truth, the picture of an idea. In the Epistle to the Hebrews the whole Mosaic law may be said to pass into a λογικὴ λατρεία, a law which, from being ceremonial, became ideal.

2. τῷ αἰῶνι τούτῳ, *this world,*] contains an allusion to the Jewish distinction between ὁ αἰὼν οὗτος and ὁ αἰὼν ἐρχόμενος, μέλλων, &c., as the times before and the times after the Messiah; expressions which are continued, for the most part in the same sense,

---

¹ Reading συσχηματίζεσθαι ... μεταμορφοῦσθαι

4 of faith. For as we have many members in one body,
5 and all members have not the same office: so we, being many, are one body in Christ, and every one
6 members one of another. ᵇBut as we have ᵘ gifts differing according to the grace that is given to us,

ᵇ Having then

in the New Testament, or with only such a modification of meaning as necessarily arises from the new nature of Messiah's kingdom. That kingdom was not merely future; it was opposed to the present state which the believer saw around him, as good to evil, as the world of those who rejected Christ to the world of those who accepted Him. This present world (ὁ νῦν αἰών 2 Tim. i. 10) was to the first disciples emphatically an αἰὼν πονηρός (Gal. i. 4), which had a god of its own, and children of its own (2 Cor. iv. 4), and was full of invisible powers fighting against the truth. Hence it is in a stronger sense than we speak of the world, which in the language of modern times has become a sort of neutral power of evil, that the Apostle exhorts his converts not to be conformed to this world, which is the kingdom, not of God, but of Satan. Comp. note on Gal. i. 4.

νοῦς is here opposed to body, as elsewhere to πνεῦμα, 1 Cor. xiv. 14. Like the English word 'mind,' it is a general term, and includes the will. (Eph. iv. 17.) It is idle to raise metaphysical distinctions about words which the Apostle uses after the fleeting manner of common conversation, or to search the index of Aristotle for illustration of their meaning which the connexion in which they occur can alone supply.

4. The connexion of this verse with what has preceded is as follows. Let us not be high-minded, but all keep our proper place, according to the measure which God has given us. For we are like the body, in which there are many members with different offices. Compare 1 Cor. xii. 14, 31, also Phil. ii. 3, 4: 'Let nothing be done through strife or vainglory, but in lowliness of mind let each esteem other better than themselves. Look not every man on his own things, but every man also on the things of others.' Where there is the same connexion between thinking of others and not thinking of ourselves, a connexion which we may trace in our own lives and characters as well as in the words of Scripture. For 'egotism' is the element secretly working in the world, which is the most hostile to the union of men with one another, which destroys friendly and Christian relations.

6. ἔχοντες δὲ χαρίσματα, *but having gifts.*] Philosophy, as well as religion, Plato and Aristotle, as well as St. Paul, speak of 'a measure in all things; of one in many, and many in one;' of 'not going beyond another;' of φρόνησις and σωφροσύνη; of a society

whether prophecy, let us prophesy according to the
7 proportion of faith; or ministry, let us ᶜuse our gift
8 in ᶠ ministering: or he that teacheth, in teaching; or
he that exhorteth, in exhortation: he that giveth, let
him do it with simplicity; he that ruleth, with
diligence; he that sheweth mercy, with cheerfulness.
9 Let love be without dissimulation. Abhor that which
10 is evil; cleave to that which is good. Be kindly
affectioned one to another ᵈin the love of the
brethren ᵍ; in honour ᵉleading the way one to ʰ

ᶜ wait on our   ᵈ with brotherly love   ᵉ preferring one

of another kind, 'fitly joined together,' in which there are divers orders, and no man is to call anything his own, and all are one. As the shadow to the substance, as words to things, as the idea to the spirit, so is that form of a state of which philosophy speaks, to the communion of the body of Christ.

προφητείαν, *prophecy*.] The gift of prophecy, common to the new, as well as to the old dispensation; not simply teaching or preaching, but the gift of extraordinary men in an extraordinary age. It was the gift of the Apostles and their converts, more than any other characteristic of the first beginnings of the Gospel, the utterance of the Spirit in the awakened soul, the influence and communion of which was caught by others from him who uttered it; not an intellectual gift, but rather one in which the intellectual faculties were absorbed, yet subject to the prophets, higher and more edifying than tongues, failing and transient in comparison with love (1 Cor. xii; xiii; xiv).

7. *ministry* may either (1) relate to the general duty of a minister of Christ; just as *faith* occurs in 1 Cor. xii among special gifts; it is not necessary here any more than there, or in Eph. iv. 11, 12, that the meaning of each word should be precisely distinguished: or (2) may refer to the office of a deacon in its narrower sense, of which we know nothing, and cannot be certain even that it was confined to the object of its first appointment mentioned in Acts vi. 1, viz. the care of the poor, and the administration of the goods of the Church. ἐν τῇ διακονίᾳ. Compare 1 Tim. iv. 15 ἐν τούτοις ἴσθι.

8. ὁ ἐλεῶν, ἐν ἱλαρότητι, *he that sheweth mercy, with cheerfulness.*] Let a man find pleasure in doing good to the unfortunate. There should be a contrast between the cheerfulness of his deportment and the sadness of his errand.

10. τῇ φιλαδελφίᾳ.] Not, as in the English version, with brotherly love, but (as in 1 Thess. iv. 9) 'in your love to the brethren, affectionate one toward another.' φιλόστοργοι, as of parents to children or of children to parents.

11 another; not backward in diligence; fervent in spirit;
12 serving the Lord; rejoicing in hope; patient in tribu-
13 lation; continuing instant in prayer; distributing to
14 the necessity of saints; given to hospitality. Bless
them which persecute you: bless, and curse not.

τῇ τιμῇ ἀλλήλους προηγούμενοι.] Not, in honour preferring one another (as in Phil. ii. 3 τῇ ταπεινοφροσύνῃ ἀλλήλους ἡγούμενοι ὑπερέχοντας ἑαυτῶν), in defence of which something may be urged on the ground of the Apostle having made an etymological adaptation of the word (cf. προεγράφη Gal. iii. 1), and the rarity, if it is ever found, of the construction with the accusative case— but as Theophylact and some of the ancient versions, 'going before or anticipating one another in paying honour:' 'leading the way to one another,' like προπορευόμενοι, and the Latin 'ante-ire.'

11. τῷ κυρίῳ δουλεύοντες, serving the Lord.] Considerable weight of MS. authority attaches to the reading καιρῷ δουλεύοντες (Δ. G. f. g.); either, 'adapting yourselves to the necessities of the time,' which comes in strangely among precepts to simplicity and zeal, though, if a good meaning be put upon the words, not unlike the spirit of the Apostle in other places, Acts xvi. 3: 1 Cor ix. 20; or (2) in a higher sense. 'serving the time;' because the time is short, and the day of the Lord is at hand: an interpretation which, like the former one, connects better with what follows, than with what precedes. Later editors, however, agree with the Textus Receptus in reading τῷ κυρίῳ δουλεύοντες, which, on the whole, has the greater weight of external evidence (A. B. v.) in its favour. Nor can any objection be urged on internal grounds, except that of an apparent want of point, the slightest of all objections to a reading or interpretation in the writings of St. Paul. And even this is really groundless, if we regard St. Paul as summing up in these words what had gone before: 'Be diligent, zealous, doing all things unto the Lord, and not unto men. Remembering in all things that you are the servants of Christ.' The difficulty is, in any case, no greater than that a χάρισμα πίστεως should occur among other special graces in Cor. xii, or that the word θεοστυγεῖς should be found in a long catalogue of particular sins. (Rom. i. 30.)

13. τὴν φιλοξενίαν διώκοντες, given to hospitality.] In the same strain as in the preceding clause, the Apostle continues: 'Relieving the wants of the saints, and given to receiving them hospitably.' The connexion leads us to suppose that the Apostle is speaking of hospitality specially to Christians, perhaps pilgrims at Rome, and not to men in general.

14. εὐλογεῖτε τοὺς διώκοντας ὑμᾶς, bless them that persecute you,] remind us of our Lord's words recorded in Matt. v. 44: 'Bless them that curse you.' The similarity is,

15 Rejoice with them that do rejoice; ᶠ⁻ᶠ weep with them
16 that weep. Be of the same mind one toward another:
ᵍ minding ᵍ not high things, but ʰ going along with
the lowly.ʰ Be not wise in your own conceits.

ᶠ add *and*   ᵍ mind   ʰ condescend to men of low estate

however, not close enough to be urged as a proof that St. Paul was acquainted with our Gospels. The word διώκοντες in the preceding verse, appears to have suggested the thought which the Apostle, as his manner is, expresses first positively and then negatively.

16. τὸ αὐτό.] Either with εἰς ἀλλήλους, (1) Thinking of yourselves as you would have others think of you — the reverse of placing yourselves above one another (μὴ τὰ ὑψηλὰ φρονοῦντες); or with φρονεῖν preserving the ordinary sense of τὸ αὐτὸ φρονεῖν in other passages (cf. τὸ αὐτὸ φρονεῖν ἐν ἀλλήλοις). (2) 'Be of the same mind one with another,' a counsel not of humility, but of unity, of which humility is also a part. Compare ver. 4.

ἀλλὰ τοῖς ταπεινοῖς συναπαγόμενοι.] It is doubted whether in this passage ταπεινοῖς is neuter or masculine: the word ὑψηλά, which precedes, would incline us to suppose the former; the common use of ταπεινός is in favour of the latter. Let us suppose the first, and take ταπεινός in the sense in which it is most opposed to ὑψηλός, not 'miserable,' as in Jas. i. 10, but 'lowly.' Then, amid precepts of sympathy and humility, or unity, the Apostle may be supposed to proceed as follows: 'Thinking of yourselves as on a level with one another, minding not high things, not struggling against lowly ones;' or with ταπεινοί as a masculine, 'Minding not high things, but descending to be with the lowly.' The two opposed clauses thus serve as a new expression of the general thought, τὸ αὐτὸ εἰς ἀλλήλους φρονοῦντες, which is again resumed in ver. 17: 'Be on a level;—there are ὑψηλά and ταπεινά or ταπεινοί;—do not seek to rise to one, or strive against descending to the other.' So far all is clear. The difficulty is how to insert the notion of 'force' or 'constraint' which is contained in the word συναπαγόμενοι. It may possibly be nothing more than the misuse or exaggeration in the use of a word which arises from an imperfect command over language; but it may also be fairly explained as referring to the struggle in our own minds, or the violence we do to our own feelings. The Apostle might have said τοῖς ταπεινοῖς συνομιλοῦντες or σὺν τοῖς ταπεινοῖς ταπεινούμενοι. Remembering that the human heart is apt to be in rebellion against lessons of humility, he uses, not with perfect clearness, the more precise word συναπαγόμενοι.

17. προνοούμενοι καλά.] It is a favourite thought of the Apostle that the believer should walk seemly to those that are without,

17 Recompense to no man evil for evil. Provide things honest [¹ in the sight of God and ʲ] in the sight of ᵏ⁻ʲ 18 men. If it be possible, as much as lieth in you, ˡ be 19 at peace ʲ with all men. Dearly beloved, avenge not yourselves, but rather give place unto wrath: for it is written, Vengeance is mine; I will repay, saith the

ʲ omit *in the sight of God and*   ᵏ add *all*   ˡ live peaceably

careful of the sight of man no less than of God. Comp. 2 Cor. viii. 21, where, speaking of the collection to be made for the poor saints, the Apostle says that he had one chosen to go up with him to Jerusalem with the alms: προνοοῦμεν γὰρ καλὰ οὐ μόνον ἐνώπιον κυρίου, ἀλλὰ καὶ ἐνώπιον ἀνθρώπων: as in this passage. Cf. Prov. iii. 4 καὶ προνοοῦ καλὰ ἐνώπιον κυρίου καὶ ἀνθρώπων.

19. δότε τόπον τῇ ὀργῇ, *give place to wrath.*] These words have received three explanations: (1) Make room for the wrath of your enemy, i.e. let the wrath of your enemy have its way; or, (2) Make room for your anger to cool, 'date spatium irae,' give your anger a respite; or, (3) Make way for the wrath of God. The second of these explanations is equally indefensible on grounds of language and sense. It is only as a translation of a Latinism we can suppose the phrase to have any meaning at all, and the meaning thus obtained, 'defer your wrath,' is poor and weak. According to the first and third explanations the words δότε τόπον are taken in the same sense (which also occurs in Eph. iv. 27 μηδὲ δίδοτε τόπον τῷ διαβόλῳ), the doubt being whether the word ὀργῇ refers to the wrath of our enemy or of God. The latter is supposed to be required by the context, 'Give place to the wrath of God, who has said, Vengeance is mine.' The last clause, however, may be equally well connected with the words, avenge not yourself; nor is it easy to conceive that if the Apostle had intended the wrath of God, he would have expressed himself so concisely and obscurely as in the words τῇ ὀργῇ. The first explanation is, therefore, the true one. 'Dearly beloved, avenge not yourself, but let your enemy have his way.' It has been objected that common prudence requires that we should defend ourselves against our enemies. This is true, and yet the fact, that the same objection applies equally to the words of our Saviour in the Gospel (Matt. v. 34-48), is a sufficient answer—ὁ δυνάμενος χωρεῖν χωρείτω.

The principle here laid down may be sometimes a counsel of perfection; that is to say, a principle which, in the mixed state of human things, it is impossible to carry out in practice. But it is worthy of remark that it is also a maxim acted upon by civilized nations in the infliction of penalties for crime. There is no vin-

¹ Reading [ἐνώπιον τοῦ θεοῦ καὶ] ἐνώπιον τῶν ἀνθρώπων·

20 Lord. ᵐRather " 'if thine enemy hunger, feed him; if he thirst, give him drink: for ⁿ it is by doing this

ᵐ *Therefore*   ⁿ *in so doing*

dictiveness in punishment, neither retaliation for the injury done to the individual nor to the state, nor, if so be, for the impiety against God. The preservation of society is its only object. Human law begins by acknowledging that God alone is the judge; it is not even the executioner of His anger against sin, much less of man's wrath against his fellows. Conscious of its own impotence and of the awful responsibilities which surround it, it only seeks to accomplish, in a superficial and external manner, what is barely necessary for self-defence.

The words which follow, τοῦτο γὰρ ποιῶν ἄνθρακας πυρὸς σωρεύσεις ἐπὶ τὴν κεφαλὴν αὐτοῦ, 'for in so doing thou shalt heap coals of fire upon his head,' are a well-known difficulty. It must not be overlooked that they are a quotation from Prov. xxv. 21, taken verbatim from the LXX, which, however, has an additional clause, ὁ δὲ κύριος ἀνταποδώσει σοι ἀγαθά. The meaning of the words, in their original connexion, has been thus given: 'Do good to your enemies, for so you shall undo them with grief and indignation at themselves, but God shall reward you.' To this it may be objected that the adversative particle δέ (ὁ δὲ κύριος) has no force, and also that the expression, 'thou shalt heap coals of fire on his head,' is an image of destruction, and cannot be distorted into the metaphor of destroying another with grief and indignation.

But, secondly, the context in the New Testament in which the expression occurs, has reference to the forgiveness of injuries, and in some way or other a meaning must be found for the words, 'thou shalt heap coals of fire upon his head,' which is in accordance with this precept. The explanation, 'thou shalt melt thine enemy like wax,' may be at once set aside as inconsistent with the words. Nor is the other interpretation, 'thou shalt make his soul burn with remorse,' really more defensible. What appropriateness is there in the expression, 'heaping coals of fire on the head,' to express inward remorse and indignation? or how would the desire even to excite remorse in an enemy be consistent with Christian forgiveness? It is impossible to harmonize such an interpretation with what precedes or follows. Better, therefore, to take the words in their literal sense as an image of destruction, which is, however, ironically appli d by the Apostle, in the spirit of the New Testament, rather than of the Old, so as to reverse the meaning. 'Instead of avenging yourselves, say rather (with them of old time), if thine enemy hunger, feed him; if he thirst, give him drink, for *this* is the right way of undoing and destroying him; *this* is the true mode of retaliation; *this* is the Christian's revenge.' There is an

THE EPISTLE TO THE ROMANS

21 that " thou shalt heap coals of fire on his head.' Be not overcome of evil, but overcome evil with good.

13 Let every soul be subject unto the higher powers. For there is no power but of God: the powers that be 2 are ordained of God. Whosoever therefore resisteth the power, resisteth the ordinance of God: and they 3 that resist shall receive to themselves damnation. For rulers are not a terror to °the good work," but to the evil. ᴾAnd wilt thou " not be afraid of the power? do that which is good, and thou shalt have praise of 4 the same: for he is the minister of God to thee for good. But if thou do that which is evil, be afraid;

° *good works*   ᴾ Wilt thou then

emphasis on τοῦτο: 'In so doing thou shalt inflict on him the true vengeance.' The omission of the final words (but the Lord shall reward thee', which would be inappropriate, if the first part of the passage is to have this turn given to it, is a strong argument that the suggested interpretation is the correct one.

21. The explanation just given is further confirmed by the verse which follows. He has just said, 'Destroy your enemy with deeds of mercy.' Following out the same thought he adds, 'Do not be carried away by his evil, but carry him away by your good.'

13. 3. οἱ γὰρ ἄρχοντες, *for rulers.*] The dative (τῷ ἔργῳ), which is supported by a great preponderance of MS. authority, is the true reading. The Apostle goes on to give another reason why it is our duty to obey magistrates, besides their being divinely appointed, because they are a terror, not to the good work, but to the evil. And would you be without fear

of the magistrate? Do well, and he shall praise you as a good citizen.

It may be observed: (1) That St. Paul cannot have intended to rule absolutely the question of obedience to authority, if for no other reason than this, that the only case he supposes is that of a just ruler. (2) That the manner in which he speaks of rulers, is a presumption that the Christians at Rome could not have been at this time subject to persecution from the authorities; whence it may be inferred also that it was in reference to the temper of the early Christians rather than to any systematic persecution likely to arouse it, these precepts were given.

4. Is the Apostle speaking of rulers of this world as they are, or as they ought to be? Of neither, but of the feeling with which the Christian is to regard them. In general, he will be slow to think evil of others; in particular, of rulers. His temper will

for he beareth not the sword in vain: for he is the
minister of God, a revenger to execute wrath upon
5 him that doeth evil. Wherefore ye must needs be
subject, not only for wrath, but also for conscience
6 sake. For for this cause pay ye tribute also: for
they are God's ministers, attending continually ᑫ for ʳ
7 this very thing. Render ʳ⁻ˡˡ to all their dues: tribute
to whom tribute is due; custom to whom custom;
8 fear to whom fear; honour to whom honour. Owe no
man any thing, but to love one another: for he that
9 loveth another hath fulfilled the law. For this, Thou
shalt not commit adultery, Thou shalt not kill, Thou
shalt not steal, ˢ⁻ˡˡ Thou shalt not covet; and if there
be any other commandment, it is briefly comprehended
in this ᵗ⁻ˡˡ, namely, Thou shalt love thy neighbour as
10 thyself. Love worketh no ill to his neighbour: there-

ᑫ upon   ʳ add *therefore*   ˢ add *thou shalt not bear false witness*,
ᵗ add *saying*

be that of submission and moderation. He will acknowledge that almost any government is tolerable to the man who walks innocently, and that the governments of mankind in general have more of right and justice in them than the generality of men are apt to suppose. And lastly, he will feel that, whatever they do, they are in the hands of God, who rules among the children of men; and, in general, that his relations to them, like all the other relations of Christian life, are to God also.

8. The precept of the previous verse is repeated in a stronger negative form: 'Owe no man any thing.' To which the Apostle adds, but 'to love one another.'

Some have taken the word ὀφείλετε in different senses in the two clauses. 'Owe no man any thing, only ye ought to love one another.' It is simpler, without such a paronomasia, to explain the words of the endless debt of love: 'Owe no man any thing, but to love one another;' that debt, we may add, which 'owing owes not' and is alway due.

9. The Apostle, quoting apparently from Exod. xx. 13: Deut. v. 18, 19, not according to the Hebrew, but according to copies of the LXX, which Philo must have had (*De Decalogo*, § 12, 24, 32), like him, places the seventh commandment before the sixth. The same order is observed in the quotation of the Evangelists, Luke xviii. 20: Mark x. 19; the places of the

11 fore love is the fulfilling of the law. And ᵘthis,
knowing the time, that now it is high time to awake
out of sleep: for now is our salvation nearer than
12 when we believed. The night is far spent, the day is
at hand: let us therefore cast off the works of dark-
13 ness, and let us put on the armour of light. Let us
walk honestly, as in the day; not in rioting and
drunkenness, not in chambering and wantonness, not

ᵘ that

seventh and eighth being also transposed in the Vatican MS. of the LXX.

11. καὶ τοῦτο, *and this too.*] 1 Cor. vi. 6-8: Eph. ii. 8.

It has been remarked that in the New Testament we find no exhortations grounded on the shortness of life. As if the end of life had no practical importance for the first believers, compared with the day of the Lord. Like one of the old prophets, St. Paul already seems to see 'the morning spread upon the mountains.' The night has endured long enough, and the ends of the world are come. Comp. 1 Thess. v. 1-5, and Essay On Belief in the Coming of Christ.

νῦν γὰρ ἐγγύτερον ἡμῶν ἡ σωτηρία, *for now our salvation is nearer than when we believed.*] So much time has elapsed since we first received the Gospel, that He cannot long delay His coming. Yet the very consciousness of this is not unlike the feeling expressed in 2 Pet. iii. 4: 'Where is the promise of his coming? for since the fathers fell asleep, all things continue as they were from the beginning of the creation.'

Comp. Ezek. xii. 22, 23 'Son of man, what is that proverb that ye have in the land of Israel, saying, The days are prolonged, and every vision faileth?

'Tell them therefore, Thus saith the Lord God, I will make this proverb to cease, and they shall no more use it as a proverb in Israel; but say unto them, The days are at hand, and the effect of every vision.'

But why should the Apostle address the Roman Christians in such startling language? Had they been asleep like the heathen around them? It is the language of the preacher now as then, and in the old time before that — 'Awake thou that sleepest, and arise from the dead,' which, however often repeated, finds men sleeping still.

12. ἡ νὺξ προέκοψεν, *the night is far spent.*] The idea of a garment is contained in ἀποθώμεθα, which is opposed to ἐνδυσώμεθα in what follows. 'And let us put on the armour of light;' compare Eph. vi. The Greek Fathers give several reasons why in the first clause the Apostle should have used the word ἔργα, and in the second ὅπλα. If any reason is

14 in strife and envying. But put ye on the Lord Jesus Christ, and make not provision for the flesh, ˣ unto ᵞ the lusts thereof.

14 Him that is weak in the faith receive ye, ʸ not to 2 judge his doubtful thoughts.ᵍ For one ᶻ has faith to ᵍ eat all things: ᵃ but he that ᵍ is weak, eateth herbs. 3 Let not him that eateth despise him that eateth not; and let not him which eateth not judge him that

---

ˣ to fulfil   ʸ but not to doubtful disputations   ᶻ believeth that he may
ᵃ another, who

---

necessary, it may be said to arise from the latter word being more appropriate to express the position of the Christian in this world, arrayed for the conflict against evil.

14. ἐνδύσασθε, *put on.*] Compare Gal. iii. 27, where the word occurs, as perhaps also here, with an allusion to the garment in which the baptized person was clothed after coming up out of the water —'For as many of you as were baptized into Christ, have put on Christ.' Compare notes on 1 Thess. v. 1-10.

14. 1. τὸν δὲ ἀσθενοῦντα τῇ πίστει, *him that is weak in the faith.*] These words do not mean him that has a half-belief in Christianity, but him that doubteth, him that has not an enlightened belief, who has not 'knowledge,' whose 'conscience being weak,' is liable 'to be defiled.' Comp. 1 Cor. viii. 1, 7.

μὴ εἰς διακρίσεις διαλογισμῶν, *not to judge his doubtful thoughts.*] From the word διακρίνεσθαι in ver. 23 being used for to doubt, it is inferred in the English version, that the word διάκρισις may be used in the sense of doubtings, 'not to doubtful disputations.'

This is the fallacy of paronymous words; the real meaning of διάκρισις is 'discerning, determining.' 'Receive him that is weak, not to determinations of matters of dispute.' 'Receive him that is weak,' says the Apostle; 'but then occurs the afterthought, 'do not determine his scruples; that might be injurious to the Church, and narrow its pale by excluding others who have another kind of scruple.'

2. ὃς μὲν πιστεύει, *one man believeth.*] Not as in the English Version, one man believeth that he may eat all things, but in the same sense as πίστις of the preceding verse, 'one man has faith so that he eats all things.' The play of words in πίστις and πιστεύει is confirmed by numberless similar instances in St. Paul's writings. Compare ver. 22 σὺ πίστιν ἔχεις.

ὁ δὲ ἀσθενῶν.] 'But the weak, of whom I spoke before;' not opposed to ὃς μέν, but referring to ver. 1.

4. The Apostle speaks generally, intending to include both the cases mentioned in the previous verse. As he argued in the last chapter, 'You ought to pay tribute,

4 eateth: for God hath received him. Who art thou that judgest another's servant? to his own ᵇ Lord ᵈ he standeth or falleth. ᶜ And holden up he shall be:
5 for the Lord ᵈ is able to make him stand. ᵈ One man approves every other day: another approves every day.ᵈ Let every man be fully persuaded in his
6 own mind. He that regardeth the day, regardeth it unto the Lord. ᵉ⁻ᵈ He that eateth, eateth to the Lord, for he giveth God thanks; and he that eateth not, to
7 the Lord he eateth not, and giveth God thanks. For none of us liveth to himself, and no man dieth to
8 himself. For whether we live, we live unto the Lord;

ᵇ master   ᶜ Yea, he shall be holden up: for God   ᵈ One man esteemeth one day above another: another esteemeth every day alike.
ᵉ add *and he that regardeth not the day, to the Lord he doth not regard it.*

for it is a debt to God;' so here he urges, that to judge our brother in matters indifferent, is taking a liberty with another man's servant. 'Who art thou who judgest the servant of another man? It is no concern of yours; not to you but to his own Master is he accountable, whether he stand or fall.' And then, as if it were a word of ill omen even to suggest that he should fall, he adds, but he shall stand, as we may in faith believe, for God is able to make him stand. He is a weak brother, I speak as a man, therefore he is likely to fall. But, believing in the omnipotence of God, I say he is so much more likely to stand also, for 'my strength is perfected in weakness.' Compare Jas. iv. 12 'There is one lawgiver who is able to save and to destroy; who art thou that judgest another?' and Rom. ix. 20.

6. As our Lord answers the difficulties put to Him by the Pharisees by stirring higher and deeper questions, as St. Paul himself concludes the discussion on marriage, by carrying it into another world, 'It remaineth, that they that have wives be as though they had none,' 1 Cor. vii. 29; as touching meats offered to idols he allows the rule of Christian charity to weaker brethren to be superseded by the wider and more general principle, 'Whether ye eat or drink, do all to the glory of God,' 1 Cor. x. 31: as the possibility of the Christian 'living in sin that grace may abound,' is dispelled by the thought of union with Christ; so too, scruples respecting meats and drinks are lost in the sense of our relation to Christ and God, which furnishes the practical rule for our treatment of them. The remembrance of this common relation is also an assurance both to the lax and the strict, that the brethren whom

and whether we die, we die unto the Lord: whether
we live therefore, or die, we are the Lord's. For to
this end Christ both died, and ᶠ lived,⸗ that he might
be Lord both of the dead and living. But why dost
thou judge thy brother? or why dost thou set at
nought thy brother? for we shall all stand before the
judgment seat of ᵍ God.⸗ For it is written, As I live,
saith the Lord, every knee shall bow to me, and every
tongue shall confess to God. So then every one of us
shall give account of himself to God. Let us not
therefore judge one another any more: but judge
this rather, that no man put a stumbling-block or an

ᶠ *rose, and revived*   ᵍ *Christ*

---

they judge or despise are believers equally with themselves.

9. It is argued that we cannot suppose the Apostle to have meant that Christ died that He might rule the dead, and rose again that He might rule the living; but that the two clauses must be taken as one; 'Christ died and rose again that he might be the ruler over all.' The remarks made on iv. 24 are applicable here. The distribution of the clauses in the present instance is to our mode of thought unnatural, but it was natural to St. Paul, who divides and subdivides Christ's life analogously to the life of the believer.

There appeared to the Apostle a certain fitness in Christ being like us, tempted in all points like as we are, and therefore able to succour them that are tempted; crucified, even as we are to crucify the lusts of the flesh; dying, that we may die with Him; rising again, that we may rise with Him. It is not simply that He once overcame death for us, or was offered up a sacrifice for sin. The Apostle's view is more present and lively, though from its not having passed into the language of creeds and articles, and perhaps also from something which we feel in it that belongs to another age, it has fallen out of daily use. Not only is Christ the source of the believer's acts, but He is the image of him in the different parts of his life. The believer is transformed into His likeness, not merely by putting on Christ, that is, by being clothed with His holiness, or invested with His merits, but by going through the stages of His existence. We cannot precisely analyse what the Apostle meant by this 'identity,' the superficial form of which is due to the peculiar rhetorical character of the age, the deeper and hidden thought being that, both inwardly and outwardly, as He was, so ought we to be, so are we in this world.

14 occasion to fall in his brother's way. I know, and am persuaded ʰ in ⁋ the Lord Jesus, that there is nothing unclean of itself: but to him that esteemeth
15 any thing to be unclean, to him it is unclean. ⁱ For ⁋ if thy brother be grieved with thy meat, now walkest thou not charitably. Destroy not him with thy meat,
16 for whom Christ died. Let not then your good be

ʰ by   ⁱ But

14. The Apostle goes on to explain the feeling under which he says all this; not that he disagrees with the stronger brethren who suppose that all these things are indifferent. Indeed as a Christian (ἐν κυρίῳ Ἰησοῦ) he knows as well as they do, that the distinction of clean and unclean meats is a mere superstition. 'Not that which goeth into a man defileth a man.' He says so broadly and generally, but his object is to show that this makes no difference in the case of another. 'Your conscience cannot judge for him, your knowledge will not pluck the scruple from his soul.' Therefore, however much he knows all this, he will not act upon it; the right use of his strength is to support his brother's weakness.

15. The Gospel is the law of freedom, and cannot by any possibility admit scruples respecting meats and drinks. But when we have not our own case to consider, but that of our brethren, when (to bring the precept home to ourselves) the difference between us is the question of a sabbath day, the very same principle of freedom leads us to avoid giving offence by our freedom. Our brother sees strongly the sin and guilt of what we nevertheless know to be our Christian liberty, and love must induce us to abridge our rights for his sake. We must not take him by force, and compel him to witness what he supposes to be our evil; still less must we induce him to follow our example and defile his conscience. Yet we cannot say that we must give up everything that offends our brother. Such a rule would be impracticable, and if not impracticable, often full of evil. It was not the rule which St. Paul himself adopted with the Judaizers, 'to whom he gave way, no, not for an hour.' It is not the rule which he enjoins when matters of importance are at stake; and the most indifferent things cease to be indifferent the moment an attempt is made to impose them upon others. Only in reference to the particular circumstances of the Church, and to the passions of men ever prone to exaggerate their party differences, the rule of consideration for others is the safer side.

16. It is a good thing, we might say, to know that Christ does not require of us the observance of the Jewish sabbath; it is a good thing to know that, without form of prayer or set times and places,

17 evil spoken of: for the kingdom of God is not meat
and drink; but righteousness, and peace, and joy in
18 the Holy Ghost. For he that in ᵏ this ᵈ serveth Christ
19 is acceptable to God, and approved of men. Let us
therefore follow after the things which make for peace,
20 and things wherewith one may edify another. For
meat destroy not the work of God. All things indeed
are pure; but it is evil for that man who eateth with

ᵏ *these things*

'neither in Jerusalem nor on this mountain,' we can worship the Father; to know that there is no rite or ceremony or ordinance that God cannot dispense with; or rather, that there is none which we are required to observe, except so far as they tend to a moral end. It is a good thing to know that Revelation can be interpreted by no other light than that of reason; it is a good thing to know that God is not extreme to mark human infirmities in our lives and conduct. But all this may serve for a cloak of licentiousness, may be a scandal among men, and humanly speaking, the destruction of those for whom Christ died.

17. χαρά, *joy*.] The Christian character naturally suggests ideas of sorrow, peace and consolation; not so naturally to ourselves the thought of joy and glorying which constantly recurs in the writings of the Apostle. These seem to belong to that circle of Christian graces, of which hope is the centre, which have almost vanished in the phraseology of modern times. ἐν πνεύματι ἁγίῳ, a holy joy, like all the other feelings of the Christian, seeking for its ground in some power beyond him, that is to say, in communion with the Spirit of God.

20. As in ver. 14 the Apostle admitted the objections which he himself put into the mouth of those who held meats and drinks to be indifferent, and replied to them, so here, he again expresses his agreement in principle with the stronger party, only to state with more force his precepts about the weaker brethren. 'It is true that all things are pure, but woe to him who eateth with offence.'

διὰ προσκόμματος.] With offence to whom? to himself, or to others? If we say to himself, the words will refer to the weak brother, who is induced to eat from seeing others eat; and his conscience being weak, is defiled; an interpretation which agrees with ver. 14 and with the parallel passage in 1 Cor. But the verses which follow, have plainly a reference to the offence given, not to a man's own conscience, but to others. We are therefore led to take the words as equivalent to ἐν ᾧ ὁ ἀδελφός σου προσκόπτει, in ver. 21. The opposite view might, however, be confirmed by observing that the Apostle returns to the other side of the subject in ver. 23.

21 offence. It is good neither to eat flesh, nor to drink wine, nor any thing whereby thy brother¹ stumbleth, 22 or is offended, or is made weak. ¹The faith which thou hast have ⁿ to thyself before God. Happy is he that condemneth not himself in that thing which he 23 alloweth. And he that doubteth is damned if he eat, because he eateth not of faith: for whatsoever is not of faith is sin.

15 ᵐ Now we ⁿ that are strong ought to bear the infirmi- 2 ties of the weak, and not to please ourselves. Let every one of us please his neighbour for his good to

¹ *Hast thou faith? Have it*   ᵐ We then

21. It is good not to eat meat, nor to drink wine, nor (to eat or drink) anything whereby thy brother stumbleth, or is entangled, or made weak.

The Apostle is using the expression to eat meat, or to drink wine generally, neither with particular reference to any customs of Nazarites or Essenes, nor to luxurious and dainty fare. He merely means, 'It is good not to eat or drink anything whatever that will give offence to our brethren.'

ἐν ᾧ is best explained by the repetition of φαγεῖν and πιεῖν.

22. Of the two readings, σὺ πίστιν ἔχεις, with an interrogative, σὺ πίστιν ἣν ἔχεις, without an interrogative, the latter has the greater MS. authority, the former is more like St. Paul. Hast thou faith, keep it to thyself. 'Blessed is he who judgeth not himself in that which he alloweth.' It is a happy thing not to have a scrupulous conscience. I admit your superiority, I am not saying that you are not better than he. Only keep it to yourself and the presence of God. Compare 1 Cor. xiv. 28 ἑαυτῷ δὲ λαλείτω καὶ τῷ θεῷ.

15. 1. The commencement of this chapter is closely connected with the preceding. 'He who doubts if he eats, is condemned.' But we who are strong and do not doubt, ought to bear the weaknesses of others. As Christ pleased not Himself, so neither ought we to please ourselves. The words of the prophets, which speak of the reproaches that fell on Him, may still instruct us. They were written beforehand, to teach us to be of one mind, that we should receive others, even as Christ received us. At ver. 8 the argument takes a new turn. While exhorting the Roman Church to unity, the other subject of discord arises in the Apostle's mind, not the disputes of strong and weak about meats and drinks, but the greater and more general dispute about Jew and Gentile, the old and the new,

¹ Reading προσκόπτει ἢ σκανδαλίζεται ἢ ἀσθενεῖ.

3 edification. For ⁿ Christ too ⁗ pleased not himself;
but, as it is written, The reproaches of them that
4 reproached thee fell on me. For whatsoever things
were written aforetime were written for our learning,
that we through patience and ᵒ through ⁗ comfort of
5 the scriptures might have hope. Now the God of
patience and consolation grant you to be likeminded
6 one toward another according to Christ Jesus: that
ye may with one mind and one mouth glorify ᵖ the
7 God and ⁗ Father of our Lord Jesus Christ. Wherefore
receive ye one another, as Christ also received ᑫ us ⁄
8 to the glory of God. ʳ For ⁗ I say that ˢ⁻⁗ Christ was

ⁿ even Christ   ᵒ omit *through*   ᵖ God, even the   ᑫ *you*
ʳ *Now*   ˢ add *Jesus*

the law and the Gospel. He returns upon the former theme, and repeats language of reconciliation, which he had used before. Christ came not to destroy the prophets, but to fulfil; the minister of the circumcision to the uncircumcision; the performer of the promises made to the patriarchs—to all mankind. The Gentiles and the Jews rejoice together; the root of Jesse is the hope of both. The Apostle then passes on to matters personal: an apology for writing so boldly; his intended journeys to Rome, Spain, and Jerusalem; the contribution for the poor saints; with the allusions to which, however, he blends religious thoughts and feelings.

we that are strong.] The Apostle identifies himself with the stronger party, to give force to his words. As if he said: 'You and I, who are strong and enlightened, should bear the infirmities of others. My side is that of the strong, not against but for the weak; we who are whole should take care of those who are sick.' It is a stage of the Gospel to know that 'that which goeth into a man defileth not a man;' it is a higher stage to know it and not always to act upon it.

3. We may ask, 'But did the Apostle suppose that words like these were intended to bear this and no other meaning? and that they were understood in this sense by their original authors?' The answer to these questions is that the Apostle never asked them. The last thought that would have entered into his mind, would have been what in modern language we should term the reproduction to himself of the life and circumstances of the writers. He read the Old Testament, seeing 'Christ in all things, and all things in Christ.'

8. *to confirm.*] It is not certain whether, in these words, St. Paul is referring to the fulfilment of

a minister of the circumcision for the truth of God, to
9 confirm the promises made unto the fathers : and that
the Gentiles might glorify God for his mercy; as it
is written, For this cause I will confess to thee among
10 the Gentiles, and sing unto thy name. And again
11 ᵗ it '' saith, Rejoice, ye Gentiles, with his people. And
again, ᵘ it saith,'' Praise the Lord, all ye Gentiles;
12 and ˣ let all the people laud him.' And again, Esaias
saith, 'There shall be ʸ the '' root of Jesse, and he that
shall rise to reign over the Gentiles ; in him shall the
13 Gentiles ᶻ hope.'' Now the God of hope fill you with
all joy and peace in believing, that ye may abound in
hope, through the power of the Holy Ghost.
14 And I myself also am persuaded of you, my brethren,
that ye also are full of goodness, filled with all know-

ᵗ he   ᵘ omit *it saith*   ˣ *laud him all ye people*
               ʸ a   ᶻ trust

the promises to the Jews (see ch. xi), or to the transfer of them which he had made in the fourth chapter to the Gentiles. Either would in his view have been a true performance of them.

9. Διὰ τοῦτο ἐξομολογήσομαι, *Therefore I will give thanks*.] These words, which are exactly quoted from the LXX, Ps. xviii. 49, are in their original meaning an expression of triumph after a victory, for which the victor says he will give thanks among the subject people. In the application made of them by St. Paul, they are supposed to be uttered by a Gentile, and the word ἔθνη receives, as elsewhere, a new sense.

12. '*There shall be*,' &c.] The quotation is from the LXX, which reads: ἔσται ἐν τῇ ἡμέρᾳ ἐκείνῃ ἡ ῥίζα τοῦ Ἰεσσαὶ καὶ ὁ ἀνιστάμενος ἄρχειν ἐθνῶν, ἐπ' αὐτῷ ἔθνη ἐλπιοῦσιν. (Isa. xi. 10.) These words are not, however, an exact translation of the Hebrew, which is as follows : ' And in that day shall the shoot of Jesse, which is set up for a banner, be sought of the Gentiles.'

Ver. 14—xvi. 27 is a resumption of the personal narrative. The Apostle began by offering commendation ; he concludes in the same spirit by apologizing for giving advice. The salutation with which he opened, like the doxology with which he ends, contained in few words a summary of the Gospel.

'But I know, brethren, that you need not these words of mine.' I myself, who give this advice, am persuaded that you ' able too (καί) to advise one ano

15 ledge, able also to admonish one another. Nevertheless, brethren, I have written the more boldly unto you in some sort, as putting you in mind, because of the 16 grace that is given to me of God, that I should be the minister of Jesus Christ to the Gentiles, ᵃ doing the work of a priest of ⁷ the gospel of God, that the offering up of the Gentiles might be acceptable, being 17 sanctified by the Holy Ghost. I have therefore ᵇ my glorying ʸ through Jesus Christ in those things which 18 pertain to God. For I will not dare to speak of any of those things which Christ hath not wrought by me, to make the Gentiles obedient, by word and deed,

ᵃ ministering ᵇ whereof I may glory

15. For the feeling, compare 1 Cor. vii. 25 γνώμην δὲ δίδωμι ὡς ἠλεημένος ὑπὸ κυρίου πιστὸς εἶναι : and Rom. i. 5. Such withdrawing of self reminds us of the quaint expression of Coleridge, 'St. Paul was a man of the finest manners ever known.'

16. The whole passage, from ὡς ἐπαναμιμνήσκων ὑμᾶς down to πνεύματι ἁγίῳ, may be summed up in two words, 'as the Apostle of the Gentiles.' The simple thought is 'transfigured' into the language of sacrifice, in which the Apostle describes himself and his office. Elsewhere he loves to identify the believer and his Lord ; here he applies the same imagery to his own work, which is elsewhere applied to the work of Christ, partly because the use of such figures was natural to him, and partly, also, because such language was intelligible and expressive to those whom ⌐ is addressing.

⌐ουργοῦντα,] performing the priestly office in relation to the Gospel.

17, 18. The train of thought in the Apostle's mind seems rather to carry him back to his opponents at Corinth, where he was then staying, than to be directed to those whom he is addressing. The delicate alternations of feeling in the verses which follow, and the transition from hesitation to boldness, remind us of several passages in the Epistles to the Corinthians. 2 Cor. x. 15, 16. There, too, he had been careful to guard against appearing to intrude in another's vineyard. Here his object is to assert in the gentlest manner possible, as in the Epistle to the Galatians in the strongest, his Apostleship of the Gentiles ; at the same time making a similar disclaimer.

19. The tone is changed, and the construction of the preceding verse forgotten. The Apostle is speaking, not of what Christ did not do, but of what He did, and

THE EPISTLE TO THE ROMANS

19 through mighty signs and wonders, by the power of the ᶜHoly Spirit ǁ; so that from Jerusalem, and round about unto Illyricum, I have fully preached the gospel 20 of Christ. Yea, so have I strived to preach the gospel, not where Christ was named, lest I should build upon 21 another man's foundation: but as it is written, To whom he was not spoken of, they shall see: and they 22 that have not heard shall understand. For which cause also I have been much hindered from coming 23 to you. But now having no more place in these parts, and having a great desire these many years to 24 come unto you; whensoever I take my journey into Spain ᵈ⁻ǁ—(for I trust to see you in my journey, and to be brought on my way thitherward by you, if first 25 I be somewhat filled with your company). But now 26 I go unto Jerusalem to minister unto the saints. For

ᶜ *Spirit of God*   ᵈ add *I will come to you*

by his means; 'I will only speak of what Christ did, and what he did was,' &c. Comp. 2 Cor. xii. 12 'Truly the signs of an Apostle were wrought among you in all patience, in signs and wonders, and mighty deeds.'

23. If the Apostle fulfilled this last-mentioned intention, no trace of his journey has been preserved. His long imprisonment at Rome and Cesarea may have hindered its accomplishment; or the stream of tradition, setting in another direction, has obliterated the memory of it. Could it be established that by the words, ἐπὶ τὸ τέρμα τῆς δύσεως ἐλθών, in the famous passage of Clement, 1 *Ep. ad Cor.* v, the Pillars of Hercules were meant, we might suppose that the true and more ancient tradition had disappeared before the later one. If we could recover a Chronicon of the end of the first century, there would be no reason for surprise in our finding mention of the martyrdom of St. Paul in Spain. So slender is the authority by which any other tradition of his death is supported, so inextricably blended in the very earliest accounts with fables respecting himself and St. Peter. Dionys. *Cor.* apud Euseb. *H. E.* ii. 25.

24. ἐὰν ὑμῶν πρῶτον ἀπὸ μέρους ἐμπλησθῶ.] 'If I be first of all filled with you in my love, in some degree;' i. e. not so much as I wish, yet as long as I am able. The rhetoric of Chrysostom adds a fine touch, which is hardly, however, contained in the original words, οὐδεὶς γάρ με

it hath pleased them of Macedonia and Achaia to make a certain contribution for the poor ᵉ among the ᵈ
27 saints which are at Jerusalem. It hath pleased them verily; and their debtors they are. For if the Gentiles have been made partakers of their spiritual things, their duty is also to minister unto them in
28 carnal things. When therefore I have performed this, and have sealed to them this fruit, I will come by you
29 into Spain. And I am sure that, when I come unto you, I shall come in the fulness of the blessing ᶠ⁻ᵍ of
30 Christ. Now I beseech you, brethren, for the Lord Jesus Christ's sake, and for the love of the Spirit, that ye strive together with me in your prayers to God for
31 me; that I may be delivered from them that do not believe in Judæa; and that ᵍ the offering of my gift

ᵉ *omit* among the   ᶠ add *of the Gospel*
ᵍ *my service which I have for*

χρόνος ἐμπλῆσαι δύναται, οὐδ' ἐμποιῆσαί μοι κόρον τῆς συνουσίας ὑμῶν.

28. σφραγισάμενος.] 'Having set my seal upon;' i. e. having given the seal of my Apostolical authority to this fruit they have borne; or, having completed and put the finishing stroke to the fruit which they offer. For the use of the word καρπός comp. Phil. iv. 17 οὐχ ὅτι ἐπιζητῶ τὸ δόμα, ἀλλ' ἐπιζητῶ τὸν καρπὸν τὸν πλεονάζοντα εἰς λόγον ὑμῶν.

29. ἐν πληρώματι εὐλογίας χριστοῦ.] I know that coming to you I will come in the fullness of the blessing of Christ.

These words naturally carry us back to the first chapter, in which he says, 'I desire to come unto you, that I may impart some spiritual gift.' So in this passage

he is thinking that he will richly endow them, even as God has endowed him. Yet how can we free the words from a sort of egotism? First inasmuch as he himself tells us that all his graces are inseparably bound up in his union with Christ, and his glorying no man can make void, because he glories in the Lord; and secondly as the thought of the good he will do them is quickened by his affection for them. Compare 2 Cor. xi. 30; xii. 1.

31. The Apostle seems to fear not only the violence of those who did not believe, but also the unwillingness of the brethren to receive offerings at his hands. The words, ἵνα ἡ δωροφορία μου . . . εὐπρόσδεκτος τοῖς ἁγίοις, imply a difference between himself and the Church of Jerusalem, such as

32 at " Jerusalem may be accepted of the saints; ¹ that
I may come unto you with joy by the will of ʰ the
33 Lord Jesus." Now the God of peace be with you all.
Amen.

16 I commend unto you Phebe our sister, which is
2 a servant of the church which is at Cenchrea: that
ye receive her in the Lord, as becometh saints, and
that ye ⁱ succour " her in whatsoever business she hath
need of you: for she ᵏ too " hath been a succourer of
3 many, and of ¹ my own self." Greet ᵐ Prisca " and
4 Aquila my helpers in Christ Jesus: who have for my
life laid down their own necks: unto whom not only
I give thanks, but also all the churches of the Gentiles.
5 Likewise greet the church that is in their house.

ʰ *God, and may with you be refreshed*   ⁱ assist   ᵏ *omit* too
    ˡ myself also   ᵐ *Priscilla*

made it possible that they might
not receive the offerings that he
brought. Why else should he
doubt, or even pray, that the collection of alms which he had undertaken at the request of Apostles 'who seemed to be pillars'
might be acceptable? Compare
the account in Acts xxi, in which
a slender line of demarcation appears to be drawn between the
multitude of Jews that believe,
all zealous for the law, and the
rest of the nation.

16. 1. Phebe, probably the
bearer of the Epistle.

To the name of deaconess of
the Church in the New Testament can only be added the conjecture, that the institution came
from the desire to avoid the scandal which would be occasioned
by the admixture of men and

women in some of the offices of
the Church. Comp. 1 Cor. ix. 5
'Have we not power to lead
about a sister, a wife, ... as the
brethren of the Lord, and Cephas.'

5. Epenetus the firstfruits. So
in 1 Cor. xvi. 15, Stephanas is
mentioned as the firstfruits of
Achaia, whence the very ancient
various reading Ἀχαΐας has probably crept into this passage.

Ewald, who admits the genuineness of the fifteenth chapter, sus-
pects that the sixteenth has been
inserted from a lost Epistle to the
Ephesians. It must be admitted
that the number of persons who
are supposed to be acquaintances
of St. Paul at Rome; the mention
of Prisca and Aquila, who are at
Ephesus both before and after
the time at which the Epistle
was written; also of Epenetus

¹ Reading ἵνα ἐν χαρᾷ ἔλθω πρὸς ὑμᾶς διὰ θελήματος κυρίου Ἰησοῦ.

Salute my wellbeloved Epenetus, who is the first-
6 fruits of ⁿ Asia ⁱ unto Christ. Greet Mary, who be-
7 stowed much labour on us. Salute Andronicus and
Junia, my kinsmen, and my fellowprisoners, who are
of note among the apostles, who also were in Christ
8 before me. Greet Amplias my beloved in the Lord.
9 Salute Urbane, our helper ¹in ᵒ the Lord,ⁱ and Stachys
10 my beloved. Salute Apelles approved in Christ.
Salute them which are of Aristobulus' household.
11 Salute Herodion my kinsman. Greet them that be
of the household of Narcissus, which are in the Lord.
12 Salute Tryphena and Tryphosa, who labour in the
Lord. [Salute the beloved Persis, which laboured
13 much in the Lord.] Salute Rufus chosen in the Lord,
14 and his mother and mine. Salute Asyncritus, Phlegon,
Hermes, Patrobas, Hermas, and the brethren which
15 are with them. Salute Philologus, and Julia, Nereus,
and his sister, and Olympas, and all the saints which
16 are with them. Salute one another with an holy kiss.
ᵖ All ⁱ the churches of Christ salute you.

  ⁿ *Achaia*   ᵒ *Christ*   ᵖ omit *All*

the firstfruits of Asia, and of others who had been fellow-workers with St. Paul in Asia or Greece, two of whom are also called his fellowprisoners at a time when he himself was not in prison, and all of whom are now at Rome, where we should not expect to find them, lends countenance to the suspicion. Whether Ewald be right or not is a matter of slight importance. It is impossible either to prove or disprove the conjecture.

7. Salute Andronicus and Junia, my fellowprisoners. The latter ('Ιουνίαν) is the name of a woman. Priscilla, Junia, the household of Chloe, the sisters who accompanied Paul and the brethren of the Lord and Cephas, the Athenian woman named Damaris, Phebe, Dorcas, the women who followed Christ and ministered to Him of their substance, besides others who are mere names to us, show the part which women took in the first preaching of the Gospel.

16. ἀσπάσασθε ἀλλήλους ἐν φιλήματι ἁγίῳ,] with the mystic kiss, the kiss that is the seal of bro-

---

¹ Reading ἐν κυρίῳ

THE EPISTLE TO THE ROMANS

17 Now I beseech you, brethren, mark them which cause divisions and offences contrary to the doctrine 18 which ye have learned; and avoid them. For they that are such serve not our Lord ^q–‖ Christ, but their own belly; and by good words and fair speeches 19 deceive the hearts of the simple. For your obedience is come abroad unto all men. I am glad therefore on your behalf: but yet I would have you wise unto that 20 which is good, and pure concerning evil. And the God of peace shall bruise Satan under your feet shortly. The grace of our Lord Jesus Christ be with you. Amen.

21 Timotheus my workfellow, and Lucius, and Jason, 22 and Sosipater, my kinsmen, salute you. I Tertius, 23 who wrote this epistle, salute you in the Lord. Gaius mine host, and of the whole church, saluteth you. Erastus the chamberlain of the city saluteth you, and Quartus a brother. ^r–‖

25 Now to him that is of power to stablish you accord-

q add *Jesus*   r add 24 *The grace of our Lord Jesus Christ be with you all.*

therly love as in 1 Pet. v. 14; or merely the kiss usual in the assembly of the saints.

'All the churches of Christ salute you.' Insert πᾶσαι, which has been omitted by the copyists, apparently because they could not understand how St. Paul could express the feeling of all Churches to the Roman Church. Compare 1 Cor. i. 2.

19. 'Avoid these deceivers, for otherwise you will mar that good fame which is gone out respecting you into all the world.'

22. That St. Paul dictated his Epistles appears from this passage, which may be compared with 1 Cor. xvi. 21, where he adds, 'The salutation of me Paul with mine own hand.' Gal. iv. 11 'Ye see in what large letters I have written to you with mine own hand.' Col. iv. 18 'The salutation by the hand of me Paul.' 2 Thess. iii. 17 'The salutation of Paul with mine own hand, which is the token in every epistle: so I write.'

25. τῷ δὲ δυναμένῳ.] The construction may be supplied by some such word as εὐχαριστῶμεν; or, more probably, was intended to terminate with ἡ δόξα. Owing to the length of the sentence, the latter end has forgotten the beginning; and consequently, ἡ δόξα is inserted in a relative clause.

ing to my gospel, and the preaching of Jesus Christ, according to the revelation of the mystery, which was 26 kept secret since the world began, but now is made manifest, and by the scriptures of the prophets, according to the commandment of the everlasting God, made known to all nations for the obedience of faith:

to stablish,] in reference to their divisions and weaknesses.

The best commentary on this verse is the first chapter, in which the Gospel is set forth as a revelation of righteousness and of wrath to a world lying in darkness. In several other places St. Paul speaks of the mysteriousness of the past, the times of that ignorance which God winked at. Comp. 1 Cor. ii. 7 'We speak the wisdom of God in a mystery, even the hidden wisdom which God ordained before the world unto our glory;' and Col. i. 26 'Even the mystery which hath been hid from ages and from generations, but now is made manifest unto the saints.' As we sometimes ask the question, not without a certain strangeness, what God 'has reserved for the heathen,' so in these passages the Apostle seems to indicate a similar feeling respecting the ages that are past.

26. φανερωθέντος δὲ νῦν διά τε γραφῶν.] But now made manifest through the writings of the prophets also. That is to say, the Gospel which had been concealed, was now made manifest, and received also a light and illustration from the prophets.

27. ᾧ] refers to God, not to Christ. In addition to the arguments urged below, we may mention the anacoluthon of the doxology, as itself affording a proof of genuineness. There can be little inducement imagined for inventing these three verses, each of which (κατὰ τὸ εὐαγγέλιόν μου, καὶ τὸ κήρυγμα Ἰησοῦ χριστοῦ . . . αἰωνίου θεοῦ . . . μόνῳ σοφῷ θεῷ) bears special marks of the hand of St. Paul.

The great majority of early authorities (B. C. D., Clement, Origen) place the doxology at the end of the Epistle. A. has it here, and at the end of chap. xiv. as well; in which latter place G. leaves a space for it, also inserting it at the end. There are several other traces of this variation, being as old as the fourth century. The antiquity of the two traditions renders it impossible to determine certainly which of them is the true one.

The doubt respecting the position of the doxology, and the circumstance mentioned by Origen that Marcion ended the Epistle at the 23rd verse of the fourteenth chapter; also certain minute coincidences, which are observed chiefly between Rom. xv. 25-29, and 1 Cor. ix. 11, 2 Cor. viii. 4, ix. 1, 5; lastly, the mention of the great number of persons resident at Rome, who were known to the Apostle, and in particular of his kinsmen and

27 to God only wise, be glory through Jesus Christ for ever ⁸ and ever." Amen. ᵗ⁻ᵍ

⁸ omit *and ever*
ᵗ add *Written to the Romans from Corinth, and sent by Phebe servant of the church at Cenchrea.*

fellowprisoners, have led to a suspicion of the genuineness of the last two chapters. To such a suspicion it may be replied : (1) that, if spurious, they would be a forgery without a motive ; (2) that they have every mark of genuineness which characteristic thought and language can supply (observe xv. 8, 9, 14, 15, 20, 21, 23, compared with 2 Cor. x. 13, 16; xvi. 13, 23) ; (3) that they present at least one minute coincidence with the history ; (4) that the occurrence of the doxology at the end of chap. xiv is no proof that this was the end of the Epistle ; the Apostle, after intending to finish, may have begun again, as in the Epistle to the Galatians, as in fact he has added a postscript at ver. 21 of the sixteenth chapter, and made a conclusion at the end of chap. xv ; (5) that the close connexion of the last verse of chap. xiv and the beginning of chap. xv, is a presumption that the doxology has slipped into that place from some accidental cause ; (6) that the evidence of Marcion is inconclusive, unless his edition, whatever may have been its object, was based on earlier documents than the received version, an assumption of which there is no proof; lastly, that the extremely close and minute resemblances between the Ephesians and Colossians, or between the Galatians and the Romans (which latter are both admitted by Baur himself to be genuine writings of the Apostle), destroy the force of the presumption derived from a few similarities, nowhere extending to a whole verse, against the two last chapters of the Epistle to the Romans.

None of these arguments, it will be observed, afford any answer to the view of Ewald, who maintains, not the spuriousness, but the misplacement of chap. xvi. See above on ver. 5.

ESSAY ON THE ABSTRACT IDEAS

OF THE

NEW TESTAMENT

RELIGION and philosophy have often been contrasted as moving in different planes, in which they can never come into contact with each other. Yet there are many meeting-points at which either passes into the circle of the other. One of these meeting-points is language, which loses nothing of its original imperfection by being employed in the service of religion. Its plastic nature is an element of uncertainty in the interpretation of Scripture; its logical structure is a necessary limit on human faculties in the conception of truths above them; whatever growth it is capable of, must affect also the growth of our religious ideas; the analysis we are able to make of it, we must be able also to extend to the theological use of it. Religion cannot place itself above the instrument through which alone it speaks to man; our true wisdom is, therefore, to be aware of their interdependence.

One of the points in which theology and philosophy are brought into connexion by language, is their common usage of abstract words, and of what in the phraseology of some philosophers are termed 'mixed modes,' or ideas not yet freed from associations of time or sense. Logicians speak of the abstract and concrete, and of the formation of our abstract ideas : Are the abstractions of Scripture the same in kind with those of philosophy ? May we venture to analyse their growth, to ask after their origin, to compare their meaning in one age of the world and in another? The same words in different languages have not precisely the same meaning. May not this be the case also with abstract terms which have passed from the Old Testament into the New, which have come down to us from the times of the Apostles, hardened by controversy, worn by the use of two thousand years ? These questions do not admit of a short and easy answer. Even to make them intelligible, we have to begin some way off, to enter on our inquiry as a speculation rather of logic than of theology, and hereafter to return to its bearing on the interpretation of Scripture.

It is remarked by a great metaphysician, that abstract ideas are, in one point of view, the highest and most philosophical of all our ideas, while in another they are the shallowest and most meagre. They have the advantage of clearness and definiteness ; they enable us to conceive and, in a manner, to span the infinity of things ; they arrange, as it were, in the frames of a window the many-coloured world of phenomena. And yet they are 'mere' abstractions removed from sense, removed from experience, and detached from the mind in which they arose. Their perfection consists, as their very name implies, in their idealism : that is, in their negative nature.

For example : the idea of 'happiness' has come down from the Greek philosophy. To us it is more entirely freed from etymological associations than it was to Aristotle, and further removed from any particular state of life, or, in other words, it is more of an abstraction. It is what everybody knows, but what nobody can tell. It is not pleasure, nor wealth, nor power, nor virtue, nor contemplation. Could we define it, we seem at first as if we should have found out the secret of the world. But our next thought is that we should only be defining a word, that it consists rather in a thousand undefinable things which, partly because mankind are not agreed about them, partly because they are too numerous to conceive under any single idea, are dropped by the instinct of language. It means what each person's fancy or experience may lead him to connect with it; it is a vague conception to his own mind, which nevertheless may be used without vagueness as a middle term in conversing with others.

It is the uniformity in the use of such words that constitutes their true value. Like all other words, they represent in their origin things of sense, facts of experience. But they are no longer pictured by the sense, or tinged by the affections; they are beyond the circle of associations in which they arose. When we use the word happiness, no thought of chance now intrudes itself; when we use the word righteousness, no thought of law or courts; when the word virtue is used, the image no longer presents itself of manly strength or beauty.

The growth of abstract ideas is an after-growth of language itself, which may be compared to the growth of the mind when the body is already at its full stature. All language has been originally the reflection of a world of sense; the words which describe the faculties have once referred to the parts of the body; the name of God Himself has been derived in most languages from the sun or the powers of nature. It is indeed impossible for us to say how far, under these earthly and sensual images, there lurked among the primitive peoples of mankind a latent consciousness of the spiritual and invisible; whether the thought or only the word was of the earth earthy. From this garment of the truth it is impossible for us to separate the truth itself. In this form awhile it appears to grow; even the writers of the Old Testament, in its earlier portion, finding in the winds or the light of heaven the natural expression of the power or holiness of Jehovah. But in process of time another world of thought and expression seems to create itself. The words for courage, strength, beauty, and the like, begin to denote mental and moral qualities; things which were only spoken of as actions, become abstract ideas, the name of God loses all sensual and outward associations; until at the end of the first period of Greek philosophy, the world of abstractions, and the words by which they are expressed, have almost as much definiteness and preciseness of meaning as among ourselves.

This process of forming abstractions is ever going on—the mixed modes of one language are the pure ideas of another; indeed, the adoption of words from dead languages into English has, above all other causes, tended to increase the number of our simple ideas, because the associations of such words being lost in the transfer, they are at once refined from all alloy of sense and experience. Different languages, or the same at different periods of their history, are at different stages of the process. We can imagine a language, such as language was, as far as the vestiges of it allow us to go back, in its first beginnings, in which every operation of the mind, every idea, every relation, was expressed by a sensible image; a language which we may describe as purely sensual and material, the words of which, like the first written characters, were mental pictures : we can imagine a language in a state which none has ever yet reached, in which the worlds of mind and matter are perfectly separated from each other, and no clog or taint of the one is allowed to enter into the other. But all languages which exist are in reality between these two extremes, and are passing from one to the other. The Greek of Homer is at a different stage from that of the Greek tragedians; the Greek of the early Ionic philosophers, at a different stage from that of Plato; so, though in a different way (for here there was no advancement), the Greek of Plato as compared with the Neo-Platonist philosophy. The same remark is applicable to the Old Testament, the earlier and later books of which may be, in a similar way, contrasted with each other; almost the whole of which (though here a new language also comes in) exhibits a marked difference from the Apocrypha. The structure of thought insensibly changes. This is the case with all languages which have a literature—they are ever becoming more and more abstract—modern languages, more than ancient; the later stages of either, more than the earlier. It by no means follows that as Greek, Latin, and English have words that correspond in a dictionary, they are real equivalents in meaning, because words, the same, perhaps, etymologically, may be used with different degrees of abstraction, which no accuracy or periphrasis of translation will suffice to express, belonging, as they do generally, to the great underlying differences of a whole language.

Another illustration of degrees of abstraction may be found in the language of poetry, or of common life, and the language of philosophy. Poetry, we know, will scarcely endure abstract terms, while they form the stock and staple of morals and metaphysics. They are the language of books, rather than of conversation. Theology, on the other hand, though its problems may seem akin to those of the moralist and metaphysician, yet tends to reject them in the same way that English tends to reject French words, or poetry to reject prose. He who in paraphrasing Scripture spoke of essence, matter, vice, crime, would be thought guilty of a want of taste; the reason of which is, that these abstract terms are not within the circle of our Scripture associations. They carry us into another age or country or school of thought—to the ear of the uneducated they have an unusual sound, while to the educated they appear to involve an anachronism or to be out of place. Vice, they say, is the moral, sin the theological term; nature and law are the proper words in a treatise on physiology, while the actions of which they are the imaginary causes would in a prayer or sermon be suitably ascribed to the Divine Being.

Our subject admits of another illustration from the language of the Fathers as compared with that of Scripture. Those who have observed the circumstance naturally ask why it is that Scriptural expressions when they reappear in the early patristic literature slightly change their signification? that a greater degree of personality is given to one word, more definiteness to another, while a third has been singled out to be the centre of a scheme of doctrine? The reason is, that use, and reflection, and controversy do not allow language to remain where it was. Time itself is the great innovator in the sense of words. No one supposes that the meaning of conscience or imagination exactly corresponds to the Latin 'conscientia' or 'imaginatio.' Even within the limits of our own language the terms of the scholastic philosophy have acquired and lost a technical signification. And several changes have taken place in the language of creeds and articles, which, by their very attempt to define and systematize, have slightly though imperceptibly departed from the use of words in Scripture.

The principle of which all these instances are illustrations leads to important results in the interpretation of Scripture. It tends to show, that in using the same words with St. Paul we may not be using them in precisely the same sense. Nay, that the very exactness with which we apply them, the result of the definitions, oppositions, associations, of ages of controversy, is of itself a difference of meaning. The mere lapse of time tends to make the similarity deceitful. For if the language of Scripture (to use an expression which will have been made intelligible by the preceding remarks) be really at a different stage of abstraction, great differences in the use of language will occur, such as in each particular word escape and perplex us, and yet, on a survey of the whole, are palpable and evident.

A well-known difficulty in the interpretation of the Epistles is the seemingly uncertain use of δικαιοσύνη, ἀλήθεια, ἀγάπη, πίστις, δόξα, &c., words apparently the most simple, and yet taking sometimes in the same passage different shades and colours of meaning. Sometimes they are attributes of God, in other passages qualities in man; here realities, there mere ideas, sometimes active, sometimes passive. Some of them, as ἁμαρτία, πίστις, have a sort of personality assigned to them, while others, as πνεῦμα, with which we associate the idea of a person, seem to lose their personality. They are used with genitive cases after them, which we are compelled to explain in various senses. In the technical language of German philosophy, they are objective and subjective at once. For example: in the first chapter of the Romans, ver. 17, it is asked by commentators, 'Whether the righteousness of God, which is revealed in the Gospel,' is the original righteousness of God from the beginning, or the righteousness which He imparts to man, the righteousness of God in Himself or in man. So again, in chap. v, ver. 5, it is doubted whether the words ὅτι ἡ ἀγάπη τοῦ θεοῦ ἐκκέχυται ἐν ταῖς καρδίαις, refer to the love of God in man, or the love of God to man. So πνεῦμα θεοῦ wavers in meaning between a separate existence, or the spirit of God, as we should say the 'mind of man,' and the manifestation of that spirit in the soul of the believer. Similar apparent ambiguities occur in such expressions as πίστις Ἰησοῦ χριστοῦ, ὑπομονὴ χριστοῦ, ἀλήθεια θεοῦ, δόξα θεοῦ, σοφία θεοῦ, and several others.

A difficulty akin to this arises from the apparently numerous senses in which another class of words, such as νόμος, ζωή, θάνατος are used in the Epistles of St. Paul. That νόμος should sometimes signify the law of Moses, at other times the law of the conscience, and that it should be often uncertain whether ζωή referred to a life spiritual or natural, is inconceivable, if these words had had the same precise and defined sense that the corresponding English words have amongst ourselves. The class of expressions before mentioned seems to widen and extend in meaning as they are brought into contact with God and the human soul, or transferred from things earthly and temporal to things heavenly and spiritual. The subtle transformation which these latter words undergo, may be best described as a metaphorical or analogous use of them : not, to take a single instance, that the meaning of the word 'law' is so widened as to include all 'law,' but that the law of Moses becomes the figure or type of the law written on the heart, or of the law of sin and death, and ζωή, the natural life, the figure of the spiritual. Each word is a reflector of many thoughts, and we pass from one reflection of it to another in successive verses.

That such verbal difficulties occur much more often in Scripture than in any other book, will be generally admitted. In Plato and Aristotle, for example, they can be hardly said to exist at all. What they meant by εἶδος or οὐσία is hard to conceive, but their use of the words does not waver in successive sentences. The language of the Greek philosophy is, on the whole, precise and definite. A much nearer parallel to what may be termed the infinity of Scripture is to be found in the Jewish Alexandrian writings. There is the same transition from the personal to the impersonal, the same figurative use of language, the same tendency to realize and speak of all things in reference to God and the human soul. The mind existed prior to the ideas which are therefore conceived of as its qualities or attributes, and naturally coalesced with it in the Alexandrian phraseology.

The difficulty of which we have been speaking, when considered in its whole extent, is its own solution. It does but force upon us the fact, that the use of language and the mode of thought are different in the writings of the Apostle from what they are amongst ourselves. It is the difficulty of a person who should set himself to explain the structure of a language which he did not know, by one which he did, and at last, in despair, begin to learn the new idiom. Or the difficulty that a person would have in understanding poetry, who imagined it to be prose. It is the difficulty that Aristotle or Cicero found in understanding the philosophers that were before them. They were familiar with the meaning of the words used by them, but not with the mode of thought. Logic itself had increased the difficulty to them of understanding the times before logic.

This is our own difficulty in the interpretation of Scripture. Our use of language is more definite, our abstractions more abstract, our structure more regular and logical. But the moment we perceive and allow for this difference in the use of language in Scripture and among ourselves, the difficulty vanishes. We conceive ideas in a process of formation, falling from inspired lips, growing in the minds of men. We throw ourselves into the world of 'mixed modes,' and seek to recall the associations which the technical terms of theology no longer suggest. We observe what may be termed the difference of level in our own ideas and those of the first Christians, without disturbing the meaning of one word in relation to another.

The difficulty while it is increased, is also explained by the personifying character of the age. Ideas in the New Testament are relative to the mind of God or man, in which they seem naturally to inhere so as scarcely, in the usage of language, to have an independent existence. There is ever the tendency to speak of good and virtue and righteousness as inseparable from the Divine nature, while in evil of every sort a reflection of conscience seems to be included. The words δικαιοσύνη, ἀλήθεια, ἀγάπη, are not merely equivalent to righteousness, truth, love, but connect imperceptibly with 'the Author and Father of lights.' There is no other righteousness or truth but that of God, just as there is no sin without the consciousness of sin in man. Consequently, the two thoughts coalesce in one, and what are to us ideas, which we can imagine existing even without God, are to the Israelite attributes of God Himself.

Still, in our 'mixed modes' we must make a further step; for as these ideas cannot be separated from God, so neither can they be conceived of, except as revealed in the Gospel, and working in the heart of man. Man who is righteous has no righteousness of his own, his righteousness is the righteousness of God in him. Hence, when considering the righteousness of God, we must go on to conceive of it as the revelation of His righteousness, without which it would be unknown and unmeaning to us. The abstract must become concrete, and must involve at once the attribute of God and the quality in man. This 'concrete' notion of the word righteousness is different from the abstract one with which we are familiar. Righteousness is the righteousness of God; it is also the communion of that righteousness with man. It is used almost with the same double meaning as we attribute to the will of God, which we speak of actively, as intending, doing, and passively, as done, fulfilled by ourselves.

A part of this embarrassment in the interpretation of Scripture arises out of the unconscious influence of English words and ideas on our minds, in translating from Hellenistic Greek. The difficulty is still more apparent, when the attempt is made to render the Scriptures into a language which has not been framed or moulded on Christianity. It is a curious question, the consideration of which is not without practical use, how far the nicer shades either of Scriptural expression or of later theology are capable of being made intelligible in the languages of India or China.

Yet, on the other hand, it must be remembered, that neither this nor any of the other peculiarities here spoken of, is a mere form of speech, but enters deeply into the nature of the Gospel. For the Gospel has necessarily its mixed modes, not merely because it is preached to the poor, and therefore adopts the expressions of ordinary life; nor because its language is incrusted with the phraseology of the Alexandrian writers; but because its subject is mixed, and, as it were, intermediate between God and man. Natural theology speaks clearly, but it is of God only; moral philosophy speaks clearly, but it is of man only: but the Gospel is, as it were, the communion of God and man, and its ideas are in a state of transition or oscillation, having two aspects towards God and towards man, which it is hard to keep in view at once. Thus, to quote once more the example just given, the righteousness of God is an idea not difficult for us to comprehend, human justice and goodness are also intelligible; but to conceive justice or righteousness as passing from heaven to earth, from God to man, *actu et potentiâ* at once, as a sort of life, or stream, or motion, is perplexing. And yet this notion of the communion of the righteousness of God being what constitutes righteousness, is of the very essence of the Gospel. It was what the Apostle and the first believers meant and felt, and what, if we could get the simple unlettered Christian, receiving the Gospel as a little child, to describe to us his feelings, he would describe.

Scripture language may thus be truly said to belong to an intermediate world, different at once both from the visible and invisible world, yet partaking of the nature of both. It does not represent the things that the eye sees merely, nor the things that are within the veil of which those are the images, but rather the world that is in our hearts; the things that we feel, but nobody can express in words. His body is the communion of His body; His spirit is the communion of His spirit; the love of God is 'loving as we are loved;' the knowledge of God is 'knowing as we are known;' the righteousness of faith is Divine as well as human. Hence language seems to burst its bounds in the attempt to express the different aspects of these truths, and from its very inadequacy wavers and becomes uncertain in its meaning. The more intensely we feel and believe, and the less we are able to define our feelings, the more shall we appear to use words at random; employing sometimes one mode of expression, sometimes another; passing from one thought to another, by slender threads of association; 'going off upon a word,' as it has been called; because in our own minds all is connected, and, as it were, fulfilled with itself, and from the abundance of the heart the mouth speaks. To understand the language of St. Paul it is necessary, not only to compare the uses of words with one another, or to be versed in Alexandrian modes of thought, but to lead the life of St. Paul, to have the mind of St. Paul, to be one with Christ, to be dead to sin. Otherwise the world within becomes unmeaning to us. The inversion of all human things of which he speaks, is attributed to the manner of his time, or the peculiarity of his individual character; and at the very moment when we seem to have attained most accurately the Apostle's meaning, it vanishes away like a shadow.

No human eye can pierce the cloud which overhangs another life; no faculty of man can 'by understanding find out' or express in words the Divine nature. Yet it does not follow that our ideas of spiritual things are wholly indefinite. There are many symbols and images of them in the world without and below. There is a communion of thoughts, feelings, and affections, even on earth, quite sufficient to be an image of the communion with God and Christ, of which the Epistles speak to us. There are emotions, and transitions, and passings out of ourselves, and states of undefined consciousness, which language is equally unable to express as it is to describe justification, or the work of grace, or the relation of the believer to his Lord. All these are rather intimated than described or defined by words. The sigh of sorrow, the cry of joy or despair, are but inarticulate sounds, yet expressive, beyond the power of writing, or speech. There are many such 'still small voices' of warning or of consolation in Scripture, beyond the power of philosophy to analyse, yet full of meaning to him who catches them aright. The life and force of such expressions do not depend on the clearness with which they state a logical proposition, or the vividness with which they picture to the imagination a spiritual world. They gain for themselves a truth in the individual soul. Even logic itself affords negative helps to the feebleness of man in the conception of things above him. It limits us by our own faculties; it guards us against identifying the images of things unseen with the 'very things themselves;' it bars remote inferences about terms which are really metaphorical. Lastly, it helps us to define by opposition. Though we do not know what spirit is, we know what body is, and we conceive of spirit as what body is not. 'There is a spiritual body, and there is a natural body.' We imagine it at once both like and unlike. We do not know what heaven, or the glory of God, or His wisdom, is; but we imagine them unlike this world, or the wisdom of this world, or the glory of the princes of this world, and yet, in a certain way, like them, imaged and symbolized by what we see around us. We do not know what eternity is, except as the negative of time; but believing in its real existence, in a way beyond our faculties to comprehend, we do not confine it within the limits of past, present, or future. We are unable to reconcile the power of God and the freedom of man, or the contrast of this world and another, or even the opposite feelings of our own minds about the truths of religion. But we can describe them as the Apostle has done, in a paradox (2 Cor. iv. 12; vi. 8-10).

There is yet a further way in which the ideas of Scripture may be defined, that is, by use. It has been already observed that the progress of language is from the concrete to the abstract. Not the least striking instance of this is the language of theology. Embodied in creeds, it gradually becomes developed and precise. The words are no longer 'living creatures with hands and feet,' as it were, feeling after the hearts of men; but they have one distinct, unchanging meaning. When we speak of justification or truth, no question arises whether by this is meant the attribute of God, or the quality in man. Time and usage have sufficiently circumscribed the diversities of their signification. This is not to be regarded as a misfortune to Scriptural truth, but as natural and necessary. Part of what is lost in power and life is regained in certainty and definiteness. The usage of language itself would forbid us, in a discourse or sermon, to give as many senses to the word 'law' as are attributed to it by St. Paul. Only in the interpretation of Scripture, if we would feel as St. Paul felt, or think as he thought, it is necessary to go back to that age before creeds, in which the water of life was still a running stream.

The course of speculation which has been adopted in this essay, may seem to introduce into Scripture an element of uncertainty. It may seem to cloud truth with metaphysics, and rob the poor and uneducated of the simplicity of the Gospel. But perhaps this is not so. Whether it be the case that such speculations introduce an element of uncertainty or difficulty into Scripture or not, they introduce a new element of truth. For without the consideration of such questions as that of which a brief sketch has been here attempted, there is no basis for Scriptural interpretation. We are ever liable to draw the meaning of words this way or that, according to the theological system of which we are the advocates; to fall under the slavery of an illogical logic, which first narrows the mind by definitions, and then wearies it with far-fetched inferences. Metaphysics must enter into the interpretation of Scripture, not for the sake of intruding upon it a new set of words or ideas, but with the view of getting rid of metaphysics and restoring to Scripture its natural sense.

But the Gospel is still preached to the poor as before, in the same sacred yet familiar language. They could not understand questions of grammar before; they do not understand modes of thought now. It is the peculiar nature of our religious ideas that we are able to apply them, and to receive comfort from them, without being able to analyse or explain them. All the metaphysical and logical speculations in the world will not rob the poor, the sick, or the dying of the truths of the Gospel. Yet the subject which we have been considering is not without a practical result. It warns us to restore the Gospel to its simplicity, to turn from the letter to the spirit, to withdraw from the number of the essentials of Christianity points almost too subtle for the naked eye, which depend on modes of thought or Alexandrian usages, to require no more of preciseness or definition than is necessary to give form and substance to our teaching. Not only the feebleness of human faculties, but the imperfection of language itself will often make silence our truest wisdom. The saying of Scaliger, taken not seriously but in irony, is full of meaning: 'Many a man has missed of his salvation from ignorance of grammar.'

To the poor and uneducated, at times to all, no better advice can be given for the understanding of Scripture than to read the Bible humbly with prayer. The critical and metaphysical student requires another sort of rule for which this can never be made a substitute. His duty is to throw himself back into the times, the modes of thought, the language of the Apostolic age. He must pass from the abstract to the concrete, from the ideal and intellectual to the spiritual, from later statements of faith or doctrine to the words of inspiration which fell from the lips of the first believers. He must seek to conceive the religion of Christ in its relation to the religions of other ages and distant countries, to the philosophy of our own or other times; and if in this effort his mind seems to fail or waver, he must win back in life and practice the hold on the truths of the Gospel which he is beginning to lose in the mazes of speculation.

ESSAY

ON

ST. PAUL AND THE TWELVE

GALATIANS II.

EVENTS of the greatest importance in the annals of mankind are not always seen to be important, until the hour for preserving them is past. There is a time before biography passes into history, when a society has not yet learned to register its acts, and individuals have not awoke to the consciousness of national or ecclesiastical life. In this intermediate period, events the most fruitful in results may lie buried (the unfolding of the germ in the bosom of the earth is not the least part of the growth of the plant); they may also be reproduced in a new form and their spirit misunderstood by the imperfect knowledge of after-ages. Two or three centuries elapse; documents are lost or tampered with, or confused; there is no eye of criticism to penetrate their meaning. The historian has 'the veil upon his face' of a later generation; he cannot see through the events, institutions, opinions in the circle of which he lives. Who can tell what went on in a 'large upper room' about the year 40? which may, nevertheless, have had great consequences for the world and the Church. Who, when Christianity was triumphant in the fourth century, would comprehend the simple ways and thoughts of believers in the first? Nor is there anything more likely to be misunderstood, than the differences between the first teachers of a religion, and the disputes of their respective followers, about a matter of discipline or doctrine which has passed away. The transition may be too gradual to be observed while it is going on. Literature is of a later date ; beginning when the Church has already arrived at its full stature, it cannot describe the stages of its infancy and growth. In the extreme distance the objects of earth are no longer distinguishable from the clouds of heaven.

All history receives a colour from the age in which it is written. This is the case with Ecclesiastical history even more than secular ; it glows with the faith and feelings of the historian; it reflects his principles or convictions—it is sometimes embittered by his prejudices. Eusebius, 'the father of Ecclesiastical history,' believing as he did that the constitution of the Church which he saw around him had existed from the first, was not likely to give a consistent account of its origin or growth. Nor was it to be expected that he should trace the history of doctrines, who, within the Church at least, could have admitted of no doctrinal difference or development. It was impossible for him to describe that of which he had no conception. Had he been disposed to write an accurate account of the progress of the Christian faith in the first two centuries, the scantiness of his materials would have prevented him from doing so. The antiquarian spirit had awoke too late to recover the treasures of the past. Those who preceded him had a similar though less definite impression of the first age, of which they knew so little, and wrote in the same way. It would be an anachronism to expect that he should sift critically the few cases in which the earlier authorities witness against themselves. In point of judgement, he is about on a level with the other 'Father of History ;' that is to say, he is not wholly destitute of critical power : yet his criticism is accidental and capricious ; most often observable in the case of Ecclesiastical writings, which his literary tastes led him to explore. But real historical investigation is unknown to him. No resisting power of inquiry prevents his acceptance of any facts which fell in with the orthodox faith of his age, or seemed to afford a witness to it. Miracles are believed by him, not upon greater, but upon rather less evidence than ordinary events. He catches, like Herodotus, at any chance similarity, such as that between the first Christians and the Therapeutae of Egypt (ii. c. 17). He feels no difficulty in receiving the statement of Justin Martyr, that Simon Magus was honoured at Rome under the title of the Holy God (Semo Sancus); or the testimony of Tertullian, that the Emperor Tiberius referred the worship of Christ to the senate. He sees the whole history of the Church through the medium of that victory over Paganism and heresy which he had witnessed in his own day. He carries the struggle back into the previous centuries, in which he finds almost nothing else but the conflict of the truth with heresy, and the blood of martyrs the seed of the Church. No one can suppose that the heresiarchs were such as he describes them, or that he has truly seized the relation in which they stood to the primitive Church. The language in which he denounces them is a sufficient evidence that he could not have investigated with calmness the character of the 'wolf of Pontus,' or the false prophet Montanus and his 'reptile' followers. Though living at a distance of a century and a half, he repeats and adopts the conventional abuse of their contemporary adversaries.

Records of the earliest heretics have passed away; no one of them is fairly known to us from his own writings. Their names have become a by-word among men; at another tribunal we may believe that many judgements passed upon them have been reversed. The true history of the century which followed the withdrawal of the Apostles has also perished, or is preserved only in fragmentary statements. It is a matter of conjecture how the constitution of the

Church arose; it is a parallel speculation, out of what simpler elements the earliest liturgies were compiled. But it does not follow that nothing happened in an age of which we know nothing. The least philosophy of history suggests the reflection that in the primitive Church there must have existed all the varieties of practice, belief, speculation, doctrine, which the different circumstances of the converts, and the different natures of men acting on those circumstances, would be likely to produce. The Church acquired unity in its progress through the world; it was more scattered and undisciplined at first than it afterwards became. Even the Apostles do not work together in the spirit of an order; they and their followers are not an army 'set under authority,' of which the leaders say to one man 'come, and he cometh,' and to another 'go, and he goeth.' The Church of the Apostles may be compared more truly to 'the wind blowing where it listeth,' or even to 'the lightning shining from one part of the heaven to the other.' Paul and Barnabas and Apollos, and even Priscilla and Aquila, have their separate ways of acting; they walk in different paths; they do not attempt to control one another. Whatever caution is observable in their mode of dealing with each other's spheres of labour is a matter of courtesy, not of ecclesiastical discipline. It is not certain, perhaps on the whole improbable, that those who came from James to Antioch (Gal. ii. 12) represented the community at Jerusalem. There is no Church which claims to be the metropolis of other Churches; nor any subordination within the several Churches to a single authority. The words of the Epistle to the Ephesians (iv. 11), 'He gave some apostles, and some prophets, and some evangelists, and some pastors and teachers,' are hardly reconcilable either with three orders of clergy, or with the distinction of clergy and laity. They describe a state of the Church in which there was less of system and more of impulse than at a later period; in which 'all the Lord's people were prophets,' and natural or spiritual gifts became offices 'in the beginning of the Gospel.' Compare Rom. xii. 6 : 1 Cor. xii. 28, 29.

Many doubts and possibilities arise in our minds respecting the age of the Apostles when we look on the picture 'through a microscope,' and dwell on those points which are commonly unnoticed. We are tempted to frame theories and reconstructions, which are better, perhaps, represented by queries. Did those who remained behind in the Church regard the death of the martyr Stephen with the same feelings as those who were scattered abroad ? or was he in their eyes only what James the Just appeared to be to the historian Josephus ? Were the Apostles at Jerusalem one in heart with the brethren at Antioch ? Were the teachers who came from Jerusalem to Antioch saying, 'Except ye be circumcised, ye cannot be saved,' commissioned by the Twelve ? Were the Twelve absolutely at one among themselves ? Are the 'commendatory epistles' spoken of in the Epistle to the Corinthians, to be ascribed to the Apostles at Jerusalem ? Can 'the grievous wolves,' whose entrance into the Church of Ephesus the Apostle foresaw, be other than the Judaizing teachers? Were 'the multitude' of believing Jews, who were all zealous for the law, and liable to be quickened in their zeal for it by the very sight of St. Paul, engaged in the tumult which follows ? Lastly, how far does the narrative of the Acts convey the lively impression of contemporaries, how far the recollections of another generation ? These questions cannot have detailed answers ; to raise them, however, is not without use, for they make us regard the facts in many points of view ; they afford a help in the prosecution of the main inquiry, 'What was the relation of St. Paul to the Twelve?'

If we conceive of the Apostles as exercising a strict and definite rule over the multitude of their converts, living heads of the Church as they might be termed, Peter or James of the circumcision and Paul of the uncircumcision, it would be natural to connect them with the acts of their followers.

One would think that, in accordance with the spirit of the concordat, they should have 'delivered over to Satan' the opponents of St. Paul, rather than have lived in communion and company with them. To hold out the right hand of fellowship to Paul and Barnabas, and yet secretly to support or not to discountenance their enemies, would seem to be treachery to their common Master. Especially when we observe how strongly the Judaizers are characterized by St. Paul as 'the false brethren who came in unawares,' 'the false Apostles transforming themselves into Apostles of Christ,' 'grievous wolves entering in,' and with what bitter personal weapons they assailed him (1 Cor. ix. 3–7). Indeed, the contrast between the vehemence with which St. Paul treats his Judaizing antagonists, and the gentleness or silence which he preserves towards the Apostles at Jerusalem, is a remarkable circumstance.

It may be questioned whether the whole difficulty does not arise from a false conception of the authority of the Apostles in the early Church. Although the first teachers of the word of Christ, they were not the rulers of the Catholic Church; they were not its bishops, but its prophets. The influence which they exercised was personal rather than official, derived doubtless from their 'having seen the Lord,' and from their appointment by Him, yet confined also to a comparatively narrow sphere; it was exercised in places in which they were, but hardly extended to places where they were not. The Gospel grew up around them they could not tell how; and the spirit which their preaching first awakened passed out of their control. They seemed no longer to be the prime movers, but rather the spectators of the work of God, which went on before their eyes. The thousands of Jews that believed and were zealous for the law would not lay aside the garb of Judaism at the bidding of James or Peter; the false teachers of Corinth or of Ephesus would not have been less likely to gain followers, had they been excommunicated by the Twelve.

The movement which, in twenty years from the death of Christ, had spread so widely over the earth, they did not seek to reduce to rule and compass. It was beyond their reach, extending to communities of the circumstances of which they were hardly informed, and in which, therefore, it was not to be expected that they should interfere between St. Paul and his opponents.

The Apostolic name acquired a sacredness in the second century which was unknown to it in the first. We must not attribute either to the persons or to the writings of the Apostles the authority with which after-ages invested them. No Epistle of James and Paul was received by those to whom it was sent, like the Scriptures of the Old Testament, as the Word of God. Nor are they quoted in the same manner with books of the Old Testament before the time of Irenaeus. We might have imagined that every Church would have preserved an unmistakable record of its lineage and descent from some one of the Twelve. But so far is this from being the case, that no connexion can be traced certainly, between the Gentile Churches of the second century and that of Jerusalem in the first. Jerusalem was not the metropolis of all Churches, but one among many; acknowledged, indeed, by the Gentile Christians with affection and gratitude, but not prescribing any rule, or exercising authority over them.

The moment we think of the Church, not as an ecclesiastical or political institution, but, as it was in the first age, a spiritual body, that is to say, a body partly moved by the Spirit of God, dependent also on the tempers and sympathies of men swayed to and fro by religious emotion, the perplexity solves itself, and the narrative of Scripture becomes truthful and natural. When the waves are high, we see but a little way over the ocean. The first fervour of religious feeling does not admit a uniform level of Church government. It is not a regular hierarchy, but 'some apostles, some prophets, some evangelists, others pastors and teachers,' who grow together 'into the body of Christ.' The description of the early Church in the Epistles everywhere implies a great freedom of individual action. Apollos and Barnabas are not under the guidance of Paul; those 'who were distinguished among the Apostles before him,' could hardly have owned his authority. No attempt is made to bring the different Churches under a common system. We cannot imagine any bond by which they could have been linked together, without an order of clergy or form of Church government common to them all; this is not to be found in the New Testament. It was hard to keep the Church at Corinth at unity with itself; it would have been still harder to have brought it into union with other Churches.

Of this fluctuating state of the Church, which was not yet addicted to any one rule, we find another indication in the freedom, almost levity, with which professing Christians embraced 'traditions of men.' The attitude of the Church of Corinth towards the Apostle was not that of believers in a faith 'once delivered to the saints.' We know not whether Apollos was or was not a teacher of Alexandrian learning among its members, or what was the exact nature of 'the party of Christ,' 1 Cor. i. 12. But that heathen as well as Jewish elements had found their way into the Corinthian community, is intimated by the 'false wisdom,' and the sitting at meat in the idol's temple. It is a startling question which is addressed to a Christian Church: 'How say some among you that there is no resurrection?' (1 Cor. xv. 12). It is not less startling that there should have been fornication among them, such as was not even named among the Gentiles. In the Church at Colossae again something was suspected by the Apostle, probably half Jewish and half heathen in its character, which he designates by the singular expression of a 'voluntary humility and worshipping of angels.' And mention is made in the Roman Church of those who preached Christ of envy and strife, as well as those who preached Christ of peace and goodwill (Phil i. 15).

Amid such fluctuation and unsettlement of opinions we can imagine Paul and Apollos, or Paul and Peter, preaching side by side in the Church of Corinth or of Antioch, like Wesley and Whitfield in the last century, or Luther and Calvin at the Reformation, with a sincere reverence for each other, not abstaining from commenting on or condemning each other's doctrine or practice, and yet also forgetting their differences in their common zeal to save the souls of men. Personal regard is quite consistent with differences of religious belief; some of which, with good men, are a kind of form belonging only to their outer nature, most of which, as we hope, exist only on this side of the grave. We can imagine the followers of such men incapable of acting in their noble spirit, with a feebler sense of their high calling, and a stronger one of their points of disagreement; losing the principle for which they were alike contending in 'oppositions of knowledge,' in prejudice and personality. And lastly, we may conceive the disciples of Wesley or of Whitfield (for of the Apostles themselves we forbear to move the question) reacting upon their masters and drawing them into the vicious circle of controversy, disuniting them in their lives, though incapable of making a separation between them.

A subject so wide is matter not for an essay but for a book; it is the history of the Church of the first two centuries. We must therefore narrow our field of vision as much as possible, and content ourselves with collecting a few general facts which have a bearing on our present inquiry.

First among these general facts, is the ignorance of the third and fourth centuries respecting the first, and earlier half of the second. We cannot err in supposing that those who could add nothing to what is recorded in the New Testament of the life of Christ and His Apostles, had no real knowledge of lesser matters, as, for example, the origin of Episcopacy. They could not understand, they were incapable of preserving the memory of a state of the Church which was unlike their own. The contemporaries of the Apostles have nothing to tell of their lives and fortunes; the next generation is also silent; in the third generation the license of conjecture is already rife. No fact worth mentioning can be gathered from the writings of the Apostolical Fathers. Irenaeus, who lived about fifty years later, and within a century of St. Paul, has not added a single circumstance to what we gather from the New Testament; he has fallen into the well-known error of supposing that our Lord was fifty years old at the time of His ministry; he has stated also that 'Papias was John's hearer, and the associate of Polycarp,' though Papias himself, in the preface to his discourses, by no means asserts that he was 'hearer and eyewitness of the holy Apostles' (Euseb. *H. E.* iii. 39); he has repeated, as a discourse of Christ's, the fable of Papias respecting the bunches of grapes; this he would have literally interpreted. Justin, who was somewhat earlier than Irenaeus, has given a measure of the knowledge and criticism of his own age in the story of Simon Magus. Tertullian, at the close of the next century, believed that the emperor Tiberius had consulted the Roman senate respecting the worship of our Lord (Euseb. *H. E.* ii. 2). Eusebius himself verified from the Archives of Edessa the fabulous correspondence of Abgarus and Jesus, and the miraculous narrative which follows (*H. E.* i. 13). In at least half the instances in which we are able to test his quotations from earlier writers, they exhibit some degree of inaccuracy or confusion. It is hard to believe the statement of Polycrates of Ephesus (about A.D. 180), that 'John, who rested on the bosom of the Lord, was a priest, and bore the sacerdotal plate' (Euseb. *H. E.* iii. 32), or that Philip the Evangelist was one of the Twelve Apostles. But what use can be made of such sandy

ST. PAUL AND THE TWELVE 377

materials? It is idle to have recourse to remote reconcilements when the facts themselves are uncertain; equally so to argue precisely from turns of expression where language is rhetorical.

The second general fact is the unconsciousness of this ignorance, and the readiness with which the vacant space is filled up, and the Church of the second century assimilated to that of the third and fourth. History often conceals that which is discordant to preconceived notions; silently dropping some facts, exaggerating others, adding, where needed, new tone and colouring, until the disguise can no longer be detected. By some process of this kind the circumstance into which we are inquiring has been forgotten and reproduced. Nothing has survived relating to the great crisis which Christianity underwent in the age of the Apostles themselves; it passed away silently in the altered state of the Church and the world. Not only in the strange account of the dispute between the Apostles, given by Origen and others, is what may be termed the 'animus' of concealment discernible, but in fragments of earlier writings, in which the two Apostles appear side by side as co-founders of the Corinthian, as well as of the Roman Church (Caius and Dion. of Corinth, quoted by Euseb., ii. 25), pleading their cause together before Nero; dying on the same day, their graves being appealed to as witnesses to the tale, probably as early as the first half of the second century. The unconscious motive which gave birth to such fictions was, seemingly, the desire to throw a veil over that occasion on which they withstood one another to the face. And the truth indistinctly shines through this legend of the latter part of the second century, when it is further recorded that St. Paul was at the head of the Gentile Church at Rome, Peter of the circumcision.

Bearing in mind these general considerations, which throw a degree of doubt on the early ecclesiastical tradition, and lead us to seek for indications out of the regular course of history, we have to consider, in reference to our present subject, the following statements:—

1. That Justin, who is recorded to have written against Marcion, refers to the Twelve in several passages, but nowhere in his genuine writings mentions St. Paul. And when speaking of the books read in the Christian assemblies, he names only the Gospels and the Prophets *Apol.* i. 67).

2. That Marcion, who was nearly contemporary with Justin, is said to have appealed to the authority of St. Paul only.

(On the other hand, it is true that in numerous quotations from the Old Testament, Justin appears to follow St. Paul. It is difficult to account for this singular phenomenon.)

3. That in the account of James the Just, given by Josephus and Hegesippus (about A.D. 170), he is represented as a Jew among Jews; living, according to Hegesippus, the life of a Nazarite; praying in the Temple until his knees became hard as a camel's, and so entirely a Jew as to be unknown to the people for a Christian; a description which, though its features may be exaggerated, yet has the trace of a true resemblance to the part which we find him acting in the Epistle to the Galatians. It falls in, too, with the fact of his peaceable continuance as head of the Church at Jerusalem, in the Acts of the Apostles; and is not inconsistent with the spirit of the Epistle which bears his name. (Comp. Euseb. ii. 23.)

4. That the same Hegesippus regards the heresies as arising out of schism in the Jewish Church. He was himself a Hebrew convert; and after stating that he travelled to Rome, whither he went by way of Corinth, and had familiar conversation with many bishops, he declares 'that in every succession and in every city the doctrine prevails according to what is declared by the law and the prophets and the Lord' (Euseb. iv. 22). This is not the language of a follower of St. Paul.

5. That in the Clementine Homilies, written about the year 160, though a work generally orthodox, St. Paul is covertly introduced under the name of Simon Magus, as the impersonation of Gnostic error, as the enemy who had pretended 'visions and revelations,' and who 'withstood' and blamed Peter. No writer doubts the allusion in some of these passages to the Epistles of St. Paul. Assuming their connexion, we ask, What was the state of mind which led an orthodox Christian, who lived probably at Rome, about the middle of the second century, to affix such a character to St. Paul? and what was the motive which induced him to veil his meaning? What, too, could have been the state of the Church in which such a romance grew up? and how could the next generation have read it without perceiving its true aim? Doubtful as may be the precise answer to these questions, we cannot attribute this remarkable work to the wayward fancy of an individual; it is an indication of a real tendency of the first and second centuries, at a time when the flame was almost extinguished, but still slumbered in the mind of the writer of the Clementine Homilies. It is observable that at a later date, about the year 210–230, in the form which the work afterwards received under the title of 'the Clementine Recognitions,' which have been preserved in a Latin translation, the objectionable passages have mostly vanished.

6. Lastly, that in later writings we find no trace of the mind of St. Paul. His influence seems to pass from the world. On such a basis 'as where the Spirit of the Lord is, there is liberty,' it might have been impossible to rear the fabric of a hierarchy. But the thought itself was not present to the next generation. The tide of ecclesiastical feeling set in another direction. It was not merely that after-writers fell short of St. Paul, or imperfectly interpreted him, but that they formed themselves on a different model. It was not only that the external constitution of the Church had received a definite form and shape, but that the inward

perception of the nature of the Gospel was different. No writer of the latter half of the second century would have spoken as St. Paul has done of the law, of the sabbath, of justification by faith only, of the Spirit, of grace, of moderation in things indifferent, of forgiveness. An echo of a part of his teaching is heard in Augustine; with this exception, the voice of him who withstood Peter to the face at Antioch was silent in the Church until the Reformation. The spirit of the Epistles to the Romans and to the Galatians has revived in later times. But there is no trace that the writings of the Apostle left any lasting impress within the Church, or perhaps anywhere in the first ages.

Yet the principle of the Apostle triumphed, though at the time of its triumph it may seem to have lost the spirit and power of the Apostle. The struggle which commenced like Athanasius against the world, ended as the struggle of the world against the remnant of the Jewish race. Beginning within the confines of Judea, it spread in a widening circle among the Jewish proselytes, still wider and more faintly marked in the philojudaizing Gentile, fading in the distance as Christianity became a universal religion. Two events had a great influence on its progress. First, the destruction of Jerusalem, and the flight to Pella of the Christian community; secondly, the revolt under Barchocab; both tending to separate, more and more, both in fact and the opinion of mankind, the Christian from the Jew.

It would be vain to carry our inquiry further, with the view of gleaning a few results respecting the first half of the second century. Remote probabilities and isolated facts are not worth balancing. The consciousness that we know little of the times which followed the Apostles is the best part of our knowledge. And many will deem it well for the purity of the Christian faith, that while Christ Himself is clearly seen by us—as a light, at the fountain of which a dead Church may receive life, and a living one renew its strength—the origin of ecclesiastical institutions has been hidden from our eyes. In the second and third centuries Christianity was extending its borders, fencing itself with creeds and liturgies, taking possession of the earth with its hierarchy. Whether this great organization was originally everywhere the same, whether it adopted the form chiefly of the Jewish worship and ministry or of the Roman magistracy, or at first of the one and afterwards of the other, cannot be certainly determined. A cloud hangs over the dawn of ecclesiastical history. By some course of events with which we are not acquainted, the Providence of God leading the way, and the thoughts of man following, the Jewish Synagogue became the Christian Church; the Passover was superseded by Easter; the Christian Sunday took the place of the Jewish Sabbath. While the Old Testament retained its authority over Gentile as well as Jewish Christians, the law was done away in Christ, and the Judaizer of the first century became the Ebionitish heretic of the second and third.

ESSAY

ON

ST. PAUL AND PHILO

'Canst thou speak Greek?' (Acts xxi. 37). 'Men and brethren, I am a Pharisee, the son of a Pharisee' (Acts xxiii. 6), 'brought up in this city at the feet of Gamaliel, and taught according to the perfect way of the law of the Fathers' (Acts xxii. 3).

CHRISTIANITY admits of being regarded either from within or from without. We may begin with our own hearts, with the study of the word of God, with the received views which have grown up within the sphere of the Christian Church; or we may place ourselves without that sphere, and look upon Christianity under the aspect which it presented to the contemporaries of Seneca or Pliny; which it continues to present to the eye of the secular historian. Those who take this latter course are sometimes said to put themselves in a false position, which has no rest or stability, until the heavenly is all brought down to the level of the earthly, and the narrative of Scripture has passed into a merely secular chronicle. The Gospel is thought to lose its sacredness when explained by secondary causes or brought into contact with ordinary events. This feeling has been strengthened by the circumstance that, of the age which immediately preceded Christianity in the land where it arose, so slight a record has been preserved to us. For the first century the Gospel stands in no relation to the contemporary history even of the Jews themselves. There is a circle of light around the forms of Christ and His Apostles; while the world, in reference to our knowledge of it, lies in darkness. Naturally, we make no attempt to supply what may be termed 'the blank leaves between the Old and New Testament,' by gathering together a few doubtful fragments; while the Christian era furnishes a new beginning, to go beyond which seems like asking 'what preceded the creation.'

Nevertheless, the really false and artificial position is not that which unites, but that which separates Christianity from the world in general.

As the 'new man' is not altogether different from the old, but retains many elements of the same character, so did the Christian world retain many elements of the Jewish and heathen world which preceded it. As in ages that we know, the earthly and the heavenly, the Church and the world, have ever been mingled together, both within and without us, so in the first age with which we are acquainted only from the record of Scripture itself, 'the wheat and the tares' were growing together; false and true brethren met together in the same Church. Nor must we confine the connexion of cause and effect to mere historical events, such as the fall of Jerusalem or the extension or decay of the Roman Empire; or to the political influences which more immediately affected the infant Communion. There is a sequence of thoughts as well, by which age is bound to age; and that which in one generation is 'sown in corruption' is in the next 'raised in incorruption;' scattered fragments unite into an harmonious whole; what was barren speculation once, becomes a practical rule of life; forms of thought spiritualize themselves; language dead for ages awakens into life.

When, turning away from the heavenly origin of Christianity, we trace the first steps of its earthly progress, we cannot avoid putting the question to ourselves, how it was made intelligible to the minds of Jews, who had been trained in a religion and way of thinking so different from it. The difficulty is analogous to that which our own missionaries experience in attempting to explain to the Chinese or the American Indians the nature of God. Their language has no words to express what is meant, or only words the associations of which confuse or mislead. We sometimes imagine that preaching the Gospel among the heathen only means persuading men who have the same minds with ourselves to be of the same opinions with us; more truly, the work which we have to do is nothing short of creating their minds anew. Now the same difficulty must have pressed upon the first teachers of the Gospel. Where did they find words in which to express themselves? How was the interval spanned which separated not only different nations, but different races of mankind? Whence came the forms of speech and modes of thought which, for nearly eighteen centuries, have been the symbols and landmarks of Christian theology? Some of them are derived from the Old Testament, but many are peculiar to the New; and those which are common to both often receive a new turn of signification in the Christian use of them, which needs explanation.

The answer may be gathered, to a great extent, from the Jewish Alexandrian philosophy. There the missing link is found supplied; we see that the Greek and Hebrew mind had already bridged the chasm that separated them, and that before the times of our Lord and His Apostles the Greek language had been forced into the service of Jewish thoughts. Persons have sometimes spoken of modern civilization including in itself two elements, a Greek and a Semitic one; but the fusion between them is not of modern or Christian origin; it dates further back, to the period of Alexander's conquests. After the establishment of the Greek kingdom of Alexander's successors, Greek became a familiar language, not only in Asia and Egypt, but also in Judea. The Jew

ST. PAUL AND PHILO

in other countries, who spoke and wrote in Greek, was not cut off from intercourse with his Palestine brethren, and new ideas and opinions readily passed from one to the other. But Alexandria was the centre of the fusion; there the Jew and the Greek may be said to have mingled minds; the books of Moses and the prophets and the dialectic of Plato and Aristotle met together, giving birth to the strangest eclectic philosophy that the world has ever seen. This philosophy was Judaism and Platonism at once; the belief in a personal God assimilated to the doctrine of ideas.

Philo, the only philosopher of this school whose works have come down to us, except in fragments, fortunately lived at a time which renders them peculiarly valuable for the purpose of our inquiry. According to the tradition of the Rabbis, he is said to have flourished about a hundred years before the destruction of the temple. But his own writings give us the date more precisely; as, from the *Legatio ad Caium*, in which he describes himself as an old man at the time of writing (ἡμεῖς οἱ γέροντες τὰ μὲν σώματα χρόνου μήκει πολιοί, Mangey, ii. 545), it appears that he went on an embassy to Rome in the hope of gaining the protection of the emperor Caligula for the persecuted Jews of Alexandria, and was at Rome at the time the emperor attempted to place his statue in the temple at Jerusalem (Mangey, ii. 573); also between the years 39 A.D., the date of the German victory to which he makes allusion (Mangey, ii. 598), and 41, which was the year of Caligula's death. He refers, moreover, to a circumstance which happened under Claudius (ii. 576), thus showing that the date of the composition of his work, though seemingly not long after, is not absolutely contemporary. His other writings—with the exception of the *Contra Flaccum*, which seems to describe the same state of continuous persecution among the Alexandrian Jews, and may have been written about the same time—are probably earlier than the *Legatio ad Caium*.

Thus we see that in reading Philo we are on the edge of

Christianity. Philo might have seen and spoken with our Lord, and possibly did so in the visit to the temple which he mentions (Mangey, ii. 646). Were it not for the distance between Alexandria and Judea, we should say that he must have breathed the same air, and been educated in the same belief and ways of thought, as the first disciples. He would have been just what Apollos of Alexandria was before his conversion, 'an eloquent man, learned in the Scriptures.' Nor is there any reason to doubt that the speculations of Alexandria and a knowledge of the Greek language had been transplanted to Judea. The traditions of Judaism expressly speak of Greek learning being cultivated in some of the Rabbinical schools. The coincidences between Philo and St. Paul and St. John are another evidence that such must have been the case. For how did these coincidences arise? Either by Philo copying from St. Paul, which is refuted by dates; or (to omit the case of St. Paul and St. John copying from Philo, as not worth considering) by the circumstance of their living in a common atmosphere and using a common language.

Philosophy has been sometimes regarded as the free effort of the human mind towards the attainment of truth by abstract ideas. Nothing could less truly describe the character of the Alexandrian school, which was the creation of circumstances, predestined from its birth to be what it was. It had no capacity of resisting new thoughts, from whatever source they were intruded. The therapeute of Alexandria could no more disengage himself from the worship of ideas than the Greek of Homer's time from the Greek mythology. Some plastic power reproduced in his mind the impressions which he received. No one asked, Is this reasonable, is this consistent, is there any proof of this? Every influence mingled and was reflected. The age was over-educated for its natural force. It was an age of imitation, the literature of which displayed no true feeling or creative power, and had no grasp of history or of life. Never perhaps has there existed another age, with so much apparent cultivation, so utterly a stranger to the first principles of knowledge.

This philosophy received a peculiar character from its connexion with Judaism. As in later times the Christian Fathers, when they passed beyond the immediate circle of Christianity, awoke to the fact that God had not left Himself without a witness, even in the writings of Greek philosophers; so too the Jew of Alexandria, first coming into contact with the stores of heathen wisdom, 'the good, the beautiful, and the true,' could not fail of receiving a more than transient impression from them. But in such a mind the difficulty arose—Whence had these men such wisdom? The received answer with Philo was that they had it from Moses himself. Plato, Aristotle, Socrates, were implicitly contained in the Pentateuch; nay, they are even blamed for not acknowledging the source whence they derived their wisdom. Moses himself 'at an early age attained the very summits of philosophy' (Philo, *De Creat. Mund.* c. 2), or, in the language of Scripture, was 'learned in all the wisdom of the Egyptians.'

The great instrument whereby Greek philosophy was brought into harmony with the Jewish Scriptures was allegorical interpretation. When the belief in the Greek mythology began to wax dim, two means were taken to give the semblance of reality to the dreams of the past. First, they were allegorized; secondly, they were rationalized. From the second of these methods, supposing it could have been applied to the Hebrew Scriptures, the mind of the Israelite would have turned away with disgust. But the first of them was just suited to his fancy; even his reverence for the letter of Scripture tended to foster rather than to discourage it. For what unknown mysteries might he not expect to find there? What wonder if God spake not to His servant Moses as one man speaks to another? It was not to be expected that the divine language should

be easy and intelligible; rather it might be imagined that
a labyrinth of truths would lurk behind every numeral or
particle. The whole system of Philo may be described as
rhetoric turned logic; ignorant of the true nature of language, presuming on its accuracy, allowing nothing for its
uncertainty and irregularity, he infers endless consequences
from trivial expressions. ' 'He says this, he does not say
that;' therefore some false and far-fetched deduction is to
be drawn. 'His expressions are the most perfect that can
be conceived, yet how do they fall short of his thought!'
'Everywhere there are marks of design, in the structure of
sentences no less than in the creation of the world.' 'It
cannot be supposed that an inspired writer would use one
word instead of another without good reason.' The worst
extravagances of mystical interpretation among the Fathers,
combined with the most tedious platitudes of a modern
sermon, will convey an idea of the manner in which Philo
'improves' Scripture.

The system of Philo is at once mystical and logical.
Mysticism is the end, logic is the means, if, indeed, that
can be termed logic which is absolutely devoid of the first
principles of reasoning. Or rather, perhaps, logic is only
the method which mysticism pursues ('though this be madness, yet there's method in it'). Philo is a kind of prophet,
as well as a rhetorician. He himself regarded the allegorical
interpretation as a sort of secondary inspiration with which
he was gifted; he had often felt its power in composition,
when, as he tells us, new ideas came into his mind, he
knew not how or whence. 'He was empty and became
full; thoughts rained into his soul from above; he was in
a trance, and had a flow of interpretation, and an enjoyment
of light' (i. 441; compare also i. 144). Those who partook
of the same gift were ἱεροί, καθαροί, μύσται (i. 147); he
exhausts in their praises all the terms which the heathen
applied to the initiated. A select few only were thus inspired; unlike 'to the poor the Gospel is preached,' τῶν

ἀγελαίων οὐδείς, says Philo, τῆς ἀληθοῦς ζωῆς κεκοινώνηκε (no common man hath part in the true life). But the allegorical interpretation was also a dialectical and traditional art. As the Patristical explanations of Scripture were under a kind of authority, as in our own interpretations of the Book of Revelation a certain uniformity may be observed notwithstanding the many discrepancies of detail, so the allegory of Philo was not without a settled principle. He himself speaks of τοὺς τῆς ἀλληγορίας κανόνας (the canons of allegory). Its first symbols, such as the sun for reason, or the tree of the knowledge of good and evil, were such as the common sense of all men, or the text itself, naturally suggested. In after-times they were neither natural nor arbitrary, but fixed by use and the authority of eminent teachers. The interpretation of them, like the interpretation of tongues in the New Testament, was a religious service. Philo speaks of the Essenes in Palestine, and the Therapeutae in the neighbourhood of the lake Moeris (ii. 458, 475), as meeting together on the Sabbath day, and above all on the Sabbath of Sabbaths, to interpret the law in its hidden sense. The Therapeutae had 'compilations of ancient men,' out of which they taught the allegorical method, and hymns which formed a part of the worship. Philo's own writings are a sufficient indication that new discoveries were not excluded. He reads the Book of the Law like a hieroglyph containing endless symbols hard to be understood, in which one sign has many meanings, and many signs are applied to the same truth.

Yet, as we wander in this labyrinth of folly, another aspect of his works must not be altogether forgotten. It is true that there is no puerility which may not be extracted from them; no exaggeration of fact or language which may not be found in Philo's pages. Even in his two historical treatises, it is hard to place confidence in his statements. And still he leaves the impression upon us of a great and good man. His whole life is a perseverance in philosophy, from which he is only called away to plead the cause of his suffering countrymen ; his precepts everywhere breathe the spirit of the purest, almost of an ascetic morality ; and in many respects he may be favourably contrasted with Plato. Unlike the Athenian philosopher, he everywhere preserves the sense of the feebleness of the human intellect in the pursuit of truth ; and he has far juster notions of the relation of man to God, and of social and family life. In point of literary merit it would be idle to compare them ; the golden age of Greece has nothing in common with 'the dregs' of Alexandria. Yet Philo, notwithstanding his intensely rhetorical tendency, is far from having lost all traces even of true dignity of style. His great object was certainly a noble one—to enlighten his own nation, and in some degree the Gentile world, respecting the nature of the Jewish religion, read as it could only be read in Alexandria, by the light of Greek learning, and adapted to the moral ideas of his own age. If discarding the method we regard only the end, Philo will stand high among ethical teachers.

His writings include nearly a complete series of commentaries on the Book of the Law. No other books form the subject of any of his separate works. Many are not even mentioned by him ; the few that are mentioned supplying but a small number of quotations, not perhaps more than one in twenty, compared with the books of Moses. It is not certain that Philo excluded any of our received books from the Canon of Scripture ; but neither is there any proof that the idea of the Canon was known to him at all. In repeating the famous narrative of the LXX (ii. 139), he confines the miracle to the Pentateuch. The prophets are commonly quoted by him in a singular manner, with the introduction, εἶπέ τις τῶν πάλαι προφητῶν, or τις τῶν φοιτητῶν Μωύσεως. Their words are chiefly used in illustration, and not made the basis of allegorical interpretations. Taking these circumstances together, it seems probable that in the view of Philo the law stood on a different footing from other writings of the Old Testament, though it does not follow that he drew any explicit distinction between them.

The inquiry tends to throw a favourable light on the mystical interpretation of the early Christian Fathers. For the utmost that can be said against them is, that they were on a level with their age, and did not shake off the scholastic trammels in which they had been brought up. The allegorical method was as natural in their day as the devotional or critical in our own. It had existed four centuries before them: it seemed to be the only means of making use of the Old Testament Scriptures. If from time to time they are found making extravagant suppositions to support a favourite theory, playing with words, numbers, or colours, reading the Old Testament backwards, that they may absolutely identify it with the New, we may compare them first with Philo, secondly with ourselves. (1) They occasionally allegorize numbers; he, it may be said, never misses the opportunity: they in a few instances supersede the historical meaning; he can scarcely be said to allow the historical meaning to stand at all. The difference, though one of degree, is yet so great as to be also a difference in kind. That the Fathers were great critics will not be maintained; but they were almost as far as any modern historian from the dreamy, inconsecutive apprehension of historical facts which we find in Philo, who is as entirely devoid of the historical sense as an Indian philosopher. In another point of view, Philo may be regarded as a witness in their favour, inasmuch as his writings show the extraordinary power which in that age the allegorical system exercised in the world. It seems as if mankind, after being raised above things of sense by the progress of the human mind, relapsed again into the world of sense; and, instead of gathering the true lesson from them, sought to find in individual objects the conductors to an invisible world. From this influence, the Fathers, in a great degree, freed themselves; in the interpretation of Scripture they are not only on a level with their age, but above their age. They must be measured not by their credulity or deficiency in knowledge— this could hardly in their circumstances have been otherwise —but by the moral purity of their writings and the intensity of their efforts, amid some extravagancies, to sanctify and ennoble human nature.

(2) It will make us more lenient, both towards Philo and the Fathers, to remember, that the method which they employ has not ceased to be practised by ourselves. It cannot be said that we have left off interpreting Scripture, by what we have brought to the text, not by what we have found there; or that we have not assumed double senses, types, allegories, either to avoid difficulties, or to adapt the Old Testament to the New, and, in general, the meaning of Scripture to the opinions of our own time; or that in portions of Scripture, such as the book of Daniel and the Apocalypse, we have not run into excesses about numbers, colours, and animals, as great as those of Philo in the book of Genesis; or that we have not argued from separate verses of Scripture detached from their connexion; or that we have not invented a system where there was no system, and asked for reasons where there were no reasons; or that we have not perverted analogies in the application of Scripture; or that we have not blended Aristotelian logic or Platonic fancies with the words of our Lord or St. Paul; or that we have not transfigured the characters of Scripture until they have become ideas rather than living persons; or that we have not sought to connect heathen mythology or philosophy, stories of Deucalion, Iphigenia, Bacchus, Orpheus, with the narrative or doctrines of Scripture; or that we have not at times unduly confined human knowledge within the circle of Scriptural truth; or that we have not misused classical learning in illustration of Scripture, introducing allusions and refinements of language where they had no place; or that we have not substituted rhetorical praises of Scripture for a true apprehension of its meaning; or that we have not

done violence to Scripture where plain words seemed to be at variance with the practice of our own day ; or that we have not sermonized over the text instead of explaining it ; or that we have not put traditional interpretations in the place of real ones, repeating probabilities until they grew into certainties ; or that we have not erected the volume of the book itself into a sort of divinity, asserting our ever-varying apprehension of its meaning to be the Unchangeable image ; lastly, that we have not degraded science or history into mere instruments for eliciting out of Scripture our own belief, when we ought to have recognized their true dignity and independent authority in the sight of God and man.

Instead of analysing in detail any of Philo's works, it will be more convenient to group our extracts around those subjects, or leading ideas, which Philo and the New Testament have in common. We must guard the reader against supposing that Philo and St. Paul or St. John are more like than is really the case, owing to the accident of all the resemblances being collected together in a short space. Surprising as these coincidences are, they are, in the writings of Philo, scattered through many volumes amidst endless platitudes. Nor can we be sure that he himself would have recognized or acknowledged the connected system which has been collected from his works. Writers like Philo always waver in their statements. There is no whole or framework which contains the parts of their philosophy, no scientific unity of idea which commands and subordinates the details. The tendency to mysticism and the habit of rhetorical exaggeration render consistency impossible.

§ 1.

The centre of our interest in the Alexandrian philosophy, is the doctrine of the Λόγος (Word). This, however, immediately flows from the prior doctrine of the nature and being of God ; to understand the former, we must begin, therefore, with the latter.

In different parts of the Old Testament there are great differences in the manner of God's revelation of Himself. In the earlier portions He is described as walking in the garden in the cool of the day, as talking to Abraham, as wrestling with Jacob, as appearing to Moses in the burning bush, or to Moses and the elders on Mount Sinai; but we should be far from expecting similar appearances in the days of David or of Hezekiah. More and more, in the course of Jewish history, God had been to the Israelites a 'God hiding Himself,' as of old in the pillar of the cloud, or in the recesses of the most holy place, so in later times seen or spoken with only by His prophets, through whom the divine will was communicated to His people. A religious feeling attached itself to the temple, breaking out in acts of rude violence at the very suspicion of its profanation; and yet this was not inconsistent with the conviction which had more and more wrought itself into the mind of the people, that 'God dwelt not in temples made with hands. Behold, even the heaven and the heaven of heavens cannot contain Him[1].' In whatever manner it was to be reconciled with the earlier history of the Jewish people, the truth 'that no man had seen God at any time' was not first taught by the Gospel.

There was another circumstance which indirectly tended to remove God further from the view of the Israelites. The glory of Israel had departed—the Lord Jehovah no longer went forth with their armies. He was known of them in wrath rather than in mercy. Was He then the author of the evils of their race? The Platonist of Alexandria would not think this. God was not the author of evil, for He was good. How then did evil arise? It seemed to remove evil

[1] Compare Philo: 'Let no such impiety enter our minds (as that God literally planted Paradise), ... for even the whole world would not be a worthy place or habitation for Him, since He is a place to Himself, and He Himself is sufficient for Himself, filling up and surrounding everything else,' &c.—*Leg. Alleg.* i. 14.

from Him to suppose that it was executed by His inferior ministers. 'He sent evil angels among them.' Thus was God, whose presence in the world had once been its life and light, more and more removed from it, that He might be free even from the shadow of a suspicion of evil.

It was the Greek philosophy, even more than the altered national belief, or the change in the circumstances of the people, that contributed to give Philo his peculiar view of the Divine nature. While he retains the Hebrew titles of King of kings and Lord of lords, he adds others which remind us of Aristotle and Plato. God is the τὸ ὄν, νοητὴ φύσις, ὁ νοῦς τῶν ὄντων; the *summum genus* (γενικώτατον), the efficient cause, the unit, better than wisdom itself, or good itself.—Many of his figures of speech are borrowed from Plato. God, he says, is the driver of the chariot, the pilot of the ship, the shepherd of the flock; over souls, and bodies, and thoughts, and words, and angels, and earth, and air, and heaven, and things seen, and powers unseen, the Ruler of all things, the Father of the world. He is omnipotent and omniscient, εἷς καὶ τὸ πᾶν, ἄλλοις ἅπασιν ἀρχὴ τοῦ ποιεῖν.

But the leading idea which, more than any other, seems to have taken possession of the mind of Philo and his contemporaries is, that the Divine Being is incomprehensible and invisible. There is nothing which he repeats so often as this; nothing for the sake of which he is so ready to pervert the meaning of Scripture. As the Eleatic philosopher of being, so of God, Philo will admit of no predicates; for which reason he says that ἐγώ εἰμι ὁ θεὸς σός (I am the Lord thy God) is an incorrect expression (i. 582). To the prophets and Moses he supposed the true nature of God to be equally unintelligible as to himself. In the same way that the Platonist doctrine of the ἰδέαι involves a chasm between φαινόμενα and ὄντα (χωριστὰ τὰ εἴδη), so did the Neoplatonist conception of the Divinity which was the embodiment of those ἰδέαι absolutely withdraw and separate Him from the world. Or as Philo said in Aristotelian phrase, τὸ ὂν ᾗ ὂν οὐχὶ τῶν πρός τι (i. 582).

Such doctrines, whether in religion or philosophy, cannot be consistently carried out. If we have no knowledge of things in themselves, what proof have we that they exist? if we have no knowledge of the Divine nature, it is useless to tell us that there is a God. Hence, in all ages, philosophy, and yet more religion, have availed themselves of the inconsistency in the human mind which allows men to believe truths not wholly reconcilable with each other. The mystic has no difficulty in dwelling on an object of faith, which is no object; the intensity of religious feeling converting a merely negative notion into a positive one. Others have introduced the fiction of a lower and a higher consciousness, the former limited by the human faculties, the latter independent of them. It is, of course, impossible to get rid of the real difficulty by any verbal distinction. Philo has his own method of smoothing the discrepancy, which is as follows: In His true nature God is incomprehensible, and yet there is a certain sense also in which He is cognizable by contemplation and by the observation of His works (i. 107). The latter is the lower way, which extracts a knowledge of God from the sight of trees and flowers, sun and stars; the other, which is the more excellent, is the way of intellectual communion or Divine imagination, as it may be termed (θεὸν θεῷ φαντασιῶσαι), imparted by God Himself, who, when we contemplate Him, is contemplating Himself in us (ii. 415). This higher knowledge of God is the knowledge of a pure unity, as of a form without shadow, such as the sun sheds upon the earth at midday. Thus, even in this sort of knowledge, little is known of the Divine Being but that He exists.

The same difficulty met Philo and the Alexandrians from what may be termed the objective side, in representing the relation of God to the world. If God is unconnected with the world, how does He act upon it? To answer this difficulty, Philo introduces the fiction of δυνάμεις. These may be described in the words of the poet as the

'Thrones, dominations, princedoms, virtues, powers,'

whereby, as in some Asiatic court, the King of kings is surrounded, his ὀπαδοί, δορυφόροι, ὑπηρέται, πρόπομποι. They are efficient causes, the bands of the world; sometimes appearing as persons, as in the visit of the angels to Abraham; also the ideas and *summa genera* of things, as well as the powers by which they are created. The highest of them are called δυνάμεις χαριστικαί and κολαστικαί; or, in another passage, ποιητικαί and βασιλικαί (*De vit. Mosis*, iii. 8); others are the δύναμις προνοητική, νομοθετική, ἵλεως (i. 431, 560; ii. 150).

These δυνάμεις occupy the same place in Philo's system, as the doctrine of emanations in the Oriental philosophy. They are interposed between God and the world, and yet designed also to connect Him with it. We ourselves, so far as we attribute any substance or reality to God's general laws apart from Himself, have recourse to a similar figure. These δυνάμεις may be said to wear a double face; one looking toward the Greek philosophy, and the other to the Old Testament Scriptures. In the first aspect they are but a new name for the Platonic ἰδέαι (ii. 261), while they themselves serve as intermediate links, now that the chasm to be bridged is thrown further back and placed not between the ἰδέαι and phenomena, but between God and the world. In another point of view they are the ἄγγελοι of the Old Testament; the beings who appeared to Abraham and Lot, themselves persons, and yet modes of Divine existence. Philo says of them, that to spirits they are spirits, but angels or men to men (i. 655). They might be described in the language of the Old Testament as the angels of the Divine presence. They abide in the Word (i. 4).

When God has been removed from the sphere of human

intelligence, it may seem absurd to dwell on His moral nature. Yet Philo, forgetful of His transcendentalism, returns in praise and thanksgiving to the natural instincts of the heart. 'His goodness and gentle power is the harmony of all things' (ii. 155). 'To whom,' he says, 'shall we give thanks but to God, and by what means but through the things that we have received?' 'In making rain to fall upon the earth, what does He, but make manifest the riches of His goodness?' It is on this side of the Divine nature that Philo delights to dwell. 'Good,' he says, 'comes directly from Him, and evil only indirectly.' 'Not only does He judge first and show mercy afterwards, but He shows mercy first, and judges afterwards : for with Him mercy is older than justice.' 'The fulness of His power He never exerts towards any creature.' So again with an antithesis of the prepositions which reminds us of some passages in St. Paul's writings as well as of Aristotle, he says, there are two ways in which God works. Some things are only $ὑπ'$ $αὐτοῦ$ (by Him); others are $ὑπ'$ $αὐτοῦ$ and $δι'$ $αὐτοῦ$ (by Him and through Him) as well (i. 51). Of the former sort is evil, of the latter good; an idea nearly answering to the modern expression, God is the Author of good, but the Permitter of evil.

Three texts of Scripture sum up Philo's view of the nature of the Divine Being. First, 'No man hath seen God at any time;' the thought of his age and nation seeking to harmonize the reverence for the Lord Jehovah with the Greek philosophy, which, however, Philo carries out consistently to the consequence that no man hath seen or known, or can conceive or tell anything of God; and then falls into the inconsistency of making Him the subject of human feelings and emotions. Secondly, 'The pure in heart see God;' not, however, in the sense of our Saviour in the Sermon on the Mount; for the purity spoken of is an ascetic or mystic rather than a human purity, such as was possessed by contemplative sects like the Essenes and

Therapeutae. Thirdly, 'God cannot be tempted of evil, neither tempteth He any man.' To execute evil, therefore, He employs inferior ministers, such as the angels, just as to make Himself known to man at all He employs the agency of the λόγος.

§ 2.

Ages which are under the power of ideas are also under the power of words. Like the names of the gods in mythology, words played a great part in the Alexandrian system. The Greek philosophy supplied the conception of a Divine νοῦς : but what was more important, the Greek language supplied the word λόγος with its happy ambiguity of reason and speech, 'outward and inward word,' itself a mediator between two worlds. How natural an expression was this of the relation between the outward and visible and the inward and spiritual, to men who had not either the consciousness of fixed laws of nature or the strong sense of human individuality like ourselves! The Alexandrian recognized as readily as a modern German philosopher, that thought and language are two aspects of the same thing.

The extreme readiness with which ideas, such as λόγος, σοφία, πνεῦμα, were transmuted into persons, is of itself characteristic of a mythological age. The Greek in Homer's time personified fire, water, and the other elements ; and in a doubtful and wavering manner, which may be termed half-personification, sought to embody also abstract ideas, such as strife, fear, and love. The Greek under the Ptolemies personified νοῦς, λόγος, πνεῦμα. In this latter process there were many stages and transitions. It was a sort of inversion of the mythological one, passing not from realities to figures of speech, but from figures of speech to realities. Gradually the abstract term began to stand out, helped by the fortunate accident of a word, and, in the case of the λόγος, by its identification with the vision of God in the Pentateuch.

The earliest form of the λόγος (word) is the ἄγγελος or εἰκὼν θεοῦ, such as was immediately suggested by the language of the Old Testament. For the word ἄγγελος itself Philo finds a verbal connexion; we may suppose, he says, that the ἄγγελος is so called ὅτι τὰ μέλλοντα γενήσεσθαι διηγγέλλετο (*De vit. Mos.* i. 13). Another germ of the same thought is the conception of wisdom in the book of Proverbs, which in Ecclesiasticus is just ceasing to be a figure of speech, and becoming a reality; it was retained in the later Alexandrianism as a sort of feminine λόγος (see infra). Both these expressions had come into use in Palestine itself, and were known in the schools of the Rabbis. But the original notion in either of its forms, whether the more concrete and allied to sense, or more abstract and ideal, was soon overlaid by the notions of Greek philosophy, which quickly resolved them into each other. Thus the ἄγγελος became a λόγος, and the λόγοι in turn became ἄγγελοι. The associations of either were endless; many were supplied by the word itself, still more by Plato and Aristotle; while every passage in the Old Testament in which mention occurred of any type or figure which could by any possibility be connected with it was transferred to the λόγος.

First came the great distinction of Philo between λόγος ἐνδιάθετος and λόγος προφορικός (ii. 154), which is a metaphor taken from the relation between human thought and language. As the thought of a man is to the speech of a man, so is the λόγος ἐνδιάθετος to the λόγος προφορικός. This, however, is not the only play of words which Philo bases on the different significations of the word λόγος. Thus λόγος is used for νόμος; the Word of God is also the Law of God; ποιεῖ ὁ ἀστεῖος τὸν νόμον, ποιεῖ καὶ τὸν λόγον (i. 456). Another meaning of λόγος assists that philosophy of number which Philo loves; in the sense of ratio of numbers the λόγος bears an important part in the κόσμος. As the Eleatic philosopher, wherever the words ὄν, ἐστί, εἶναι occurred, seemed to see a confirmation of his favourite theory; so the

Alexandrian, whatever might be the sense in which the word λόγος was employed, eagerly adapted it to his purpose, and found the evidence of the universality of the idea in the ever-recurring use of the word. Or, to look nearer home for an illustration, as commentators on the Old Testament, wherever they met with the word spirit, have identified it with the third person of the Trinity; or as the early Fathers, in the accidental mention of bread and wine in the Prophets, saw a type and figure of the Eucharist.

The associations derived from Plato and the Greek philosophy so often blend with those of the Old Testament, as to make it difficult to separate them. In a few only the genuine language of Plato is retained. Thus, the λόγος is ἰδέα ἰδεῶν, εἶδος εἰδῶν, the habitation of the ἰδέαι, in which they seem to reside. So, again, according to that explanation of the ἰδέαι which made them γένη, the λόγος is said to be γενικώτατον, the *summum genus* which comprehended all things in itself. In like manner the λόγος is also termed τομεύς, that is, the divider of the genus into its species (i. 504). Here, however, a secondary thought enters in, which gives a curious insight into the network by which the Old Testament and Plato are woven together; the λόγος is not only the divider of the genus into its species, but of the sacrifice into its parts (i. 491). In the New Testament similar language occurs, though in a different sense; 'the word of God is quick and powerful, and sharper than any two-edged sword' (τομώτερος ὑπὲρ πᾶσαν μάχαιραν). (Heb. iv. 12.)

As Plato divided the world into νοητά and αἰσθητά, Philo makes a corresponding division of the λόγος. It is not quite clear whether he designed this to be the same with the one above mentioned of the λόγος ἐνδιάθετος and προφορικός. Where language is the soul of philosophy, we can scarcely suppose a variation of the word without a change of the idea; if indeed it be not the truer view that the word is the idea. In modern phraseology the first of the two pairs of opposites seems to express the more subjective, the other the more objective, aspect of the distinction ; the λόγος ἐνδιάθετος and προφορικός standing in the same relation to each other as human speech and human thought, the soul and body of thought; while the twofold λόγος, which answers to νοητά and αἰσθητά, is but an adaptation of the Platonic distinction (ii. 154).

A curious blending of Greek philosophy and of Jewish and Christian notions occurs in the account of the λόγος μεσίτης. All things, says Philo, are in pairs, right and left, good and evil, Israel and the Egyptian hosts ; and between these two the λόγος stands as a mean, neither begotten as man, nor unbegotten as God ; standing by God as a pledge that the whole race will not utterly rebel, and by man that he may have a good hope that God will not overlook the work of His hands. Have we not here the Pythagorean συστοίχια, the Aristotelian doctrine of a mean, and the Mediator of the New Testament, jumbled together in one ? (i. 509).

Another transition is formed from the Alexandrian to the Jewish aspect of the λόγος by the idea of νόμος; also an ambiguous term, at which the fancy caught, which was common to the Greek and Jewish world. As the λόγος is the first emanation and energy of the Divine Being, whereby the world was created, so also is it the law or bond of the world, ἀπὸ τῶν μέσων ἐπὶ τὰ πέρατα συνάγων τὰ μέρη πάντα καὶ σφίγγων (i. 562). In all the workings of God in nature the λόγος is the intermediate link. Neither is it only the law of the physical, but of the political world, and orders the changes of states. In the spirit of Sulpicius' letter to Cicero, Philo says, 'Look at Pontus, Macedonia, Carthage ; their vicissitudes are not chance, but Providence. The Divine Word brings round its operations in a circle which the vulgar call fortune ; it is ever running about the world to establish the perfect form of government—universal democracy' (*De Immut. Dei*, c. 36). Νόμος, equally with λόγος, had become a power, almost a person; a conception of both, which naturally led to their identification with each other. Thus Philo says, in a passage which at once reminds us of Plato and of St. Paul: 'Every bad man is a slave,' ὅσοι μετὰ νόμου ζῶσιν ἐλεύθεροι. Νόμος δὲ ἀψευδὴς ὁ ὀρθὸς λόγος, οὐχ ὑπὸ τοῦ δεῖνος ἢ τοῦ δεῖνος θνητοῦ φθαρτὸς ἐν χαρτιδίοις ἢ στήλαις ἄψυχος ἀψύχοις, ἀλλ' ὑπ' ἀθανάτου φύσεως ἄφθαρτος ἐν ἀθανάτῳ διανοίᾳ τυπωθείς (ii. 452). Do we not trace here the beginning of that wider and more expansive notion of the law which we find in the Epistles; a law above a law, not written on tables of stone, such as those had who, 'not having the law, were a law unto themselves?'

A still more remarkable parallel with St. Paul is found in Philo's explanation of the law of Leviticus xvi. 36, according to which the house was not pronounced unclean until seen by the high priest. Philo, after his usual manner of setting aside the text where its meaning seems inappropriate, says that the literal interpretation of this cannot be accepted: for the priest's coming to the house would make it clean and not unclean. Here, therefore, as elsewhere, the priest is the λόγος, and the meaning is, that before the λόγος enters into the soul it is innocent in all things: ἕως ὁ θεῖος λόγος εἰς τὴν ψυχὴν ἡμῶν καθάπερ τινὰ ἑστίαν οὐκ ἀφῖκται πάντα αὐτῆς τὰ ἔργα ἀνυπαίτια (i. 292-299).

We have here a dimmer expression of St. Paul's often repeated thought, 'Sin is not imputed where there is no law;' 'I was alive without the law once;' 'the law entered in that sin might abound.' But the parallel is also carried further. For as in many passages of Scripture we have the law spoken of with scarcely any reference to the Mosaic law for the workings of the human soul under the sense of sin, or, as we should say, for the conscience, Philo has also his λόγος ἔλεγχος—ὁ ἑκάστῃ ψυχῇ συνοικῶν καὶ συμπεφυκὼς ἔλεγχος, κατήγορος ὁμοῦ καὶ δικαστὴς ὁ αὐτὸς ὤν (ii. 195). When convicted by our own conscience, he says we should pray God to save us by chastisement, and send His λόγος ἔλεγχος into our minds. So the angel who appears to Balaam is the type of the ἔλεγχος attacking the soul disposed to sin. This ἔλεγχος is likewise the παράκλητος, the intercessor and instructor also (ii. 247).

The parallels with the New Testament are not yet exhausted. For example, the λόγος is the living stream (i. 560), the river of God in Paradise, the bread that came down from heaven (*Leg. All.* ii. 59)[1], the garden of Eden itself, the sword that turned every way. It is, however, in the personifications of the λόγος that the most striking parallelisms are found; the word seeming to draw to itself all the passages in which manifestations of angels, or of the Divine presence occur in the Old Testament.

Our own idea of personality does not admit of degrees. To us it is not natural to think of either man or angel as more or less a person. Nor, again, is it easy to imagine, except in poetry, an outward form of personality, such as is assigned to the Homeric heroes in the world below. Neither is it possible to us to conceive two persons in one. Such distinct ideas of personality did not, however, exist for the age of which we are speaking. In the same manner that any one deity in the heathen pantheon might have many statues and images, without thereby implying the notion that these statues were mere representations of him—in the same way that by some anomaly of the human mind saints are worshipped in many places at once with hardly a thought of attributing omnipresence or pluripresence to them; so to the Alexandrian in Philo's time the λόγος might be many persons, and exist in many

[1] The soul is taught by the prophet Moses, who tells it: 'This is the bread, the food which God has given for the soul, explaining that God has brought it, his own word and reason; for this bread which He has given us to eat is this word of His' (*Leg. Alleg.* ii. 60). Again, c. 61: 'Let God enjoin the soul, saying to it, that "man shall not live by bread alone," speaking in a figure, " but by every word that proceedeth out of the mouth of God."'

persons, and have many shadows and images of himself without thereby losing his original personality. On this view only can Philo be made intelligible. When we raise the question whether the λόγος was a person, it must be allowed that the word 'person' has a definiteness and unity which belong not to that age, but to a subsequent one, and is therefore used in a somewhat different sense from that in which we ordinarily employ it. And we may further distinguish what may be termed this growing idea of personality from the personal appearances of angels or the Divine Being in the Old Testament, which are also attributed to the λόγος. On the other hand, it must be admitted that when Philo speaks of the λόγος as ἀρχάγγελος (*Quis. rer. div. haer.* § 42), or δεύτερος θεός (*Frag.* ii. 625), he had at least an indistinct conception of a person. The word λόγος itself, both in its superficial meaning of human speech, and in its deeper intention of 'the Word by which the worlds were made,' naturally suggested the idea of personality.

A critical question more difficult of solution is the origin of the personification. An earlier form of the λόγος, as has been already mentioned, is the σοφία of the book of Ecclesiasticus. Wisdom and the Word of God are there described as real powers, almost as persons. It has been doubted, however, whether we are to look here for the personality of the λόγος. Gfrörer is of opinion that the personal notion is originally Jewish, and that the Platonism was an after addition. In the absence of much positive evidence, the following seems to me the most probable conjecture on this subject.

It can scarcely be doubted that to the Jew everywhere, whether at Alexandria or in Palestine, the aspect of the religion of his fathers had much changed. To neither could the law in its original meaning have been wholly intelligible. To both probably, whether under the influence of Egypt or of Chaldea, the visible appearance of God in the altered state of the world seemed strange and discordant. That this was the case appears to be proved by the observation of Gfrörer, that passages in which such appearances occur in the LXX have been altered by the translator. The dread of mentioning the name of God was a native superstition, older than the Christian era. Both therefore, the Jew of Alexandria and of Palestine alike, might be said to be prepared for the doctrine of the λόγος, that is, to feel the need of an intermediate being, who might take the place of the God who had guided His people Israel. The Alexandrian, coming more under the influence of the Greek philosophy, sought and found it in the Platonic νοῦς; while the Jewish Rabbi, confining himself to the Hebrew Scriptures, exalted the angels into the place of mediators, and found in the law the answer to his own difficulty. The λόγος itself implied the idea of personality, so far as this can be separated from individual form and character, while on the other hand it derived a kind of outward figure or embodiment from the angels, or the patriarchs, or the high priest. From these latter it gained a new personality, while it was itself the pantheistic link by which they were connected together, εἷς ἐν πᾶσι. And although from the few facts bearing upon the question we are obliged to argue *à priori*, there is no reason, notwithstanding the absence of positive evidence, to doubt that the personality was partly supplied by both; so far as it is involved in the idea of mind, mainly by Greek philosophy; so far as it seems to connect the idea of an outward form or embodiment, by the Old Testament itself. The λόγος may have been identified with the angel of His presence, or the angel of His presence identified with the λόγος; the conception of Philo includes both.

There is scarcely an angelic or divine appearance in the law which Philo does not attribute to the λόγος. He is the instrument by which the worlds were made, 'the word of the Cause' by which also Moses, the perfect soul, is raised to God Himself[1]; He is the guide of the Patriarchs, the angel who appeared to Hagar, the avenging angel who destroyed Sodom and Gomorrah, the God who appeared to Jacob in Gen. xxviii. 11, 19, the Divine form who changed the name of Jacob to Israel, the angel of the Lord in the burning bush, the cloud at the Red Sea, the angel who appeared to Balaam, the guide of the Israelites in the wilderness. Individuals are also types of Him. Melchizedek is 'the reason' to which we offer the first fruits; Aaron and Moses are also symbols of Him; Bezaleel is a τρόπος ψυχῆς, who makes the shadows of things even as Moses makes the realities; the sons of Jacob are one man's sons, ἕνα πατέρα ἐπιγεγραμμένοι, that is, the ἄνθρωπος θεοῦ, the λόγος. Both these last passages may be illustrated by another passage in Philo's account of the creation, in which he says that God made the image first—a seal, an idea, a genus, immortal, without sex; afterwards He made the species Adam (διττὰ ἀνθρώπων γένη· ὁ μὲν γάρ ἐστιν οὐράνιος ἄνθρωπος, ὁ δὲ γήϊνος).

The Platonic image of the copy and the reality is constantly recurring in Philo; that of the ἄνθρωπος θεοῦ is more important for the purpose of our present inquiry (i. 411). In some sense the λόγος is man as well as God— He is God and also man. He is the Son of God, who is the Father of all; the eldest born of being (πρεσβύτατος τοῦ ὄντος λόγος), who puts on the world as it were a garment (ii. 562); the second God (ii. 625); the image of God (i. 6, 454), by whom men swear in their imperfect state[2], for He is the God of us imperfect beings (i. 128, 656); above the angels (i. 561); the incorporeal light that is with God Himself (i. 414); who is eternal (i. 330, 332); and nearest to

[1] 'The shadow of God is his word, which he used like an instrument when he was making the world.'—*Leg. Alleg.* ii. 31; compare also *De Sacrific. Cain.* iii. 3.

[2] The reason Philo gives for this is remarkable. 'For no man swears by himself, for he is unable to determine about his own nature.' And it is impiety to swear by God (cf. Matt. v. 33-37).

God without any interval or separation (i. 561); the shepherd who has the care of the flock (i. 308); the angel who is, as it were, the physician who heals evil (i. 122). What may be termed the humanity of the λόγος is not the humanity of one who was in all points tempted as we are; it arises out of his being the image of God, in which man also is made. Philo sometimes identifies, sometimes distinguishes, divine and human reason. There are two temples, he says: the first the world, of which the λόγος is the high priest; the second, the rational soul, of which the high priest is the true man (i. 653). Being neither begotten as man, nor unbegotten as God, he is able to mediate between God and man. Words which imply human virtue are also applied to him, such as would not be applied to God Himself. He is the ἱκέτης in Moses, who intercedes for the people (i. 653); the παράκλητος, who is with the high priest when he goes in to intercede for the people (ii. 591); the ἱερὸς λόγος, who, in Num. xvi. 48, stands between the living and the dead (i. 501); the cloud that divided the Egyptians and Israelites; above all, the ἀρχιερεύς (i. 270, 562), who mediates between God and man; who is not to be defiled by touching the corpse of his father, i. e. the Spirit, or his mother, i. e. the sense; who is married to a virgin, even the pure sense, and wears for his priestly garment the world and the elements.

Two accessory ideas remain to be considered, σοφία and πνεῦμα. The first is in most respects identical with λόγος. Like the λόγος, it is the creative power and inner principle of the soul, and has the same predicates attributed to it. A difference in its use arises from its feminine termination, which renders its employment more appropriate where a feminine, such as πηγή, μήτηρ, θυγάτηρ, is the symbol under which it is expressed. Further, the second meaning of λόγος conveys a conception of energy or action, which is wanting in σοφία; the word λόγος is at once a simpler, as well as more philosophical expression of Divine energy.

Hence σοφία which also occurs less frequently, is not so completely personified as λόγος; always retaining in some degree the nature of an abstract term, for which reason it is in some passages opposed to λόγος, as inward to outward. One place in which Philo uses it for the rock in the wilderness, which is also the manna, affords a remarkable parallel to St. Paul: ἡ ἀκρότομος πέτρα ἡ σοφία τοῦ θεοῦ ἐστιν ἣν ἄκραν καὶ πρωτίστην ἔτεμεν ὁ θεὸς ἀπὸ τῶν ἑαυτοῦ δυνάμεων (i. 82, 213).

The other modification of the λόγος is the πνεῦμα, on the double meaning of which latter Philo himself remarks. Altogether it has four principal uses : (1) The wind ; (2) The breath of the soul ; (3) The wisdom that is from above ; (4) Prophetic power. It is a synonym of λόγος, except so far as the word itself suggests different associations. Thus it is used more naturally wherever the communion of men with one another, or with God, or the inspiration of man, is spoken of. So Philo says that the Spirit cannot endure among divisions ; and those who are under its influence are borne upward as by wind, and hence are said to be ἀνακαλούμενοι.

The parallelisms between Philo and the New Testament, which have already presented themselves, may be summed up as follows :—

1. The invisibility of God (John i. 18).
2. The ministration of angels in giving the law (Gal. iii. 19 : Heb. ii. 2).
3. The 'Word,' as the instrument of creation.
    as prefigured by the manna.
    as the living stream.
    as a sword (τομεύς).
    as the image of God.
    as the high priest.
    as the cloud at the Red Sea.
    (under the name σοφία) as the rock in the wilderness.

The 'Word,' as the first-begotten son of God.
> as begotten before the world, which is God's second Son (compare πρωτότοκος πάσης κτίσεως).
> as the man of God.
> as a second God.
> as the Paraclete and Intercessor.
> as the Mediator.
> as Melchizedek.
> like the νόμος in St. Paul's Epistles, under the title of ἔλεγχος, the convincer of sin.
> as the heavenly man, who is opposed to the earthly.

These parallelisms between Philo and the New Testament have different degrees of resemblance. Thus, for example, the λόγος as μεσίτης is mixed up, as we have seen, with Pythagorean follies; that of the οὐράνιος and γήϊνος ἄνθρωπος is not exactly the same with St. Paul's first and second Adam. But whatever may be the difference in their meaning, the fact that such expressions exist alike in two writings separated from each other by an interval of twenty or thirty years cannot be attributed to accident; while, on the other hand, neither of the two presents the slightest trace of having borrowed from the other. The only supposition that remains is, that they belonged to the mode of thinking of the age, whatever inflections or adaptations of meaning they may have received.

§ 3.

A question which is in some degree connected with Philo's conception of the λόγος remains to be considered; viz. how far he partook of those Messianic hopes which occupied the minds of the Jews of Palestine in the time of our Saviour and His Apostles? The answer is, that very little trace of them can be found in his writings. He has no desire to return to Jerusalem and build up the house of David. Like the Jews in later ages he acquiesces in the dispersion of his countrymen among the Gentiles. The kingdom for which he looks is a heavenly, or rather an ideal, one. He knows nothing of the prophecies in the sense in which they are interpreted in the New Testament. It is a philosophical more than a national pride which he takes in the Jewish institutions. He belongs not to the school of those who called no man master on earth, 'whose blood Pilate mingled with their sacrifices;' for even amid persecutions he is a loyal subject of 'the powers that be.' There are places in which philosophy makes him a sort of Cosmopolite. The book of the law, not the Jewish nation, forms the circle within which his hopes and aspirations are contained.

One passage forms an exception to this statement (*De Exsecrat.* ii. 435), in which Philo, enlarging on the book of Deuteronomy, chap. xxviii, describes the restoration of the Jews to liberty at a given signal, 'their sudden and universal change to virtue causing a panic among their masters; for they will let them go, because they are ashamed to rule over those who are better than themselves. . . . When they have received this liberty, those who a short time before were scattered about in Greece and other countries, rising up with one impulse, and coming some from one quarter, some from another, hasten to a place which is pointed out to them, being guided on their way by some vision, more Divine than is compatible with its being of the nature of man, which is manifest to those who are saved, but invisible to every one else.' Philo goes on to mention the three intercessors or 'comforters' of the Jewish nation in their reconciliation with God: (1) the goodness of God; (2) the holiness of the departed Patriarchs, who pray for their descendants; (3) the improvement of the nation itself.

It has been doubted whether in this passage the Divine vision is the same with the λόγος. The λόγος had just been mentioned in the previous sentence. 'If,' it is said, 'they receive their chastisement in a humble and contrite spirit, . . . they will meet with acceptance from their merciful Saviour, God, who bestows on the race of mankind His especial and exceedingly great gift, namely, relationship to His own Word, after which as its archetype the human mind was formed.' It is hardly consistent with the laws of language to suppose that what in one paragraph Philo has called 'the word,' he speaks of in the next as 'the vision.' It is more natural to see in the latter a manifestation of the word only. The tendency which Philo shows to connect the λόγος with the apparitions of the Divine presence, such as that of the angels to the Patriarchs, and with several Messianic passages (i. 414), makes it probable that he intended such a reference here. At any rate, he would not have excluded the λόγος from the authorship of any good. His system is too Pantheistic to allow of his distinguishing the Messiah, or the apparitions which heralded His advent, from the Word.

§ 4.

Philo's conception of the creation is different from that which we gather from the Old Testament. The world, he says, is not without beginning; but his idea of γένεσις is the working of God upon matter which pre-existed. Creation is with him rather the ordering and arrangement of the world than the actual bringing of it into being. Yet he, too, uses the same expression as St. Paul (τὰ μὴ ὄντα εἰς τὸ εἶναι καλεῖν ii. 367), 'to call the things that are not into being,' though in a different sense. There was no subject in which Greek and Oriental modes of thought so naturally, almost necessarily, came into conflict with Jewish ; Philo sought to remove the incongruity by Pythagorean triads of numbers, which, however strange it may seem, were more agreeable and intelligible to that age than the simplicity of the Mosaic narrative.

He holds the Platonic doctrine of the pre-existence of the soul, though in a different way (ii. 604). The wise man—Abraham, Jacob, Moses—confesses that while on earth he is a stranger in the Egypt of sense. In its origin, the human soul is an ἀπόσπασμα or ἀπαύγασμα θεῖον, or, to speak more religiously, ὅπερ ὁσιώτερον εἰπεῖν τοῖς κατὰ Μωϋσῆν φιλοσοφοῦσιν εἰκόνος θείας ἐκμαγεῖον ἐμφερές (i. 208). Sometimes the ether is represented as the source of the soul (i. 119); in other passages λόγοι, or ideas bearing the image of God and the stamp of the Divine Spirit. This participation in the Divine Spirit makes man free, and therefore capable of virtue, without which freedom is impossible.

There is also another point of view, which is Jewish, in which Philo regards the soul as opposed to the body. The body is the source of evil; the Egyptian house, in which, as in a living tomb, the soul is forced to dwell: δεδεμένη σώματι φθαρτῷ, ἐντετυμβευμένη, νεκροφοροῦσα (ii. 367, 387). In vain does Divine wisdom take up its abode in the body: διὰ δὲ τὸ εἶναι αὐτοὺς σάρκας οὐ καταμένει. Marriage, and the education of children, and the provision for daily life, and meanness, and avarice, and occupation are apt to wither wisdom, ere it can come into bloom. Yet does nothing so impede this growth of the soul as the fleshly nature. This is the foundation of ignorance and want of understanding on which the others are built (i. 266). In the language almost of the New Testament, he describes the life of the bad as τὰ φίλα τῇ σαρκὶ ἐργάζεσθαι καὶ μεθοδεύειν. There is an original sin in the flesh, and in man as a created being, against which the Spirit of God is ever striving. There is a strife in the camp, says Moses; that is, the Spirit within us cries out. Not that the bodily substance of the flesh is to be regarded as the source of evil, but the flesh comprehends in itself the ideal evil will, ever seeking to satisfy the lusts of the flesh.

Hence Philo is led to make a new division of the soul into two parts: the one in alliance with the flesh, the other separate from it. There are two kinds of men, he says—

those who live in the flesh, and those who live in the Spirit. And there is an outer soul, ψυχὴ σαρκική, the essence of which is blood, corresponding to the first of these two classes; and an inner soul, ψυχὴ λογική, which answers to the latter, into which God puts His Spirit. That is the true soul; the soul of souls, as it were—the apple of the eye (ii. 241, 356). In like manner he seems disposed to confine immortality to the souls of the good.

The chief parallels with the Epistles which occur in the preceding section may be summed up as follows:—

The idea of Creation, τὰ μὴ ὄντα εἰς τὸ εἶναι καλεῖν.

His conception of the human soul as an ἀπαύγασμα θεῖον, εἰκόνος θείας ἐκμαγεῖον ἐμφερές.

The body, as the tomb of the soul, which is said to be ἐντετυμβευμένη, νεκροφοροῦσα.

The strife of the soul and the body.

The flesh conceived of as the seat of sin.

The ideal soul inspired by God.

The innumerable company of angels and aerial beings.

The distinction of the ψυχὴ σαρκική and λογική, taken from the good and bad man, like St. Paul's φρόνημα σαρκός and φρόνημα πνεύματος.

§ 5.

The end of human life, according to Philo, is to follow God, and become like Him, and the mean to this is virtue. Philo, however, sometimes proposes the mean, without reference to God, as in itself the end. It is the seed which is also the fruit. It consists in bringing αἰσθητά under νοητά, and is the same with wisdom.

But how is man to attain to virtue? He is corrupt, and may justly be punished by God. Like St. Paul, Philo just touches on the sin of Adam, as the source of misery and death to his descendants (ii. 440). His answer to the question which has been asked is, in general, the same with that of the New Testament. God gives men grace to enable them to serve Him. The λόγος is the source of every good. Even virtue without the care or grace of God is of no avail (i. 203, 662). 'He says that he sets his tabernacle, the place of his oracle, in the midst of our impurity, that we may have wherewithal to cleanse ourselves and wash away all the filth and pollution of our miserable and ignoble life' (i. 488, on Lev. xvi. 16). The λόγος is the food (i. 120) and also the temple of the wise soul. By its power, by whom all things were created, God will also raise the just man, and advance him to be near Himself in heaven (i. 165).

Philo entwines with his theological theory the ethics of Greek philosophy. There are three ways upwards, διδαχή, φύσις, ἄσκησις, of which he finds types in the three patriarchs, Abraham, Isaac, and Jacob. Of these the lowest is the way of ἄσκησις; he who practises this is described as in a perpetual state of strife and struggle, the image of which is Jacob on his pillow of stones, of which also the Homeric heroes are a figure, as described in the line ἀλλότε μὲν ζώουσ' ἐτερήμεροι ἀλλότε δ' αὖτε τεθνᾶσιν. Next to him stands the διδακτός, of whom Abraham is the type; and yet, strange to say, the διδαχή consists in nothing but the ordinary elements of Greek education; viz. grammar, music, geometry, rhetoric, and dialectic. Before Sarah, who, according to Philo's allegorical method, is virtue, can bear a son to Abraham, who is the representative of νοῦς, he must betake himself to Hagar, that is, the slavery of knowledge. The soul must have its food of milk and plain sustenance first, afterwards its strong meat; νηπίοις ἐστὶ γάλα τροφή, τελείοις δὲ τὰ ἐκ πυρῶν πέμματα (i. 302). So near a parallel to St. Paul as this image affords, which occurs three or four times in Philo, is not supplied by the whole writings of Plato.

But the highest way is the way of nature, of which Isaac is the type. Here nothing but the word φύσις affords a vestige of the Greek philosopher. The way of nature is the way of God, attained only by withdrawing from the flesh. It might be described almost in the language which St. James applies to the 'wisdom that is from above.' First, it is peaceable, and is accompanied by a joy which God communicates from His own attributes—the joy of resignation, which looks with pleasure on the whole world. Secondly, it is pure, and reveals the sight of God to the pure in heart: ἰδεῖν οὐκ ἀδύνατον, εἴη δ' ἂν μόνῳ τῷ καθαρειοτάτῳ καὶ ὀξυωπεστάτῳ γένει, ᾧ τὰ ἴδια ἐπιδεικνύμενος ὁ τῶν ὅλων πατὴρ ἔργα, μεγίστην πασῶν χαρίζεται δωρεάν. (Compare John v. 20). He who has it becomes a steward of the mysteries of God, μύστης τῶν θείων τελετῶν (ii. 427). (Compare St. Paul, οἰκόνομος τῶν θείων μυστηρίων.) Lastly, it consists in the contemplation of God, ὥσπερ διὰ κατόπτρου (ii. 198), an image which occurs again and again in Philo, and is repeated more than once in St. Paul —'For now we see through a glass darkly, but then face to face.'

Many other striking parallels with the description of the Christian life are found in Philo. Such are the expressions—διψᾶν καὶ πεινᾶν καλοκἀγαθίας, διψᾶν εὐνομίας, δουλεύειν θεῷ, εὐαρεστεῖν θεῷ, γνωρίζεσθαι θεῷ, by which Philo denotes the relation of the perfect man to God. Another mode of expression with which he is familiar, is that of the 'true riches'—οἷς ἀληθινὸς πλοῦτος ἐν οὐρανῷ κατάκειται διὰ σοφίας καὶ ὁσιότητος ἀσκηθείς, τούτοις καὶ ὁ τῶν χρημάτων ἐπὶ γῆς περιουσιάζει, ... οἷς δὲ ὁ κλῆρος οὐκ ἔστιν οὐράνιος δι' ἀσέβειαν ἢ ἀδικίαν οὐδὲ τῶν ἐπὶ γῆς ἀγαθῶν εὐοδεῖν πέφυκεν ἡ κτῆσις (ii. 425). 'Lay not up for yourselves treasures on earth, ... and all these things shall be added unto.' A more general parallel with our Saviour's sermon on the mount is furnished by the figure of the way of life, which there be 'few who find': ἄτριπτος ὁ ἀρετῆς χῶρος· ὀλίγοι γὰρ βαίνουσιν αὐτόν, τέτριπται δ' ὁ κακίας (i. 84).

To the four cardinal virtues of Plato and the Stoics, which he delights to recognize in the four rivers of Paradise and elsewhere, Philo adds what we may term three Christian graces. These are: hope, which is the seed of life, of which Enos is the type (i. 218); repentance, which is prefigured by Enoch, ὅτι μετέθηκεν αὐτὸν ὁ θεός (ii. 4, such is the strange turn which Philo gives to Gen. v. 24); righteousness, which is typified by Noah, the last of the ancient evil race, and the preserver of the new. In addition to these, there occurs a second triad, of πίστις, χαρά, and ὅρασις θεοῦ (ii. 412), which is yet higher than the preceding, and of which Abraham, Isaac, and Jacob are the examples (ii. 2, 3, 5, 8). Faith, according to Philo's conception, is trust in God. It is that which says to the soul in the name of God—'Do thou stand here with me.' It is the adhesive force which binds us to God: τίς οὖν ἡ κόλλα; εὐσέβεια δήπου καὶ πίστις· ἁρμόζουσι γὰρ καὶ ἑνοῦσιν αἱ ἀρεταὶ ἀφθάρτῳ φύσει διάνοιαν· καὶ γὰρ Ἀβραὰμ πιστεύσας ἐγγίζειν θεῷ λέγεται (i. 456). In another passage he comments on the words—'Abraham believed God, and it was counted to him for righteousness.' What could make his faith so praiseworthy? Has not the evil also faith in God? To which we reply: If you look not at the surface, but at the substance of things, you will know that it is infinitely hard to trust God alone; to loose the bands of ambition, lucre, power, friendship, and other earthly goods; to set thyself wholly free from the creature, and trust to God, who is alone to be trusted—μόνῳ πιστεῦσαι θεῷ τῷ πρὸς ἀλήθειαν μόνῳ πιστῷ (i. 485, 486).

The faith of Philo has not the depth or associations of that of St. Paul; it bears a nearer resemblance to faith in the sense of the Epistle to the Hebrews. That is, it is not faith, the negative of the law, faith that makes men free, but the faith of one 'who endures as seeing Him who is invisible.' Almost in the language of Heb. ix he describes Abraham as seeking a better country which God would show him, and finding his reward in regarding the things that are not as though they were: ἀρτηθεῖσα καὶ κρεμασθεῖσα ἡ διάνοια ἐλπίδος χρηστῆς, καὶ ἀνενδοίαστα νομίσασα ἤδη παρεῖναι τὰ μὴ παρόντα διὰ τὴν τοῦ ὑποσχομένου βεβαιοτάτην πίστιν, ἀγαθὸν τέλειον ἆθλον εὕρηται. In another passage he speaks of faith as the only true and living good, the consolation of life, the substance of good hope: πλήρωμα χρηστῶν ἐλπίδων, ἀφορία μὲν κακῶν, ἀγαθῶν δὲ φορά, κακοδαιμονίας ἀπόγνωσις, εὐσεβείας γνῶσις, ψυχῆς ἐν ἅπασι βελτίωσις ἐπερηρεισμένης τῷ τῶν πάντων αἰτίῳ καὶ δυναμένῳ μὲν πάντα, βουλομένῳ δὲ τὰ ἄριστα. 'This is the strait and smooth way, in which, if a man walks, he stumbles not, in which he avoids the slippery path of bodily and external things. He who trusts these latter has no faith in God, he who has no faith in these has faith in God' (ii. 39).

In other passages the more general term εὐσέβεια takes the place of πίστις. Εὐσέβεια and φιλανθρωπία are often mentioned together. Thus, almost in the words of the Gospel, he declares that there are two great commandments —piety and holiness towards God, and love and justice towards men. Under these, innumerable lesser details are comprehended. ἔστι δὲ τῶν κατὰ μέρος ἀμυθήτων λόγων καὶ δογμάτων δύο τὰ ἀνωτάτω κεφάλαια, τό τε πρὸς θεὸν δι' εὐσεβείας καὶ ὁσιότητος, καὶ τὸ πρὸς ἀνθρώπους διὰ φιλανθρωπίας καὶ δικαιοσύνης (ii. 391). But the highest form of virtue is love to God, which Philo describes as the last stage of mystic initiation. They who possess this gift are inspired, ὑπ' ἔρωτος ἁρπασθέντες οὐρανίου καθάπερ οἱ βακχευόμενοι καὶ κορυβαντιῶντες ἐνθουσιάζουσιν μέχρις ἂν τὸ ποθούμενον ἴδωσιν (ii. 473); they are free, and participate as friends in the power of the king—they are gods themselves, as Moses has ventured to call them.

Philo, like the Apostle Paul, describes faith, hope, and love as the fairest graces of a religious soul. In Philo as well as in St. Paul, in different senses and under different points of view, faith and love seem either of them to occupy the first place, while hope lies more in the background, and is the germ of the other two. In both, faith is almost sight; love has nearly the same position in Philo as in the Gospel and Epistles of St. John. Hope, as with the early

Christian it was closely connected with the sorrowfulness of his life in this world, so in Philo seems to arise out of the degenerate state of the Jewish race, from which the righteous could by hope only escape.

Philo regards the law in a different manner from the Scribes and Pharisees at Jerusalem. He speaks of certain who laid aside the letter, and considered only the spirit of the sacred writings, who, like St. Paul, would have said— 'Let no man judge you of a new moon or of a sabbath;' and of such he disapproves. Yet he too, in a spirit which partakes both of Greek philosophy and Hebrew prophecy, utters warnings against lip service and superstition; the whole of the sacrificial language of the Old Testament receives from him a spiritual or ideal meaning. Thus he calls πίστις κάλλιστον καὶ ἄμωμον ἱερεῖον; in the same spirit he says that the holiest and most acceptable sacrifice is a soul purified by virtue and age; 'from holy men the least gifts find acceptance with God, and even if they bring nothing else, in bringing themselves, who most perfectly fulfil the law of goodness, they bring the best sacrifice—It is not of the sacrifice, but of the virtue, that God takes account' (ii. 151, 253, 254). On such a theory it would be unnecessary that sacrifices should be offered at all. Nevertheless, by reason of the frailty of men, God, he says, was pleased to give them a temple made with hands, which is one only temple, even as God is one, and to this He compelled men to assemble as a test of their piety. This temple is the image of the world, as the passover is of a change of life, and the rite of circumcision of purity of heart (ii. 222, 223); or as the Jewish people are the priests and prophets of the whole human race (ii. 15).

With this idealizing tendency he seems to have united the more popular belief of ransom and sacrifice. Thus he speaks of the Levites as the ransom of the children of Israel, and says, on Lev. iii. 12, that what the sacred writer probably intends to teach, is, that every good man is the ransom of the bad (*De Sacrif. Cain et Abel*, c. 37). In like manner his interpretation of the offering up of Isaac implies that he believed in the efficacy of sacrifice in its most literal sense (ii. 27–29).

Points of parallelism in the preceding section are as follows:—

1. The view that righteousness is the gift of God to man, not of debt, but of grace.
2. Faith, hope, and love. Faith is the substance of things hoped for. What a man seeth, why doth he yet hope for? The greatest of them is love.
3. The two great commandments in the law.
4. The metaphorical use of sacrifice and of circumcision.
5. Particular expressions: 'stewards of the divine mysteries,' 'the true riches,' 'hungering and thirsting after righteousness.'

§ 6.

We have completed a sketch of the principal points of Philo's system, if indeed that can be called a system, the connexion of which is chiefly made by the continuity of the Mosaic writings. On those writings were incrusted the fancies of the Alexandrian philosophy. They soon worked themselves into the fabric, which they covered with grotesque and monstrous fictions. More precisely considered, the writings of Philo are not a system in the sense in which the writings of Plato and Aristotle form a system, but a method of applying the Greek philosophy to the Jewish Scriptures.

This method, however, was not the fancy of an individual; it was the method of a school. The age which compares the present with the past, seeks to adapt ancient monuments to itself. In a place of learning, like Alexandria, swarming with teachers and rhetoricians, the natural tendency of the human mind was not likely to be without an expression. Plato himself had found the allegorical interpretation an instrument of implanting his lessons too convenient to be neglected. The instant that the bright thought occurred to some Euhemerus that all these things were an allegory, an idea which many of the fictions of Greek mythology readily suggested, it might be indefinitely expanded and applied. The 'ill weed grew apace' in a congenial soil; it was suited to that stage of human culture. But for the disposition to receive it, such an interpretation of the law of Moses would have seemed as singular to the Alexandrian, as a similar allegorical explanation of Blackstone's Commentaries to ourselves. Like other methods of knowledge, it was relative to the age which gave birth to it. It is curious to trace the manner in which the same tendency is restricted among ourselves. If a person were to apply the allegorical method to the Prophets generally, he would be thought fanciful—to the books of Kings or Chronicles absolutely insane; while in the treatment of the book of Revelation, it would seem to have a natural application. The simplicity of the Alexandrians admitted every use of it; nor did they see any absurdity in the grammatical studies of Abraham, or the Greek instructors of Moses (ii. 8).

The effects of such a predisposing belief may be traced still in modern commentaries and paraphrases. The mystical interpretation of Scripture, though more common with the Fathers and schoolmen than among Protestant divines, has found supporters in our own days. It is regarded by many as 'tending to edification.' Is this conceivable, unless it had been based on some principle of human nature? Could a method of interpretation which, though destitute of objective truth, has survived 2000 years, have been due only to the genius of Origen or of Philo?

We might reply, 'impossible,' on such *a priori* grounds only. No system like that of Philo could have sprung, fully equipped, out of the brain of an individual; it would have been an unmeaning absurdity, unless many generations

of teachers and hearers had preceded. No system which
was the idiosyncrasy of a philosopher, could have retained
so tenacious a hold on the human mind. Reason and feeling
must have married in some natural conjunction, the links
of which have never been entirely untwisted. There is
no need, however, to rest the position that Philo was the
representative of his age on mere *a priori* arguments. More
direct proofs are the following :—

First, the 'undesigned' coincidences between Philo and
the New Testament can be explained on no other hypothesis
than the wide diffusion of the Alexandrian modes of thought.
Was it by chance only that Philo and St. John struck upon
the same conception of the λόγος, or that the Alexandrian
philosophy transferred to the λόγος the manifestations of
God in the Old Testament which we commonly refer to
Christ? Was it by chance that the same figures of speech
are applied to the λόγος, which we receive in the New
Testament from the lips of our Lord and His Apostles,
such as the manna, the living water, the rock that flowed
in the wilderness? It may be doubted whether they are
used in the same sense by both, but there can be no doubt
that they are a part of the language and mode of thinking
of the age.

Secondly, it may be observed, that in several passages of
his work Philo refers to the allegorical interpretation as
already of ancient date. In some places he gives several
explanations of the same verse, showing that he was not
himself its first interpreter. In speaking of the Therapeutae and Essenes (to whom he seems to stand in nearly
the same relation as Basil or Chrysostom to St. Antony
and the Christian hermits), he gives a description of their
preaching, and speaks of the allegorical method as peculiar
to them. He says that they are scattered in many parts of
the world: 'for it must needs be, that Greece and the
stranger should have part in the perfect good' (ii. 474, 477).
He also uses the expression, οἱ τῆς ἀλληγορίας κανόνες (as

though an art of allegorizing existed just as much as an art of rhetoric), and everywhere presupposes the idea of his method as well known.

Thirdly, there are traces of the same application of the Old Testament much older than Philo. The 'Word of God' in the Mosaic narrative of the Creation, and the 'Spirit of God' which moved on the face of the deep, are the first germs out of which the Alexandrian λόγος afterwards developed itself. 'Ideas must be given through something;' it was natural to men to describe the operations of God in the world in symbols and figures of speech derived from Scripture. These figures were spiritualized and personified; the 'God who brought up Israel out of Egypt' became more and more abstract, and the language which had been applied to Him was transferred to the hypostatized λόγος, and also to the written word. But in the Old Testament the personification, whether of wisdom or of the word of God, is only poetical. In Philo and the Alexandrian writers, on the other hand, poetry has already been converted into philosophy. Words have become facts, and the great truth of the unity of God has passed into an invisible essence, which no man has seen or can see. All the gradations of this transition can no longer be traced; there are sufficient intimations, however, to prove its reality. Gfrörer's remark has been already quoted, that in several passages in which apparitions of the Divine Being occur in the books of Moses, alterations have been made by the translator. The Book of Jesus, the son of Sirach, probably a work of Palestine origin and of the second century before Christ, written upon the model of older writings of the same class, the fragments of Aristeas and Aristobulus, also of the second century, portions of the Sibylline oracles, which are supposed to be the work of an Alexandrian Jew, and the Book of Wisdom, which is also probably of Alexandrian origin, contain the same idealism, the same conception of Wisdom or of the Word of God, and the commencement of the same allegorical method. The writings just mentioned were all older than Philo: and if we turn to those who followed him,

Fourthly, the remains of the Alexandrian Fathers, not more than a century and a half after Philo, bear the impress of the same school. It would be absurd to suppose that the whole system sprang up afresh in the mind of Clement or of Origen. Whence could they have derived it? Or how happened it in their writings to be much more freely and commonly applied to the Old Testament than to the New? No other answer can be given to these questions but that they were the natural heirs of the traditional method of Alexandria.

Philo, then, was neither the first author of the system, nor did it end with him, though he represents probably its highest development. There preceded him writers who, by a series of steps, led up to the entrance of the mystical temple. The Christian Fathers who followed him had a higher aim, which freed them from many of his puerilities. The power of the Gospel imparted to them, even in a literary point of view, a great superiority over their Jewish or Gentile contemporaries. Still they were his natural successors. Alexandrianism gave the form to their thoughts; hence they also derived a mystical and rhetorical character. The spirit with them had taken the place of the letter, and the hieroglyphic written on the walls was read by the light of a new truth. But they remained wandering in the labyrinth, though the roof had been taken off, and the sun was shining in the heavens.

§ 7.

It is a great proof of the importance of Philo's works for the illustration of Christianity, that some early Christian writers show an inclination to claim him as a Christian. Eusebius, for example, believes Philo to have had intercourse with St. Peter at Rome, and has no doubt that in describing the Therapeutae, he has in view the first heralds of the Gospel, and the original practices handed down from the Apostles. Photius preserves a statement that he was a Christian who relapsed. To us Philo is unmistakably a Jew. What is there in his writings that has produced this opposite impression on the Fathers and on ourselves?

1. They found in his writings what was unintelligible to them, unless identified with Christ and the Gospel; the conceptions of 'the Word,' 'the Holy Spirit,' 'grace,' 'faith;' of 'the Spiritual,' or rather 'the Ideal, Israel.'

2. They found these ideas drawn from the Old Testament by the same method of interpretation they were themselves in the habit of employing.

3. They found the same, or nearly the same, language with that of Philo in Christian writers.

4. His writings appeared to them orthodox in their tone; that is to say, they inclined to the mystical and spiritual.

5. The influences that produced Philo were still unconsciously acting upon them.

6. That they should have seen Christianity in Philo, was far less strange than that Philo should have traced Greek philosophy in Judaism, and Judaism in Greek philosophy.

A Jewish philosopher [1] was asked when he would become a Christian: he replied, 'When Christians cease to be Jews.' In the spirit of this reply it might be said: $\mathring{\eta}\ \Pi a \hat{v} \lambda o s\ \phi \iota \lambda \omega \nu \acute{\iota} \zeta \epsilon \iota\ \mathring{\eta}\ \Phi \acute{\iota} \lambda \omega \nu\ \chi \rho \iota \sigma \tau \iota a \nu \acute{o} s\ \acute{\epsilon} \sigma \tau \iota$—either Philo is a Christian, or St. Paul learned Christianity from Philo. And it must be admitted that Philo cannot but exercise a great influence on our conception of the Gospel. As we read his works, the truth flashes upon us that the language of the New Testament is not isolated from the language of the world in general: the spirit rather than the letter is new, the whole not the parts, the life more than the form. There is a great interval between Philo and the Gospel when looked at under a practical or moral aspect. But they

[1] Mendelssohn.

approach far nearer when Christianity is drawn out as a system, and theological statements are substituted for the simple language of our Saviour and His Apostles.

In the preceding pages, the chief similarities in the writings of Philo and St. Paul have been brought together; the differences between them remain to be considered.

I. Philo was strictly a Jew. It was his reverence for the law which led him to evade the law, and then to regard this evasion as its original intention. The law, though perverted to such a degree that no trace of its meaning was suffered to remain, he conceived to be of everlasting obligation. It was not 'destroyed,' but 'fulfilled,' by Greek philosophy. Though living on the edge of a volcano which was to open and swallow up his race, he had no conception that the Jewish way of life could ever cease, or the daily sacrifice fail to be offered. At the moment the law was departing, it seemed to him to contain everlasting treasures of wisdom and knowledge. The zealot or Pharisee at Jerusalem could not have clung with greater tenacity than Philo to the hope and privileges of the Jewish race.

II. Philo's system has been already described as the interpretation of the law by Greek philosophy. Hence in many places he uses the language of morality rather than of religion, and often mixes up both in a sort of rhetorical medley. Ideas are brought together in a way that sounds tasteless and strange to modern ears. Logic, ethics, psychology are ascribed to Moses, who is made to mean what he ought to have meant in the second century before Christ. Aristotle, Plato, the Sceptic, the Pythagorean, the Stoic, are Philo's real masters, from whom he derives his forms of thought, his tricks with numbers, his methodical arrangement, his staid and rhetorical diction, and many of his moral notions. Of this classical or heathen element there is no trace in the New Testament. If there be ground for thinking that St. Paul had attained considerable Greek culture, there is no trace in him of a classical or heathen spirit. There is no sentence of any philosopher recorded in his Epistles ; no doctrine of which we are able to say that it derives its origin from Plato rather than from Aristotle, from the Stoic more than from the Epicurean. While the writings of Philo are a coat of many colours, a patchwork in which the individuality of the writer is wellnigh lost, in St. Paul there is nothing composite or eclectic, nothing that is derived from others in such a manner as, in any degree, to interfere with the harmony and unity of his own character. In his hymns of praise, in his revelation of the human heart, in his conception of the universality of the Gospel, he breaks away from the conventionalities of his age, bursting the bonds of Greek rhetoric as well as of Greek or Rabbinical dialectic.

III. Less prominent than Greek philosophy, but still discernible in Philo, is the influence of that widely spread and undefined spirit which may be termed Orientalism. It is the spirit which puts knowledge in the place of truth, which confounds moral with physical purity, which seeks to attain the perfection of the soul in abstraction and separation from matter. It is the spirit which attempts to account for evil, by removing it to a distance from God ; letting it drop by a series of descents from heaven to earth. It is the spirit which regards religion as an initiation into mystery. How little of all this we find in the New Testament ! Of the abhorrence of matter, that deeply-rooted tenet of the East, absolutely nothing. The purity of which St. Paul speaks, is not and cannot be mistaken for the putting away of the filth of the flesh. Though he often introduces the thought of angels and spirits, yet he nowhere regards them as links in the chain let down from the Author of all good to the evils and miseries of mankind. And if he sometimes speaks of mere earthly and human relations as mysteries, in a sense in which we can scarcely realize them to be so, or uses associations and figures of speech which had a force and meaning to his own age which they have lost to ourselves, yet the spiritual reality is never far off—under this mystical or allegorical language is the 'life hidden with Christ and God.'

IV. There may often occur a similarity of language between two writers, although their first and leading thought is different. Two systems of philosophy may be described: the one as practical the other as speculative, the one ideal and the other real; they may have an analogy in the details, while their first principles are different; just as there may be an analogy between the animal and vegetable worlds, while the idea of the one is quite distinct from that of the other. Such a difference and similarity there is between Philo and the New Testament—a difference not so much in the parts as in the whole, a similarity not in the whole but in the parts. Philonism may be truly characterized as mystical and ideal, while the New Testament is moral and spiritual; the one a system of knowledge, the other a rule of life. Yet the terms wisdom, knowledge, prudence, faith, charity, as well as many others, may be common to both, and be applied by both, in senses which have a relation to each other, yet are really different. The wisdom and knowledge of Philo mean chiefly allegorical explanations of the Scriptures; the wisdom and knowledge of the New Testament are inseparable from life and action, and denote the perfect moderation of Christian life and character. A similar difference is traceable in the use of the Old Testament Scripture. The allegory which to the one is but a thin fiction that overspreads the Greek philosophy, to the other is the instrument of preaching a moral or religious lesson. What is everything to the one, is but secondary and subordinate in the other. What is the greater part of Philo, is but rare and occasional in St. Paul.

V. Another aspect in which the religion of Philo differs from the Gospel, is that the one is the religion of the few, the other of the many. The refined mysticism which Philo taught as the essence of religion, is impossible for the poor.

That the slave, ignorant as the brutes, was equally with himself an object of solicitude to the God of Moses, would have been incredible to the great Jewish teacher of Alexandria. Neither had he any idea of a scheme of Providence reaching to all men everywhere. Once or twice he holds up the Gentile as a reproof to the Jew; nothing was less natural to his thoughts than that the Gentiles were the true Israel. His Gospel is not that of humanity, but of philosophers and of ascetics. Instead of converting the world, he would have men retreat from the world. There is no trace in him of that faith which made St. Paul go forth as a conqueror. In another way also the narrowness of Philo may be contrasted with the first Christian teaching. The object of the Gospel is real, present, substantial—an object such as men may see with their eyes, to which they may put forth their hands; and the truths which are taught are 'very near' to human nature—truths which meet its wants and soothe its sorrows. But in Philo the object is shadowy, distant, indistinct; whether an idea or a fact we scarcely know—one which is in no degree commensurate with the wants of mankind in general or even with those of a particular individual. As we approach, it vanishes away; in the presence of the temple services, and of the daily sacrifice, it could scarcely have sprung up; if we analyse and criticize, it will dissolve in our hands; taken without criticism, it cannot exert much influence over the mind and conduct.

VI. The Gospels and the Epistles of St. Paul have a real continuity with the Old Testament; they echo the voice of prophecy; they breathe the spirit of suffering and resignation which we find also in Isaiah and Jeremiah; they teach the same moral lesson in a more universal language. The inner mind of the Old Testament is—the New. Not, as some suppose, that the ceremonial law had any other relation to Christianity but one of contrast. 'Sacrifice and offering thou wouldest not, then said I, Lo I come.' But as, in the history of Greek thought, laws and customs are prior to

that higher idea of law which philosophy imparts, so, in the
Hebrew Scriptures, the law of Moses comes first; afterwards
that under-growth of Christian morality which is given by
prophecy. Now Philo has no connexion with the prophets,
and no real connexion with the law. To the former he
seldom refers, while to the latter he assigns, as we have
seen, a purely arbitrary meaning. With the single exception
of the great truth of the unity of God, it cannot be said that
he derives his ideas from the Old Testament. He does not
catch the real preparations and anticipations of a higher
mode of thought in the books of Moses themselves. He is
unable to see the light shining more and more unto the
perfect day in the Psalmist and the Prophets. The world
is fifteen hundred years older than in the days of the giving
of the law; philosophy and political freedom have come
into being; the culture of one race is working upon the
culture of another. These external influences Philo and
the Alexandrians receive and amalgamate with the Mosaic
Scriptures. But of the development of the Jewish religion,
in itself, they have no perception. Nor are they conscious
of the incongruity of the elements which they bring together
from different ages and countries.

§ 8.

These general differences may be illustrated further by
a short comparison of the particular subjects which are
common to Philo and the New Testament: (a) For example,
the words λόγος and πνεῦμα occur in both, and in both have
a relation to each other. Neither can it be said, that the
λόγος in Philo is a merely physical notion; or denied, that
most of the predicates attributed to Christ are applied also
to the λόγος. The great difference is, that the idea in the
one case proceeds from a real person, whom 'our eyes have
seen, and our hands have handled, the Word of Life;' in
the other case, the idea of the λόγος just ends with a person,
or rather leaves us in doubt at last whether it is not

a quality only or mode of operation in the Divine Being. It begins with being unintelligible. It is not the 'open,' but the 'closed, secret' of Divine Providence. The λόγος, in the Alexandrian sense, occurs in the New Testament only at the commencement of the Gospel of St. John; it has a single definite application to the person of Christ. It is like an expression borrowed from another system, the language of which was widely spread, and for once transferred to Him; no further doctrinal use is made of the term. In Philo the whole system centres, not in a person, nor in a fact, nor in a moral truth, but in the term λόγος. Everywhere, both in the book of nature and the book of the law, the λόγος only is seen. If in Scripture the same predicates are applied to Christ as in Philo to the λόγος, it is not that they were transferred from one to the other, but that the same words naturally suggested themselves in both cases to the Jewish mind to express an analogous idea. Christ is called μεσίτης or ἀρχιερεύς; not because these designations had previously been appropriated to the λόγος, but because the disciple now believed the same attributes to belong to Christ which the Alexandrian philosophy had attached to the λόγος. The λόγος of Philo is not an historical Christ; he is diffused over creation, and has hardly any connexion with Messianic hopes.

The difference between Philo's conception of the πνεῦμα and that of the New Testament may be summed up as follows: (1) In Philo it occurs less frequently, and has a less important place. (2) It is more of an abstraction, being scarcely distinguishable from a quality in the human mind, or an attribute of the Divine Being. (3) It is blended with a physical notion of the wind. It has hardly a separate existence at all, but is a sort of modification of the λόγος.

(β) Analogous differences are traceable in the moral and spiritual character of the doctrines of Philo when compared with the Gospel. We have seen that it would not be true to say that Philo knew nothing of the Christian λόγος or πνεῦμα. Neither would it be true to say that he knew nothing of the doctrines of grace. Like St. Paul, he would have acknowledged that God was the Giver of all good; like St. Paul, he believed that the good suffered for the evil, 'even as Christ, the just for the unjust.' He could have said, 'When ye have done all, count yourselves to be unprofitable servants.' Such a doctrine would have been by no means new to him. But it is rather theoretical than practical; it flows with him out of a consideration of the Divine nature; it is a part of his theosophy, not a rule of life. The language of a school pervades all his writings; the teacher never allows his reader to forget that he is the rhetorician also. Plain duties he involves in dreamy platitudes; no word comes from or goes to the heart of man. And as his view of religion and morality is wanting in depth and reality, so also it is wanting in breadth. It does not embrace all mankind, or all time. It could never have attained to the sublimity of St. Paul: 'In Jesus Christ there is neither Jew nor Greek, barbarian, Scythian, bond or free;' though often assuming in the Israelite the ideal of humanity (*De Victim.* c. 3).

(γ) Philo, in his conception of faith, falls equally short of St. Paul. Both in Philo and St. Paul faith is trust in God, and belief in His promises. But in St. Paul it is more than this, a faith such as may remove mountains, a confidence that 'all things' are ours, 'whether life or death, or things present or things to come.' It is the instrument of union with Christ, and, through Him, of communion with all mankind. The faith of Philo is bound up in the curtains of the tabernacle; it is the faith which believes that God will keep His covenant with the sons of Abraham, not that 'God is able of these stones to raise up children unto Abraham;' the faith of St. Paul is absolute and infinite; it breaks down the wall of partition which divides the Jew from the Gentile, and earth from heaven.

(δ) Once more: it is fair to estimate the difference between

Philo and the Gospel by the result. The one may have guided a few more solitaries or Essenes to the rocks of the Nile or the settlements of the Dead Sea; the other has changed the world. The one is a dead literature, lingering amid the progress of mankind; the other has been a principle of life to the intellect as well as the heart. While the one has ceased to exist, or only exists in its influence on Christianity itself, the other has survived, without decay, the changes in government and the revolutions in thought of 1800 years.

From the above statements, as we pass from the Epistles of St. Paul to other parts of the New Testament, a slight deduction has to be made. Philo may be allowed to stand in a nearer relation to the Gospel of St. John, and to the Epistle to the Hebrews, than to any of the writings of St. Paul. There is truth in saying that St. John wrote to supply a better Gnosis, and that in the Epistle to the Hebrews a higher use is made of the Alexandrian ideas, and the figures of the Mosaic dispensation. That is to say, the form of both is an expression of the same tendency which we trace in the Eastern or Alexandrian Gnosis. But admitting this similarity of form, the difference of spirit which separates St. John or the author of the Hebrews from Philo, is hardly less wide than that which divides him from St. Paul. The λόγος of Philo is an idea, of St. John a fact; of the one intellectual, of the other spiritual; the one taking up his abode in the soul of the mystic, while the other is the indwelling light of all mankind. Philo would have shrunk from 'the idea of ideas,' as he termed the λόγος, being one 'whom our eyes have seen and our hands have handled;' he would have turned away from the death of Christ. And although the author of the Epistle to the Hebrews approaches more nearly to Philo in his conception of faith, and carries the allegorical method further than St. Paul, both in the particular instance of Melchizedek, and in his application of it to the whole of the Mosaic dispensation, and seems even to regard such knowledge as a sort of perfection (Heb. vi. 1), he too never leaves the groundwork of fact and spiritual religion.

Alexandrianism was not the seed of the great tree which was to cover the earth, but the soil in which it grew up. It was not the body of which Christianity was the soul, but the vesture in which it folded itself—the old bottle into which the new wine was poured. When with 'stammering lips and other tongues' the first preachers passed beyond the borders of the sacred land, Alexandrianism was the language which they spoke, not the faith which they taught. It was mystical and dialectical, not moral and spiritual; for the few, not for the many; for the Jewish therapeute, not for all mankind. It was a literature, not a life; instead of a few short sayings, 'mighty to the pulling down of strong holds,' luxuriating in a profusion of rhetoric. It spoke of a Holy Ghost; of a Word; of a divine man; of a first and second Adam; of the faith of Abraham; of bread which came down from heaven: but knew nothing of the God who had made of one blood all nations of the earth; of the victory over sin and death; of the cross of Christ. It was a picture, a shadow, a surface, a cloud above, catching the rising light ere He appeared. It was the reflexion of a former world, not the birth of a new one. It lifted up the veil of the temple, to see in a glass only dreams of its own creation.